VIDEO, WAR AND THE DIASPORIC IMAGINATION

Video, War and the Diasporic Imagination is an incisive study of the loss and (re)construction of collective and personal identities in ethnic migrant communities. Focusing on the Croatian and Macedonian communities in Western Australia, Dona Kolar-Panov documents the social and cultural changes that affected these diasporic groups due to the fragmentation of Yugoslavia. She vividly describes the migrant audience's daily encounter with the media images of destruction and atrocities committed in Croatia and Bosnia, and charts the implications the continuous viewing of the real and excessive violence had on the awakening of their ethno-national consciousness.

The author provides a valuable and unique insight into how migrant cultures are shaped and changed through the reception and assimilation of images seen on video and television screens. Using the combination of close and powerful semiotic analysis of video texts with an informed account of social, political and historical contexts, Kolar-Panov recalls the complex relationships between ethnicity, technology and the reconstruction of identity.

Foreword by Michael O'Toole, Professor of Communication Studies, Murdoch University, Western Australia.

Dona Kolar-Panov is Associate Professor in Communication Studies at Skopje University, Macedonia. She previously taught Communication Studies at Murdoch University, Western Australia.

ROUTLEDGE RESEARCH IN CULTURAL AND MEDIA STUDIES

David Morley and James Curran

Series Advisors

VIDEO, WAR AND THE DIASPORIC IMAGINATION
Dona Kolar-Panov

REPORTING THE ARAB–ISRAELI CONFLICT
How Hegemony Works
Tamar Liebes

VIDEO, WAR AND THE DIASPORIC IMAGINATION

Dona Kolar-Panov

London and New York

First published 1997
by Routledge
2 Park Square, Milton Park, Abingdon, Oxfordshire OX14 4RN

Simultaneously published in the USA and Canada
by Routledge
711 Third Avenue, New York, NY 10017

First issued in paperback 2014

Routledge is an imprint of the Taylor and Francis Group, an informa business

British Library Cataloguing in Publication Data

A catalogue record of this book is available from the British Library

Library of Congress Cataloging in Publication Data
Kolar-Panov, Dona.
Video, war and the diasporic imagination / Dona Kolar-Panov.
p.   cm. — (Routledge research in cultural and media studies)
Includes bibliographical references and index.
1. Mass media—Australia—Audiences.   2. Bosnians—Australia—Ethnic identity.
3. Croats—Australia- –Ethnic identity.   4. Mass media and minorities—Australia.
5. Yugoslav War, 1991—Mass media and the war.   I. Title.   II. Series.
P96.A832A85   1996
302.23'0994—dc20   96–7698

ISBN 978-0-415-14880-1 (hbk)
ISBN 978-1-138-00700-0 (pbk)

For my mother, Elizabet Kolar

CONTENTS

CONTENTS

FOREWORD

The traditional stance of the social scientist involves a grammar dominated by the third person and the passive voice. The favoured method is the objective scrutiny – and, if possible, the counting – of empirical facts in relation to a theoretical hypothesis, and the resulting discourse is objective, dispassionate, remote from the scene of social action: 'Victims of childhood rape have been shown to be 200 per cent more likely to suffer from identity problems as adults'. Human experience of inadequacy, loss and suffering becomes a written record for other social scientists, politicians and bureaucrats to contemplate or neglect. Process is turned into product.

Dona Kolar-Panov's book is about the rape of a country, the loss of a national identity, and the attempts of individuals, families and ethnic communities to construct an identity for themselves within a different and often alien culture. The records they use to preserve their past, to learn about their present loss and to establish an individual and collective face for their future are not written documents by social scientists, historians, journalists or politicians, but video tapes. Here the grammar is dominated by the first person – the 'I' (and eye) of the cameraperson and the active voice, which is both responsible and audible. The process of the lived human experience is visible and audible in these video tapes; to an extraordinary degree it is conveyed in this document.

The author of this book is wholly, and consciously, involved. As a citizen of the Socialist Federative Republic of Yugoslavia, so recently a political and social entity and now irretrievably fragmented, and with a profound and intimate knowledge of the histories and cultures of the ancient yet emergent republics of Croatia, Serbia, Slovenia, Macedonia and Bosnia, Dr Kolar-Panov is unmistakably 'an insider'. As an overseas student at an Australian university, she identified, and was identified, closely with the migrant communities of the Yugoslav diaspora. As a student of culture, her view was informed by theories of ethnic and cultural interaction, diasporic studies and modes of communication, but the cultures, the languages, the modes of social interaction were her own. As a student of electronic media, she found herself among groups of migrant viewers cast as actor and agent as well as interpreter and theorist.

The video tapes which became the main focus of her research were not officially produced newscasts, documentaries, dramatised reconstructions of fictional drama. War makes people highly inventive, and the communities of the Yugoslav diaspora evolved their own genres of video, which the author dubs 'infotainment'. These combined private family or community footage with excerpts from films, documentaries, news programmes, plays, concerts – and even opera; the important criteria were that they would be relevant both to the moment and to the target audience. Both their production and their distribution testify to the ingenuity and community organisation of the migrants and their friends and relatives in 'the old country'. We witness here an emergent technology – one which is born out of the situation of civil war and migration, but which also comes to have its own effects on the conduct and perceptions of that war. From a semiotic perspective, Dr Kolar-Panov's study powerfully combines a close and perceptive analysis of the video texts with an informed account of the social, political and historical context in which they are produced and viewed. Most importantly, and movingly, she brings alive the moods engendered by their viewing at particular moments in particular living rooms and ethnic social clubs.

The war and its current aftermath in all the 'new' Balkan republics makes depressing reading and viewing in the newspapers and television newscasts and documentaries of the outside world. Sociological and political analysis – to say nothing of the propaganda war still raging about who did what to whom – increases our depression about the tragedy that has overtaken this beautiful and deeply cultured part of the world and about how easily something similar could happen in our own backyards. Dr Kolar-Panov's engaged and vivid account of some of the ways meaning about the tragedy was reconstructed and interpreted in Croatian and Macedonian homes and clubs in Western Australia would have found the approval of Aristotle himself: we experience the terror and monumentality of the tragic events, but the form of the drama – the refraction of video tellings through the reactions of their audiences and the perceptions of the author – brings *catharsis*, a purging of the emotions and a new understanding.

Michael O'Toole,
Professor of Communication Studies,
Murdoch University,
Western Australia
January 1996

ACKNOWLEDGEMENTS

Many people have in one way or another played supportive and indeed crucial roles in the creation of this book. My thanks are due above all to the members of my 'audience'; those who allowed and welcomed my intrusion into their daily lives over a period of four, as it turned out, increasingly difficult years.

Murdoch University, and my colleagues and students there, provided the appropriate intellectual atmosphere and support, and I was indeed fortunate to find myself, as they say, in the right place at the right time.

The two supervisors of my research, Professor Michael O'Toole and Dr Tom O'Regan never failed to support me through the 'murky waters' of interdisciplinary research. I owe them more than just 'thank you' – but thank you Tom, for initially giving me the opportunity to develop some of the arguments in this book; and thank you Michael for being not only the best possible teacher and mentor, but also a true friend.

Special thanks go to Ien Ang for her intellectual and emotional support and to Bob Hodge for his good-humoured encouragement. Support, wide-ranging and beyond the limits of professional duty, was also provided by Grant Stone, Librarian, and Irene Finlay, Secretary, of Murdoch University. Both friends have my heartfelt thanks.

There are many other people without whose generous help in my research and the preparation of the manuscript this book would never have appeared. To them also, my warmest thanks.

Last, and most particularly, I wish to thank David Morley for his endless patience and encouragement in guiding me towards the publication of this study.

Some of the material in this book has seen publication in different forms. Part of the pilot study from chapter 2 was published in *Macedonian Review* under the title 'Video as a cultural technology: the Macedonian experience in Australia'; a differently edited version of chapter 6 was published under its present title in *Continuum*; and an essay based on parts concerning video and Croatian cultural identity formation in the diaspora, was published in *Cultural Studies* under the title 'Video and the diasporic imagination of selfhood: a case study of Croatians in Australia'.

ACKNOWLEDGEMENTS

The research for this book was made possible by the generous support of an Overseas Postgraduate Research Scholarship and a Murdoch Scholarship.

The translation of all written and oral material used in the text is my own, unless stated otherwise.

GUIDE TO PRONUNCIATION

This is compiled from Babić, Finka and Moguš, 1994: 3–5; and Ristić, Simić and Popović, 1973: x–xi.

Croatian alphabet	*Pronunciation*
A, a	**a** in father
B, b	**b** in bed
C, c	ts in lots
Ć, ć	A sound between **t** in tune and **ch** in chalk
Č, č	**ch** in chalk
D, d	**d** in day
Dj, dj (Đ, đ)	A sound like **j** in Jew but slightly softer
Dž, dž	j in John
E, e	e in pet
F, f	**f** in few
G, g	**g** in go
H, h	**h** in loch
I, i	**i** in machine
J, j	y in yet
K, k	**k** in key
L, l	**l** in let
Lj, lj	**lli** in million
M, m	**m** in met
N, n	**n** in not
Nj, nj	**ni** in onion
O, o	o in hot
P, p	**p** in pen
R, r	**r** in red
S, s	ss in glass
Š, š	**sh** in shop
T, t	t in top
U, u	**u** in rule

V, v	v in view
Z, z	z in zero
Ž, ž	s in pleasure

ABBREVIATIONS

6EBA–FM	West Australian Ethnic Public Broadcasting call sign
6KY	West Australian Radio Metropolitan commercial call sign (former)
6WF	West Australian ABC Radio Metropolitian call sign
6WN	West Australian ABC Radio Regional call sign
ABC	Australian Broadcasting Corporation
ABC–US	American Broadcasting Company
ABS	Australian Bureau of Statistics
ACWA	Australian–Croatian Women's Association
AFC	Australian Film Commission
AGPS	Australian Government Publishing Service
ASTRA	European satellite system
BBC	British Broadcasting Commission
Beta	A proprietary home video recording system (Betamax)
BRACS	Broadcasting in Remote Aboriginal Communities Scheme
CBC	Canadian Broadcasting Corporation
CNN	Cable News Network
ESL	English as a second language
EU	European Union
FAX	facsimile
FYRM	former Yugoslav Republic of Macedonia
HDTV	high definition television
HDZ	Hrvatska Demokratska Zajednica (Croatian Democratic Union)
HSS	Hrvatska Seljačka Stranka (Croatian Peasant Party)
HTV	Hrvatska Televizija (Croatian Television)
ITN	Independent Television News (British)
IUC	International University Centre for Graduate Studies (former)
IVS	International Video Studios
JAT	Yugoslav Airlines

ABBREVIATIONS

JNA	Jugoslovenska Narodna Armija (Yugoslav People's Army – former)
JRT	Jugoslovenska Radio Televizija (Yugoslav Radio Television – former)
JVC	Japan Victor Company
MNT	Makedonski Naroden Teatar (Macedonian National Theatre)
MTV	Music Television
NBC	National Broadcasting Company (United States)
NDH	Nezavisna Država Hrvatska (Independent Croatian State)
NES	non-English speaking
NESB	non-English speaking background
NFM	new composed folk music
NTSC	National Television Standard Code (US video)
OMA	Office of Multicultural Affairs (Australia)
OTV	Opuzen Television (Opuzen TV)
PAL	phase alternative line (German colour television system)
RAI	Radio Televisione Italiana (Italy)
RCA	Radio Corporation of America
RTB	Radio Televizija Beograd (Belgrade Radio and Television)
RTS	Radio Televizija Srbije (Serbian Radio Television)
RTV	Radio Televizija (Radio Television)
SBS	Special Broadcasting Service
SBS–TV	Special Broadcasting Service Television Network
SECAM	French colour television broadcast system
SFR	Socialist Federative Republic
SFRJ	Socialist Federative Republic of Yugoslavia
SR	Socialist Republic
SRM	Socialist Republic of Macedonia
TWA	Trans World Airlines (former)
UN	United Nations
UNESCO	United Nations Educational, Scientific and Cultural Organisation
UNHCR	United Nations High Commission(er) for Refugees
VCR	video cassette recorder
VHS	video home system
VMRO–DPMNE	Vnatrešna Makedonska Revolucionarna Organizacija - Demokratska Partija Za Makedonsko Nacionalno Edinstvo (Internal Macedonian Revolutionary Organization – Democratic Party for Macedonian National Unity)
WA	Western Australia
WTN	World Television News

INTRODUCTION

Much has changed since this study was completed, and the major part of this book was written. The completion of the manuscript coincided with the signing of the Dayton Peace Agreement in Paris, and with the first signs of peace visible in Bosnia (and Croatia) as the American troops moved in. While CNN's reporters, with the same kind of feverish excitement as in Saudi Arabia, Somalia and Haiti, reported – live – the arrival of the 'cavalry', the only thing I could think of were the images of naked dead bodies lying on a cement table being washed down by a green garden hose . . . And I am fully aware that as long as those images of the anonymous victims of the war, images I watched day in day out with the audiences I was studying, as long as those images are so strongly present on the margins of my consciousness it would be impossible to write this book any differently.

While I have attempted to update some of the interpretative framework, I have left the structure of the descriptive ethnographic account of the fieldwork intact. Given the amount of writing on the former Yugoslavia and the war in Bosnia, together with the recent theoretical shifts in cultural studies in general and audience ethnography and studies of cultural identity in particular, any further rewriting would mean writing a whole new study. More importantly, such extensive rewriting would jeopardise and perhaps completely eradicate the most valuable part of this book, and that is the description of the moments of socio-cultural change in the Croatian diaspora in Perth, Western Australia. And according to Edmund Leach (1976) and Victor Turner (1974) the best time to study the underlying structure of culture is in that marginal state that arises from the moment of change, or in the *liminal zone*.

INSIDE THE LIMINAL ZONE

This book began as a study of the role of entertainment video in the cultural maintenance strategies of the diverse (former) Yugoslav communities in the Australian context. I expected it to centre on the Australian host and immigrant minority dynamic; and I anticipated making a case for the ongoing

1

importance of the homeland–diaspora relation in the triangular relation of diaspora–homeland–host country. What I hoped to show was the relationship between media discourses and the institutional context in which they gain relevance. I intended to conduct an ethnographic participant research inquiry and through a descriptive audience research allow glimpses of how mass-mediated meanings have an impact beyond the immediate context of the media (video) use. But it was not to be so. Instead the study was overtaken by the disintegration of (former) Yugoslavia and the ensuing and continuing war there.

This war reconfigured all of the anticipated relationships. It especially prioritised the homeland–diaspora relationship; and it did so for the most part at the expense of the immigrant–host relationship which was largely in abeyance during the period of this research. Additionally, the anticipated kind of video – video entertainment – itself changed towards information and propaganda video. With this the relationship of the ethnic audiences – particularly the Croatian community – towards video and broadcasting was transformed. This transformation was following the larger changes brought about by the unravelling of Yugoslavia and the ensuing and ongoing crises there.

The audiences were now naturally concerned with news from the homeland in ways they had not been before; with this came a demand for timely information the existing mainstream media simply could not provide. New types of video came into existence and accounting for these became a central focus, particularly in the second half of the study. These new videos – some of which featured graphic images of atrocities – had a considerable impact upon those who viewed them, including myself. If there is a point at which this research changed direction it is when I first encountered these videos and the reaction of the audience to them in the larger public setting of the packed Croatian Community Centre in Fremantle, Western Australia (WA) in late 1991. During the screening, occasional sobs in the dark rose from members of the audience as they came face to face with brutal and unedited images of death; images largely kept out of the mainstream media. These videos, translated from many realities and fragments of personal experience, conveyed portraits of men, women and children along the long path to exile and death. Displayed alongside this was a disjointed and spurious glorification of such death as being for the homeland. Lyrics and musical scores of newly composed folk music (NFM) accompanied the shots of recently defaced landscapes and mutilated human bodies.

I could not remain outside these videos in a way that I could with entertainment videos or remain impervious to their impact on cultural maintenance and reproduction dynamics. I was witnessing the physical destruction of landscapes – urban and natural – that I knew too well; friends and relatives were being killed or made homeless; the friendships I had made across the ethnic divisions in both former Yugoslavia and Perth became increasingly

2

strained as the different communities became increasingly polarised. In this context it was impossible not to be involved. I became a part of the audience I was studying as I also shared its bewilderment, uncertainties, fears and grief about what was happening. Because of my more recent and extensive knowledge of former Yugoslavia I was often called upon to explain, translate or otherwise facilitate the understanding of these video tapes. In these circumstances I had ceased to be a 'fly on the wall' but had become an agent in the very processes of meaning-making I had come to observe. Consequently it became necessary to write myself into my account of the ethnographic research undertaken so as to make this presence and its influence transparent.

What was happening here was not simply something personal affecting family, friends and one's identity, but something ineluctably public. The same videos became important in transforming a cultural identity into a national political identity mobilisable on behalf of the newly emerging nation states in former Yugoslavia. They served to create and in some instances further reinforce ethnic animosity between the different nationalities in the diaspora. At the start of this research in 1989 the rhetoric about the possible disintegration of Yugoslavia was already becoming deafening. Then as now the country/countries I so loved seemed to be unified only by discourses of hatred, and any discourse of peace was dismissed as evidence of weakness, sentimentality and lack of patriotism. It only got worse. Inevitably questions of ethnicity, nationalism and human rights became central not only to the conflict and its playing out in the diaspora in Perth, but also dictated the course of the present research. Thus this book reflects the wider issues arising from the geo-political and socio-cultural changes in (the former) Eastern Europe and the world more generally in a 'New World Order' where globalisation and ethnic revivals exist side by side.

In this context the questions driving this research became: what are the relationships between ethnicity, media technologies and nationalism? Do diasporas grow more encapsulated and localised with the availability of technologies such as video that permit cultural identification and maintenance outside the traditional information corridors? Do the symbolic ethnicities based on the timelessness of myths and traditions carried from distant homelands become transformed under technological and political conditions which facilitate more ongoing and extensive homeland–diaspora *cultural* connections? How does the vertiginous development of media technologies such as the video cassette recorder (VCR) and satellite television influence the simultaneous creation of globalised general audiences, globally linked diasporas, and polarised divisions between ethnic communities? Do diasporas now linked with each other and with the homeland become more visible in their marginality? If so, how does this visibility affect the processes of acculturation and assimilation into the perceived mainstream in the land of their present existence? These questions crystallised as I was observing and describing people in their intimate worlds as they watched video tapes, not only in their homes with family and friends, but also in larger groups in church halls and community centres.

PUTTING THE AUTHOR BACK INTO THE TEXT

I soon discovered problems faced by, and common to, all research that ambitiously sets up an agenda of interdisciplinary approach. However, the paradigm shift currently taking place inside discussions of the wider discipline of cultural studies (see e.g. Ang 1992; Grosberg, Nelson and Triechler 1992) allowed me to describe the cultural dynamic of VCR inside the flexible category of 'interpretation' (Eco 1990a, 1992), ethnographic audience research (e.g. Lull 1990; Ang 1990, 1991; Morley 1992) and cultural anthropology (Rabinow 1986; Clifford 1986, 1988). This made it possible to move freely between ethnography and semiotic and textual analysis in order to understand the 'multiplicity of voices' (Bakhtin 1981) and the meaning-making processes of the audience from videos as cultural texts (Lotman 1990). These voices were not always easily and readily translatable, and the cultural production of that multiplicity of voices is taken as a starting point for the exploration of marginal positions I was and am occupying as a researcher and simultaneously a member of the very community that is the 'subject' of this research (Fischer 1986).

Additionally, there has recently been a significant and ongoing discussion about ethnography as a discipline at the centre of the intersection of other disciplines (Marcus and Fischer 1986; Rabinow 1986), and ethnographically oriented audience research is increasingly seen as appropriate and acceptable for studies of media consumption (Lull 1990; Ang 1990, 1991; Morley 1992). This movement towards qualitative research in studies of mass communication (Jensen and Jankowski 1991) in general, and ethnographic inquiry into audiences in particular, can provide us with a closer look into audience–media relationships (VCR in this case), allowing us to examine the audience inside its historical, cultural and contextual specificity.

Moreover, it is the analysis of examples of cultural descriptions from the past, and the most recent explorations into the function of cultural technologies, when taken in conjunction with the power of ethnographic writing and cultural representations, that is challenging researchers and writers into re-thinking the processes of production and reproduction of discourses and the creation of new knowledge. Ethnographically oriented audience research might be seen as most suitable to unravel 'the minutiae of difference and variation' in everyday video consumption, but it still remains controversial and problematic (Ang 1990: 8). One of the more frequently discussed problems is the level of intervention and interference of media ethnographers in audience meaning-making (Walkerdine 1986; Lull 1988; Ang 1990; Morley 1992). However, it is the very position of a researcher who is at the same time a member of the culture under inquiry that James Clifford (1986) is describing (and I can identify with) when he argues that 'different rules of the game for ethnography' apply and that advantages exist for what he calls an 'indigenous ethnographer', since 'insiders studying their own cultures offer new angles of vision and depths of understanding. Their accounts are empowered and restricted in unique ways' (*ibid.*: 9). Just how 'restricted' and how empowered my position was I soon found out by positioning myself as observer and participant in the heart of the very cultural production I was attempting to describe.

First of all, watching video tapes with a group, a family or in the ethnic community hall could not be reproduced afterwards in the manner of written notes. Second, the *ad hoc* character (in montage and content) of the ethnic video tapes is full of specificities and peculiarities and presents a specific form (or genre) different from the generic forms of mainstream video (Court and Maddox 1989, 1992; Cubitt 1991) and was and still is causing an additional limitation in recording the audience response (apart from my own response as a member of the audience). In addition, the personal responses to both events and audience responses inevitably raised questions about the validity and significance of the present work as 'reliable cultural data'. This, in turn, could raise legitimate questions about the validity of the data obtained, as well as become a problem about the acceptability of ethnographic inquiry as the best possible mode of inquiry for VCR research; mainly due to the position of the participant observer as an instrument of data generation and as an intermediary between the occurring events (Fiske 1990).

However, it is the final articulated description and the analysis, which should form the basis for acquired knowledge of the audience responses to the VCR, that reveals the circumstances that have made the process of the ethnographic contextualisation possible. Thus, it would be most useful at this point to shift from questions of ethnographic audience research towards the fundamental interest of the processes of interpretation by making the author – researcher – observer – me – accountable for not only the data collection and informed interpretation, but also the generation of the data, the construction of the interpretative processes and the very realisation of these in the auto-reflexive models of the interpretative strategies which were the result of the author's dichotomy, which I call 'schizophrenic positioning', on the margins of the community in question on one·side and of academia on the other.

It soon became obvious that this book, and the research on which it is based, departs from 'traditional' or even the 'new' audience research methods as proposed by Ien Ang (1991), Klaus Bruhn Jensen (1991) and David Morley and Roger Silverstone (1991). It also departs from classic and critical ethnography (Clifford and Marcus 1986; Clifford 1988). It does so in a number of ways. I don't disguise my role as participant (observer) with the invisible and omniscient third person-narrator, but rather allow the claims on the privileged position I was occupying as a researcher to become transparent. Thus, the first-person reference always means my own, singular interpretation, while the ambiguous 'we' becomes the inclusive 'we', inclusive of the audiences and myself.

This approach is also far removed from the writings on culture sensitised by Michel Foucault (1975, 1980, 1982) and the premises of the power–knowledge dichotomy which left ethnography and fieldwork 'to hang as an unwarranted intrusion' in the lives of vulnerable and threatened peoples – as 'other' (Scheper-Hughes 1992). I do realise the danger of a malaise of ethnography that could set in if this led to a personal sort of postmodernist alienation as questioned by James Clifford (1988), who sees this nostalgia as belonging to traditional anthropologists pursuing lost worlds in an anxious and postmodern age (cf. Rosaldo 1989). Taking into account all this, it almost seems as if media ethnography is some hostile act that reduces subjects or audiences to objects of scientific gaze. As a consequence, the practice of descriptive ethnography in audience research is often displaced by highly formalised methods of discourse analysis or other extremes of academic particularism or resorts to using quantitative methods as the only 'way out' (Lull 1990; Ang 1991; Morley 1992).

However, in any act of writing culture what emerges is always subjective, fragmentary and partial (Clifford 1986). The present work is no exception. It is in part a deeply felt personal account (or a chronicle) of at least four years (eight years if we take into account the years I spent in Australia as a diplomat's wife) of my life as a part of the migrant community in Perth, Western Australia. And all along while researching and writing this study I lived with the realisation that in the process of accounting for those years, the danger of engaging in an obsessive, self-reflexive hermeneutics in which the self, not the audience, could become the subject of inquiry, was always 'lurking just around the corner'.

Thus all the limitations of the adopted methodologies and the model of personal interpretative strategies, always coupled with its resonating emotion, make the present work tentative and partial, bringing with it the realisation that as a researcher I represented an instrument of cultural translation, a position which is always inherently flawed and biased (Rabinow 1977: 150). It is impossible to remove from my writing (or any writing) the traces of cultural self, and as I struggled to do my best, that best was often reduced to an ability to listen and observe carefully, empathically and compassionately. My position as a media ethnographer was a privileged position, and the readiness of the audiences to share with me their private lives and life-cycle events like births, marriages and deaths, enabled me to understand the fragile web of human relations that binds the ethnic community together. But there are and were differences in class or, as Pierre Bourdieu (1984) would call them, differences in cultural and educational capital that necessarily separated me from my audience, preventing me from completely understanding and thus taking part in the life of the community (cf. Walkerdine 1986).

As Nancy Scheper-Hughes (1992: xii) in the 'Prologue' to *Death without Weeping* poetically describes it:

> The ethnographer, like an artist, is engaged in a special kind of vision quest through which a specific interpretation of the human condition and entire sensibility is forged. Our medium, our canvas, is 'the field', a place both proximate and intimate (because we have lived some part of our lives there) as well as forever distant and unknowable 'other' (because our destinies lie elsewhere).

This is, then, a self-reflexive or 'autobiographical' (Fischer 1986) ethnographical study of video audiences carried out and interpreted through an interdisciplinary approach. It is also a study which surveys the possible effects of the free flow of information through video upon a small and fragile ethnic community.

WHAT IS THIS BOOK ABOUT?

The book – effectively but not formally – is in two parts. The first and more general part revolves around video as a cultural practice and involves a comparative study of audiences in the small and geographically isolated migrant communities of former Yugoslavia in Perth, Western Australia. The audiences for this part of the study are mostly, but not exclusively, of Macedonian and Croatian descent. The second part provides a more detailed examination of video within the Croatian communities in Perth under the impact of the break-up and wars in Croatia and Bosnia and Herzegovina (often referred to as 'the war in the former Yugoslavia').

The research for the first part was mostly carried out over the period of three years from 1989 to 1992. There is, however, some comparative analysis based on personal notes and diaries dating back to 1985; additionally, there are data about aspects of video use in the fragments of the same community in the Western Australia provincial centres of Carnarvon and Manjimup. The concern in this first part is with establishing ethnic video dynamics as an important but relatively neglected component in the emergence of video technology; with establishing the often different patterns of video usage and, indeed, of types of video material circulating in the Croatian and Macedonian communities; and with providing a profile of these communities within the West Australian and, to a lesser degree, in the Australian context.

The second part of the study, conducted in the Croatian community, is dominated by the analysis of VCR dynamics in the context of everyday life and in the light of the rise of Croatian national consciousness in the diaspora, and later by the course of the unfolding war in Croatia and then Bosnia and Herzegovina (often referred to as Bosnia). As the study progressed, so did the hunger for information by Croatian audiences given the limited information on the conflict offered in Australia's mainstream media. This created changes not only in the Croatian diaspora's community viewing habits, but also induced a reliance on video tapes 'from home' as sources of 'accurate' information. In turn this brought about changes to the everyday life of the community. (As a result of those changes I was spending twenty to thirty hours a week watching videos with the audience.) The increased anxiety about the war in the homeland seemed to require people to come together in face-to-face interaction so as to create meanings from often contradictory and conflicting media reports intertwined with popular narratives and emerging myths around the 'homeland at war'.

The chapters are organised chronologically. However, within each chapter the sequence is often broken as I move from the present to the past and back depending on, and together with, my audience.

In chapter 1 the central themes of the research are defined. This chapter includes a review of the available literature tracing the history of VCR research through its development, dissemination and use, from surveillance to entertainment and to home-video use. It addresses the place of VCR in audience studies, with special attention to studies – where they exist – of marginal audiences. Because the fluidity of cultural processes of hybridisation (Hall 1993) or creolisation (Lotman 1990) reveal themselves throughout this study, theories of nationalism, culture and the production of cultural texts are also touched upon in this chapter (but they are mostly developed as the need arises in subsequent chapters). And finally, as traditional audience studies do not tend to account for the existence of minority audiences inside the mainstream, it is important to claim a space for the ethnic audience as a minority audience, albeit in terms of their visibility as the 'other'.

Chapter 2 summarises the pilot project: a participant observation study of two ethnic audiences – Macedonian and Croatian – in Western Australia. This study was undertaken, first, to investigate video as a cultural practice of a minority audience; second, to gauge the influence of the VCR on cultural maintenance and cultural familiarisation strategies within the community; and third, to interrogate the consequences of the extended use of VCR, not only as 'entertainment' and 'infotainment' in commodity exchanges, but also in forging new communication corridors, and therefore cultural linkages, between diaspora and homelands. This study not only revealed the negotiation of cultural identity through video tapes and the (re-)creation of cultural and historical memory, but it also indicated considerable shifts in loyalty and interaction between various ethnic groups from the former Yugoslavia. This coincided with the increased ethnic divisions and politicisation of the ethnic identification taking place inside former Yugoslavia. As the attention of the ethnic audiences moved from cultural-maintenance strategies within the Australian context towards cultural production and reproduction of nationalist ideologies directly imported from the homelands, by formal and informal means, not only the dynamics of video use in the community, but its influence on my research inevitably changed too. Just as the audience was no longer innocent, so too the VCR and other electronic media were no longer simply guilty.

Within this context this chapter includes a description of the formation of the commodity market for ethnic video as a result of the absence of public access to video material that would satisfy the community needs for information and entertainment in community languages. As a result of this absence, alternative structures based on the already existing 'community webs' developed. In the course of the research for this chapter, I noticed that a certain stagnation had set into the dynamics of video use and related cultural practices in the Macedonian community at about the same time as the Croatian ethnic revival (using A.D. Smith's terms (1991)) influenced and altered the established video-consumption patterns in the Croatian community. This, among other reasons, caused the field of inquiry in the second part of the thesis to be narrowed down to the Croatian community of Western Australia.

The research for this chapter indicated that the VCR and video cameras (camcorders) allowed the Macedonian and Croatian communities to assert their cultural existence within the larger frame of Australian culture and national political identity (as in citizenship). The resulting politics of cultural identity negotiations through the VCR only augmented the symbolic existence of these communities as ethnic minorities inside Australian multicultural policy.

The existence of these communities as 'migrant' communities inside Australia drives the concerns of chapter 3. Since there is no comprehensive socio-historical account of migration from former Yugoslavia to Australia in general and Western Australia in particular (save for some internal reports to multicultural commissions), I needed to write this chapter as a background to the disintegration of the Yugoslav community in Western Australia described in chapters 4 and 5. Here I trace the formation of the Perth Yugoslav community through a brief historical account from the establishment of various ethnic clubs to the break-up of these communities in the 1990s. Since the ethnic communities are not stable and structurally fixed formations – any studies of migration patterns are a researcher's nightmare – the patterns and events described in this chapter could only emerge from the account of informants, and individual perceptions and accounts of migration. Because in many cases the stories about the community go back only as far as the memories of my informants, this chapter revolves around people's knowledge and interpretations of the historical record which often cannot be independently assessed. Given this dependence upon individual memory, some reservations must be noted about the historical veracity of this account.

As the investigation into the history of ethnic clubs revealed that there existed two parallel diasporas not only from Croatia but also from Macedonia, in order to understand the parts of this work concerned with them it was necessary to describe some of the socio-political and cultural circumstances that made their existence possible. The Macedonian nation has maintained its language and culture through centuries of oppression and has managed to retain a distinct cultural identity in spite of all hostile claims and influences of various conquerors passing through its lands (Kennan 1993). It did so by carefully preserving oral traditions enabling the passing on of myths and legends of national origins. Today the oral tradition is supplemented by the VCR, and the video tapes circulating in the Macedonian community form a kind of 'cultural manual' for younger generations. However, the acceptable existence of two parallel Macedonian communities, one whose homeland is in northern Greece and the other in the Republic of Macedonia (within the former Yugoslavia), shows how the diaspora's past, including its distinct patterns of migration (whether through exile or voluntary migration), provides a model for current relations inside the community.

In contrast to the Macedonian diaspora, the Croatian diaspora was always 'robbed' of its open display of Croatian-ness. This, in turn, often provided a vehicle for interpreting and acting upon those events in the present conflict in former Yugoslavia that the Macedonian diaspora largely stayed out of. This opens out on to the second part of the book, the specific case study of cultural identity negotiation within the Croatian community within which the VCR played a pivotal role.

Chapters 4 and 5 directly address the explosive subject of Croatian nationalism. They trace the gradual and often nervous formation and re-invention of Croatian cultural identity in the Croatian diaspora in Western Australia. With the inception of the war this cultural identity turned into a fully fledged ethnic nationalism. As everyday events and relationships in the community are interpreted by evoking the collective past as a kind of 'blueprint' (or template) for cultural identity, the VCR was used as an active engagement in the historical ordering and reordering of the Croatian past for the audiences observed. This preoccupation with narrating and reconstructing the past is traced in these two chapters. They also follow and analyse the production of Croatian national identity via VCR, and the contingencies surrounding it. The very active and long-standing competition over the question of 'What is a good Croatian?' inside and outside the powerful sources of Yugoslav unitarism, created conflicts within the Croatian community which added to the already complex identity negotiations arising from immigration and exile.

As a direct consequence of the disintegration of former Yugoslavia, the Yugoslav community in Western Australia also dissolved. Faced with the increased 'call of the homeland on the diaspora', the Croatian community consolidated its ranks, finding short-term reasons for celebrating their new-found freedom of cultural expression. Chapter 5 describes one video viewing session at some length in order to show how the (re)construction of Croatian history became a powerful collective discourse on nationalism. These 'historical' videos are concerned with narratively establishing Croatia as a primordial nation. Their assemblage techniques – the beat of drums, the newest nationalistic song, the national anthem – helped to create a deep cultural allegiance that individuals used as markers of their identity (literally, as we will see). However, with increased ethnic tensions in former Yugoslavia and later with the aggression by the Yugoslav People's Army (JNA) and Serbia on Croatia (in which a third of the Croatian Republic's land came under Serbian control in the space of a year), the Croatian community was no longer content to build only a cultural identity. They attacked the very definition of the 'other' – that is, Serbia – using every means available to vilify the enemy. (My limited contacts within the Perth Serbian community reveal a similar process happening from that end, with the enemy being Croatia.) These changes came accompanied with a degree of standardisation presented in the stories and narratives of the videos in which the past struggles for Croatian independence were glorified, to be soon joined by a celebration of Croatian Catholicism providing religious memories as cultural national memories. The video tapes circulating within the community by now fell only just short of open propaganda.

Chapter 6 examines the 'atrocity' video tapes in circulation in the Perth Croatian community. It notes the impact of these videos on those who watched them; speculates on the reasons behind their continued viewing; analyses their presentational and rhetorical strategies; and traces their unusual source providing an account of an interview with one of their producers. Even though I did not share the passion of my audiences for their newly found (or reconstructed) ethnic identity, I was often sickened by the butchery and brutality of these video tapes. This affected how I could write about them as, at the time, it felt as though this research project had been overtaken by events as the accounts of massacres produced meanings of multifold significance. On the one hand, accounting for the details of massacres seemed to be a means of asserting the veracity of events that the victims, talking often directly into the camera, had experienced or witnessed. On the other, these narratives only heightened the existing ethnic tension between the communities in Perth, providing a proof of the perception (by now common in the community) that all Serbs were essentially evil.

This chapter explores the meaning of the powerful phrase 'ethnic cleansing' first developed to describe the wars in Croatia and Bosnia and Herzegovina. Furthermore, the chapter describes the everyday confrontation with death and dying from the television screens fed through the endless supplies of videos and the current affairs television viewing reaching saturation by community members. Yet nowhere on these video tapes is the anonymity and disposability of the bodies of thousands of civilians and their shattered lives made more explicitly clear than on the videos produced by Opuzen

11

Television (OTV). As information and disinformation about the war was readily picked up by the world media and disseminated worldwide by satellite television, the rumours and stories about atrocities were spreading rapidly. An interview with one of the producers of OTV exposed the reality and the cost (in human lives) of the production of the footage of war shown through broadcast and satellite television channels and through informal video networks around the world.

Chapter 7 surveys the other, often overlooked, component of the 'ethnic cleansing' strategies in former Yugoslavia, the attack upon cultural heritage and artefacts – such as historical buildings, museums, libraries, bridges, and so on. After the scenes of death and dying (courtesy of OTV) became accepted and naturalised (Fiske 1987) as conditions of war, the spatial dimension of collective cultural memory belonging to the mnemonic markers of culture (Lotman 1990; Eco 1992) such as religious icons like churches, mosques, cemeteries, monuments and whole cities were attacked and destroyed during the course of the war. This involved a levelling and destruction of natural and cultural landscapes. After establishing some theoretical coordinates for the analysis of national mythology, I describe the Serbian attack and siege of the city of Dubrovnik in 1991 as a calculated assault on a city which has long represented and represented itself as a symbol of freedom. My audiences and I found this assault on a world cultural icon deeply troubling. The bombing of Dubrovnik disturbed everyone because it was one of those extraordinary events which signalled the collapse of the rules of war and the absence of any morality (if there is morality in war).

There are many examples of 'uncivilised' behaviour recorded on video tapes circulating in the Croatian community. These were often told by those raped, victimised or incarcerated in detention camps. And video tapes of more of the same kept coming into the community, especially in the two-year period between 1991 and 1993. But how are we to understand the fragmented accounts of deeds defying any inner logic, and why did we keep watching them? I don't know. Certainly the viewing practices described in the last three chapters were not autonomously culturally produced. Rather they were embedded in the socio-cultural history of both the audience who kept watching them and the producers of the tapes who kept supplying them.

If at first the reinvention of the Croatian past served as a political ideology for the present war, the three years of the war itself have already produced its past creating in turn new myths, among which is the myth of blood-revenge so powerfully and presently being enacted in Bosnia; and to a lesser degree it is a part of everyday contacts between Croatians and Serbs. Chapter 7 ends on this rather sombre note. By this time it was written by a tired and disillusioned researcher without her audience. As I saw increasingly dangerous ethnic hatred forming from the subtexts of the popular discourses around the war, discourses that justified violent actions of

Croatians against Muslims and Serbs (and vice versa), staring at me from the frame of the television screen was the ugly face of a hegemonic discourse justifying violence and defiance, a face accepting the appropriateness of military butchery. I wanted out. It was impossible to continue functioning as a part of the community who, although equally tired and disillusioned as this ethnographer, could still accept the death of others as justified revenge. Of course this last assertion applies only to a section of the community, as a lot of people felt the same as I did, but were afraid to express it publicly. Six months later – towards the end of 1993 – many others were prepared to take the same stance as the Federation of Croatian Community Clubs in Western Australia dissolved under the impact of the ongoing war in Bosnia and Croatia. It seemed that the national and cultural revival, at least for some in the community I studied, was now able to be disconnected, once again, from the institutions of the (Croatian) national state and its politics.

The concluding chapter, chapter 8, serves a variety of purposes. First, it considers the relationship between issues raised in previous chapters, especially the enormous diversity of the data collected in the course of the study. It also assesses the relevance of the research findings to a number of areas of scholarly concern, such as the formation of cultural identity in the light of the globalisation–localisation dichotomy and discussions around it. But like any study in which culture and its processes of production constitute a significant variable, and where, in addition, relationships between media and meaning-making are actively sought, this chapter attempts to place the present study in a historical context of the time in which the research took place.

In no way is chapter 8 a conclusion to this study. This is because its subject is so like 'a cultural chameleon' and because it proved impossible to settle issues of ethnicity, technology and war inside a rapidly changing global and regional politics. If the breadth of focus revealed in this chapter is puzzling, I can only say that it was necessitated by the historical embeddedness of the issues studied within such disjointed and fragmented frames – historical, communitarian and indeed the frames offered by shifting trends of academic discourse. In spite of all the above I was able, for a moment, to catch a glimpse of the structural changes in the cultural organisation of the communities I was studying, and I was most surprised to find that marginal audiences do indeed form real, not 'imagined', communities across space and time, and that these communities function along the lines of traditional interpretative strategies establishing common values and general commonality, discovering their togetherness in their shared otherness.

1

A SILENT REVOLUTION

When video cassette recorders (VCRs)[1] entered the public sphere in 1965 (Marshall 1979: 109) the new technology formed a full circle with the already established medium of television.[2] It appropriated the representational practices not only of television but also of film and photography and of the cinema. The convergence of cybernetics, communication and aesthetics into the technological interface of what is often referred to as the 'home-video terminal' has turned the television screen into an all-purpose device. First, video games were played on it, then rented or pirated cassettes of feature films or time-shifted television programmes were watched. However, the cheapness and flexibility of the portable video camera (portapac, camcorder, etc.) allowed a broad cross-section of the public to produce their own programmes. This turned VCR from a reproductive technology into the first widespread postmodern communication medium.[3]

The domestic use of the video cassette recorder signalled a shift in the control and power of the medium from the control rooms of television stations and the boardrooms of the television and movie corporations to the living rooms of audiences. The excitement that came with the ability to time-shift and record television programmes in absentia, as well as 'bring the movie theatre home' still lingers on, even if today with the help of the computer and modem we are able to create everything from simple video graphics to virtual realities. Today, VCRs have proliferated around the world, with the VHS format almost as widespread as the audio cassette (Nmungwun 1989: 112-99; Secunda 1990). The earlier Betamax and video Phillips V-2000 technologies are still available, especially Betamax due to its use for portable video cameras, but it is VHS, which is (despite other technological advances such as videodisc and higher resolution formats), the most popular format with producers, distributors and users.[4] It is possible to send anyone a VHS cassette as a form of 'video letter', and for them to find a VCR to play it on. Multiformat VCRs are also increasingly available to enable NTSC, SECAM and PAL videos to be viewed. The international success of VCR is such that video cassettes (both programmed and blank) are distributed or sold in corner shops, pharmacies, libraries, and now even in vending machines, side by side with Coca Cola and condoms. Not only has the VCR made its presence felt in 'The West', but also in India, Thailand, Indonesia and in countries of what used to be Eastern Europe, as well as in many other Third World countries where video cassettes are available in almost any market place (Boyd, Lent and Straubhaar 1989). Just as VCRs can be seen in a small Dalmatian village (Croatia) without electricity, run off truck batteries, so too they can be seen in remote Central Australian Aboriginal communities.[5]

However, most of the tapes distributed are of commercial cinema, mostly rented rather than purchased (Nmungwun 1989: 166–79). Since the distribution of these video tapes is ultimately a commercial matter involving a hierarchy of producers, distributors and consumers with a profit-making goal, early studies of video audiences were naturally concerned with issues related either to the video technology's impact on related industries (*ibid.*: 199–243), issues of piracy or copyright laws, or its wider impact on television audiences (Levy and Gunter 1988). VCR is considered first and foremost (in its domestic use) a major innovation in home entertainment, whose rapid diffusion into the home media environment necessarily attracted a lot of attention from film and television industry oriented research (see, e.g. de Sola Pool 1984; Tydeman and Kelm 1986).

In August 1988, *The Bulletin* ran a cover story on the VCR entitled 'Captives of the VCR: how we became a couch potato culture' (Jarrat 1988). Alarmed by the statistics from major audience research agencies such as Nielsen in Australia and the United States which showed Australia's video ownership as being over 50 per cent (in television households), and even more alarmed by the projection for the future that claimed that by the early 1990s the video penetration will be 90 per cent (a bit off – as we will see later), the question posed in the essay was whether VCR offered liberation and more choice to the consumer or whether it was creating a nation of 'couch potatoes'. But, more importantly, the question was in line with the type of audience research addressing the video-rental business and the effects on the advertising industry of the nation's 'flippers', 'zippers' and 'zappers', given that advertising is the largest revenue-generating source for commercial television. Since then, the concerns of the movie industry have been put to rest and Terry McGann reports that:

> A decade ago, who could have predicted where the humble VCR would lead. Certainly not the big Hollywood movie houses which tried and came close to getting the VCR banned in the US for fear of what it would do to first-run movies. Now the studios make more money out of videos than movies.
>
> (1993: 29)

There are also indications that time-shifting and 'zipping' and 'zapping' does not affect the television advertisements as much as was predicted, since

the television advertisements today are sophisticated, technologically as well
as content-wise, and are often 'better than the average television programme'
(Ang 1991: 69).

The high VCR penetration in Australia, together with inflexible government policies (O'Regan 1993) and the highly dispersed population, has
postponed the introduction of satellite television/cable television (pay TV)
and narrowcasting. Additionally, geography has limited the extent of trans-
mission overspill; satellites, by and large, have to be specifically 'trained' on
Australia to reach the high population centres. In the United States and
some European countries these new television technologies have been introduced prior to, or at the same time as, the domestic video cassette recorder.
This has created a unique media environment in Australia that relies on
video-rental structures, and, to a lesser degree, on the informal channels of
distribution for viewing products alternative to broadcast television.

Watching pre-recorded material, mostly rented from the video shops
(video-rental outlets, video libraries), is the most common use of the VCR in
Australia and elsewhere. This is so much the case, that Nmungwun (1989:
219) has found in the United States that 62 per cent of the surveyed audience preferred viewing a movie on tape compared to 34 per cent who chose
to go to a movie theatre. David Court and Garry Maddox (1992) suggest
that even though the number of video stores in Australia was reduced from
3,000 in the mid-1980s to 2,500 in 1991, it is still an $840 million rental
industry, with five top rental distributors in the fiscal 1991 earning $45 mil-
lion before interest and tax, on a turnover of $170 million. Court and
Maddox also estimate that approximately 72 per cent of all television
households in Australia own a VCR, that is, some 3,850,000 Australian
homes, out of which 62 per cent rent videos at least once a month (*ibid.*:
1–3).

One significant point in their report is that they have found that the VCR
penetration in Perth, Western Australia, is significantly higher than the national average at 78 per cent – other capitals range from 71 to 73 per cent
and 'the recession has hardly influenced Australian rental habits' (*ibid.*: 10).
Indeed the Australian rental market is seen as one of the healthiest in the
world with per capita rentals significantly higher than in Britain and France.
Australia continues to have one of the highest levels of VCR penetration in
the world. The *Screen Digest* 1991 (cited in *ibid.*: 2) shows that only one
country – Kuwait – has a higher penetration of 85.5 per cent while the
United States (71 per cent) Canada (70 per cent) Japan (70 per cent) and the
United Kingdom (71.5 per cent) are slightly behind Australia. The worldwide penetration is quoted as 38.8 per cent (*ibid.*: 2) and Australians still
regard renting a video as an alternative to seeing a film at the cinema (*ibid.*:
3). Not surprisingly, then, 120 to150 hit movies made in the United States
form the 'core' of the rental 'titles' (*ibid.*: 7). The 'core' of 'A' titles together
with 'B' titles (movies which don't achieve major cinema release) are con-

sidered by the industry as 'mainstream' videos. (I use 'mainstream' differently, by contrasting it with 'minority' or ethnic video.) The 'non-mainstream' categories are made up of a large proportion of new releases of martial arts (Kung-Fu) movies, R-rated and soft porn films, low-grade thrillers, and horror movies (often made specially for release on video). The next category in the Court and Maddox report is that of 'foreign films' and 'art-house' releases. These films are usually produced in Britain, France, Germany and Italy (*ibid.*: 8–9). The remaining video industry categories include sport, music, live comedy and children's videos including cartoons (animated film) (*ibid.*: 18).

Many distributors and retailers claim to be reflecting the 'needs of the audience' based on the general and demographic characteristics of the populations in their video-rental area (as shown later). These 'needs' in turn are based on the market research classification of the targeted audience which includes: population mix, relative affluence, unemployment levels, numbers arriving during holiday periods (for resort areas), the range of other leisure options available and the number of broadcast television channels in regional Australia as well as competition from other 'local video stores' – video outlets whose main business is other than video rental, such as news agencies, pharmacies, and so on. Since most of the video cassettes rented by the ethnic population surveyed in this research are not rented from the mainstream video outlets but rather from 'local video stores' and circulated through the community networks (see chapter 2), these audiences are uncharted in the official records and reports on VCR use by both software or hardware manufacturers and distributors. With most of the research into VCR use being industry driven, the dynamics of ethnic video remain largely invisible.

(IN)VISIBLE AUDIENCES

This invisibility of ethnic-video markets in Australia is even more marked than in the United States and the United Kingdom, where some statistical data, however limited, are available – in the United States on Hispanic audiences (Albarran and Umphrey 1993; Meyrowitz and Maguire 1993) and in the United Kingdom on Indian audiences (Gillespie 1989). This is mainly due to the fact that both markets are covered by official rental structures owing to the size of the ethnic group concerned and the fact that the Spanish language and Indian audio-visual productions are large and sophisticated industries. The semi-legal structure of ethnic, mainly Greek, Italian, Chinese, Vietnamese and Indian, distribution channels in Australia are in part a consequence of an absence of economies of scale and ethnic dispersal. Consequently the ethnic video depends on the distribution by 'ethnic' outlets and small businesses in Australia – making neighbourhood video less available as an option. This structure has not been accounted for in any

17

official reports to my knowledge except for some Chinese, Indian and Italian films which are accounted for (by Court and Maddox 1992) in the 'non-mainstream' category mentioned above.

The invisibility of ethnic video audiences only reflects their wider invisibility in broadcast television research. Furthermore, the only television station broadcasting materials in languages other than English in Australia, the Special Broadcasting Service (SBS-TV or SBS), is watched by both English and non-English-speaking background (NESB) audiences (Bailey 1980; H. Evans 1989; O'Regan and Kolar-Panov 1993a). SBS-TV audience research is typically concerned with its reach amongst the different ethnic communities and the extent to which it reaches the broader Australian (and anglophone) population (Connor Report 1985). This tends to be broad-brush research since there are so many ethnic communities in Australia, that the surveying of any differences between their use of SBS-TV and video remains largely undeveloped and unnoticed.

Apart from occasional reports in print media, such as on the occasion of SBS's proposal to set up a pay TV, when it was noticed that 2.3 million people in Australia go home every night to an NESB environment (Simper 1993), NESB audiences tend to be invisible and therefore appear to be irrelevant.

However, there is a large body of research which addresses not only distribution, piracy and copyright laws, but raises questions of the VCR's possible social impact. Initially this research raised concerns about the impact of VCR on Third World countries (Boyd, Lent and Straubhaar 1989), continuing to some extent a debate on television and cultural imperialism (Tomlinson 1991). Since most inquiry into the dynamics of VCR use worldwide was carried out before the end of the Cold War, when the world was still divided comfortably into two blocs, such research was concerned with the power of VCR to shift time and space allowing for the free flow of information into those countries 'deprived' of the free flow of information enjoyed in the democratic West. For example, Gladys D. Ganley and Oswald H. Ganley found that:

> The means of control thus far instituted by even the most restrictive governments do not appear to be commensurate with the threat posed by VCRs and video cassettes to the information monopolies claimed by many nations. Where controls have been rather rigorously attempted they have usually been ineffective. This is true even in those countries where information suppression is a high art, such as the USSR and the countries of Eastern Europe.
>
> (Ganley and Ganley 1987: xi)

Appropriately, VCR was seen to enable such 'deprived' audiences to view material prohibited and censored on official channels. Sometimes the researcher's own fascination with the medium is inherently present in this writing and works such as Pico Iyers' *Video Night in Kathmandu* (1988) provide valuable insights into new 'image spaces' (Morley and Robins 1995: 31–7) created by VCR as well as raising numerous questions related to its 'powers'.

Manuel Alvarado's (1988) study, *Video World-Wide*, written for UNESCO, is regarded as the first collection of a unique body of data concerning 'the global distribution of video hardware and software', providing a chronicle of the extraordinary explosion of video around the world. It approaches the VCR as 'a whole new medium of communication which is fundamentally individualistic, anarchic and most of the time beyond the reach of institutional organization' (meaning difficult to police). But contributors to the study only touch upon the social impact of VCR in passing. As Michael Tracy in the Foreword to Alvarado's study writes:

> The social role of video, however, clearly remains as one of the most beguiling problems we face in establishing a proper understanding of the place that audio-visual culture plays in the life of nations and peoples.
>
> (Tracy 1988: ix)

Although this study of video use worldwide does not address its aesthetic, perceptual, and social impact, the VCR is shown to go hand-in-hand with almost anything. It can go with 'alternative', with illegal, and semi-legal networks. Extensive networks of video pirates are described in the Gulf States, especially Kuwait and Saudi Arabia, which have one of the highest VCR penetrations in the world (Boyd and Adwan 1988). The fact that there are so many video recorders in the Gulf States is often ascribed to religious restrictions which reduce the range of public entertainment to virtually nil (cf. Boyd, Lent and Straubhaar 1989: 81). Moreover, before the Gulf War there were no cinemas in Saudi Arabia, and since Arab culture has always strongly focused on entertaining people at home, this, together with the high average income and short working day, created ideal conditions for VCR use. American and European film companies could exercise little or no control over the Gulf States whose governments tolerated piracy to an extent. Only erotica was handled with a certain circumspection. These tapes always begin with five minutes of heartwarming video album (family album) in order to escape censorship (cf. Boyd and Adwan 1988: 169–70). The study (Alvarado 1988) also describes some ingenious methods employed against all obstacles and restrictions to get hold of VCRs or to view an illegal tape. For example, in a case study of Poland (Pomorski 1988) it was shown that the only way to find out where the special screenings were was through friendship networks, since, in order to divert the authorities before the end of the cold war, the screenings were often dubbed 'technical demonstrations' (*ibid.*: 189). In Chile, passwords gave access to VCR screenings (Ulloa and

Donoso 1988: 308). In Brazil, for every legal tape the study showed there were 100 illegal copies in circulation (Santoro 1988: 269–70).

But the most interesting study in Alvarado's book is the case study of Belize (Petch 1988: 311–22), a small Caribbean state with 27,000 homes. Broadcast television had not reached there by 1981. The advent of the video recorder in the late 1970s provided the upper class in Belize with the latest American films and television programmes. It was a lucrative business for the ingenious 'pirates' and distributors of illegal tapes, until one day some-one decided that not only the affluent should be able to see programmes and films. He bought a satellite dish, a transmitter, a video recorder and began broadcasting. The video business collapsed, but at last Belize had television. It is interesting to note that remote Australian Aboriginal communities (except the Aboriginal community which has Imparja Televison) are utilis-ing the narrowcasting technologies offered by VCR and satellite, and lately microwave technology through the BRACS (Broadcasting in Remote Abo-riginal Communities Scheme, see O'Regan and Batty 1993). The rigidity of the Australian communication policies regulating television broadcasting which are often protectionist towards existing television networks have in-hibited the broader uptake of narrowcasting (O'Regan 1993), as too has the fact that Australia has the second largest private ownership of VCRs in the world (Court and Maddox 1992: 2).

While SBS-TV is arguably a narrowcast national broadcaster (see O'Regan and Kolar-Panov 1993a, 1993b) the proposed SBS pay TV will be develop-ing narrowcasting in 'foreign languages' and the initial service should range 'through Italian, Greek, Arabic, Cantonese, Mandarin and Vietnamese' (Simper 1993: 4). It is difficult to predict how successful pay TV will be, given the strengths of the firmly established video-rental business together with a well-functioning video exchange through ethnic community networks. It is most probable that any narrowcasting in Australia in the mid-1990s will never have the same impact as the 'video for people' in Belize (Petch 1988), or, for that matter, as any form of pay cable television or pay TV in other countries in the 1980s, such as in the United States or Canada, since the absence of cable television in Australia has fostered and utilised the alterna-tive viewing possibilities offered by the VCR and created viewing habits which will be slow to change. In addition, the communication services offered by Internet and the possibilities of such services as 'video on demand' will all together create a very different media environment.

Eric Michaels (1985, 1987, 1990) in his work on Central Australian Aboriginal communities has described the influences of VCR use on remote Aboriginal communities and Peter Kulchyski (1989) and Kate Madden (1990) have given us an insight into the ways in which the Inuit people in Canada have utilised video technology to create the first Inuit television.[6] However, all three examples of the Belize, Aboriginal community and Inuit broadcasting show the uses of VCR in the communities which are well defined, with visible boundaries that separate them from the 'mainstream' audience. The borders of their difference or 'otherness' are twofold, as in the case of Belize through their isolation from the rest of the world, or as in the cases of Michaels' Aboriginal communities and the Inuit people by the fact that they are an indigenous minority inside nation states. The indigenous status of Inuit and Aboriginal people when coupled with their significant population presence in remote regions automatically removes them from the mainstream and allocates them a 'special status' in the wider pull of 'marginal audiences' (O'Regan and Kolar-Panov 1991).

Indigenous audiences such as the Aboriginal or Inuit are visible in their difference to the mainstream, just as the television audiences of 'Hispanics and Blacks' in the United States (Albarran and Umphrey 1993) are made visible on the basis of their race (colour), or their number or linguistic and cultural differences. There are other marginal audiences which form a significant part of the population in some countries, such as overseas Chinese or Indians in Malaysia, and they all use VCRs as 'alternative' entertainment. Boyd, Lent and Straubhaar (1989) describe Chinese and to a lesser degree Indian audiences' use of the VCR as a reaction to the imposition of Islam as state religion and of Malay culture as the national culture as the main reason for the development of significant rental structures offering mainly Hong Kong, Indian and Taiwanese movies and serials.[7] Australia's ethnic minorities – while cumulatively large – are individually small with no single ethnic group approaching the Malaysian Chinese or Indian levels. Indeed no single NESB ethnic group makes up more than 5 per cent of the total population (see O'Regan and Kolar-Panov 1993a).

One of the first researchers to note VCR usage in 'maintaining cultural ties' was Julia Dobrow (1989). She noticed that some immigrant groups in the United States use VCR to view videos in languages other than English. Dobrow suggested that the role of VCR in cultural maintenance could represent an important question to scholars of ethnic identity (cf. Ganley and Ganley 1987: 44–50). Moreover there are some available ethnographic studies into VCR use that go beyond statistics and inquire into usage to study the meaning of the technology as well as VCR's effects on the dynamics of the daily lives of audiences. Marie Gillespie's (1989) study of the position and social significance of video viewing inside a South Asian community in London is perhaps closest to my own inquiry into the uses of VCR by the Macedonian community in Perth. In this study, Gillespie highlights two important issues – ethnicity and generation – by examining the way in which first and second generations relate, often differently, to 'Bombay films'. Gillespie's study is something of a landmark in what I see as an immensely rich and important field of inquiry which could bring us closer to an understanding of what Ien Ang calls 'a multifarious and intractable social world of actual audiences' (Ang 1991: 14).

From an examination of the main body of work on the dynamics of VCR it could be argued that it has given rise to two markedly different approaches to inquiry into VCR. The first is concerned with the dissemination of 'hardware and software' (video cassette recorders and video cassettes) mainly through the sell-through structures and video-rental structures such as video shops, video-rental outlets and video libraries. These show the extension of what Tom O'Regan (1990) refers to as 'international information monopolies', the multinational companies such as Sony, JVC, Toshiba, General Electric, RCA and Panasonic.[8] This research is principally concerned with the penetration or dissemination of VCRs in the world as well as with the rental of pre-recorded video tapes. However, it is also concerned with 'time-shifting', scrutinising VCR use to determine 'how time-shifting affects the audience maximising effectiveness of their carefully arranged schedules', including the effect of video on television advertising revenues (Ang 1991: 73).

The second approach deals with, on the one hand, the dynamics of VCR lying outside the concerns of 'international information monopolies'. It addresses the mainly non-commercial video production of video art on one side (Cubitt 1991) and audiences on the other, drawing heavily on qualitative television-research methods and concerning itself mainly with the domestic and family context of viewing and its possible social impacts, stressing the active role of the audience (Lull 1990; Gray 1992; Morley 1992). However, it is the reception model for audience research (Jensen and Jankowski 1991) that allows for inquiry into the interpersonal dynamics of television (and other media) viewing of what Hermann Bausinger (1984) called 'the specific semantics of everyday'. So far this research has been concerned with audience practices within a *mainstream* but often with inquiries into gender relation and including VCR-related issues (see Gray 1992). Thus the recent developments in television-audience research reflects on the VCR research, moving it further and further from the picture painted by the industry-oriented research, that is, the picture of audiences using VCR for passive playback with occasional 'zipping' of advertisements (Sims 1989).

VCR AND AUDIENCE STUDIES

Ien Ang (1991) has demonstrated that the boundaries of audiencehood are inherently unstable. In the Introduction, using Ang's argument (*ibid.*), I have claimed that the ethnic video audience has to be understood in the context on two levels, that is to say on the discursive level and inside the social world of actual audiences. On the discursive level, John Hartley makes the point that in all cases audiences are 'the product of a fiction which serves the needs of imagining institutions' (1987: 125). In no case is an audience 'real', or external to its 'discursive constructions'. The elusive character of the audiences is just that: 'elusive', and represents a debatable point in any examination of media. Perhaps Ien Ang comes closest to an answer to the dilemmas posited by such debates by proposing that we should retain 'the crucial distinction between "television audience" as discursive construct and the social world of actual audiences' (Ang 1991: 13).

Thus the second level of understanding ethnic audiences has to come from the 'social world of actual audiences'. The family unit (i.e. a household) is seen as the most basic site for such research (Lull 1990; Silverstone, Hirsch and Morley 1992), bringing the researcher closer to the everyday world of the audience. But in analysing the uses of ethnic video we are not dealing only with its consumption or the micro-politics of family life. The capacity of media technology, radio, television, VCR, satellite, and so on to join the private world sphere of home and family with the larger public realm beyond the boundary of the front door, has enabled the Croatian and Macedonian audiences in Australia to be in touch with places that are distant in time and space, creating symbolic communities which in turn have offered identification points often of a transnational character to audience members.[9] Thus Ang (1990) and Morley (1991), by tracing the shifting points of identification for consumers, identify the intersection and meetings of 'the local' and 'the global' as the major challenges facing media ethnographers in the 1990s.

David Morley's The 'Nationwide' Audience (1980) has been followed by a number of qualitative research projects centring on viewers' interpretations of news broadcasts and current affairs. I will mention only the ones pertaining to this project. For example, John Corner's (1991) research is concerned with the media's power to define issues and meanings in the information sphere, while Justin Lewis (1985, 1991) has attempted to explain the different readings with reference to 'channels of access' that open up only certain parts of television messages (Lewis 1985: 210). Lewis's argument is especially important here because it is about the extra-textual narratives drawn on by viewers in their attempts to understand the news. As we will see later, extra-textual narratives were of immense significance to the ethnic video audiences under examination here, helping to make sense of the often fragmented and randomly assembled news reports from their homelands.

Peter Dahlgren's (1988) distinction between 'official' and 'personal' modes of talk (cf. Bernstein 1971, on 'elaborated' and 'restricted' codes) proved useful to me, since on occasions during my fieldwork, trivial associations were made by the ethnic audience between the images or narratives shown on the video tape. They were, nevertheless, worth recording, because such trivia pointed to the association on the part of the viewer of the personal experience and the elements of the video as cultural text.

As the boundaries of ethnic audiences become more visible through the course of this current project, I often recalled Hartley's critique of Morley's work that: 'Morley's audience is . . . produced by his project' (Hartley 1987: 126). Since the attempt in this project was to understand the experiences of the ethnic video audiences of Croatian and to a lesser extent Macedonian background, this is also an attempt to see things 'from the virtual point of actual audiences' (Ang 1991). This required my constant presence in the lives of the audience, giving some validity to Hartley's critique. But the micro-setting of the everyday lives of the audience in question – and my presence in it – are as much the 'context' to the meaning-making as is the larger context of history in the making as shown on the video tapes at the time of the inception of the war in former Yugoslavia.

There have been numerous studies of the uses of television in family life, (such as: Lull 1980, 1988; Morley 1986), most of them based on data collected during long periods of participant observation. The data were compiled by a group of researchers who 'ate with the families, performed chores with them, played with the children, and took part in group entertainment, particularly television watching' (Lull 1980: 201). I did this too. The significant difference between my study and the above-mentioned studies is that I was the sole researcher. If being a sole researcher had the advantage of minimal disruption of the family life of my subjects, it was also a disadvantage in that there was too much personal investment in the interpretations of the data collected as well as in my analysis of the video texts. As the 'analysis of any act of media reception, no matter how cleverly interpreted, risks dramatic mistakes in interpretation' (Lull 1990: 18), I do not for a moment imagine that I can disentangle myself from the subjectivity of my shared experiences with the audience.

Although I might have made a minimal intrusion into the lives of the audience, since I was received as a friend and 'one of them', the question of the influence of my presence on their viewing habits remains an open one. As I shall describe later, some video tapes were viewed at times when I was present either for the purpose of gaining new information about the war in the common homeland, or in order to help audience members with the understanding of the content and context of the video tape itself.

Since the precise degree of disruption to people and places in conditions of ethnographic inquiry is debatable, I would like to point out that Valerie Walkerdine (1986) is less optimistic in her assessment of the possibilities for an unobtrusive recording of audience behaviour or meaning-making than is James Lull (1988, 1990). Walkerdine raised questions concerned with the larger issue of the social identification of and the differences between media researchers and the non-academic audience members. Her questions will resonate often in this study, especially in those parts where I could identify with members of the audience in their shock and horror over the war in our homeland, but was burdened with my knowledge or educational capital which set me apart from the audience's strategies of interpretation. Even though I often achieved a close cultural proximity to the Croatian audience, I can understand the position Walkerdine found herself in when as an 'escapee from the working class into a middle class environment of higher education' she could no longer be like her audience (Walkerdine 1986: 183–8).

At the same time my memories as someone brought up and educated in the socialist system in former Yugoslavia often acted as an obstacle to understanding the fears and anxieties of the Croatian migrant groups. (This issue is dealt with in the next chapter.) Indeed I repeatedly had to question my personal distaste for the feverish nationalism expressed in that community. I wanted to take a 'neutral' and 'objective' academic stance at a time when even my pacifist orientation came into question as I found myself hoping for foreign intervention to end the conflict that was destroying my country. Class and other boundaries became permeable when the whole community was subjected to the invasive dynamics of identity management under crisis, such as the war.

Perhaps Pierre Bourdieu's (1984) arguments on the matter of taste are useful here, since rejection, revulsion and often a sense of disgust towards certain objects and/or practices – like the cake with the Croatian coat of arms, or the singing of songs calling for the slaughter of Serbians – could be explained in terms of a complex intersection of class, gender and often generational subjectivity. Issues raised in Bourdieu's (*ibid.*) study challenged my prejudices against such cultural practices since Bourdieu argues that such activities can be innate. He also challenges the notion that the meanings of cultural objects are fixed and given. With the proliferation of popular cultural goods such as items of everyday use among the Croatian community bearing Croatian flags or coats of arms, or the use of the portrait of Goce Delčev (a Macedonian revolutionary and folk hero) on wall hangings and bedspreads in the Macedonian community, Bourdieu's (*ibid.*) focus on the socially constructed character of all interpretations, preferences and value judgements in matters of taste are very important, as is his model of culture which is all about the process of identification and differentiation which produces cultural identities through practices of distinction.

For Bourdieu (*ibid.*), the meanings of cultural objects and practices are negotiable within the relational dynamics of cultural domains. For example, the popularisation of opera by Luciano Pavarotti over recent years which points towards processes of change in popular taste starting with the 1990 World Cup soccer concert (or 'Three Tenors Concert' – Placido Domingo and José Carreras also took part in the performance) is an example of how opera exists in a parallel cultural space of 'high' culture and 'mass' culture. I draw a parallel here with the performances seen on the video tape by the Croatian audience including a mixture of opera, folk music and the recitation of poems on the occasion of the first democratic elections in Croatia and on the re-erection of the monument to Ban (Viceroy) Jelačić. This clearly shows the existence of a dynamic cultural 'economy' of the 'cultural capital'. Thus, the organisers of the two celebratory concerts in Croatia (seen on those video tapes), by using opera, clearly relied on the negotiability of the meaning and the possibility of the existence and circulation of such cultural texts in the 'two taste zones', one universal and the other cultural, nationalist and particularist (Bourdieu 1984: 21).

If most of the available research on VCR viewership within audience studies discusses technology in the domestic arena (Silverstone and Morley 1990) and its relationship to pre-existing patterns of television audience behaviour, Anne Gray's (1992) study *Video Playtime* pursues the connections between gender labour, leisure and power, usefully following up Morley's (1986) model laid out in *Family Television*. For example, Gray (1992: 36–41) has noted that the respondents in her study were not content to merely talk about VCRs, but would frequently want to talk and relate details of their life experiences. This corresponds to my own experiences in the Croatian and Macedonian communities where I was often presented with whole family histories or at least stories of migration. This in turn proved to be extremely useful in helping to piece together the contextual circumstances in which the video was made sense of.

Furthermore, the use of VCR could not be examined as predominantly feminine or masculine due to the fact that technology acquires gendered meaning as a consequence of cultural 'circulation' such as different uses of television, for example, watching soap opera (Brunsdon 1981; Hobson 1982; Ang 1985). Thus, apart from their embarrassment, the inability of Gray's interviewees to operate the video controls corresponded to the situation of Croatian and Macedonian women at the inception of this study. However, in the Croatian community, this has changed quickly, as the women were often the only ones at home at the times that a certain item from news or other television information programmes required their quick reaction to record so as to 'catch' the news item on the war in the homeland, for later replay to family and friends.

SOCIAL AND CULTURAL SEMIOTICS

Roland Barthes (1973) applied his *Mythologies*-style semiotics to media studies, while Stuart Hall's (1980) essay 'Encoding and decoding in the television discourse' attempted to account for the active consumption as well as the production of the textual organisation of media sound and images. Furthermore, Hall (1982), in his article 'The rediscovery of ideology', signalled the return to some fundamental questions about mental and material production reintroducing questions of ideology into audience research. Hall recognised that the language of media does not only transmit ideas: it is not a 'tool', or a transparent 'window' of the social world, but rather a refractive sign system. He gives examples from television news and current affairs in which issues are 'made to mean'. They are subjected to the symbolic work of encoding and constantly shaped into textual forms which are then easily recognisable as news or current affairs. This recognition on the part of audiences happens through interpretative processes which 'may not be perfectly symmetrical' with the encoding process. Hall (1980) calls this 'decoding'. The reasons for this asymmetry are first of all the polysemic nature of texts (Vološinov 1973), which makes them open to multiple readings. (Broadcast television and the VCR rely on audio-visual signs and are perhaps more open to such readings than any other media.) Both Barthes (1973) and Hall (1980) qualify the semiotic fact of the textual openness by stressing the constraints of the ideological forces which constrain and close down the range of available readings.

Social semiotics (see the work with the same title by Hodge and Kress 1988) could be seen as having developed from the work of Valentin Vološinov (Bakhtin) (1973) which postulated the 'multi-accentuality' of the sign. Vološinov (*ibid*.: 46) located the sign in living social interaction. According to him (*ibid*.), there are no fixed meanings in language because the sign is continually the site of class struggle, an arena for the clash of differently oriented 'social accents'. Thus, signs such as 'nation' or 'the people' (in the context of class relations) are not wholly organised around a single hegemonic connotation. According to Vološinov (*ibid*.: 23), the leading social class will always endeavour to reproduce the conditions of its dominance by proposing certain meanings as taken for granted and obvious by attempting 'to impart a superclass, eternal character to the ideological sign ... to make the sign uni-accentual'. We will see later on how the Croatian government has partially succeeded in creating that taken-for-granted meaning of being Croatian.

The second reason for the possible difference between encoded and decoded meaning, according to Vološinov (*ibid*.), is the varied social 'accents' given to the sign by its users. Umberto Eco (1972: 115) has usefully extended this point about the interpretation of a television message which he sees as being dependent upon the reader's 'general framework of cultural references ... his ideological, ethical, religious, standpoints ... value systems etc.'[10] In 'Overinterpreting texts', Eco discusses the mechanisms of analogy as:

[When it] has been set in motion there is no guarantee that it will stop. The image, the concept, the truth that is discovered beneath the veil of similarity, will in turn be seen as a sign of another analogical deferral. Every time one thinks to have discovered similarity, it will point to another similarity, in endless progress. In a universe dominated by the logic of similarity (and cosmic sympathy) the interpreter has the right and the duty to suspect that what one believed to be the meaning of a sign is in fact the sign for further meaning.

(Eco 1992: 47)

Eco's view of analogy (*ibid*.: 46) is often used in this study when examining the meaning-making of the video audience, and his list of criteria 'for associating images or words' from 'a sixteenth-century mnemonics' or *ars memoriae* together with Jurij Lotman's (1990) 'iconic continuum' (*ibid*.: 203) are the most important theoretical proposals for analysis and often for just 'making sense' of the wartime videos watched in the community. The concept of 'iconic continuum' is an important element in Lotman's semiotic theory of culture, in which cultural semiosphere is described in analogy to biosphere and at first defined 'as the semiotic space necessary for the existence and functioning of languages' (*ibid.*: 123). But it is also 'a cluster of semiotic spaces and their boundaries and outside the semiosphere there can be neither communication nor language' (*ibid.*: 124). More importantly 'the semiosphere is the result and the condition for development of culture' and 'semiosphere is marked by its heterogeneity' (*ibid.*: 124). This points towards Lotman's argument that the multiplicity of codes present at any time in a given culture gives rise to creolisation (*ibid.*: 142) or creates a culture of hybridity. In order to understand how the semiosphere functions, Lotman invites us to:

> imagine a museum hall where exhibits from different periods are on display, along with inscriptions in known and unknown languages, and instructions for decoding them; there are also the explanations composed by the museum staff, plans for tours and rules for the behaviour of the visitors. Imagine also in this hall tour leaders and visitors and imagine all this as a single mechanism (*which in a certain sense it is*). This is an image of the semiosphere. Then we have to remember that all elements of the semiosphere are in dynamic, not static, correlations whose terms are constantly changing. We notice this specially at traditional moments which come down to us from the past.
>
> (*ibid.*: 126–7)

Parts of that cultural past are organised as spatial spheres, and:

> The importance of spatial models created by culture lies in the fact that, unlike other basic forms of semiotic modelling, spatial models are constructed not on a verbal, discrete basis but on an iconic continuum.
>
> (*ibid.*: 203)

It was this iconic continuum that was disturbed when the war, still raging in Croatia and Bosnia, destroyed the cultural space that was the basis for the organisation of our (mine and my audience's) spatial sphere. Since 'the spatial picture of the world is many-layered' including 'both the mythological universum and the scientific modelling and everyday "common sense"' (*ibid.*), the complex semiotic mechanism which creates our image of the world has to accommodate this disturbance in the iconic continuum, creating a new mythology and with it a new 'common sense', which in this case was an acceptance of the inevitability of the war. Thus Lotman's (1990) work as well as his joint work with Boris A. Uspensky (Lotman and Uspensky 1978a, 1978b, 1984) on the semiotics of culture, together with Eco's

28

(1976, 1979, 1990a, 1992) work, largely underpins my analysis of both video tapes as cultural texts and the 'meaning making mechanisms' (to use Lotman's term) of my audience. There are many visual-media theorists and authors who apply semiotic theory in one way or another to the analysis of the media. However, a successful combination of semiotic theory and sociological concerns is achieved in Fiske's (1987) *Television Culture*, and his work together with Ien Ang (1985, 1991), and the work of a number of other culture and media theorists is frequently called upon in order to either aid in the analysis of videos as cultural texts or to facilitate understanding of audience behaviour. I use their arguments, concepts and theories freely and will refer to them as the present work progresses and the meaning construction and the influences of institutional and cultural power and their relation to ethnic identity construction are revealed.

THEORISING TECHNOLOGY

Anthony Giddens' (1990) account of the spatial and temporal dimensions of modern culture is important to this work since it offers a theoretical base from which to examine forms of video such as the 'video album' or the 'video letter'. As Giddens points to the effects of the forces of modernity as to separation of time and space, the 'continuity of self identity' is threatened because places are no longer sufficient to provide the constancy of 'the surrounding social and material environment' (*ibid.*: 92). Giddens suggests that the transition from traditional to modern societies has brought about a fundamental restructuring of time and space relations. Whereas traditional social activity was centred around localised face-to-face interactions, which in turn were dominated by 'presence' and a strong sense of place, modern social activity is restructured in terms of relationships with absent others which may extend over vast geographical areas. This is a consequence of technological development and was characterised by Giddens (1984: 114) as 'time–space convergence'.[11] I propose here that the face-to-face interaction described as being specific to traditional society today is effectively mimicked by technologies such as VCR and that this might be the reason why societies which have remained traditional, such as the Aboriginal communities in Central Australia described by Eric Michaels (1985, 1987) or the Inuit people of the Canadian North described by Kate Madden (1990), have embraced VCR and its communicative functions more readily than other societies who consider themselves modern. On the other hand, the permeability of cultures brought on by modernity has replaced the 'concept of a fixed, unitary and bounded culture' (Wolf 1982: 387), causing a break in the cultural identity and creating a need for a relationship with the past (Rustin 1987: 33–4). The ontological security and the continuity of self-identity that was rooted in kinship systems, local community, religion and in the continuity of tradition is now increasingly re-created through attachment to various ethnic organisations, clubs and regional and village associations in order to re-capture the forms of 'trust relation from attributes of local context' (Giddens 1990: 108). The proliferation and the freedom in information and communication flows made possible by communication technology such as video (and satellite television and the Internet, etc.) allow those organisations to have access to a choice of regional traditions, languages, dialects and cultures and create a basis for more than one way to 'belong'.

One other theoretical approach which has informed the present research shifts the emphasis from *what* television and video programmes mean to *how* television and video produce meaning, contextualising video and television as a technological form and thus moving away from interpretations of ideological content (Baudrillard 1988). The twentieth century has seen the development of many technological forms, but the arrival of electronic technology is of crucial significance since it has altered the means of communication and brought the global political and economic fragments together in what is today an instant global communication, establishing what Marshall McLuhan perceived as an implosion:

After three thousand years of explosion, by means of fragmentary and mechanical technologies, the western world is imploding. During the mechanical ages we had extended our bodies in space. Today after more than a century of electronic technology, we have extended our central nervous system in a global embrace abolishing both time and space as far as our planet is concerned.

(McLuhan 1964: 19)

Twenty years later, Jean Baudrillard (1983a) saw industrial modernity as a fragmentary, explosive process, a massive liberation of force and energy, which eventually, in the electronic media, reaches its limits, crosses a threshold of oversaturation and begins to involute and implode. While McLuhan (1964) envisages implosion as abolishing fragmentation and ruling the global village, Baudrillard (1983a) in a postmodernist, somewhat nihilist fashion reads implosion as increasing fragmentation, abolishing meaning, the social reality itself and establishing a state of absolute non-communication, where the media saturate the environment, with seductive images and spectacles. Implosion, as a radical contracting phenomenon, overtakes postmodernity at every level.

Baudrillard's (*ibid.*) concept of simulation as applied by Michael Sorkin (1986) to the analysis of television argues that television as a simulation model shows substitute signs of the real for the real itself and implodes the difference between them, making the real and the substitute-real indistinguishable (*ibid.*: 176). Simulation models can be found across chains of signification, and while 'simulation thrives on the migration of categories' (*ibid.*: 175) it evaporates reality via its simulated reproduction which brings about ontological destabilisation.

This ontological destabilisation of the boundary between the real and simulated could be seen as one of the reasons why the Croatian audiences reacted positively to the rise of nationalism and ethnic consciousness through the highly structured media campaigns of their homeland (cf. Meeuwis 1993). Baudrillard's (1983a) argument that television extends its simulation throughout the whole culture can be applied to the analysis of ethnic video in the Macedonian and Croatian communities (at least prior to the commencement of war). The VCR extends its simulation not only throughout the whole culture (in this case Australian culture) but also across the cultural and linguistic boundaries of Australian 'multicultural society', erasing the lines between real and unreal, producing the radical reduction of the real to its constructed simulation.

In addition, Kevin Robins (1994) argues that 'screen has the potential to extend and amplify human awareness and sensibility' affording 'experiences beyond the ordinary' (*ibid.*: 313). The (television, video) screen also 'displaces (rather than supplements) reality, the very presence of the screen image testifies to the absence or remoteness of the screened reality' and because the 'screen is fundamentally inert' it does not necessarily 'involve us in the processes of dialogue and negotiation' (*ibid.*: 314). However, this 'remoteness of the screened reality' has changed drastically since the first 'atrocity videos' started to circulate in the Croatian community and the audience found it necessary to engage in 'dialogue and negotiation' during and after screenings mainly in order to come to terms with the excessive violence. The documentary nature of such video tapes in contrast to the television images which do not 'involve us in the plight of those distant others' (Morley and Robins 1995: 144), removed a 'separation a shield, a protection' that the screen should afford us. Thus we ceased to be 'armchair anthropologists' (*ibid.*: 145) while the images of violence and death, rape and the vicious cycle of destruction of 'our' people and 'our' countryside confronted us with moral issues and personal dilemmas, based not on the fact that it was excessive violence we were watching but rather that this excessive violence was happening to us, to our people, and to places, however distant, we considered a home.

THE VCR AS 'SHADOW SYSTEM'

Lili Berko (1989: 289) argues that 'the first years of video's development found it shifting through the heteroglossic debris of its prehistory in search of its own ontological specificities', and that 'the entire history of photography and cinema, broadcast television, serial and electronic music and computer language can be considered as prehistory of video'. In saying this she reinforces my argument that VCR and the whole videographic apparatus[12] operate not on some other level or in some other space, but rather in the space between television, film, radio and all other communication and reproductive technologies such as the telephone and the photographic lens. This in turn coincides with Stephen Hill's (1988: 7) notion that 'experience of using a particular artefact is housed in what the "shadow system" of other technological systems make possible'. If the VCR is a 'shadow system' of both television and film it also draws heavily on the knowledge systems located outside television and film – since the reproductive quality of VCR has allowed it to become the focal point (together with a screen) of the multimedia system. Through its reproductive function, the VCR appropriates the specialised area of the existing technological parameters such as photography – VCR as a family album and VCR as phonograph – video hits, appropriating with it a certain authority, properties inherent and belonging to those media forms.

As a 'shadow system' the VCR acquires its place by becoming a cultural property capable of being translated into any of the systems it is shadowing. It even functions as a form of substitution for traditional cultural systems and cultural forms such as story-telling, just as such story-telling has appropriated VCR to ensure the continuation of the qualities of an oral culture (cf. Ong 1982). Hidden behind the technologies of television and film and embodied in photograph and phonograph lies the entire 'shadow' form of VCR technology which has its potency expressed in every act of its use of photography or phonography, appropriating their properties and escaping at every point along the specific technology path of diffusion. Thus the VCR creates its own frame and commands the development of new productive practices that transform the pre-existing patterns of cultural meaning production of the technologies it is shadowing. It creates an objectification of the symbolism ascribed to those other technologies, thus expanding, *not* replacing, the cultural technologies of the past.

The most powerful property that video has appropriated from all visual (and other) technologies is the claim to a reality of representation, a claim to the representation of 'truth'. Moreover, this claim to the 'reality' of representation is not specific to the ethnic video tapes under analysis here, rather it is inherent in video as a technology. According to Sean Cubitt:

> [T]he politics of cultural identity in which so much video is engaged is caught up in its own dialectic: people making meaning, but not in conditions of their own choosing. But still making meaning: their own meaning, despite circumstances.

> (Cubitt 1991: 43)

The circumstances Cubitt is talking about are the circumstances of 'difference', for instance, in the use of video by marginal-values groups such as gay lobby groups in their struggle to claim cultural space through the use of alternative media such as video, given that cultural space is largely denied to these groups in the mainstream media such as television (*ibid.*: 140–1).

But broadcast television, which was first with programmes like *Candid*

Camera, and later introduced *The Funniest Home Video Show* and *TV Bloopers and Practical Jokes,* created the climate for claims on reality for VCR, and later reclaimed some of VCR's credibility producing television shows like *Hard Copy, Real Life, Cops* and the latest, *Rescue.* All these television programmes are based on the notion of the authenticity of the recorded material, often using what was claimed to be 'authentic' footage.[13] They utilise the aspirations to the representation of the real which are in turn based on the accepted practices of television stations and global news corporations (such as ITN, WTN) of purchasing home-video tapes or amateur footage in order to dramatise their news and current affairs programmes.

The use of such 'incidental footage' is often the subject of ethical concerns, sometimes igniting heated public discussions presented on television itself or in other media. Headlines such as 'Woman regrets filming shooting by police' regularly appear in newspapers and magazines, which only adds to the VCR's claims to the true representation of reality, thus further blurring the boundaries between archival and doumentary uses of video and the production of highly structured shows such as *Cops, Rescue* or *Real Life.*

Toby Miller (1992: 5) describes the perhaps most famous amateur video tape today, the 'Rodney King Beating' as 'truth in motion'. He demonstrates how the video tape was used by both prosecution and defence as a basis for their arguments. Miller also raises the question of admitting in court a video tape of the testimony of a witness, instead of the witness in person, and using the tape as evidence. The example Miller quotes is the case tried by the Supreme Court of Victoria in 1987, when the court admitted as evidence a video tape recorded by a terminally ill lung-cancer patient in the hospital and gave it the same validity as personal testimony. However, the first admission of the video tape into a court as evidence was in early 1976 in the United Kingdom (Geake 1993b: 21) in a blackmail case, and the validity of video tape as evidence was strengthened further in 1982 when a judge ruled that the testimony given by someone who had seen a video tape of an event was as good as an eyewitness account.

Today the video camera and the whole videographic apparatus is irreplaceable for surveillance of all kinds, from public security to private investigations, and its claims to truth and reality are such that 'most people who are arrested after being caught on video tape confess as soon as they are told of the tape's existence' (Geake 1993a: 20). It is often argued that video cameras have such deterrent power that just telling people that they are being watched cuts crime. 'For example, Britain has an estimated 200,000 video surveillance cameras' and 'it is argued that [they] make people feel safer' (Robins and Levidow 1995: 112).

THE 'SHADOW SYSTEM' AT WAR

Video cameras in the war in Croatia and Bosnia and Herzegovina were welcomed by victims as a means of telling the truth to the world. Because of this, the occupying Serbian (and later other) forces often banned filming, while journalists, especially photographers and camera operators, were frequently sought out as targets.[14] The war images captured on video tape and later replayed 'in the comfort of suburban Perth homes' call into question all dominant discourses and discursive constructs of cultural texts, not only the glorifying of wars, but also the 'sanitised' images of the world media reports. As the visible results of war are everywhere (Goldberg 1991: 8) they are easy to capture on video tapes which are then widely circulated and accepted as part of everyday life.

Jorge Lewinski (1978: 222) argues that 'the closer images of war are to us in time, the more vivid and savage they appear'. He attributes this effect to technological advancement speeding the process of image production and reproduction and the greater freedom of the press, in addition to mass distribution, and to the general trend away from historical documentation and towards photographers' individual expression. This supposedly produces new visual awareness as a part of the production and consumption of new icons created by such photographers (*ibid.*: 201). Video tapes, just like photographs, are visual records accepted both as legal evidence and historical record. This acceptance is based on the appropriation of 'reality effects' of photography by VCR as a 'shadow system' of photographic technology. Thus audiences which generally recognise that photographic representation 'cannot be made . . . without the presence of the matter presented' (Beloff 1985: 2), usually ascribe the same property as inherent to video. Today video, like photography, presents a 'piece of reality' for its viewers, even though the audience often recognise the paradox inherent to photography and mirrored by television and video in which the image is both an 'objective rendition as well as a cultural construction of reality' (Jayyusi 1993: 25).

In the case of the representation of the war in the former Yugoslavia through both photography and video, the context of these spatially and temporally inaccessible events to the viewers in diaspora is authenticated by eyewitness accounts on video tapes. Just like war photography, video becomes 'a part of science, part of reading history' (Beloff 1985: 20) and provides evidence of social change happening outside our immediate environments. The Croatian audiences watching tapes of atrocities (as described in chapter 6) readily understood that 'the camera can enter the secret places of our civilization. It can literally take, steal, the hidden scenes that are closed to our gaze' (Beloff 1985: 5). Like photography, video is perceived as isolating and fixing an event in time and space, hence preserving it 'for ever' (Berger 1980: 50). As such, video functions to extend the life of a momentary event through each and every subsequent viewing. Furthermore, the 'rewind' and 'freeze frame' functions of the VCR allow audiences to view the moving image in its static form many times, allowing for close scrutiny and analysis, and aiding in the meaning-making by virtue of repetition. Moreover, media audiences already literate in photographic, television and film discourses draw on their intertextual knowledge (see Fiske 1987: 108–27) and are easily able to recognise – in their intertextuality – representations of persons/casualties, places/war zones, action/slaughter, event/war and objects/weapons (see Jayyusi 1993: 31). Such understandings (for example, the ethnic videos dealing with the history of Croatia) involve the construction (or reconstruction) of a 'proto-narrative' which mobilises the 'expected trajectory of action' (*ibid.*) in which the image was captured on the video tape or on the photograph. In addition to this common visual literacy, the audience I examined makes meanings according to the structure of their own referential knowledge and 'transforming the image into a site of meaning' (Burnett 1993: 16).

MEANING-MAKING AS POACHING

Meaning-making (or semiosis) takes place through a subtle dialogue (Bakhtin 1981) between the viewer and the video as a cultural text. This 'poaching' (de Certeau 1985: 122–45) involves a process of making personal meaning through exploring the text in 'whichever way one chooses', personalises the routes of meaning-making and the site for its users. The poaching of the text often positions the viewer within the narrative flux of an historical and real time which is captured by video camera. In this way the audience simultaneously inhabits two separate spaces, the physical space of their momentary existence and the represented space on the video tape (cf. Batchen 1993: 83).[15]

This dual existence only reinforces the impact of the destruction of mnemonic markers (Lotman 1990) as a result of the war. In this context most viewers studied felt betrayed by the discourses of the mainstream media which often showed 'toned down' versions of events or archival footage as 'most recent news' (Kolar-Panov and Miller 1991: 76). Compared with video tapes 'from home', this discrepancy enabled those tapes to be seen as the 'true pictures' of the war. Nor did the audiences ever seem to question the inevitable (and often accidental) manipulation of the video tapes either by their producers or by the editors. On the other hand, this acceptance of video as 'reality' (Hodge and Kress 1988: 23) is not to be confused with the audience's reactions to the often surreal quality of such videos. Images seen on such videos come into a 'head on' collision with moral values not only of the ethnic but also of the general population, 'acquiring such potency as to deeply affect basic definitions of good and evil' (Craig 1993: 114). This induced not only outrage against senseless killings but also vilification of the enemy in unabated hatred.

Thus a sense of shock and disgust often accompanied the audience response to the war videos circulating in the community. A similar account to those of my audience describes the aftermath of the images of nuclear war:

> [T]hey are so horrifying as to leave me weak-kneed and sleepless for several nights after seeing them, which has nothing to do with their artfulness or lack of it; it has everything to do with the fact that they are photographs of those two atomic explosions and the aftermath, since there is no escape from the reality they document.
>
> (Coleman 1979: 38)

There is a common experience of helplessness and condemnation as expressed by my audiences in the later stages of my research. Watching from the distance of Australia the destruction of our homeland, we felt 'helpless and hopeless' (Berger 1980: 38), feeling a 'moral guilt for our own safe position' (*ibid.*: 39). This was expressed by the common apologetic statement 'I feel sorry for those people, but there is nothing we can do.' Thus the video tapes of war in their unedited 'nakedness' introduce yet another level into the discourses about and around war, in a sense becoming 'the "site" of a continuous process of reinterpretation', and 'altering the viewer's mental taxonomy' (Burnett 1993: 6).

E PLURIBUS UNUM

Immanuel Wallerstein (1991) argues that racism and sexism have a constant form and function, although they are each different and flexible categories. He argues that the three modal social categories of race, nation and ethnicity are based on three basic cleavages in the capitalist world-system. Race is predicated on a core-periphery level, nation is based on nation states, and ethnicity is founded in households (*ibid.*: 77). This model offers a useful starting point for a short account of various theories of nationalism and ethnicity. This was necessitated by the larger context to this study and by the persistent presence of the same in all accounts of the fall of Communism before – and more so after – the 'end of the cold war', and especially in all descriptions of the war in former Yugoslavia.[16]

The contemporary study of nationalism has gone through a number of different phases. The first phase was dominated by comparative historians such as Hans Kohn (1944) who saw the national 'roots' of European states deriving from enlightenment, liberalism and the American and French Revolutions. These works are important only as a background to current theories. The second phase is embedded in the rapid decolonisation of Asia and Africa which revived interest in the subject. The scholarship of this phase was dominated by explanations of nationalism such as those written by Karl W. Deutsch (1966) and Hechter (1975), which shared the view that explanations of nationalism were to be found first of all in social structure rather than in ideology.

Today, studies of nationalism and the politics of cultural identification are addressed across various scholarly disciplines. These are also, by and large, discussions of – and the product of – European ideologies of nationalism. There are some works in particular, such as A.D. Smith (1988, 1990, 1991), Ernest Gellner's *Nations and Nationalism* (1983), Eric J. Hobsbawm and Terence Ranger, *The Invention of Tradition* (1983), and Eric J. Hobsbawm's *Nations and Nationalism Since 1780* (1990) which are important in more than one way to the present research. Works by others, like Donald Horowitz (1985), Miroslav Hroch (1985), John Armstrong (1982) and Benedict Anderson (1983), have informed parts of this research. What all these have in common is an emphasis upon the homogeneity and stability of socio-cultural formations which, if linked inside a nation state of common origins, present a 'workable' solution (Anderson 1983: 203). This often stands in opposition to the reality of heterogeneity of most modern nation states, including examples such as the United Kingdom, Spain or even France (Armstrong 1982; McNeil 1985).[17]

Carleton Hayes (1960), for example, gives priority to language in the formation of a common tradition, but also argues that five 'types' of past are important elements in the construction of a mythical base for tradition and peoplehood. These types are: territorial, such as a sentimental regard for the homeland; a political element, such as detachment from some governmental unit; fighting for homeland as a memory of exploits and valour; industry and economy as relative degrees of progressive development (or 'progressiveness' and 'backwardness'); and finally, a culturally distinctive literature and architecture. The accent on homogeneity as 'a kind of naturalizing purity of a nation in the myths of national origin' is investigated also by Gellner (1983), by Hobsbawm (1990) and Smith (1988, 1991) as well as by many others.

However, the study of the cultural production of ethnicity and cultural identity in the ethnic diaspora and its implications for the production of Australia as a nation state complicates this picture. Ethnographic inquiry into the range of adoptions and adaptations required to build everyday life (in the host country) makes visible how the 'ethnic' as 'the other' is constructed by the host culture and the community itself, not only through policies on their and the host culture's part, but also by the insistence on cultural differentiation inherent in the very concept of the 'migrant' or 'immigrant'. Gillian Bottomley (1992) in her informed study *From Another Place* moves away from the 'invention of tradition' (Hobsbawm and Ranger 1983) towards the construction and manipulation of the 'ethnic' in her examination of the experiences in the Greek migrant community in Australia. Bottomley's study provides a useful foil to mine. She also approaches the subject through an examination of everyday-life practices (such as dance), allowing the competing solidarities and identities revealed there to be examined at the levels of economic and political productions of class and gender, and not simply of ethnicity.

The ethnic audiences from former Yugoslavia build and seek their dual cultural identity within these same Australian national ideological configurations and processes of cultural production that Bottomley (*ibid.*) describes. Moreover it is often assumed that these ethnic identities are finally constituted and legitimated from wider domestic multicultural politics. But my research indicates a more complex interaction where ethnic identities are as much constituted actively through the diaspora–homeland relation as they are in reaction to exclusion or marginalisation by the host culture. Just as the Australian state and society as the host community was largely innocent of any significant influence, inasmuch as the Australian state basically tolerated and permitted the circulation of propaganda in the community (or simply did not know about it), first the Yugoslav and later the Croatian, Serbian and to a lesser degree Macedonian, Slovenian and Bosnian influences were responsible for ethnic nationalistic revivals. Clearly the development and state of multiculturalism in Australia is critical to an understanding of these legitimation processes, but the present work only addresses these issues as they arise within the frame of the present research (see Chapter 3). It is rather through the analysis of processes of particular cultural production, in this case through the medium of VCR, that understanding of such processes is sought. Only in such a way can the nationalist or ethnic (or cultural) configurations as they occur in historical time and space reveal the mutability of structures of domination and the means by which they are (re)produced, and thus make them transparent.

As the studies based on the assumption of an isomorphic relation between territoriality and nationalism (as mentioned above) have shown, nationalism presumed a social integration of everyone into politically and ideologically defined nation states seen 'as one culture, one people, one country' (cf. Stalin 1953–5: 307). Clearly, nationalism needs to take a different route in poly-ethnic societies formed by immigration such as Australia and the United States. In this context it is assumed that the assimilation and acculturation practised in Australia desired the creation of an Australian nation state still dominated by whites and Anglo-Australian culture and anglophone culture more generally. These priorities for many years legitimised the criteria for migrant intake and created what has been called in the US context (Meyrowitz and Maguire 1993) 'standardized diversity' or 'accepted difference' as a part of the homogenising processes already in motion. This creates a paradox which could be seen as a 'transformist hegemony' (Gramsci 1971). The paradox lies in the fact that legitimation inside Australian multicultural policy allows for symbolic levels of heterogeneity (symbolic ethnicity) *and* the production and legitimation of Australian national culture. Consequently, classificatory systems exist simultaneously inside parallel cultural spaces, coming into conflict only occasionally, such as with ethnic communities (such as the Croatian one studied here) where it appears that forces from outside, from the homeland, lay exclusive claim on the loyalty and resources of their diaspora and have disrupted the degree of equilibrium already in place.

We cannot, of course, assume that nationalist ideologies which are introduced from the homeland into the diaspora will result in the same processes and dynamics of production of nationalist ideologies as existed in the former Yugoslavia; nor should we assume that the newly produced ethnic nationalism amongst Serbs, Croats (and others) represents only a backward form of loyalty. In fact, in the course of this study I have learned not to expect anything. Mostly I have learned to observe and to note, looking for what Geertz in his 'Rituals and social change' (in Geertz 1973: 147) calls 'balanced syncretism'. Even if Geertz is describing the cultural production of religious traditions in colonial Indonesia, the processes of that cultural production are similar to, if not the same as, the present situation in Australia.

The question which remains to be answered concerns how such balanced syncretism can happen in multicultural Australia under a policy of 'unity in diversity', and if this does happen, how coherent will it be? Also, how will (or perhaps could) the 'traditions' within tradition function as a part of the Australian 'national character' in the making? Perhaps the answer can be found in Geertz's subsequent work where he addresses the interpretative strategies of processes of national homogenisation, concluding that only through observing the processes in their progress – as they happen – might we understand the character of 'integrative revolutions' (*ibid.*: 255–310). We should expect the formalised institutional processes designed to foster a policy of 'unity and diversity' to encapsulate the politics of meaning, because 'political processes of nations are wider and deeper than formal institutions' (*ibid.*: 316), and at the same time we have to recognise that the politics of meaning has a shape, trajectory and force of its own. This study shows that this 'balanced syncretism' involves the homeland–diaspora relations just as much as it relies on the poly-ethnic relations within the Australian nation state.[18]

DIASPORAS AS MARGINAL AUDIENCES

Minority audiences are usually, but not exclusively, defined in terms of their difference to the mainstream, and always inside the boundaries of a certain nation state. Under certain conditions this relation can change and the minority can define itself in opposition to other minorities which are seen as antagonistic, and in relation to other nation states or would-be nation states. Most nation states have within their administrative boundaries more than one people or ethnic group, even states like Great Britain and France. The multi-ethnic composition of nation states as they are today is a product either of annexation or the unification of different territories occupied by different ethnic groups; or the result either of large immigration programmes such as is the case with the United States, the United Kingdom, Canada and Australia, or of the accommodation of immigrant labour from less developed countries (i.e. Turkish migrant workers in Germany, or Filipino maids in Arab countries, Singapore and Hong Kong).

With the development of communication technology, especially VCR and satellite technology, it is easy to cross cultural boundaries with television images which do not require literacy, just as it is easy to cross territorial boundaries. The boundaries of cultural spheres (Lotman 1990) are becoming more, not less, permeable. In the past, this permeability of cultural and territorial boundaries has given rise to concerns about cultural imperialism, Americanisation, globalisation and standardisation (Tomlinson 1991). My research suggests that, at least for the marginal audiences I examine, the VCR and satellite have maintained and often reinvented traditions rather than bypassed them. Thus, for present purposes, it is necessary to use different terminology for different minority or marginal audiences. They can be usefully divided into four categories:[19]

1. indigenous audience cultures (such as Aborigines and Torres Strait Islanders in Australia or the Inuit people in Canada);
2. ethnic minority audience cultures (such as ethnic Chinese in Malaysia and Indonesia; the Bretons in France, the Welsh in the United Kingdom or Macedonians in Greece);
3. ethnic immigrant audience cultures (such as the different NESB groups in the United States, Canada and Australia);
4. marginal values audience cultures (such as gays and lesbians, religious groups and other partially encapsulated communities formed around different values and lifestyles).

This division is based mainly on the degree of difference in relation to the mainstream and the gaps between the interpretative strategies of mainstream and marginal audiences. The largest difference exists between indigenous audiences and the mainstream, followed by the two different types of ethnic audience – the minority and immigrant audience cultures – and lastly, the marginal values audiences which share the knowledge of mainstream value systems and which organise their marginality around the difference from and partial antagonism to the mainstream morality. Of course, there will always be differences even within these proposed categories. For example, the barely literate Australian-born and the illiterate non-English speaking migrant audience in Australia have far greater gaps in their interpretative strategies from the Australian mainstream than the ethnic immigrant cosmopolitans, who are often those bilingual educated professionals from Europe or Asia that are so favoured by immigration policy – outside its refugee, humanitarian and family reunion programmes (O'Regan and Kolar-Panov 1993b).

My focus in this study is upon ethnic immigrant audiences and the influence on their claim for cultural space created by technological changes, most importantly VCR and satellite television. These communication technologies, as it is proposed, have created a different audience dynamics overall and have impacted most upon ethnic immigrant cultures.

Thus the ethnic immigrant cultures (category (3) as above) can be divided further into those immigrants who seek permanent settlement in traditional migrant countries like Australia or Canada; those which are the result of migration from former colonies such as is the case with South Asians in Britain or Indonesians in the Netherlands and Arabs and North Africans in France; and finally, ethnic temporary immigrants such as South European guest workers, for example, Turks and Greeks in Germany, or Filipino maids in Arab countries and in Singapore. (The category of the refugee audience warrants further research and will not be dealt with here.) The ethnic audiences under inquiry here are the immigrant audiences which result from permanent migration, such as in the case of Canada and Australia, and which have already been accommodated by the multicultural policies of both countries. These policies in turn provide cultural space for immigrants in the host media systems. In Canada this involves programming in migrant languages on cable television. In Australia the main manifestation is SBS-TV and as of August 1993, *Tele Italia*, the first ethnic pay-TV television station, began narrowcasting films and variety programmes in Italian in Melbourne. Until *Tele Italia*'s inception SBS-TV was the only official source of programmes for ethnic audiences in Australia. I stress 'official' because in Australia the second largest penetration of VCRs in the world (72 per cent), and the VCR's special importance for ethnic communities have, according to my own research, created an uncharted, and thus unofficial, mediascape where the penetration of VCR into ethnic households I studied was near-total saturation.

The VCR has changed the relationship between the marginal and the mainstream in Australia, offering an alternative to the mainstream media and allowing the marginal audience to deal with the mainstream culture on their own terms. The desire of the permanent migrants to fit into the host culture and eventually become Australians, does not, these days, have to clash with their desire to maintain a separate cultural identity based on the homeland culture. Moreover, the present research into Croatian and Macedonian audiences has shown that the fragments of the homeland which have maintained a separate cultural identity are easily called upon by the homelands in time of ethnic revival in that homeland. For a short time such mobilisation can cause increased antagonism between ethnic immigrant groups in the host countries such as the potentially explosive tensions in the case of Australia with Croatian–Serbian and Greek–Macedonian. What we

41

see here is that changes in various homelands can and *do* impact upon particular ethnic immigrant communities, often widening the gap between groups which were a part of a carefully constructed multicultural identity or 'standardised diversity' (see Meyrowitz and Maguire 1993).

Mary Gillespie's (1989) short essay on the use of VCR for the negotiation of cultural identities in Southall, England (as mentioned earlier in this chapter pp. 17, 21) addressed the position and social significance of video viewing inside a South Asian community in England. Gillespie's work highlights themes of ethnicity and generation, showing the difference of interpretations of what she calls 'Bombay Films' which are often watched as a ritual by whole families. However, since the time Gillespie wrote her article, British South Asian audiences have gained access to satellite channels, for example *TV-Asia*, which started as an after-midnight service on Murdoch's SKY satellite channel and now as a result of demand, operates a full satellite service. This may have altered the audience dynamics as described by Gillespie, in so far as there is now an immediate and readily available source of South Asian news, films, variety and children's programmes. This only shows the risk of categorising audiences which are always 'historically embedded' (Ang 1991) and which undergo the same changes which are occurring in society at large.

The best examples of this historical embeddedness are the temporary migrant categories as guest workers in Western European countries who, as was the case of temporary migrants from former Yugoslavia, before the advent of the VCR depended on half-hour or hour-long weekly mixture of variety and news programmes carried by the mainstream television (Letić 1989). VCR has dramatically changed this and allowed these audiences access to programmes in their own language, most often produced and aimed towards the audiences in their homeland.

In contrast to Australia, whose ethnic audiences still depend on VCR for programmes from the respective homelands (with the exception of SBS and *Tele Italia*), the European temporary migrant audiences now have direct access to homeland programmes on satellite television. This is a part of a 'new media order' (Morley and Robins 1995: 12) where the 'new media technologies and markets make a mockery of borders and frontiers' and 'in Europe . . . the order of the day is now a free circulation of audio visual products and services' (Robins and Conford 1994: 233). This is seen as a tendency towards globalisation, and the mainstream media's answer is the creation of regional broadcasting since 'local and regional media are coming to be seen as fundamental resources of both community and identity' (*ibid.*: 234).

This new European global–local or international–regional change in media-development strategies reflects the broader processes of socio-cultural changes taking place in Europe (*ibid.*: 226–36).[20]

As for the European migrant audience, the global free flow of information and entertainment is not only a 'world bazaar of local and exotic' (Morley and Robins 1995: 112), it is first and foremost an opportunity to bring the language and the culture of their homelands into their living rooms.

This in turn confirms the findings of Meyrowitz and Maguire that:

[T]he majority of minorities express their 'special' desires to blend into the mainstream, to know what everyone else knows, to experience what everyone else experiences, to work in the same professions, go to the same schools, compete in the same sports, live in similar homes – and, yes, have some of their own distinctive history and culture presented to the larger culture in entertainment, news, and education.

(1993: 43)

2

THE CULTURAL FUNCTIONS
OF VIDEO

We don't know English as we are blind; we don't know driving as we are
crippled. The only thing we can do every morning is to take the bus to
visit the video shops, then to a tea-house for dim-sum (brunch). In the
afternoon, we enjoy the video tapes rented in the morning. At night we
may need to suffer by watching the local television programmes with
them (referring to the young ones in the family). On the next day the
same steps are repeated.

(Lee 1993: 6)

It is often argued that the national and network television in Australia,
centrally controlled as it is, promotes an 'artificial' national monoculture
when it does not contaminate it with American popular culture (University
of Technology, Sydney 1990). Existing television services – even those like
SBS-TV with a multicultural remit – often leave out or distort the multiplicity of voices and viewpoints of the many different communities that exist
in Australia (Seneviratne 1992). And it is commonplace in cultural studies
that broadcast television focuses and promotes the 'ways of looking' at the
world of a few socially privileged producers concerned with producing
images for large television audiences (Lewis 1991). This means that broadcast television must speak in general terms addressing audiences in a safe
language and images so as not to upset television ratings or, more importantly, the television advertisers.

   The difficulties facing the multicultural television station, SBS-TV, in catering adequately for Australia's diverse ethnic population or its 'other'
marginal audiences, and the structure of the mainstream video market
which carries very few titles in languages other than English except for a few
'art' films (Court and Maddox 1992), have resulted in the development of
alternative often semi-legal video-rental structures catering for the NESB
audiences.

   As my work with Tom O'Regan (O'Regan and Kolar-Panov 1993a,
1993b) has discussed the influence of SBS on Australian ethnic and other
marginal audiences, it is not my intention to repeat our discussion here;

44

nevertheless I would like to highlight the fact that SBS is a unique broadcast television service by world standards that has provided alternative programming for the ethnic, marginal and cosmopolitan audiences, thus fulfilling needs left unaddressed by both state television (ABC) and the commercial stations. Although over half of SBS broadcasts are in languages other than English, SBS can never satisfy or meet the needs of all ethnic groups in Australia, since no single non-English speaking (NES) community audience makes up more than 5 per cent of Australia's population.[1] This is important to note also in connection with the absence of ethnic narrowcasting. For example, *Tele Italia*, the first 'ethnic' cable television, had only 350 subscribers in August 1993. If we compare this with 15–20 million Hispanics or 16 million black Americans in the United States and what Meyrowitz and Maguire (1993: 41) see as 'American society splintering into subcultural clusters of race, religion and ethnicity', we can understand why the VCR still remains the most suitable medium for a special kind of ethnic narrowcasting regulated and practised by the NES communities in Australia.[2]

The quotation at the beginning of this chapter is from an interview (conducted by a student of mine, Albert Lee, for a research exercise) with an elderly Chinese couple who had recently emigrated to Australia from Hong Kong. It is indicative of the everyday video uses in NESB households. The invisibility of such video uses follows the trends in audience research in general where there is a noticeable absence of accounts of ethnic audiences. Perhaps when it introduces narrowcasting (Simper 1993: 4) the SBS will solicit some data that will make such audiences visible, and thus relevant, and hopefully this will lead to improved programming. However, the quoted Chinese couple, as well as hundreds of thousands of members of the Chinese-, Indian- and Italian-speaking audiences in Australia are in a way privileged in their ability to obtain a large variety of entertainment videos through the more or less well organised (even though sometimes semi-legal) video-rental structures. This is due to the fact that the Hong Kong, Indian and Italian film industries are large and established and turn out numbers of titles comparable only to the scale of Hollywood (O'Regan 1992). While these often tend to be community-based, some videos, particularly those from Hong Kong, increasingly are being organised in stand-alone video libraries.

The other NESB communities in Australia are not in such privileged positions, and have to rely on the extensive community and family networks in Australia and abroad in order to satisfy their need for entertainment and information from their homelands. This is partly a result of the disposition of homeland markets, or the lack of technological developments, or the slow development of proper information channels required for the production and circulation of audio-visual products for export. Furthermore, the poverty of Australian audio-visual markets in products from countries such as former Yugoslavia could also be partly due to the fact that most of the time there were complicated bureaucratic procedures involved in negotiation for exchange or import of these products. These negotiations were often conducted on the highest state and diplomatic levels and usually ended with a compromise. In the case of former Yugoslavia, the suitability of audio-visual products for import to Australia was usually measured by criteria relating to their 'non-offensive' content to any of the Yugoslav ethnic communities.[3] This in turn resulted in increased circulation of semi-legal or illegal audio-visual products in those communities.

The study presented below is a limited ethnographic study of two such communities as audiences, the Croatian and Macedonian communities in Western Australia. It is the result of a participant-observation oriented research into such communities, mainly in Perth, but also to a lesser degree in the rural towns of Carnarvon and Manjimup, Western Australia.

ETHNIC COMMUNITIES AS VCR AUDIENCES

Australia's Croatian and Macedonian ethnic communities have been formed principally through immigration. In fact most of the present-day Australian ethnic groups are the product of voluntary immigration (Martin 1978), but at times they carry the stigma of enforced exodus, as with the Macedonians from Greece (Stardelov, Grozdanov and Ristovski 1993) in 1949 or, more recently, refugees from Bosnia.[4]

Immigration to Australia typically means entering a poly-ethnic society with a culture that differs in varying degrees from the homeland left behind. Australian immigration policies ensure that, from the moment of their arrival in Australia, ethnic communities are oriented towards the host culture, because of its critical importance to the resources available to the family, community and the individual. As a result of these policies, there is a typical dual orientation among the ethnic communities towards the homeland and the host culture, leading to varying degrees of participation in both (cf. Stratton and Ang 1994: 128).

A.D. Smith (1988: 150) makes a number of important general observations in general about 'ethnic migrants'. He notes that 'ethnic migrants were offered citizenship and mobility within a single division of labour' in return for 'assimilation into a common political culture and the shedding of old attachments and vernaculars'. Such migrants neither aspired to 'nationhood for themselves' nor saw themselves as constituting a separate nation. However:

> [T]hey (or many of their members) were loath to . . . lose their ethnicity. So they accepted the offer of citizenship and mobility, but retained a 'primordial' ethnic attachment. In this way, there arose a familiar modern phenomenon: the sundering of citizenship from solidarity.
>
> (*ibid.*: 151)

Thus for the ethnic groups (like the Macedonians and Croatians in Australia), a 'dual' attachment was formed through loyalty to the most political unit as citizens of the Australian state, with its 'rights and obligations', and 'a sense of affiliation and solidarity with the ethnic community into which one's family was born and socialized' (*ibid.*). Smith observes two sets of allegiances and loyalties evolving from this situation 'one public and political with its official symbolism and all-embracing mythology' and 'one semi-private and cultural for each ethnic community' (*ibid.*).

Smith argues that for the most part 'citizenship and ethnic solidarity operate in separate spheres, public and private, political and cultural, so there is little friction or unease between them' (*ibid.*). The possibility of obtaining dual citizenship for migrants from the former Yugoslavia and Australia's multicultural policy of promoting 'unity in diversity' are examples of how citizenship and ethnic solidarity have been able to coexist in Australia on a sometimes frictionless continuum. SBS-TV – the 'ethnic' television station – could be seen as another example of a vehicle by which both kinds of loyalties were placed on that continuum (see O'Regan and Kolar-Panov 1993a, 1993b).

Because the ethnic fragments of the Croatian and Macedonian communities are dispersed across Australia, their need for 'ethnic solidarity' and ethno-specific information as well as entertainment have only partially been met by the development of Australia-wide distribution and information networks such as the ethnic press, ethnic radio and SBS-TV (Arena 1985; Young 1986). The former Yugoslav diplomatic missions and the former Yugoslav-based migrant associations were other available sources. Thus the former Yugoslav diplomatic missions and the various migrant organisations attached to the Multicultural Commission of Western Australia functioned as official information networks which provided both Australian and home-land information, political viewpoints and entertainment products, not available in the mainstream media or not readily available to the ethnic fragments due to their lack of English-language competence. The other sources – and the more important ones for this argument – were the ethnic clubs and the web of information networks developed around them, often based on local, familial and regional affiliation. Such organised ethnic networks extended the community through time and space in a new location, and served to repair, but also to maintain the boundaries of the ethnic group and culture in the Australian context. They also helped to govern the nature and the extent of acculturation by helping to negotiate publicly the selection of characteristics and behaviours that are appropriate to the definition of their ethnicity.

Ethnic communities are inevitably weakened by the very process of immigration and by their geographical dispersal, their time of arrival in Australia, and their diverse levels of knowledge of the English language at the time of their arrival. Obviously the higher the language competence is at the

47

time of arrival, the higher is the level of participation in Australian social and cultural life. This leads to various degrees of adoption of many ways and styles of living, including the use of Australian symbolic goods and benefits. (At the same time, of course, these all contribute to a necessary and barely recognised divergence between the homeland and the immigrant 'fragment' over time.) These engagements in turn ensure that the ethnic group soon becomes a 'cultural hybrid'.[5] These are made up in varying degrees of elements of the host (Australian) and homeland culture (Macedonian and Croatian). What is created in this process is a new culture which is neither authentically host (Australian) nor homeland (Croatian or Macedonian).

This process not only makes it increasingly difficult for any kind of ethno-separate politics and ethno-specific culture of the homeland to be sustained continuously across generations, but also ensures that the 'cultural' hybrid (or creolised culture) that develops will retain its ethnic dimensions, but in a form of symbolic ethnicity, accepted and favoured as a form of ethnicity by the host culture. Finally in this levelling process, the 'homeland' and the language of the homeland often lose the importance they had for the first- and second-generation migrants (and less often the third generation), and are replaced by an identity within Australian culture and English language, but still more often than not remain marginalised. Thus, under these conditions ethnic communities have permeable cultural boundaries (Lotman 1990), with their shape and identity changing from generation to generation and often depending on continuing immigration, if any, from the homelands. Nevertheless, the typical forms of ethno-specificity are characteristics of the first- and second-generation migrants, where the character of the cultural hybrid (or creolised culture) permits dual orientations and dual identities. In subsequent generations the cultural distance between the host culture and the ethnic culture narrows and tends to result in a greater degree of self-identification as Australian (cf. Price 1989; Betts 1991). However, what follows is a study of the uses of the VCR by the Croatian and Macedonian communities in Western Australia (between 1989 and 1991, with some data going back as early as 1985), and it can be expected to engage with the class, the professional and the value orientation of each community only in connection with their media habits.

As I have argued, ethnic video use has a fundamentally dual character, since VCR is used for the same purposes as among mainstream audiences involving time-shifting or watching rented videos (Ganley and Ganley 1987; Levy and Gunter 1988; Cubitt 1991), but is also used for viewing non-English videos of different types, some of which could be seen as ethno-specific, such as 'video letters'. On the basis of the present research I would claim that the degree of difference in VCR viewing patterns between the ethnic and mainstream audiences depends on the extent to which an ethnic minority is incorporated into the host (mainstream) culture. This is one of the most important factors in the determination of the ethnic audience's viewing patterns. The other factors which may influence the ethnic viewing patterns are the nature of the immigration – whether voluntary or enforced; there is also a direct relationship, to the length of the residence in Australia, as I show later, and, of course, the class and occupational base (of my informants).

Similarly, public policy initiatives like SBS's multiculturalism are designed to facilitate and guide integration in ways that enlist ethnic communities by giving them a public forum. The rapid penetration of VCR into ethnic households saw SBS programmes, mainly the multilingual programmes and the ethnic affairs reports such as *Vox Populi*, being used to construct and maintain ethnic separation and disconnection while simultaneously creating solidarities and connections with the mainstream (see O'Regan and Kolar-Panov 1993a).

Moreover, since Australia has the second highest level of VCR ownership in the world, next only to Kuwait (Court and Maddox 1992), we can be certain that the choice offered by non-English (ethnic) videos did not displace the consumption of Hollywood and other mainstream programmes (cf. McGann 1993). VCR is also used in time-shifting broadcast television programmes, but the consumption of non-English videos increased progressively, first, in proportion to the users' facility with English and later independently of it. Hollywood feature films could also be seen as offering a kind of 'buffer' between the immigrant and Australian cultures. In the first place, Hollywood films often provide a point of continuity for more recent migrants, as Hollywood films and series are screened nearly everywhere and most of the ethnic audiences have already appropriated a particular Hollywood imagery into their lives prior to migration. In addition, Hollywood productions also constitute a shared cultural resource with the broader Australian audience, which builds up common informational resources, though not necessarily common readings, as Eric Michaels' research in the Walpiri Aboriginal Community indicated (1990: 29).

Ethnic video, which is usually, but not always, a non-English production, is quite another matter, relying as it does upon a certain knowledge of the symbolic resources shared by the community in question and not by the mainstream.

However, as a result of the local nature of television and the absence of cable television and satellite services at this time coupled with the predominantly anglophone cinema exhibition structures and the geographic dispersal of the Croatian and Macedonian population across Australia, the entertainment industry has afforded ethnic markets and audiences only limited recognition. Before the establishment of SBS, and before and immediately after the availability of VCR, the two communities in question depended on the limited repertoire of feature films, information and propaganda material available from the Yugoslav Consulate in Perth, which were usually shown in the local ethnic clubs.

However, the increasing availability of the VCR for home use saw many individual households obtaining one, so that group viewing of material from the homeland in clubs slowly came to an end – but not for long, since the Croatian ethnic clubs quickly came to use collective viewing of war reporting as one of the strongest means to mobilise the diaspora.

Since there are virtually no controls over ethnic video imports in Australia, the ethnographic evidence assembled below cannot be backed up by any statistics or relevant numerical data. Consequently the account of viewership and its patterns is unavoidably fragmentary. Furthermore, the mainstream market is regulated through enforced copyright laws, while the ethnic market is remarkably free of such policing. The ethnic-video outlets operate through different types of shop, for example, corner 'delis' (variety stores), butchers' shops and hairdressers as well as an under-the-counter service in the regular video-library outlets. This makes for a semi-formal, non-transparent video market which is tightly wedded to ethnic community structures.

THE FORMATION OF A COMMODITY MARKET FOR ETHNIC VIDEO

In the study compiled by Alvarado (1988) for UNESCO three main uses of VCR in thirty-nine countries are defined, uses which are later taken as official UNESCO categories. They are:

1 Time-shifting
2 Viewing non-broadcast professional material
3 Viewing non-broadcast non-professional material, e.g. 'home movies'.

(*ibid.*: 5)

This and other similar categorisations of the uses of video (cf. O'Regan 1991) have presented some difficulties for this study, and I have used the third category of 'viewing non-broadcast non-professional material' in order to accommodate the various uses of video encountered in the course of this research, such as video letters and video albums.

The first UNESCO category of 'time-shifting' appears to be the least used function of the VCR by the participants in this study, if we do not count as time-shifted the pirated broadcast television programmes from Yugoslavia (more specifically from Croatian and Macedonian television). However, the VCR was and is used for time-shifting of feature films by the younger generation and often used for taping the daytime soap operas by housewives at times when they are unable to watch them for one reason or another. The long-running American soap opera, *The Young and the Restless*, was cited as the one most frequently taped. The apologetic reason, 'I have watched it

50

since I arrived in Australia', was given to me by one of the participants (M.M.) during an informal interview in early 1989. A lot has been written about soap opera and I don't intend to enter that discussion at this point (see e.g. Hobson 1978; Brunsdon 1981; Ang 1985; Katz and Liebes 1985).

Two years later, the same participant, a housewife in her forties, mentioned in the follow-up interview that she has no time to watch *The Young and The Restless* any more if she wanted to keep up with all the news about the war in her homeland, and said:

> M.M.: I cannot be bothered to watch the imaginary problems of the Americans while my people back home are dying. Anyway the Americans did not help much, did they?

What we have here is a change in the dynamics of ethnic-video viewing which has been and still is being directly influenced by socio-political developments in the homeland. When asked whether she still exchanges the programmes with her friends, the answer was positive, but no interest was shown in the usual time-shifting of feature films and serials. Rather, current affairs programmes such as *Dateline* (SBS), *7.30 Report*, and *Lateline* (ABC) were taped, as well as the segments of the news programmes directly concerning the 'Conflict in the Balkans'. (A detailed account of the changes in the practices of time-shifting will be given in Chapter 5. We will also see that two years after abandoning watching *The Young and the Restless*, the same participant, fatigued by the prolonged war, resumed watching her favourite soap but did not time-shift it any more.)

UNESCO's second category of 'viewing non-broadcast professional material' usually refers to Hollywood or other films such as Indian or Chinese feature films (cf. Ganley and Ganley 1987). Most of the videos in this category are rented from video libraries (less often purchased e.g. music videos). The study carried out in the United Kingdom (Alvarado and Davis 1988: 10) revealed that amongst the numerous video outlets for Asian films in an area with a heavy migrant population, one of the video outlets carried as many as 5,000 titles for a membership of 30,000.

The development and the dynamics of ethnic-video viewing in the two communities in question has been greatly influenced by a number of factors such as the wide dispersal of ethnic audiences in Australia and the fact that the homeland(s) of the Macedonian and Croatian communities did not have a film or video industry oriented towards their diaspora, let alone commercially developed industries on a large scale like the Asian film industries of Bombay, Calcutta and Hong Kong which successfully compete with the Hollywood product in East and South Asia.

The lack of interest in the developing of the 'ethnic market' by the main video distributors and the equally sluggish response of the homeland institutions in Australia, when coupled with the increased demands for 'videos from home', has led to the widespread use of established community organisations such as clubs and churches for the exchange and distribution of tapes. It might also be argued that the relative integrity and separateness of the ethnic dynamic, not to mention the 'informality' (semi-legality) of these software providers and distributors through the ethnic businesses, made it difficult for 'outsiders' to establish any business contacts or enter into transparent business dealings. With the disintegration and the war in the former Yugoslavia, an extensive community network of 'solidarity' developed, which only served to make the community more encapsulated.

A survey carried out in February 1990 in twenty video libraries in the suburbs of Perth and also in Spearwood, Hamilton Hill in the City of Fremantle area (all in Western Australia), all with a high concentration of Croatians; and in eight video libraries in the Balcatta and Wanneroo (suburbs of Perth) with a high concentration of ethnic Macedonians, showed that, except for limited titles of Italian feature films in rental outlets in Fremantle and Hamilton Hill, none of the surveyed video libraries carried any material in languages other than English.[6] However, other local shops which offered video rental as a 'sideline', such as newsagents, pharmacies, and most of all, the local 'delis', offered video tapes in languages other than English. The language and the origin of such video tapes was determined by and directly linked to the ethnic background of the shop owner. Two types of video tapes were available from such video outlets: Indian, Chinese, Greek and Italian tapes which were legal and available through a regular procedure – over the counter; and others which were pirated tapes from broadcast television of professional videos mainly of music from music festivals and variety programmes taped off-air which were available under the counter. Of these 'under-the-counter tapes' I can only speak about those circulating in the Croatian community in the Perth suburbs of Hamilton Hill and Spearwood and the City of Fremantle, since this part of my fieldwork – visiting video outlets – usually involved being accompanied by an informant who personally knew the owner of the rental outlet. We normally purchased a newspaper or a carton of milk, and I would stand aside while the shopkeeper conspiratorially brought out a selection of video tapes, generally unmarked on the outside.

There was also a noticeable absence of videos in the Macedonian language – even though a certain interconnection exists inside what is often characterised as the Mediterranean or southern European community (O'Regan 1993: 112). An Italian 'deli' frequently carried tapes in Croatian and Spanish, but there was not a single shop where Macedonian video tapes were available for rent or purchase outside the Yugoslav-oriented businesses with strong governmental links.

The oldest and the most popular 'multicultural shop' on James Street, Northbridge, in Perth which carried newspapers, books, records, audio and video tapes in all European languages did not have a single title or item in

Macedonian. Perhaps the fact that the owner of the Hellenic Emporium is a Greek Australian had something to do with it. I constantly made enquiries to the owner regarding some figures on video rentals and general stock. I never received any answers, and others acting on my behalf were also unsuccessful. The influence of the Greek lobby in Australia and its impact on the position of Macedonians is evident from the fact that Australia has only partially recognised Macedonia as an independent state (see Danforth 1995). For that matter, the same Hellenic Emporium did not carry any Asian items or titles either, most probably due to the strong Asian business-community interest already established, and formalised Chinese video rental and cinemas in that area.

In the only available account of circulation of video tapes from former Yugoslavia in other countries, Firdus Džinić (1988) found that the Yugoslav market is closely tied to the international video market. He also gave an example of how some ten Yugoslav families in the opal mine in the middle of the Australian desert had jointly bought a video recorder and regularly receive video tapes of popular songs and television programmes by air through a variety of 'Yugo' businesses.

His findings reflect the political situation of their historical time, since the 'Yugo firms' mentioned were usually collaborating with the Yugoslav diplomatic and trade missions. The source for the videos mentioned by Džinić, therefore, was the capital of Yugoslavia, Belgrade. A comparison of my research with the above account by Džinić (ibid.) cannot be made since I do not have any data on the wider Serbian community in Australia, which would be the most likely source for Džinić's records. My intended research into the Serbian community was one of the first casualties of the war, as my access to Serbian informants deteriorated. (I also lost most of my Serbian friends in Perth because of the war.)

As the former Yugoslav official policy was 'brotherhood and unity', and the Yugoslav diplomatic missions were often openly hostile towards the display of one's ethnic identity, apart from the euphemistic generalised term 'Slav', alternative channels for obtaining video (and other cultural) material were developed by the Macedonian and Croatian communities. In this case they were helped by official Australian multicultural policy being geared towards 'cultural maintenance' (as discussed earlier). By contrast, the Serbian community had all the official channels available to them including a steady flow of off-air pirated tapes directly from Belgrade – compliments of Yugoslav Airlines (JAT). For its part the much smaller Slovenian community (approximately 600 members) never joined in the so-called 'Yugoslav Community of Western Australia' in any way.

Nevertheless, Džinić (ibid.: 219) gives examples of many individuals with initiative who either bought the rights for the distribution of Yugoslav films or otherwise dealt with the pirated (off-air) video cassettes in what Džinić calls the 'Yugoslav languages'. He gives an example of a Yugoslav businessman in Sydney, Australia, who sold cassettes of popular songs ranging in price from DM70–80 to $50, in both Australia and the United States.

The price of $50 is low in comparison with the prices which members of the isolated Croatian community in Carnarvon were paying in the mid-1980s.[7] These were priced at anywhere between $60 and $100 with the usual price being about $80 for a single 1–2 hour video cassette, most often of very poor quality. When I visited Carnarvon in 1986, the VCR technology available was not sophisticated enough to enhance the quality of the second-generation tapes. However, with the availability of the appropriate technology, the quality of the tapes improved and the prices dropped, mainly because the advances in technology meant that a home reproduction of the tape could be made by linking two videos. Prices today vary from $25 to $50, depending on the length of the tape and also on whether it is 'legal' or pirated. Until recently, when the video tapes started to be used for fundraising for a cause, the practice of re-taping from a friend instead of purchasing an original copy was very common.

Among the tapes circulating in the Croatian and Macedonian communities were also tapes of ethnic programmes and films taped off SBS-TV, and with the availability of portable video cameras and camcorders there appeared a type of video tape which I call a 'video letter', examples of which are described later.

With the availability of portapaks and the camcorders, various different genres of home-videos emerged, such as videos of weddings, graduations, funerals and other family events which were often filmed by professionals (especially before the camcorder) since more and more photo studios offered video services (cf. Levy and Gunter 1988). These videos I classify as 'video albums' and I will refer to them as such from now on.[8]

VIDEO AS DISTRACTION AND ENTERTAINMENT

The first wave of video viewing was oriented more to the community than to the family, with the use of the VCR mostly being confined to wide video screens in ethnic clubs in Western Australia. Not all the ethnic clubs owned this still expensive equipment, but the video player and the screen were circulated from the Yugoslav Club in Perth which owned them as required by other clubs in the Yugoslav community in Western Australia. This practice of video use was an extension of the usual 16 mm or 8 mm film screenings which, in the absence of ethnically oriented cinemas in Perth, was a regular event in the clubs. It is interesting to note that the Yugoslav Club in Carnarvon used the equipment to screen not only tapes from the homeland but also taped events from other clubs in Perth.

The video tapes were at first supplied by diplomatic missions and homeland-based migrant organisations, but soon off-air pirated drama series, music videos and other broadcast entertainment found its way to the clubs. With the increased availability of material on video cassettes the repertoire of 'film evenings' suddenly became richer and more interesting. This more interesting material was provided mainly courtesy of Yugoslav Airlines' (JAT) stewardesses and pilots or by relatives and friends travelling abroad.

In the period between 1976 and 1980, before the VCR became accessible for domestic use, the variety and choice of video tapes was poor and the same programmes were recycled endlessly. For example, among the earliest mass viewed television serials in the Croatian community in Western Australia were the two long running serials from Zagreb Television (a sort of 'soapy' series like the long-running *Peyton Place* with a Dalmatian slant) called *Moje Malo Misto* (My Little Town), and *Velo Misto* (The Big Town). Both series dealt with the lives of several families in cities and villages in Dalmatia, mainly along the Adriatic coastline. *Moje Malo Misto* was set between the two World Wars and *Velo Misto* during and immediately before the Second World War.[9]

At the time of my arrival in Perth in 1984, the serial *Velo Misto* was at its peak of popularity. Many families purchased a VCR at that time in order to watch the reruns at home. The family of my principal informants, whose roots are from the Dalmatian provincial centre of Split, which is the setting for the plot in *Velo Misto*, was one of those families. However, the episodes, which were shown usually more than one at a time, were still watched in the clubs, since the group-watching offered more opportunity for comment and gossip.

It could be reasonably argued that the messages carried by *Velo Misto* actually promoted the perspective on the Second World War held by the Socialist government of Yugoslavia. However, the interpretation of the separate subplots by the audience completely overshadowed the ideological messages the series carried. *Velo Misto* was interwoven with many complex storylines in subplots, all of which are based on Dalmatian popular mythology, occasionally slow developing and full of double meanings and innuendoes. It would be counterproductive to outline all twelve episodes at this point since at the time of its showing in the Yugoslav Club I had not yet embarked on the present research, and I do not have reliable ethnographic notes. Indeed the only record I have is my personal diary, from the time when I had an opportunity to participate in the viewing of several episodes in the Yugoslav Club. It was in July 1984 and I noted the different interpretations by the mainly female audience (cf. Gray 1992), who besides noticing the relevance of the series to life 'back in the old country', followed the lives and numerous individual portrayals of what might be considered somewhat stereotyped (and easily recognisable) urban characters, such as the rubbish man and the mayor. Like all such series this one was full of family tragedies and love affairs, which were then endlessly analysed and retold by the audience (cf. Ang 1985: 28–34).

In the absence of any reliable evidence about the ways in which actual readings of *Velo Misto* took place, I can add only that comments during and after the viewing reflected not only the feelings about the show itself but also the stability of the shared cultural symbols and most of all the common cultural memory of the viewers (Lotman 1990), which 'enabled [them] to participate in the "world" of the serial' (Ang 1985: 28).

At approximately the same time, the Macedonian community, which includes a large number of Macedonians from Aegean Macedonia (P. Hill 1989: 14), showed a strong resistance to being put into the same category as 'other Yugoslavs', a fully justified resentment, since most of them had little or no connection to Yugoslavia, and most fled their homes during the civil war in Greece (Stardelov, Grozdanov and Ristovski 1993). They demonstrated a preference for watching 'historical' dramas and mini-series which dealt directly with their flight from Greece or with the destiny of the Macedonian nation in general and the destiny of displaced Macedonian children during the mass exodus of 1949. The video tapes that recorded the destinies of families displaced all over the world were often produced as documentaries by Television Skopje (RTV Skopje).[10] So too there were taped (pirated) theatrical performances of modern and historical plays written by contemporary Macedonian authors dealing with the historical fight of the Macedonian nation for independence, or plays like *Pečalbari* by Anton Panov (1938/1983) dealing with the tradition of migration and the reasons behind it, which are described later in this chapter. Nevertheless, the most popular genre for viewing were video versions of Macedonian popular and folk music and dance.

VIDEO AND CULTURAL MAINTENANCE

The television programmes produced in the former Yugoslavia, in this case in Skopje (the capital of the Republic of Macedonia),[11] were at first the only programmes available in the Macedonian language. Until 1944 Macedonians did not have a separate (official) language and schools or other cultural and educational institutions operated in the languages of the current administration of the region. (Unfortunately the remaining Macedonian population in Greece and Bulgaria still does not have the right to cultural self-determination.) Thus as a result of centuries of foreign rule, Macedonians have been denied the basic cultural technologies such as schools or even the printing press, and were often persecuted if they used their native language (Stardelov, Grozdanov and Ristovski 1993). Tome Sazdov in *Macedonian Folk Literature* argues that this denial of the literate use of the language led to the development of a mainly oral culture and that 'under such conditions of cultural and educational injustice the enslaved Macedonian could express his [sic] creative instincts and aspirations only through the medium of oral literature, in the form of folklore' (1987: 11). Thus traditions, folk tales, songs, aphorisms, proverbs and riddles have been handed down from generation to generation, preserving the cultural heritage. Perhaps the oral basis of what, today, is a fully literate culture is the major reason for specific genres of ethnic videos in the Macedonian community such as tapes of short sketches, even fairy tales (watched not only by children), usually accompanied by song and dance (cf. Michaels 1988).

The pirated videos from Macedonian broadcast television (RTV Skopje) very often contained overt communist propaganda, but as with the Perth Croatian audiences, this propaganda was more or less ignored. From the beginning of the penetration of the VCR into Macedonian households every available video tape was watched carefully. Later, as a larger selection of tapes began to circulate in the community, information and variety programmes were increasingly favoured and sought after; indeed even if a segment of a news programme was accidentally included in the course of the off-air taping it was fast forwarded in search of the music and dance. This period (especially between 1985 and 1991) was a golden time for the business-minded television officials from RTV Skopje, since the ever-growing hunger of the Macedonian communities abroad was such that all material was marketable, even if the quality of the videos produced was technically, and content-wise, often about twenty years behind what was available on Australian broadcast television. The other popular genre of video tapes were the tapes of the performances of local folklore groups, popular and folk music of questionable quality, sketches and stand-up comedians. Everything happening in the community was taped and then circulated overseas between Macedonia, Australia and Canada.

With the re-establishment of a democratic government in Greece (1975) which saw Greek policies towards Macedonian immigrants from Aegean Macedonia relaxed, at least in formal terms, the Aegean Macedonian migrants were for the first time since 1949 able to travel to Greece. The simultaneous advance in video technology (the camcorder), and possibility of travel to the homeland produced a new mode of communication between the ones abroad and the ones left behind, a form of video production which I have called a 'video letter'.[12]

Most of the Macedonians from Aegean Macedonia who visited their devastated villages in northern Greece had a mission other than just a visit. They had a duty to record on video tape those villages or their ruins; they had to tape messages from long-lost or never-seen relations and friends. And they did this not only for their families, but more often for half of the Macedonian community they were coming from. The tapes were then shown at group screenings mainly in private homes with the heroes or heroines who successfully brought the tapes back being at the centre of attention. He (mostly, but sometimes she) would tell the story of the visit and tell anecdotes from the trip to as well as giving her interpretations of the images on the television screen.

I have watched several times with different audiences a tape showing the trip to what used to be one of the most prosperous villages, which was almost completely destroyed after 1949. The proud baker turned video artist enriched the texture of his story with each and every new viewing. The camera lingered on the piles of rocks and ruins to which the host gave meaning by identifying them as 'so-and-so's house', or the village school or shop. Only during the part where the village priest, the only remaining in-habitant (then over 90 years old), is interviewed, did the narration stop. Each time I saw this tape, the audience would pay close attention to the story of how the priceless iconostasis of the once rich Macedonian Ortho-dox church was saved in the crypt of the church, which still served as living quarters for the priest.[13] The sound was poor and the voice of the priest often interrupted by coughing, but the audience listened attentively as though they were attending a church service. All activities ceased and the children were often silenced with angry 'shushing' from their mothers.

The same tape contained footage of other villages in the vicinity, since the camcorder was bought with funds raised by several families and the 'Austral-ian tourist' was obliged to tape as much as possible of their homeland and life in it. We were told by authors that this activity was most of the time extremely dangerous, since the Greek authorities had relaxed their policies only on the surface. The Greek government was willing to make a show of easing the visa requirements for visitors of Macedonian origin, but they were not prepared to let too much visual documentation of the effects of the civil war and what is seen by the Macedonian community as a 'genocide of a nation' to circulate around the world, particularly not interviews with sur-vivors of the 'genocide' like the village priest mentioned above. For this reason a lot of the taped material was confiscated (often together with the rest of the video equipment) either by the Greek police who closely followed the movements of the 'Australian tourists', or by Greek immigration offi-cials on the border crossings. One such incident made the news on the Macedonian ethnic radio in late 1986, when one of the most prominent members of the Aegean Macedonian community in Perth had his video equipment confiscated and was 'escorted' out of Greece.[14] The video tapes that made it safely back to Australia for this reason were cherished even more, and the authors celebrated as heroes by the community.

VIDEO LETTERS: AN ETHNO-SPECIFIC VIDEO GENRE?

Due to the private nature of these particular video tapes, most of the Mac-edonian families purchased VCRs relatively early in the 1980s, even though market prices were still high and the massive consumption of VCRs in the rest of the Australian population did not develop until somewhat later. Very often families invested in two VCRs, mainly for the purpose of retaping the most frequently borrowed tapes, and less often to overcome the noncompatibility of the VHS and Beta systems. Owning two VCRs also lessened the possibility of disagreement between parents and the younger generation who often got bored with the endless reruns of the same tapes and preferred to watch rented (mainstream) tapes or broadcast television.

The practice of watching these *ad hoc* assembled ethnic videos at home is different from any other practices described in media-related research, including my earlier description of community video-viewing practices, since the home atmosphere of viewing ethnic videos allowed for interruption by comments and story-telling. This was most noticeable during the viewing of the videos which I refer to as 'video letters'.

Many tears were shed when suddenly on the television screen someone recognised a relative or a friend, or when a grandmother or mother or sister appeared on the screen and filled the room with emotionally charged messages to a sister, daughter or grandmother, some of whom they had never met or had not seen for a very long time. Time and space lost their meaning and those present were transported 12,000 km into another culture, and often back in time. Families and friends were reunited in an instant, if only just for a moment or two. A number of the people interviewed commented that these tapes provided them with a strong sense of belonging, and often evoked recollections of their childhood.

One viewing experience particularly stands out. I visited a Macedonian migrant family in Perth who had just received a video cassette from Toronto, Canada recording the reunion of a family from Skopje, Macedonia. Let me first provide some background. In 1948 four infant sisters were among a number of children sent to orphanages around Europe due to the forced exodus (today we would call it 'ethnic cleansing') of the Macedonian population from northern Greece (Macedonia). Let's label them sisters A, B, C and D. Sister A was sent to Hungary, sister B to Romania, sister C to the USSR and sister D to Poland. The father of the family went to Australia, for *pečalba* (temporary work), and the mother managed to join him during the Greek civil war. After a long wait and enormous difficulties, they managed to find sister A in Hungary, with the help of the Red Cross, and they organised her escape from Hungary to Australia just days before Hungary was invaded and taken over by the former USSR in 1956. Sister B, who was sent to Romania, married and migrated to Toronto, Canada. Through the community network and with the help of the Red Cross, sisters A and B established contact with each other and together embarked on a twenty-year-long quest to find the two younger sisters, C and D, in USSR and Poland. When in the late 1970s, Yugoslavia sponsored a relocation programme for the return of displaced Macedonian children from the USSR, sister C was among the lucky ones. Again with the help of the Macedonian Migrant Association and the Red Cross, the fourth sister, D, was located in Poland. However, the political situation in Poland at that time was such that it was almost impossible to obtain visas to leave the country. Finally in 1984, sister

D managed to obtain a permit to come to visit her sister, C, in Skopje, Macedonia (then Yugoslavia). Sister B from Canada as well as sister A from Australia, together with their families, attended the family reunion.

The reunion was taped, and the video cassette was brought back to Australia for the mother, who was by now too old and fragile to travel. The father was long dead, but the mother was able to see for the first time her four daughters together, as well as their spouses, her fourteen grandchildren and two great-grandchildren. I was told that the mother had watched the same video tape at least once a day. Besides that tape there are many others, which in the form of video letters circulate in the triangle of Macedonia–Canada–Australia, providing the otherwise illiterate mother with a more than adequate means of communication with her family. Moreover, the daughter in Perth bought a video camera (at the time when they were still considerably expensive) so the mother could send video letters to her other daughters. These video letters are full of motherly advice, recollections of the past and even recipes. When I visited sister C, who now lives in Skopje, I was entrusted with one such video letter. There I found that sister B who lives in Canada (and I believe is more affluent than the sister who lives in Perth) had bought her sister a VCR on her last visit to Skopje, just so that they could keep in touch with their mother.

Today, there is a well-developed and well-established communication link between families and friends via video tapes. With the development and availability of more affordable production equipment, video cameras, camcorders and VCRs have slowly become accepted by the community (alongside photography and the telephone) and are used as a means of personal communication. However, the use of video equipment did not come with a 'Big Bang' since video comfortably fitted into the cultural spaces occupied by the existing technologies, and has done so in such a way that it has not significantly affected their patterns of use. Video, today, exists side by side with photography as a recorder of family histories and the only visual technology that video has nearly eradicated is the 8 mm and 16 mm camera as used for the production of 'home movies' (Slater 1991).

There are many types of video letters that serve as a link between people, and the structure of the video tape depends to a large extent on its producer. If the video has been taken by a professional video agency (part of a previous photographic studio), the tape is more or less structured and easily recognisable by its use of computer graphics in editing and titling techniques identifying the producer. More often than not, there is also music accompanying the images, music which is determined by the producer's idea of what is 'suitable' for the contents of the video. For example, most of the tapes of weddings start with Mendelssohn's *Wedding March (Here Comes the Bride)*, while tapes of funerals tend to be accompanied by appropriately sombre music, thus following the well-established musical encoding used by the film industry. I believe that most of us have by now been treated to a viewing of such video tapes, since video records of family history are not confined to ethnic video practices exclusively.

Such tapes can also come under the category which I call 'video album'. Together with the amateur videos taken by members of the family, these are used the same way as family photo albums. Domestic photography (Slater 1991) served the purpose of sustaining private domestic lives, helped construct family biographies and just like video albums, has become a part of the mass-market medium of recording family history. The video camera and the whole videographic apparatus have become parts of our daily lives, but at the time of this research video equipment was still considered as a 'luxury item'. Or as Slater puts it: 'the "maturity" of the market seems evident' and 'we'd all love a camcorder, but for the moment we will wait patiently and knowingly for the prices to come down' (ibid.: 59). However, the ethnic audiences under consideration here acquired camcorders as soon as they became available for domestic use. At first, a few families would share in the cost; later, individual families would purchase one. Also, the 'duty free' shopping system as in place in Australia meant that camcorders and VCRs could be acquired for far less than the retail price, during travel abroad. This meant that a camcorder would be purchased (and often an extra VCR) by members of the Croatian or Macedonian community travelling to their homeland, often used for the duration of the holiday and then left as a gift to the fragment of the family in the homeland, in order to enable them to produce and send tapes to Australia.

Even though the complete video package required a considerable investment,[15] most of the participants in the research considered it worthwhile, since it enabled the family fragments to establish a mode of contact which is considered as second best to face-to-face personal communication with their loved ones. Given that the video equipment typically included a VCR with recording ability, an ethno-specific genre of video letter was produced which contained a mixture of programmes taped off-air and family-album type records of family situations such as holidays, reunions and very often 'rites of passage' occasions – such as christenings, weddings and funerals. The usual records of celebrations of birthdays, anniversaries, graduations, and so on, as well as the records of such dramatic moments as the first words or first steps of a grandchild, (or the loss of a first tooth) are mixed on these video tapes with more ordinary moments from everyday life, like showing 'why the roses got spoiled this year in grandma's garden', or 'how well the vineyard is doing'.

Each of these video letters is unique and they are all very different, not only because they combine the personal letter and the snapshot, but also because, besides representing the personal account of the producers, they contain pirated off-air television (broadcast and satellite) programmes thus fostering an *ad hoc* cultural exchange between Australia, the former Yugoslavia and Canada. For example, the video tape recorded on the occasion of the birth of a child, a grandson and a nephew to one of the families taking part in the research, was rounded off with a taping of off-air segments of *Hey, Hey, It's Saturday* (a variety show on Australian commercial television that was being watched by the younger members of the family at the time when the tape was prepared for sending to Croatia by an acquaintance travelling abroad that night). I asked why that show? And the answer given to me was:

> M.R.: Because there is some space left on the tape, and there is no time to add anything else; besides they should see what rubbish we have on television here.

Above all it is the random selection of the content which places the above described video tape in a category of its own. It is on the basis of the participation in viewing such video letters produced in Croatia and Macedonia which also contained many more taped off-air programmes, that I am arguing that they should be considered an ethno-specific video genre. I will describe many such tapes throughout this book. However, at this point I would like to explore further how the VCR has been embraced in the Macedonian community as a form of cultural and communication practice without reservation.

SOME ASPECTS OF VCR: THE MACEDONIAN COMMUNITY IN WESTERN AUSTRALIA

A VCR was placed on the priority list of consumer items together with other necessities such as a refrigerator, stove or television, giving lower-income families the same access to this alternative means of communication as that enjoyed by mid- and high-income families. In some ways this took the 'status' out of VCR ownership, making it almost a necessity and not a luxury item at a time (mid-1980s) when among the rest of the Australian population, VCR was viewed as a relatively expensive entertainment medium (Connor Report 1985). When, in 1978, VCRs started to be marketed commercially, not many Macedonian families purchased one, but as soon as the communicative possibilities were discovered, the ownership of VCRs reached such proportions that in 1984 approximately 75 per cent of the Macedonian migrant households in Western Australia had one. (This figure is based on my initial research in Perth and Manjimup, the two largest Macedonian communities in Western Australia.) For these communities video technology did not mean bringing the cinema into their home, rather it meant bringing their roots, their heritage, their culture, squeezing their nostalgia into the format of a video cassette and letting it flow from the television screen any time they desired it.

Once the VCR was purchased and had occupied its rightful place among other precious possessions, it rapidly became an extension to an already important and dynamic range of ethnic community cultural practices. It is clear, then, that VCR use in this ethnic community varied greatly from its use in the mainstream English-speaking Australian population. The VCR in migrant communities performs a *dual* function. Besides providing a cultural link with their homeland or families and friends, VCR is also used for the same purposes as by the mainstream population, for example, for watching rented films (in English), time-shifting, or watching music videos. The emphasis on music-video viewing and film renting is often a more extended practice among younger people, often second- or third-generation migrants. Nevertheless, these videos are in most cases watched habitually by other members of the household, even by the older people with negligible fluency in English.

The social ritual of watching videos from the 'old country' is very different from watching rental videos and time-shifted English-language programmes. However, the VCR and the television screen are still the focus of an interaction which stresses the notion of togetherness and communality. Another interesting observation that I have made during hours spent watching videos with various families (and in the course of informal interviews) is that, while conversation is welcome during the viewing of videos in (their first language) Croatian or Macedonian, one is often silenced if one attempts conversation during English-language programmes either on broadcast television or on video. There are probably many reasons for this, but two aspects are of special interest for this project. First, the 'ethnic' videos are usually watched over and over again, so the content is familiar, while broadcast television or rented films in English are not readily available. The other aspect might be degree of language competence. While English-language fluency among the majority of migrants is variable, videos in English require closer attention, whereas videos in their mother tongue are readily understood. The interesting point here is that the same thing happens among the younger, Australian-born family members, whose fluency in English is expected to be higher than their fluency in Macedonian or Croatian. Whatever the reason, such different cultural practices in watching videos warrant further research.

The power struggle over VCR and television controls in ethnic families has the same characteristics as that in mainstream families as evidenced in television and video research (Morley 1989). This power struggle, particularly between children and parents, is very often overcome by the simple solution of purchasing another television – and very often another VCR.

If the power struggle over television and VCR controls in the ethnic households surveyed shows the same gender- and age-based characteristics as in the mainstream, the control of the mothers over the socialisation of ethnic children could be said to be even greater than in the families of the mainstream culture (cf. Bottomley 1992). If there are living grandparents, they often take an active part in the child-rearing practices of the two communities under discussion. My informants tell me that children of Macedonian and Croatian ethnic origin most often initially reject their ethnicity and very often rebel against anything that would 'make them different', as a consequence of extreme peer pressure. Yet once they reach young adulthood and come to terms with themselves as individuals, they very often return to seek their 'roots'. In this, they are assisted by Macedonian and Croatian government policies towards the diaspora, which actively support language seminars and summer schools for migrant students.[16] This tendency to maintain their culture and language is also fostered by Australian multicultural policy (see Clyne 1991, especially ch. 3). This renewed interest in one's cultural roots might be one of the reasons for the considerable popularity of ethnic video tapes among second- and third-generation Australians of Macedonian and Croatian origin. The viewing practices of young married Australian couples, when either one or both partners is of Macedonian or Croatian origin, are also different. In the case of a marriage to a partner of the same ethnic origin (intermarriages inside both communities are very frequent) or at least to a partner of European NESB descent, the maintenance of the 'ethnic' culture is far stronger than in the case of intermarriage to a partner from an English-speaking background. The greater the propensity towards cultural maintenance, the more the cultural practice of ethnic-video viewing is favoured.

There is an interesting variation in attitude regarding language maintenance and use among the Macedonian ethnic community from Aegean Macedonia (territorially now in Greece). Most of the migrants from Aegean Macedonia speak Greek as well as the archaic form of Macedonian. Many of them watch Greek films, mainly commercially distributed and available in local video libraries, or taped off SBS-TV. However, there is no community practice involved either in viewing or in exchanging such films except among close friends and within the family.[17] There is even a strong reluctance to discuss such films, almost as if these involve some sort of taboo, while the same is not the case with videos in English or even other community languages such as Spanish or Italian. Films and television programmes in these other community languages are very often pirated from SBS-TV and sent to friends and relatives outside the metropolitan area where SBS-TV is not received. For this reason, available statistics on the SBS-TV audience, which are calculated to be between 1 and 3 per cent of the overall audience in Australia (O'Regan and Kolar-Panov 1993a: 121), could be rendered partially redundant. Ethnic community members tape off SBS-TV, and distribute relevant programmes and films through the community web. They dispatch SBS-TV programmes on video tapes to the country areas, mainly the day after they are broadcast. In this way, SBS programmes pertaining to Croatian and Macedonian culture as well as films that are screened reach the majority of that audience (approximately 300,000 people in Australia).[18] Even more importantly, there is a practice of repeated viewings of most of the 'ethnic' videos, which only strengthens the impact of SBS programmes. If this tendency of off-air taping and subsequent distribution of SBS programmes is so strong in Macedonian and Croatian, it is likely that other ethnic communities such as the Italian and Greek, use the same practices. This would give SBS viewing a much higher true audience rating.

Migrant families are more inclined to watch SBS-TV or to time-shift SBS broadcast programmes than to time-shift programmes from the commercial channels or ABC. This is true even with SBS programmes which are not in their mother tongue. However, this has changed drastically for Croatian audiences as they began watching and taping news items and current affairs programmes from mainstream broadcast television in their quest for information about the homeland which was becoming increasingly confusing and perceived as incomplete. By taping (time-shifting) such information programmes as *7.30 Report* (ABC), *Dateline* (SBS) and *Lateline* (ABC), the Croatian audiences could watch and discuss them at a later time, rewind and rerun them or stop them in order to make sense of the reports and images. Very often, for the older generation with limited competence in English, such programmes were simultaneously translated by other members of the household and I have served as an interpreter on numerous occasions. One particular family taped news items and other information programmes for a whole week and then reran them for me when I visited at weekends, in order to help them understand the English-language commentary and the international politics being reported (e.g. the fall of the Berlin Wall).

From the outset of this research project it seemed very important to record and detect the basic functions and regularities of ethnic audience practices. But this research has led to somewhat fragmented results, making it difficult to draw conclusions with regard to the role of the VCR as entertainment and as a 'tool' for cultural maintenance. The problem was the constant element of change in ethnic video dynamics in the (mainly Croatian) community which made it dificult for anything like a stable picture to emerge. This was further heightened by the socio-political changes taking place in the homeland due to the disintegration of Yugoslavia. These changes saw the Croatian ethnic audiences in Perth continuously expressing a strong preference for what Paul Attallah (1991) has called 'cultural nationalism' type videos (he uses this term to qualify certain Canadian television programmes). Due to the fact that most Croatian videos of 'cultural nationalist' orientation were pirated from HTV (Croatian Television) this orientation is not perhaps a surprise. Indeed, as we will see later the provision of these videos was a part of a wider campaign by Croatia to reclaim its migrant fragments (or diaspora) and mobilise them in support of the Croatian nation.[19]

Because of its family and community base (rather than commercial base) ethnic video tends to be invisible outside its use in the respective community. There are also connections between ethnic-video viewing practices and cultural reproduction of ethnic identity, which not only makes such videos into a powerful medium of communication but also brands it as a marker of 'otherness' or 'difference'. Younger people in general – and teenagers in particular – show an understanding of how ethnic-video viewing practices may be disapproved of and ridiculed as 'backward' and foreign, especially by their non-ethnic peers (cf. Gillespie 1989).

Within this context, organisations such as the Office of Multicultural Affairs (OMA) and the Australian Broadcasting Authority (ABA) should develop a greater interest in researching ethnic video dynamics as it has become an important part of the everyday experience of television and video in Australia.

PEČALBARI

The geographical proximity of the Macedonian and Croatian people and their common Slav origins have created similar motifs in the folk culture not only of the two nationalities in question, but also with those of other people in the Balkans (Sazdov 1987). It is no wonder, then, that the migration traditions and the cultural patterns show similarities as both cultures have developed under such strong mutual cultural and economic influence as being under foreign rule. While Croatians (mainly Dalmatians from the Adriatic coast) had a tradition of seamanship which took them overseas to America, New Zealand and Australia, the Macedonians at first migrated seasonally to neighbouring countries like Greece, Bulgaria, Serbia, Turkey and sometimes the Middle East, especially Cairo in Egypt, and only later to America and Australia (Andonov 1973). Poor economic circumstances were the main reason for migration in both communities and the Croatian author Anthony Splivalo (1982: 2–3) in his autobiographical account of migration describes the same situation of poverty, debt and migration that is the theme of the highly acclaimed Macedonian play *Pečalbari* (The Migrant Workers) by Anton Panov (1938/1983). (I will use the original title *Pečalbari* since it means much more than 'migrant workers' and itself carries the whole history of the Macedonian people.) This play is particularly important for Macedonians worldwide. Besides dealing with a theme so close to their own personal and collective destinies, it also includes the description of different traditions and rituals accompanied by folk singing and dance. Due to its dramatic simplicity the play does not require an elaborate setting (or choreography and scenery), making it easy and inexpensive to produce. It is understandable, then, that Panov's *Pečalbari* is the most frequently staged play in Macedonian immigrant communities worldwide. For example, in his book *Macedonians in Australia*, Peter Hill (1989: 106–7) includes as an illustration of the theatrical production by various amateur theatre groups, three photographs of three different productions of the play.

With the increased ownership of VCRs and the availability of the play in different versions on tape, from feature-film version (Vardar Film), televised theatrical production by the Macedonian National Theatre and mini-series (RTV Skopje), to taped performances by community members, almost every Macedonian household in Perth has at least one video tape of *Pečalbari* in their video library. All versions seem equally popular, since it is not the production of the play, but rather the storyline, the narrative, that matters. It tends to be the community performance recording that is usually shown to visitors, since it provides space for comments and friendly gossip as well as providing an opportunity for the hosts to tell their own story of migration.

Pečalbari is often translated as 'migrant workers'. However, its meaning is closer to 'seasonal worker', and *pečalba* is the money earned that way. As mentioned above, any translation of it loses this emotionally charged meaning since it symbolises a whole set of particular economic, historical and emotional circumstances of migration. Peter Hill describes *pečalba* as 'a widespread Macedonian custom' asserting further that Macedonians 'did not think initially of Australia as being anything but a temporary workplace' (*ibid.*: 10). Thus the strongest connotation of the word *pečalba* is that of temporary absence from home and from the family, and above all, of the hope for a prosperous and happy return to the village. This hope that is still present among Macedonian migrants somehow becomes one of those connotationally charged codes that can be evoked and set in motion by the mere mention of the word *pečalba*. The structure of expectations and assumptions which lie behind the desirability of cultural continuity, the social stability of the community and the existence of moral behavioural absolutes, all are epitomised in this single word.

Discourses that have evolved throughout different times and in that 'other' (than home) space, and the emerging 'creolised' culture accommodating the traditional and the new order of the emerging situations still rely on images of the homeland, which persist throughout time and which are constructed and sustained through a positive mythology of the imagined past (Lotman 1990). What is important about this play which is so cherished among the Macedonian ethnic audiences is the fact that it represents exactly the kind of positive mythology so vital for the activation of the cultural memory (*ibid.*: 64). This makes it into a part of what Lotman calls 'a system of texts' which is actually 'tradition' (*ibid.*: 70). And the element of choice in tradition is relatively constrained once tradition has become an integral part of the functioning of a culture. Representing the way in which people recognise themselves as continuous entities, traditions (such as *pečalba*) exist over long stretches of time as connections, ties and extensions without which the ethnic (or other) group becomes disassociated (Shils 1981). While tradition can serve as a conventional shorthand for the values of the larger culture (presenting a useful way for outsiders to enter the culture), this does not obliterate the diversity of tradition or the varying degrees of adherence to it by its members. To qualify this, a short description of Panov's *Pečalbari* and its reception by the Macedonian audiences is given below. We will see how *Pečalbari* invoked commonly shared and understood associations and provoked elaboration, idiosyncratic themes or individualised versions.

Pečalba is a kind of tradition that Panov (1938/1983) calls *adet*. *Adet* is a word of Turkish origin (used in vernacular Macedonian with a stronger connotation than just a tradition) and is called upon throughout the play showing that behind the 'tradition' lurks the most elementary of all reasons, survival. By means of a simple and unpretentious plot Panov tells the story of a personal tragedy with which so many viewers are able to identify.

The hero of *Pečalbari*, Kostadin, borrows money from the local 'money shark' in order to pay for his bride (the bride is the money shark's daughter; cf. Bottomley 1992 on the similar tradition of dowry in the Greek community). Kostadin is an unlikely hero – indeed an anti-hero – and does not fit the stereotype of a *pečalbar*. The *pečalbar* is usually a strong young man who is willing to go to unknown lands, a hero who builds the transcontinental railway in America, a hero who works in the goldfields and opal mines of the Australian outback, a hero to whom local legends and folk songs are dedicated. Kostadin is a rebel, he does not want to go to *pečalba*, he wants to stay in his village with his bride and his widowed mother. He loathes the very thought of leaving, perhaps afraid of the same fate as his father whom he had never known, who died abroad.[20]

However, on the occasion of viewing the video tape of *Pečalbari* with an Aegean Macedonian family in Perth, I noted the comment by a male member of the audience (an Australian-born man in his early thirties) that Kostadin is not a coward. It was argued that Kostadin rather understood the futility, the hardship and the pain of leaving a family behind and that he should have considered taking his young bride with him if he was forced to go, just as the young man's father did. Meanwhile, the two elderly women in the audience were attempting to explain that behind the plot is a love story between Kostadin and Simka (the bride). These two women have time after time retold me the plot of how really Kostadin died for his love, overlooking selectively the parts of the play where he at first rebelled against another *adet* of paying for his bride (buying her from her father) and only did so after being coerced by his mother into accepting a loan. The widowed mother of Kostadin who, never having experienced happiness herself, poor but proud, had forced her son into obeying both customs by giving her word to Jordan (the 'money shark') that Kostadin would go to *pečalba*, pushing her son closer to his unfortunate destiny, was not loathed by the audience for her deeds, but was rather considered as 'doing the right thing'.

I have found that especially the older Aegean Macedonian audiences strongly agreed with the mother and often repeated that 'one's word should be kept under any circumstances'; and moreover, 'what would the village say' if her son did not uphold traditions? On several occasions the teenage members of the audience would make the point that 'parents should not interfere in any way', but they would be silenced immediately and scolded for disrespect.

The tragic end of the young hero, who finally bowed to the pressure from his mother and father-in-law and left for Belgrade (Serbia) in order to earn enough money to repay the loan, leaving behind his young bride pregnant with a son, a son who will never know his father who dies of tuberculosis at the end of the play, usually brought tears to the eyes of the audience. The discussion during and after the play usually included people's personal histories of immigration and very often a vivid account of the similar destiny of someone they knew back home in the village. The conversation would stop at places which involved singing and dancing and children tended to be silenced at what I have noticed to be the same four points in the play. The first of these is during the engagement party, actually a sort of official proposal, when Simka has been promised to another man. The second point is the wedding; the third is when the group of men from the village, including Kostadin, depart for the *pečalba*; and the fourth point is the return of the group of villagers from *pečalba*, the same group with which Kostadin was expected. At all four points in the play, singing of traditional folk songs (and sometimes dancing) is foregrounded.[21] Even though the script for the play offers lyrics and descriptions of traditions, the productions staged by the migrant communities show an interesting tendency to substitute the 'original' songs and traditional ceremonies with their local rituals and songs which make the play even more accessible to the audience. I have also noticed that the video tape was frequently rewound to the places showing the ceremonies and traditions and quite often an argument would develop about leaving out or misinterpreting one or other aspect which differed from some personal recollection and knowledge of the same.

There are thirteen different songs in the play altogether, and even though some of them pertain to traditional engagement and wedding rituals, the most haunting and the most powerful are the *pečalbari* ones. Tome Sazdov characterises the *pečalbari* songs as follows:

A wasted youth, nostalgia for the family, home, fatherland, unfulfilled desires and hopes are present in every line of such songs. The worker's poverty proved stronger than his boundless love for his wife and family, whom he was forced to leave in order to make a living. The youngest child, in these songs usually a year old, will come to call a stranger 'father' without having met his father.

(Sazdov 1987: 45)

Sazdov (1986: 304–11) also argues that Macedonian folk music is a living process due to the absence until recently of a literate culture, and that it lends itself to the constant production of oral forms of poetry, which then become lyrics for 'new composed folk songs'.[22]

NEW COMPOSED FOLK MUSIC

The influence of technology such as the gramophone and tape recorder, as argued by Sazdov (1986: 305; and I would add VCRs), has made the new composed folk music (NFM) enormously popular and a part of everyday life, as a continuation of 'folk production'. Sazdov's argument is based on the fact that the NFM is transmitted orally and that the theme of the lyrics, as well as the music, are so close to traditional folk songs that the boundaries between them become blurred. This blurring of the boundaries between the new composed and traditional folk songs is even more evident when both are available on video tapes often being performed by the same artists. I have noted cases when audience members have attempted to explain to me that a particular song is a 'very old' folk song, and yet I distinctly remembered that the song in question such as *Makedonsko Devojče* (Macedonian Maiden) was composed by one of the pioneer artists of Macedonian traditional and new composed folk music, Jonče Hristovski. The obvious blurring of the boundaries here has occurred for two reasons. First, Jonče Hristovski is a well-known Macedonian artist, interpreter and composer who has in his long career toured and visited most of the Macedonian ethnic fragments in the world and is well known as an interpreter of traditional folk music. I first met him in 1976 in Toronto, Canada, and again on several occasions in Perth between 1984 and 1988. The second reason is the fact that the song *Makedonsko Devojče* has all the elements of Macedonian traditional poetry and it has a history of collective authorship with the most famous Macedonian folk group Tanec from Skopje (*ibid.*: 309), the group that is also at the forefront of traditional folk dance.

The song is a celebration of the beauty of a young Macedonian maiden, compared in the song with the beauty of the Macedonian fatherland. (Croatians call Croatia 'Motherland' but Macedonians call their native soil 'Fatherland'.) The video spot we were watching was an interpretation by Jonče Hristovski, but the images accompanying the music were a mixture of the shots of a young woman (perhaps considered as a cultural stereotype of Macedonian feminine beauty) intercut with candid tourist-like shots of the Macedonian countryside composed of iconic representations of Lake Ohrid and close-ups of churches, monasteries, and so on.

However, the Croatian community, where a literate and urban culture has been present for a longer period, and universal education together with social communication and mobility of a different type from that of Macedonians, has produced a specific genre of popular music. This music is a mixture of an Italian canzonet type of material characteristic of the Eurovision Song Contest, together with traditional folk music, and often dance. This type of popular music (NFM) has retained many of the characteristics of folk music, and has undergone a further transformation through the availability of VCR. It fulfils the functions of traditional folk music (ritual music, etc.) since it has substituted its lack of 'folk' originality with the vivid visual representation of a folk ambience. Anna Czekanowska-Kuklinska (1986: 64) mentions that there is a special and 'authentic' interest in folklore in traditional peasant communities, communities 'where historical trad-itionalism' is very strong, such as in Norway or Sweden, and among immi-grants. She gives the example of immigrants to Canada but does not offer any further elaboration on immigrant communities other than a generalised conclusion that 'the functions of folklore in modern society are diversified and often contradict one another' (*ibid.*). She also argues that the 'func-tional dualism' of folklore has simultaneously 'stabilizing and revolution-izing functions', and that the most basic function of the folklore includes relaxation and reflection. In these terms we can argue that, if the first func-tions of the 'recreative and reflexive' type are what would in this research be considered the entertainment and cultural maintenance functions of ethnic-music videos, the second type which 'gains significance occasionally as a reflection of abnormal and eventful periods' (*ibid.*) fits the description of the militant and nationalist-oriented folk songs which gained immense popu-larity immediately before the disintegration of Yugoslavia alongside de-mands by Croatia and Macedonia for independence. The mass production of such NFM had an even more substantial impact on the immigrant com-munities of all three nations (Serbian, Croatian and Macedonian), and has had a long-range effect especially in the Croatian community since their homeland has been engaged in a war since 1991.

Less noticeable changes have occurred in the Macedonian community, mainly due to the fact that a large part of the Macedonian ethnic fragment in Western Australia is from Aegean Macedonia, who see the struggle for freedom and independence as continuing, thus upholding musical traditions seen by others as archaic, part of which stem from a nineteenth-century epic song glorifying Macedonian heroes of that time. The Republic of Macedo-nian (or Vardar-Macedonian) fragment of the community had a genre of soldiers' songs which were created during the Second World War (similar to most of the soldiers' songs of partisans fighting against Nazism) and these are rediscovered in such times of need as the recent Macedonian struggle for independence. Current changes in folk music circulating on video tapes, often performed live by a visiting artist from the 'homeland' (who then uses the opportunity to sell the illegally imported and reproduced tapes of their songs), are of particular interest to me, and the possible impact of the traditional and especially NFM as a 'social value' itself and a trans-mitter and cause for changes in ethnic migrant communities is analysed in chapter 5.

CONCLUSION

To conclude this chapter, and in a way the first part of this study, I will draw comparisons and parallels between the social and cultural experiences of viewers of ethnic video. These experiences vary from nostalgia – a key element for the older members of the ethnic community – through to the shared ritual for family and friends, while also functioning as a way of teaching the culture and language of their forbears to second and later generations of the community. For the elders, videos showing the folk rituals or other aspects of the way of life in their homeland as they remember it appear to act as a form of collective popular memory. Also some parents are more able to convey a sense of their past to their children through video, especially if the children are not literate in the Macedonian language. With the emergence of the second generation of children as parents and grandparents, the nostalgic element is usually lost and the socio-cultural use of ethnic video is primarily defined in terms of linguistic, ritual and other cultural learning (cf. Gillespie 1989).

Ethnic-video viewing provides one of the very few occasions when Macedonian and Croatian ethnic communities come together in the family environment on a shared linguistic basis. This does not happen in day-to-day life, since a common practice, even if the parent addresses the child in Croatian or Macedonian, is for the child to answer in English (cf. Bungey 1993). Most of the people interviewed shared a common enthusiasm for ethnic videos, often commenting that 'videos help the new generations to learn or to hold on to their mother tongue', frequently comparing the times when video was not available and pointing out the difficulties they were faced with when attempting to teach the children the language of their ancestors. In the case of the Macedonian language it was even more difficult since the Macedonian alphabet is a form of Cyrillic, and the levels of literacy required for fluent reading of original Macedonian material were seldom achieved. Regardless of the availability of a different font, and 'desktop publishing', due to the advancement of computer technology, the ethnic Macedonian newspapers often use the English alphabet for printing Macedonian texts. In addition, Aegean Macedonians are not literate in contemporary Macedonian. It is obvious that for many migrant children ethnic videos provide the only opportunity outside communication within the family and community (e.g. Sunday school in the ethnic church) to hear the Croatian or Macedonian language in its natural/cultural environment.

The notion of language as a transmitter of culture is still prevalent in these communities (Clyne 1991), as was also evident from the very heated debates over language policies (even under the Communist government) which have taken place throughout the history of both nations. And it is a shared view of both the communities involved in this research project that 'if children do not speak the language they lose their culture'.

Language for Croatians and Macedonians is a potent symbol of their collective identity as a nation, and is often the site of fierce loyalties and emotional power. In Yugoslavia from 1945 to 1990, a country which was artificially constructed from several Slavic and non-Slavic nations, the right to read and write in one's national language was one of the guaranteed constitutional rights. However, the dominant Serbo-Croatian language (which was also artificially constructed) was made the official language of administrative and other state and social institutions and was perceived as more powerful than the languages of 'other' nations inside Yugoslavia. (On the role of the Serbo-Croat language in the break-up of Yugoslavia, see Magaš 1993: 330.) This was reflected in the desire to defend and maintain the linguistic (and with it the cultural) heritage, especially in the Macedonian and Croatian communities led by an intellectual diaspora which very often claimed a dissident status within Australia, Canada and the United States.

These orientations are not surprising once we realise that the Macedonian nation was faced with cultural genocide in Greece and Bulgaria (Stardelov, Grozdanov and Ristovski 1993) and given that the Croatian fear of possible Serbian domination (which ended in a war) followed the long history of foreign linguistic domination by Hungarians, Austrians and Italians. The struggle by both nations – Macedonian and Croatian – for independence, was and is based not only on territorial rights, but also on the 'construction of the culture which is partly perceived as being based on linguistic continuity' (Gellner 1983; Smith 1988).

Since many second- and third-generation migrants and migrant children are illiterate in their mother tongue (and the Aegean Macedonians have been either illiterate or partly literate), the role of ethnic video as a means of communication with the 'old country' and among friends and family living in the old country, together with its role in familiarising them with the culture of the parents, seem to be viewed as most important by the Macedonian and Croatian migrants interviewed.

It has also become clear in the course of this research that ethnic videos generate discussion between young people and their parents and grandparents (frequently with three generations of the same family together), discussions that otherwise would very seldom take place. Both generations, the elders and the young people, use ethnic video to negotiate and argue about a whole range of customs, traditions, values and beliefs. Thus ethnic video, it could be argued, functions as a catalyst or as a tool for eliciting attitudes and views on what are quite often taboo themes (cf. Gillespie 1989). Family problems and extended family affairs, romance, courtship, marriage, as well as other cultural practices, are discussed with a strong bias towards what can be called the 'Australian' way on one side and towards the 'old ways' – generally considered part of the generation gap – from the other. Recognition of the differences between values and norms between the mainstream Australian and the ethnic community is a recurrent feature with most of those interviewed. It would appear that ethnic videos serve to legitimate a particular view of the world migrants have left behind. Ethnic video also functions to open new avenues for comparison and for contradiction since the process of acculturation flows both ways. While parents use ethnic videos to foster some traditional attitudes and beliefs in their children, the same videos are used by the younger generation to deconstruct the same 'traditional culture' their parents want them to learn, and through discussion, to help their parents to accept some of the Australian cultural practices faster and more wholeheartedly than they would without those discussions.

Many parents in Macedonian and Croatian communities voiced their concern over what they perceive as a progressive cultural loss with each new generation of children. While young people born and raised in Australia are striving to endure not only cultural but also peer-group pressure and desperately want to fit in with what for their parents or grandparents is an alien culture, their parents are still attempting to recreate the traditional culture of their past. The influences of ethnic video on the process of striving after cultural continuity and holding on to the ethnic cultural identity is specific to each generation of migrants. Nevertheless, the impact of the VCR on the very process of negotiating the cultural identity of every individual is far-reaching and overshadows the 'fun' aspect of the entertainment value of the VCR.

The notion of video viewing as a social activity which takes place in families needs to be extended to include more detailed explorations of the wider social, cultural and ideological implications of uses of VCR in migrant families. This is an important task, especially given the contexts of cultural and linguistic maintenance inside the wider context of acculturation into Australian society.

What has become clear from the above research is that the sense of national and cultural identity does not displace or dominate the equally dominant and equally powerful age and gender differences, and out of what is often called the 'communication revolution' of the 1980s strange alliances have been forged. However, as we will see later (Chapters 5, 6 and 7), the conditions of war have largely displaced the established age, gender and class dynamics, under the strain of 'living the war from afar'. Furthermore, the Macedonian and Croatian communities, even though they have emerged from common origins, have different experiences in the different countries they have settled in, and are not re-creating but rather creating the Macedonian and Croatian cultures out of their shared heritage, because culture is a dynamic process and no culture stays the same but rather develops and combines old and new cultural practices (Lotman 1990).

Ethnic video, as a cultural practice involving a detachment from its original place and time, creates and extends new cultural patterns and gives rise to new shapes of collective consciousness which in turn give rise to new common identities and new cultures, just like the pieces of coloured glass in the ever-changing shapes of a kaleidoscope.

3

CLAIMING A CULTURAL SPACE

The dynamics of video viewing by Croatian and Macedonian audiences is inextricably linked with the socio-historical formations of the two ethnic communities in Western Australia. This is because the positioning of the audience, as well as of the individual viewer, towards the cultural texts, in this case video tapes, depends on the viewers' cultural competence (Bourdieu 1980, 1984). The cultural competence of the two ethnic audiences is constructed and informed by their collective and personal histories and cross-cut by their class or social status, gender and other differences such as their political and religious affiliations. According to John Fiske 'cultural competence' also 'involves a critical understanding of the text and the conventions by which it is constructed, and involves a constant and subtle negotiation and renegotiation of the relationship between the textual and the social' (1987: 19). The video tapes circulated and watched in the Croatian and Macedonian communities in Perth were a potent kind of cultural text, which when mixed with the socio-cultural circumstances of migration and with the pressures of everyday confrontation with changes in the homeland and the existing cultural competence, could be accommodated only by re-negotiation of the cultural identity.

In such a cultural context the dramatic transformations that took place in the former Yugoslav community in Perth over the course of this research could be seen partly as a result of the mutual interplay of socio-political developments in the homeland and the availability of communication technologies such as the VCR (but also including others). In order to understand these transformations it is necessary to explain briefly the formation of the 'Yugoslav' community in Perth and its relation to the homeland or homelands.

Cultural technologies such as the telephone and television have already helped to overcome the 'tyranny of distance' to some degree, but the imperative need of migrants not only for communication with the homeland but also for more immediate communication on a day-to-day basis by a local clustering of social and personal relationships is reminiscent of a village or even an extended family and has brought about the creation of what are most often referred to as 'ethnic clubs'. These clubs were organised mainly according to national, ethnic and regional affiliation. Like any club or organisation whose members share common interests or meanings, the 'ethnic club' provides migrants with a cultural space in which they do not feel marginalised (even if their club is perceived as marginal from the outside). It provides a space which members claim as theirs, a space which creates a feeling of belonging even if only through speaking the common language of its members, by being able to share common memories and remembering and retelling stories from the homeland, and by sharing news and information. Most importantly, it provides the sense of belonging created by the pull of shared cultural symbols. Ethnic clubs have made it possible to claim a cultural space which is perceived as standing clear of the common cultural spaces which migrants share with the rest of multicultural Australia.

At the same time, ethnic clubs foster to some extent the process of acculturation into the wider Australian society by allowing the created space to display dual loyalties to the homeland on the one hand and to Australia on the other. This is most visible in the display of various insignia side by side, including the flags of Australia and the homeland together with portraits of the leader of the homeland on one side and the British queen, also head of state of Australia, on the other.

Western Australia, especially Perth, has traditionally been one of the strongest centres of immigration for migrants from the Dalmatian coast, and later Macedonia. This was so even before the Second World War.[1] The wave of patriotism and solidarity that overwhelmed the Yugoslav community in Western Australia during and immediately after the Second World War saw a massive return of migrants to Yugoslavia to help to rebuild the country. They returned mostly to the villages from which they had emigrated. The ship *Partizanka* became a legend among the migrants from the Dalmatian coast, since it served as a commuter between the Adriatic coast and Western Australia. Most of these families subsequently re-migrated to Australia after finding themselves unable to survive the post-war economic hardship in Yugoslavia. The return migration brought about a depletion of the various organisations and it was only in the early 1950s that a restructuring and renewal of the Yugoslav community in Western Australia began to take place. It is important to note that the survivors of the *Partizanka* era and their children during the later period of disintegration of Yugoslavia were the last to accept the fact of the disintegration of the country. These groups mainly refused to choose a 'new' national identity, opting instead to be simply Australian and thereby often coming into conflict with the newly founded Croatian and Serbian nationalism in the community.

In the immediate post-war period (1945–50) the largest and most influential ethnic clubs in Western Australia were the Perth-based clubs, since the initially large Kalgoorlie Croatian community had declined due to internal migration to Perth and Fremantle, Western Australia.

The anti-communist paranoia of the 1950s and 1960s caused a large number of migrants to join nationalist-oriented Croatian (and Serbian) clubs, and when coupled with an immediate post-war migration to Australia of people less than enthusiastic about the Yugoslav Communist state, it is understandable that they embraced the anti-communist sentiment of the time. At the same time the increasingly popular Yugoslav-oriented clubs steadily gained membership and strength from two sources: first of all, they enjoyed the full support of the newly established consular and other official representations of the Socialist Federative Republic of Yugoslavia (SFRJ); and second, the larger number of economic migrants from the new Yugoslavia gained entry permits to Australia and contributed to the idea of Yugoslavism. As a result of this, a new Yugoslav Club was established and registered in 1968 and functioned until late 1993. It is significant that Macedonian migrants from Yugoslavia joined this club in large numbers. Meanwhile the migrants from the Adriatic coast who were living and working in Fremantle and in the Perth suburbs of Spearwood and Cockburn established a sports organisation around a soccer club, Dalmatinac, in 1962. Dalmatinac soon became a member of the First Division Soccer League (1967) which drew in a large number of new members. As such it represented a competitor to the Yugoslav Club. In 1979 it became the Spearwood-Dalmatinac Club Inc. Soccer clubs based on or associated with various ethnic clubs became the first openly nationalist-oriented organisations at the time of 'ethnic revival' in the Yugoslav community in Perth. Not surprisingly the soccer fields often became a 'battlefield' between rival teams (*Sunday Times*, 25 April 1993, p. 11).

However, the post-war migrants from the new Yugoslavia were not all from Dalmatia. The ethnic Serbs and Macedonians (from the Yugoslav Republic of Macedonia) felt a need to organise their own clubs which would nurture and maintain the culture and traditions of their homelands. Depending on their individual orientation, 'old' Macedonian migrants from mainly Aegean Macedonia attended either Greek or Yugoslav functions. This changed when in 1963, in Skopje, the capital of Socialist Republic Macedonia (SRM), an organisation was formed to unite and represent Macedonians in Western Australia. During 1964–5 this campaign saw the unification of the Macedonians from both Aegean and Yugoslav Macedonia, and finally in 1969, the first United Macedonian Club in Western Australia was opened. The subsequent political pressure for the 'Yugoslavisation' of all ethnic clubs organised by migrants from the geo-political territory of the SFRJ caused a division in the Macedonian community, but more recently the clubs have joined ranks in the campaign for international (and Australian) recognition of Macedonia as an independent country.

In the meantime, the internal political changes in Yugoslavia (see Tripalo 1990) brought the Yugoslav federation a new constitution (1974) and a tightening of unitaristic policies. This increased the unitaristic activities of the diplomatic missions and their personnel. It directly resulted in the foundation of yet another club. The Yugal Club was envisaged as representing a miniature Yugoslavia, and even though it had only 250 members, the club was to become a favoured venue for campaigns by Yugoslav official representatives as well as for different campaigns by Australian political parties. The 'Yugoslav orientation' of this club became symbolic for what was going on not only among the Western Australia Yugoslav community but also in the diaspora from the territory of Yugoslavia all over the world. Ethnic orientation was discouraged as much as possible, so that even regional cultural identification became less desirable. However, the Slovenian Club (in Guildford, Western Australia) with approximately 600 members and the Macedonian community of Western Australia never joined the newly founded Yugoslav Community of Western Australia. They continued to celebrate their cultural and national heritage largely undisturbed. The Croatian clubs remained openly hostile towards SFRJ and carried the stigma of being fiercely nationalistic and attracted much negative publicity. Any attempt on the part of these non-Yugoslav-oriented Croatian migrants to gain legitimacy and equal status as Yugoslav-oriented clubs was met with suspicion. For instance, in 1986 the newly opened Croatian Information Centre in Midland, on the outskirts of Perth, was effectively closed down due to a campaign by officials from the Yugoslav Consulate in Perth. As a result of that same campaign, the remote and mainly Croatian community in Carnarvon, Western Australia was targeted. Carnarvon is approximately 800 kilometres north of Perth and is situated on the estuary of the Gascoyne river. The 'Yugoslav' migrant community was formed mainly after the Second World War and consists mostly of farmers and market gardeners of Croatian descent. The nature of the work on banana plantations (and in orchards and vegetable gardens) is such that the internal migration is high, both frequent and seasonal. Most of the families move to Perth or send their children to Perth for the purposes of higher education as soon as they accumulate sufficient capital. The fruit and vegetable business was, and still is, so structured that this was possible, while there was a mass change in the ownership of plantations from Yugoslavian to mainly Vietnamese and Portugese families, in the mid- and late 1980s.

In 1984 when I visited Carnarvon for the first time, the number of ethnic Yugoslavs, mainly Dalmatians, was estimated at about 500. The market gardens and plantations owned by migrants from Yugoslavia were producing 70 per cent of Carnarvon's fruit and vegetables.[2] The isolation and the seasonal nature of the work meant that the Carnarvon community developed fairly independently from the rest of the Yugoslav community in Western Australia, and also remained isolated from other Yugoslavs in Australia. Their cultural maintenance has depended mainly on the extended families and on informal community networks. Family and other ties with Perth helped in organising the Carnarvon Yugoslav community along the same unitarian lines as the clubs in Perth, and had split the otherwise cohesive Carnarvon community in half. The increased activities of Yugoslav diplomatic and other representatives only deepened these divisions and the establishment of the Yugoslav Consulate in 1972 in Perth brought the final split in the Carnarvon community. The increased activities of the economic migrants of the younger generation who had completed primary and often secondary education in post-war socialist Yugoslavia, and who had come to Carnarvon mainly through marrying the Australian-born members of already established families, in turn brought the spirit of unitarism into this isolated community. Carnarvon quickly became the most targeted community for Yugoslav socio-political (or cultural-political) propaganda, and when the Western Australia Lands Department donated land for the use of the Yugoslav community, it took less than a year to build the club and amenities. The Carnarvon community remained, for a long time, divided between the 'Croatians' and some families that insisted on calling themselves 'Yugoslavs' which often sits uneasily with the newly formed Croatian collective consciousness in the light of ethnic revival.

The unitarist activities of the leaders of the Yugoslav community in Western Australia and those of the agents of the former Yugoslav government coincided with the newly adopted multicultural policies of Australia (Fraser 1981). This produced a flurry of activities such as dances, picnics, and so on, in celebration of the ethnic diversity of the 'promised land'. Even though the aim of most of these activities was to bring people together, and very often for specific fundraising for a hospital or club or other such campaigns, the political activities of the Yugoslav and Australian governments were ever-present. The Australian political activity was simple and open, consisting mainly of lobbying by one or other of the main parties (mainly both) for the ethnic vote, and very often celebrating the new-found bliss of the 'unity in diversity' policy promoted by Australian multiculturalism.

However, with the illness and later the death of the leader and the founder of modern Yugoslavia, Josip Broz Tito, in 1980, the largely hidden and well-camouflaged quest for a 'Greater Serbia', which had operated up till then under the disguise of Yugoslav unitarism, resulted in increasingly – even if not openly – pro-Serbian behaviour of mainly younger-generation migrants from Serbia. They were not satisfied by the unitarist- and centralist-oriented policies of the existing clubs and formed their own organisations.

Even though these new clubs manifested openly Serbian nationalistic policies, including a display of old Serbian royalist insignia, and operated a Saturday Ethnic School teaching the Serbian rather than the Serbo-Croat language, the new clubs received open support from the official Yugoslav agencies which turned a blind eye to the increasingly nationalistic tendencies of these organisations. During the 1980s, the open display of Serbian nationalistic tendencies under the guise of 'Yugoslavism' and the activities of the Serbian Orthodox Church in Western Australia increased. These activities led to the first signs of discord within the Yugoslav community in Western Australia. As a result of these, together with the fact that the world had started to see Serbia as responsible for the carnage in the former Yugoslavia (Thompson 1992; Magaš 1993), the Serbian community found itself increasingly isolated. However, the very successful propaganda machine working from Belgrade kept the Serbian diaspora misinformed and increasingly xenophobic (cf. Copley 1992). Video tapes circulating in the Serbian community were tapes either made by the Belgrade regime for 'information' in English or, just like other ethnic video tapes, were collages of off-air taped news and entertainment. As I had limited access to the Serbian community I cannot offer a closer examination of the cultural dynamics of this group at this time.

According to official records from the Australian Ministry of Foreign Affairs (1988: 21), the number of immigrants in Western Australia who declare themselves as Macedonian (not Greek, Yugoslav or Australian) is about 15,000. The majority of these are from Aegean Macedonia and, according to a popular myth (P. Hill 1989: 12), the first Macedonians arrived in Australia at the end of the nineteenth century (incidentally, the same popular mythology is present among the Dalmatians), and they have worked and lived in harmonious relations with the Dalmatians (Croatians) for a very long time (*ibid.*: 16–17).[3]

From before the Second World War and up to the early 1960s the Macedonian community was cohesive and even those who had accepted the Greek political line usually identified themselves as ethnic Macedonians. However, with the arrival of a large number of economic migrants from the newly formed Republic of Macedonia within the Federation of Yugoslavia the disagreement in this relatively cohesive community surfaced and started to erode the mostly friendly relations with the Yugoslav community. The insistence of some self-appointed leaders who argued that the Macedonian community should unite and identify itself as a part of the larger Yugoslav community with ties and affiliations to the Yugoslav Socialist Republic of Macedonia was the main reason for this long-lasting disagreement. This was because the symbols of the newly founded Yugoslav nation and its newly formed and still forming traditions were as alien to the Aegean Macedonians as to anyone else outside the borders of SFRJ.

It is understandable, then, that the conflict and confusion caused by this development created a kind of 'double orientation' which has remained until recently, so that when the two communities united officially in 1992 the identification and declaration of one's nationality and ethnicity as Macedonian remained just as confusing. There are numerous and, of course, differently oriented accounts of this split within the Macedonian community (cf. P. Hill 1989). However, for the purposes of the present argument it is sufficient to say that the two Macedonian communities in Perth, even if in disagreement on the surface, have kept the channels of communication open. This has only proved that cultural unity based on collective consciousness can and will override or absorb newly introduced cultural elements which are foreign to it (Lotman 1990).

This short account of the formation of 'Yugoslav' ethnic clubs in Western Australia closely matches the self-perception of the past by the ethnic communities. It also shows how these ethnic communities are neither 'fixed' nor unchangeable natural formations. They are rather shown to depend on and reflect the conditions and socio-historical context they migrated from and presently live in. Gillian Bottomley similarly suggests that 'Ethnics are devalued minorities not a central part of the nation' (1992: 63). She sees them as being constituted from commonly shared complexes of language and culture which are embedded in more or less elaborate cultural codes essential for communication and constituting only the base for a wider cultural consciousness which is necessary for their survival as the 'other' in their new homelands. My own research does not foreground disadvantage and marginalisation as a central component to the cultural maintenance of Croatian and Macedonian communities in Western Australia. This component of 'otherness' has been overshadowed by the disintegration of Yugoslavia and the recent quest for and gaining of independence for Croatia and Macedonia. The diaspora–homeland relations favoured the open display of national feelings and/or required clear ethnic and national identification, and created a need for re-negotiation of cultural identity. It is possible that the self-marginalisation and the resulting encapsulation of ethnic communities which has been happening as a result of the increased orientation towards the homeland is only a short-lived phenomenon.

It is early to speculate on this issue, because the process of the fragmentation of the community is still going on, and here I will address and discuss issues relating only to the function of ethnic clubs. It is important to note, however, the extent to which the traditional cultural base of the homeland still regulates the cultural and social dynamics and interactions in the Croatian and Macedonian communities. It is also important to note that ethnic clubs serve as a kind of substitute kinship base for the newly arrived migrants to Australia, offering them points of identification with the lands they have left behind. At the same time, ethnic clubs have offered a necessary bridging point for the slow process of acculturation by providing a space in which the Australian government and its institutions can address a large number of migrant issues, such as availability of community services and support systems.

The present research into the use of VCRs in the two communities shows just how important the maintenance of the real and substitute kinship relationships is for both communities. As the increasing availability of the technologies for communication with relatives and friends at home became of immense importance, the role of the ethnic clubs in everyday life began to diminish and weaken. This was because the need for social and personal interaction was now being fulfilled by smaller gatherings in private homes and around the television and VCR watching either 'video letters' or entertainment videos from the homeland. This weakening in the position of ethnic clubs did not last. The movement towards democracy and, soon after, the inception of the war, drove people back to the clubs. If anything they became even more prominent. The clubs functioned as places to enlist the diaspora, first into the politics of democratic elections and later for the purposes of collecting humanitarian aid for the war-ravaged country. However, by late 1993 the Perth Croatian community had almost exhausted its capacity to give aid and an increased disillusionment had set in.

The kinship-like ties in the community allowed the members access to information networks which developed as a result of networking based on territorial and national identity and which served as a base for the exchange of information 'from back home', thus allowing the private video tapes containing information about the war to be circulated and copied in the community at large. Regional and village associations were at the forefront of such circulation and exchange of information. In the following section I show the dynamics of such exchange of information, taking into account particularly the historical circumstances. Both the occasions described are symptomatic and can be seen as typical of the changes in audience behaviour.

In mid-1990 I was invited to a private party to honour a village saint which was attended by more than fifty people originating from the same village, on the Dalmatian coast and now living in Perth, Carnarvon and over rural areas of Western Australia.

The 1990 'village-saint celebration' was held immediately after the first democratic elections (in April 1990). The hosts already proudly displayed the new Croatian flag, not only on the flag-pole but also on almost everything that had enough white surface for the three significant colours – red, white and blue – from paper serviettes to the cake. Almost two years later I attended the celebrations of the christening of the first grandson in the same household. There was an even greater number of people present (around eighty), and I could notice the absence of the 'display of colours' and of the celebratory spirit among most of the guests. In 1990, the atmosphere had been full of hope and high spirits. Old Croatian revolutionary songs were played and the video tape that the host had produced himself 'just a month ago' while 'back home' in Croatia was shown. This tape was a mixture of 'taped off-air' popular songs intermixed with video messages from relatives and neighbours from the same village whose saint was celebrated that day. The audience paid little or no attention to the tape and there was only an occasional comment when a familiar face or landscape was spotted.

The carefree festive atmosphere of this gathering was in stark contrast to the christening celebrations held in the same home in 1992. The tape shown then was obviously an amateur edited tape made up of pirated off-air fragments of more than one news programme from Croatia. It displayed a documentary type of account of damage to churches and historical monuments, and straight after that an account of an alleged massacre in the geographic area close to where most of the audience originated. The audience gathered around the television set, some sitting, some standing, and watched in silence the devastated countryside, half-burned-down buildings and deserted streets. The only comment came from a young woman in her twenties when the body of a dog lying in the village street was shown towards the end of the tape: 'They even kill animals.' (The comment was in English.) No one asked who 'they' were and it was as if she brought the audience to life as they broke off into smaller groups to comment on the tape and exchange opinions about the war.

I had a private name for interaction of that type; I called it 'Serb-bashing', as most of the people's comments were limited to repetition of the popular myths produced in the course of the war, and the majority of the stories were accounts of the video tapes that the audience had watched on some other occasions. At this time, I realised that the free circulation of such video tapes was aiding the creation of an enormous hatred and animosity toward Serbs, and that the cohesion and solidarity of the audiences was forged on the anti-Serbian anti-Yugoslav and pro-Croatian sentiment.

We may be inclined to see these developments in terms of cultural reversion caused by Croatian–Serbian conflict or by the revival of ethnic animosities repressed by the unitaristic orientation of the former Yugoslavia and its politics, but what was happening here had very little to do with cultural reversion (to tradition, religion or whatever). What I was witnessing during this study was rather a creation of new myths on the basis of the 'blueprints' of old ones (Geertz 1963: 312). The stories emerging from video viewings of ethnic tapes were variants of the existing stories with the internal pattern of the theme itself being the question of the 'difference' between Croatians and Serbs (between self and the other). Placing this in a theoretical framework, we can trace all the stories and myths about 'Serbian bestiality' to some original, because all stories are part of a chain of variants. As Vladimir Propp (1968) asserts, the new is born of existing forms (and from the design of functions that he sees as plot), and the processes of story transformation are largely made up of substituting a function or character in limited spaces. Claude Lévi-Strauss (1963) sees transformation as a key element of compositional modelling, for if myths grow in a continuous process (as he believes they do) then some form of transformational logic can be assumed. As we witnessed the transformation of the myths of Croatian and Serbian 'age-old hatred' into new myths about the war in Croatia and Bosnia, the mythic map of the underlying structure of the culture has revealed itself. We were now in the 'liminal zone' (Leach 1976; Turner 1974).

ONE PEOPLE: TWO DIASPORAS

The anti-Yugoslav sentiment was not entirely new among the Croatian diaspora in Western Australia. The Croatian community existed as a parallel organisation, organised and functioning separately from the Yugoslav community. It was made up from numerous 'pockets' of Croatian migrants who did not identify themselves as Yugoslavs and were clustered around the Croatian Church in North Fremantle, Western Australia, which served as both a spiritual and political centre. The membership of this community varied in its political orientation towards the former Yugoslavia, from fairly disinterested members who used the community to fulfil their spiritual needs and disassociated themselves as much as possible from political activities, to fiercely nationalistic groups such as the above-mentioned Croatian organisations in Carnarvon, Western Australia, which had grown to resent everything that had any connections to Yugoslavia.

This stratification of the Croatian community was in sharp contrast to the openly expressed nationalistic orientation of the Serbian migrants whose often overt antagonism towards the Croatian community was in terms of their claim to 'Yugoslavism' and their despising of the fascism and racism embedded in the myth of the Serbian–partisan victory over Germany in the Second World War (cf. Magaš 1993: 318). The Croatian community worldwide had carried a stigma as fascistic and terrorist, and was viewed by the majority of Australian people and the Australian government as 'extremist'. This was particularly noticeable after the improvement of diplomatic relations between Yugoslavia and Australia in the early 1970s. Because of this, and in defiance of the Yugoslav community, Croatians displayed insignia and proclaimed loyalty to the Croatian independent state, NDH, which had once been a puppet state allied to Hitler's Third Reich (e.g. Paris 1981; Banac 1984; Thompson 1992).[4]

Some 'real' terrorist actions which were carried out or allegedly carried out by Croatian extremists from around the world, such as attacks on the offices and officers of Yugoslav diplomatic or trade missions, or the hijacking of an American (TWA) plane in 1976 remain a highly controversial issue and I will not enter this debate here. However, it is important to note that the infamous 'Case of the Croatian Six', which was always cited as an example of Croatian terrorist activities in Australia, turned out subsequently to be a set-up organised by the Yugoslav secret police. It was investigated by ABC's *Four Corners* current affairs team and the findings were broadcast just as the disintegration of Yugoslavia became topical. ABC's timing was impeccable since the Yugoslav community was then starting to show the first signs of disintegration in Western Australia. This *Four Corners* programme was taped by the members of the Croatian ethnic audiences and the video tape was watched over and over again, especially when the VCR audience was mixed with the 'Slavs' (Croatians of Yugoslav orientation) who needed some persuasion to change their alliances.

The labels of extremist, fascist and terrorist and especially the 'Nazist' orientation of Croatians most recently fuelled by the fact of the existence of a political party in the newly formed Republic of Croatia which was and is based on the former Ustaša movement during the NDH were a potent part of the popular mythology operating in the everyday discourses about the war in former Yugoslavia. These discourses are also operational inside the wider discourse of the Balkans as the 'powder keg' of Europe.

IDEOLOGY IN ACTION

In 1993 when I finished my research, the infernal fire of war was still raging in Bosnia and Herzegovina and to a lesser degree in Croatia. This war was a realisation of the worst nightmares of the 'Balkan watchers' who had been predicting the collapse of SFRJ as a 'blood bath'.[5] However, most of the 'Balkan watchers' had been surprised by the fact that Macedonia, which was seen as the overshadowing issue in Balkan politics, has effectively stayed out of the war. The decisions of the Macedonian government in Skopje (Republic of Macedonia), which minimised the possibility of armed conflict, was to denounce any aspirations towards territory inhabited by ethnic Macedonians in Greece and Bulgaria and to respect the rights of minorities within its borders (*Constitution of the Republic of Macedonia* 1991).

The reassurances of the Macedonian government regarding any territorial claims might be one of the factors responsible for the relative stability in Macedonia at this time but it has not altered the position of the Greek government which still insists that Macedonia as a name is exclusively Hellenic property (Martis 1984) and that 'recognition of Macedonia as an independent state would imply approval of territorial pretensions' (Glenny 1992: 182). Greece's implacable opposition to recognition of Macedonia has led to disastrous results for the Macedonian economy and has caused more than embarrassment to the European Community and the United Nations, which have been practically blackmailed into accepting Greek demands (see, e.g. Thompson 1992; Liakos 1993; Toševski 1993).

The decisions which are made by the current Macedonian government in the Republic of Macedonia are carefully followed and examined not only by the neighbouring states but are equally carefully watched by the members of the Macedonian diaspora worldwide, especially by the Macedonian diaspora which left their homes during the forced exodus from Greece during what is generally known as 'the Greek civil war'.[6]

There are no reliable statistics on the number of Aegean Macedonians who migrated to Australia as a result of this policy, since the exodus did not happen at once and in a controllable fashion. Moreover, Macedonian migrants in Australia have a long and colourful history of migration (P. Hill 1989). In the official records of ABS (the Australian Bureau of Statistics) they are categorised by country of origin – country of birth, which in turn could be Serbia, Turkey, Bulgaria, Greece or Yugoslavia according to which of these countries were ruling over Macedonia. But by and large, the Macedonian migrants in Australia are the result of the forced exodus before, during and after the civil war in Greece (P. Hill 1989). The stigma of forced exodus and the loss of the homeland for Aegean Macedonians has created specific cultural dynamics in the Macedonian communities worldwide, which relate best to what Ernest Gellner describes as 'diaspora nationalism' (1983: 101–9).

Given the position of the Macedonians in diaspora who have never lived in the Republic of Macedonia and who are more often than not illiterate in the Macedonian language, the possibility of communication with the homeland and fragments of the homeland worldwide via audio-visual technology such as the VCR was more than welcome. As I have already described some viewership patterns, I would just like to add here that the Aegean Macedonian community – which used to frown at what they perceived as 'technologically inferior' programmes taped from Skopje television and fast-forwarded the news segments – once recognising the possibility of Macedonian independence, started to seek out and watch video tapes containing information about the political decisions of the Macedonian government. However, the passing of the new Macedonian Constitution has removed any immediate hopes among the exiled Macedonians of a possible return or even the continued existence of a Macedonian homeland, in Greece. Because of this, the Aegean Macedonian community has grown to resent the current Macedonian government's policies, accusing the Macedonian state of abandoning them. The reason for this is that the Macedonian government is opting for respecting borders and speaks of a spiritual rather than political unity (Reuter 1993: 168). There is however a radical wing to the VMRO-DPMNE, the Macedonian nationalist party, which supports the dream of a 'greater Macedonia with Solun or Salonika' (Thessaloniki) and has supporters in the diaspora. It is worth noting, that this party was the largest political party at the time of the first democratic election in Macedonia, in 1990. However, it has since lost support in the Republic of Macedonia. The alliance of the diaspora and the radical wing of VMRO-DPMNE nevertheless adds to the irrational fear within Greece of possible claims on the northern Greek province of Macedonia by either the government of the Republic of Macedonia or by its exiled inhabitants scattered throughout the world.

Returning now to the concept of 'diaspora nationalism' (Gellner 1983: 101–9) we can understand the basis for such Greek fears, given the fact that the Macedonian diaspora shows similar cultural dynamics to the Jewish diaspora before the establishment of Israel. Since the 'extraordinary transformation' that resulted in the existence of modern Israel 'was achieved, no doubt thanks in large part to the incentive provided by persecution, first in Eastern Europe and then throughout the Holocaust' (*ibid.*: 107) the continuing denial by Greece of Macedonians' right to a cultural identity is more likely to have an effect opposite to the one desired. I will resist at this point speculating on the possible fate of the Macedonian state in the future, but it is clear that, given the state of flux in economic and political conditions in the world since the fall of Communism, the risks are high for any such a state. Indeed, I agree with Sotiris Wallden who concludes that:

> Though certain recent Greek policies in the Balkans, particularly those toward FYR [Former Yugoslav Republic] of Macedonia, have run counter to the stabilising role the country can play in the area, and have harmed its own interests, there is evidence that this situation is presently changing. Such a change would allow Athens to play a constructive role that would correspond to its real weight in the area. The economic dimensions would probably be decisive in this context.
>
> (Wallden 1993: 192)

However, it was not clear at this time (late 1995) if and how the recognition of the Republic of Macedonia by Greece would change the cultural dynamics of the Macedonian diaspora, and it is even less predictable what influence it would have on the preservation of the cultural memory and collective consciousness which form the basis for its ethnic identification. The whole complex of change taking place in Republic of Macedonia is fraught with dangers. There is no room for illusion or complacency. Given the fact that the Republic of Macedonia is a multi-ethnic country with a large population of Albanians (Lazarov 1995) the potential exists for a resurgence of Macedonian nationalism, in response to both ethnic separatism (of Albanians) and to the stubborn politics of the Greek government (Danforth 1995). As there is a profound anxiety among a part of the Macedonian diaspora in Australia (and I believe worldwide) about the potential unrest in the Republic of Macedonia, all the news about Macedonia is carefully monitored. This is reminiscent of the situation in the Croatian diaspora at time of the Croatian quest for independence and ethnic revival.

I pointed out in the conclusion to the previous chapter that the change in ethnic-video dynamics in the Croatian community due to the socio-political changes in SFRJ and later the war in former Yugoslavia altered the course of the present research, focusing it more towards the Croatian community, and this forced me to conclude the participant observation among the Macedonian community in early 1991. I also argued that the patterns of VCR ownership and the consumption patterns differ in the Croatian and Macedonian communities as established by my research up to that date. But what is important for the following argument is that further differences in viewing preferences are noticeable in the Macedonian community itself.

I would like to propose that these differences in viewing preferences are largely historically embedded and are the result of 'a complex game of positions' between the text and the viewer (Lotman 1990: 62–5). Thus by reconstructing the type of 'common memory' which the video tape as text shares with the ethnic audience it was possible to understand the 'readership image' or, to paraphrase Lotman, it was possible to make the audience visible even if it was 'merely inherent to the text'. For example, I analysed briefly the ways in which the play *Pečalbari* (recorded on video tape), especially the versions performed by the members of the ethnic community itself, have acquired a high cultural currency in the Macedonian community. Thus the fact that the tapes were often inferior productions of the play was less important than the fact that the play itself is based on, reflects and includes a large number of elements of everyday life, traditions and of folklore including thirteen songs which are all part of the larger pull of popular narratives from Macedonian popular mythology. The viewing of the tapes also frequently invited an avalanche of personal extra-textual narratives which are more or less versions of the same story (Propp 1968). More importantly, even if today the play is already canonised in Macedonian national literature, it has retained its original function of an oral narrative in which the past becomes the present through the utterances of actors, and the audience relives the story (Ong 1982: 141–2; cf. Muecke 1985: 41). The hardship and the tragedy of the young hero vividly epitomise the Macedonian economic struggle; however, it is the history of the forced exodus of the Macedonian people from Greece, which is an equally or even more popular subplot in the story of migration. I have described the video letters circulating in the Aegean Macedonian community and argued that it was the impossibility of a return visit due either to 'the tyranny of distance' or to Greek government policies that enhanced the impact of the first video tapes in Perth. These tapes, smuggled out from Aegean Macedonia, brought the popular narratives and the memory of the Macedonian community suddenly alive with images of the desolate landscapes which used to be home. At the screening of such tapes it became obvious that the two Macedonian communities shared a common language and used similar or identical strategies for meaningful negotiation based on a common cultural memory. However, the final and decisive factor for the preference of one video text over another was based on each personal family history of migration.

As the recurrent differences in responses of Macedonian audiences to the play *Pečalbari* have shown, the oral narratives of personal experiences of migration usually determine the final interpretation of the play. The collective memory of the Macedonian diaspora is tied to a territory other than where they reside, but neither the space nor the memory of the two Macedonian migrant groups is the same. The differences in their perception of homeland became even more evident when it came to the existence and the formation of the Socialist Republic of Macedonia (SRM) within the Yugoslav state (and later the Republic of Macedonia), since that territory does not include in its boundaries the Aegean Macedonia that is a part of Greece. Thus the processes leading to the social reconstruction of memory, that depend on the link between territory and cultural identity, could be seen as two parallel processes in the identity construction by the Macedonian diaspora. Cultural-identity construction occurs as social actors draw boundaries around their groups and include some groups through 'imagined' criteria (Anderson 1983), and we can trace how the two Macedonian communities 'constructed' their identity through interactions with their 'imagined' and real homelands. The very construction of their cultural identity depended on the existing structures of both Greece and the Macedonian state (SRM) inside the former Yugoslavia. The recurrent denial in Greece of the existence of Macedonians as a distinctive ethnic group is well known and well documented (see Stardelov, Grozdanov and Ristovski 1993: 82), and I shall not describe it here. However, it is important to note that, until today, the two groups of Macedonians exist in a somewhat uneasy alliance.

The mythic map and its structure that revealed itself in this moment of change allow us to see the differences in the stories and myths of the two Macedonian communities. While the Macedonians from former Yugoslavia had a cultural memory of relative safety inside the Socialist Republic of Macedonia (1945–91), the Aegean Macedonians nurtured memories of exile and genocide. What are at issue here are not political disagreements, but something more elemental, the difference in a historical memory of a nation. In theoretical terms, Geertz's (1963) view of culture as a collective experience not of consensus but a naturally felt 'we', and his argument that cultural patterns are understood to provide a template or a blueprint for social and cultural processes, is most relevant here. This is because some of the underlying reason for the differences between two Macedonian communities revealed themselves during interpretations of cultural texts, in the case of this study during and after viewing video materials from 'home'.

This is why the first video tapes smuggled out from Greece showing the lush green vegetation growing over the ruins of churches and flat fields where once prosperous villages stood, caused considerable excitement in the Aegean Macedonian community, while they left most of the members of the other community only with a sense of compassion. Macedonian Television (former Television Skopje) had shown (in 1993) a short documentary assembled from such video tapes, and had created considerable interest in Macedonia. On the basis of a large interest shown by audiences, it could be argued that documentaries shown on Macedonian Television together with other cultural texts showing the exodus of Macedonians from Greece is part of an attempt by the Republic of Macedonia to reclaim its diaspora by introducing to those segments of Macedonian population who did not experience the plight of Aegean Macedonian that part of the cultural memory that is not their own.

The myth of the exodus, as we have seen, is a strong binding myth in the creation of a nation (Gellner 1983; Smith 1988). The passionate intensity with which the issue of Macedonian exile from Greece is described and

retold, even by third generations of Australian Macedonians, and the renewed interest in that part of the history of the Macedonian nation among
the population in the Republic of Macedonia, suggests that this myth will
continue to be a living part of their cultural consciousness. This was also
visible in the passionate outbursts of anger and grief which occurred every
time I participated in viewing video tapes dealing with the plight of Aegean
Macedonians. It also shows us that the tragedy which was experienced only
by a certain number of Macedonian people is slowly claiming a symbolic
place in the collective cultural memory of the Macedonian nation. The influence of such myths and symbols is evident in the fact that the nationalist
party VMRO-DPMNE in the Republic of Macedonia which favours territorial unification with the ethnic Macedonian territory currently in Greece
and Bulgaria, won a relative majority in the first democratic elections in
1990.

Meanwhile, the Macedonian community in Australia has to confront the
difficult task of claiming its cultural space inside Australian multiculturalism, and is facing the difficult task of creating an Australian–Macedonian
cultural identity while avoiding regression to ethno-nationalism. This is a
difficult task given the fact that the Australian state and its institutions are
inclined to give up easily under pressure from the Greek lobby (Danforth
1995), and as a consequence they have decided to rename the Macedonians
in Australia as Slavo-Macedonians, thus committing an act of symbolic
violence. But that is another story.

4

RE-INVENTING CROATIA

The divisions inside the Croatian community described in the previous chapter led to a differentiation in the representational practices of cultural texts, codes of behaviour and often in the organisation of the narrative structures of popular myths regarding the homeland. The very existence of Croatian ethnic groups and clubs in Australia outside the Yugoslav community (of Western Australia) meant that their definition as a 'different' ethnic social formation from the Yugoslavs depended on maintaining a sense of difference from and antagonism towards the other groups. Eric Hobsbawm (1983, 1990) characterises nationalist movements of the late twentieth century as essentially negative and divisive with their insistence on ethnicity and linguistic differences, and Hobsbawm's perspective on the 'invention of traditions' provides a useful model for examining how Croatia was reinvented in the light of the break-up of Yugoslavia into separate political nationalism. Thus on the level of ethnic markers and display of 'holy icons' of nationhood (the flag, emblem, anthem, etc.), Croatians outside the Yugoslav community often relied on symbols and myths appropriated mainly from the Independent Croatian State (Nezavisna Država Hrvatska, NDH). This reliance on symbols of a puppet Nazi regime reproduced and strengthened the popular mythology concerning the fascist tendencies of Croatians that already existed not only in the Yugoslav community but also in the world at large.

Within the Croatian community itself the former ustašas and advocates of Nazi policies for the government of the NDH were just a minority, but the photographs of the NDH leader, Ante Pavelić (Krizman 1980), together with the coat of arms and flag of Independent Croatia became symbols of that 'otherness' and differentiation of the Croatian community from the Croatians in the Yugoslav community. The majority of Croatians in the Yugoslav community have resorted to referring to themselves euphemistically as 'Slavs', first, to escape the negative connotations of the name 'Croatian', and second, to distance themselves from the historical fact of the existence of the Croatian Independent State as a collaborator with Nazi Germany. It is often stated fallaciously that Yugoslav partisans were mainly

Serbs and most of the Croatians were collaborators (Magaš 1993: 314). The actual numbers of Croats involved in the resistance under Tito in the Second World War are most probably lost, not only because of the nature of the history of the Second World War, but also because so much of the data on them was retrospectively fabricated for different purposes, ranging from the personal scale of obtaining war pensions, to the international scale of getting war damages from Germany, or to simple propaganda purposes by the various parties involved.[1]

However, the myth of Croatians as terrorists and Nazis operated on multiple levels of society both in the Socialist Federative Republic of Yugoslavia (SFRJ) itself and worldwide. There can be no denial that the NDH took part in the execution of the policies and aims of Nazi Germany, but the Croatian people have never been allowed to forget this or even to seek reconciliation. While Germany, Italy and even Japan have been allowed to apologise and seek reconcilation with the world, the Croatian alliance with Nazi Germany persistently haunts Croatians. This is so much the case that it is customary among journalists to mention this alliance in almost every article dealing with the war in former Yugoslavia. The past is simply an easy reference point for all that is negative in the Republic of Croatia. It has also provided a simplistic justification for the non-interventionist policies of the rest of the world when it came to the question of defending the Croatian Republic from open aggression by Serbia and the Yugoslav People's Army (JNA) in 1991 (Harries 1993: 44). The creation of the modern Croatian state, the Republic of Croatia, in 1990 (Letica 1990; Bilandžić et al. 1991) has revived and refuelled the old (but not forgotten) mythologies about Croatians, leaving a residue of suspicion towards the Croatian Republic. The suspicion and distrust by the world community was rooted in the fact that the ruling Hrvatska Demokratska Zajednica (HDZ: Croatian Democratic Union) led by Dr Franjo Tudjman, besides basing their election promises on promises of an independent Croatia, adopted and later made official the modified flag, the coat of arms and the national anthem, all of which were used by the NDH during its brief existence from 1941 to 1945.

The symbolically charged insignia of the newly established Croatian Republic might have helped to unify to a large extent the Croatians in Croatia and in the diaspora, but the negative symbolism inscribed in the Croatian flag and coat of arms signalled to the rest of the world not merely the revival of Croatian nationalism but the danger of a revival of fascism. This negative symbolism of the Croatian insignia is always pointed out by the Serbs, and the world media follow (cf. Glenny 1992: 1–30). The unification of the Croatian nation in the late twentieth century was not an easy task since the former socialist regime of the SFRJ discouraged displays of regional national sentiment other than inside the framework of a wider Yugoslav orientation. The traditions and custom of Croatian people were thus absorbed into the creation of a larger national Yugoslav people's tradition.[2]

Of course there was considerable dissidence from the official line of the SRFJ and a large number of Croatian intellectuals in the diaspora have appointed themselves as guardians of Croatian culture (see Hefer 1959). Over forty-five years of modern Croatian development inside the Yugoslav Federation saw Croatian national and cultural history manipulated into an often uneasy symbiosis with the cultural history of other Yugoslav nationalities, in which language was the most powerful weapon. Each Yugoslav republic had a constitutional right to use of both languages – the Serbo-Croatian (official language of the SFRJ) and Slovenian, or Macedonian, and in some cases the languages of large minorities were used as second languages, for example, Hungarian in the former Serbian province of Vojvodina or Albanian in the (former) province of Kosovo (Socialist Federal Republic of Yugoslavia 1974).

However, contrary to A.D. Smith's claims that Serbo-Croat represents a unified language which affords no basis for nationalism,[3] the creation of a Serbo-Croatian or Croatian–Serbian language was always highly controversial and doomed to failure, not only because the respective languages used two distinct alphabets: Croatian the Roman alphabet, and Serbian the Cyrillic one (cf. Hobsbawm 1990: 54–5), but also because language is a central, indeed often the decisive, element in a national culture (cf. Gellner 1983). Even though linguistically the Serbian and Croatian languages might be very similar they are not the same, largely due to the fact that historically they have developed differently. The larger social semiotic conditions for the development of the Croatian and Serbian languages were provided by the socio-historical conditions of the two countries which had until the late nineteenth century been very different indeed. Because of the complexity of this issue I will not even attempt to enter the discussion about the formation and difference of the Serbian and Croatian languages (see Singleton 1976; Banac 1984).

It will suffice to say at this point that besides the alleged genocidal tendencies of the Croatian nation, the acceptance by the world community of the Croatian and Serbian languages as one and the same, was and is one of the larger obstacles for the young Republic of Croatia to overcome. The persistence of such notions in the discourses surrounding the modern state of Yugoslavia has always been enhanced by the artful and very successful propaganda machinery working from centralised foreign affairs departments operating from Belgrade. Its success is exemplified in the fact that Yugoslavia was always regarded as a nation, not as a multinational state with the most complex ethnic composition on the Balkan peninsula. It was summed up nicely by A.D. Smith (1988: 149–50) who takes Yugoslavia as his example to support his argument that no 'nation-to-be' can survive without a homeland or a myth of common origins or descent. He argues (*ibid.*: 150) that Josip Broz Tito built Yugoslavia on 'a compact territory, citizenship rights, a common code of law and secular political culture', pointing out that the Communists always:

recognized the ethnic distinctiveness of Yugoslavia's six nations, and institutionalised it, the Communists also tried to bind them together in a territorially defined 'Illyrian' homeland, with its common division of labour, common citizenship right and common laws – and even a shadowy common culture 'Yugoslavism', with its non-alignment, self-management and confederalism.

(*ibid.*: 151)

The intermixing of the population in the SFRJ, via intermarriages and largely unobstructed internal migration due to the centralised law and social policies, has further blurred the question of the national identities of the inhabitants on the territory of the SFRJ, with the possible exception of Slovenia which has largely maintained its 'pure' ethnic composition by implementing a series of by-laws restricting settlement (Magaš 1993: 140–1).

UBI PEDES IBI SERBIA[4]

I have described earlier how the Yugoslav community was formed in Western Australia, but what I would like to add here is that the large dissenting factions among the Serbian and Croatian intelligentsia in the SFRJ itself and in the diaspora have been busy persuading the Croatian and Serbian population respectively, about grandiose plots by the other side. Due to the well-known stigma of 'Croatian fascism', the Croatian dissidents could be active only outside the country. Consequently they had very limited influence either on the formation of the national consciousness of Croatians within the Socialist Republic of Croatia or among the large section of the diaspora who considered themselves as Yugoslavs. In the meantime the Serbian dissidence operated relatively freely both inside the SFRJ and in the diaspora under either the guise of Yugoslavism and in opposition to the supposed genocidal tendencies of Croatians, and anti-communist sentiment which has culminated in (the by now well-known) 'Memorandum of the Serbian Academy of Arts and Sciences' in 1986 (Beljo *et al.* 1992). The 'Memorandum', carefully engineered and convincingly written, has presented to the Serbian people a picture of modern Yugoslavia as a general conspiracy to rob Serbs of their cultural heritage as well as to rob them economically, 'only stopping short of calling for war for the creation of a Greater Serbia' (Magaš 1993: 4).

At the same time, Croatian people were still locked inside their fear of retaliation and persecution, gathering courage to voice their quest for national identity only inside the larger democracy movement (1988–90) which brought sweeping changes to Eastern Europe and to the world. Whereas in Serbia under the Serbian nationalists' jingoistic slogan of 'keeping Yugoslavia as a nation' nationalism grew unobstructed and under the leadership of

Slobodan Milošević (Magaš 1993: 282–4), in Croatia the movement for democracy was divided between those who wanted to have a democratic state of Croatia inside the larger federation of the Yugoslav state, and those who wanted secession from Yugoslavia altogether and the formation of an independent state along democratic principles.

When the current president of Croatia, Dr Franjo Tudjman, formed the HDZ, he had played all his cards along nationalistic lines and the HDZ won the first elections in Croatia in April 1990 (Republic of Croatia 1991). But before it was possible to build an election campaign along the lines of re-building the Croatian State to its 'former glory', some major re-invention of Croatia itself had to be achieved.

For almost forty-five years in the SFRJ, the building of the Yugoslav nation was based mainly on the myths and heroes of the epic struggle of the partisans against Germans during the Second World War. The other pool of collective popular myths was to be found in the history of battles with the Ottoman Empire.[5] Since Croatia at that time itself was divided mainly between Italy and the Austro-Hungarian Empire, only a small part of Croatian land was ruled by Turks and the mythology of those times is either lost or was considered secondary for Croatian cultural consciousness. Croatia was at war with the Turks from 1463 to 1527, but from 1671 to 1918 it was a part of Austria and Hungary, and in 1918 entered the Kingdom of Serbs, Croats and Slovenes as an independent state. In 1928 the kingdom was renamed Yugoslavia (Šišić 1975; Klaić 1980). However, one myth of the two noble families, Šubić and Zrinski, has survived, since the story was used as a libretto for the opera *Nikola Šubić-Zrinski*.[6] The heroic deeds of the battle for Siget (a military outpost) and the death of the Croatian patriots in that battle became a cultural text, and as such entered the common memory of Croatians. However, even if the battle for Siget was perceived as a symbol of Croatian resistance against Turkish invasions, it was the battle for Kosovo, 1389, that was used most often in illustrating the 'Yugoslav' nation's struggle against the Turks.[7]

The strength of the popular memory of a nation which resides in the timelessness of its myths is exemplified by the myth of the 'Battle of Kosovo'. The Belgrade regime led by Slobodan Milošević, used the celebration of the five hundredth anniversary of the 'Battle of Kosovo' as an occasion not only to call for a greater Serbia but to justify the Serbian cultural and other genocide that is taking place against the Albanian population in the province of Kosovo (Magaš 1993: 161). When describing 'proto-nationalism', Eric Hobsbawm (1990: 75–6) sees 'belonging or having belonged to a lasting political entity' as the 'last and the most decisive criterion' and illustrates his argument as follows:

There is no reason to deny proto-national feelings to pre-nineteenth century Serbs, not because they were orthodox as against neighbouring Catholics and Muslims – this would not have distinguished them from Bulgars – but because the memory of the old kingdom defeated by the Turks was preserved in song and heroic story and perhaps more to the point, in the daily liturgy of the Serbian Church which has canonized most of its kings.

(*ibid.*: 76)

Thus history not only becomes a legend but through the simple structure of the myth simplifies the more complex historical conditions of the Serbian past. I would like to propose here that, through the construction of a particular image of Serbia and the mythology behind it, the normative conditions for Serbian nationalism were constantly present, so allowing for an easy mix of everyday reality and the imagined history. Thus there was a great difference between Croatia and Serbia in 1988 because Serbia possessed a ready-made mythology which was also rooted deeply in the Serbian Orthodox Church. It possessed a carefully preserved pool of myths, customs and traditions on which Serbian nationalism could build its future. In addition to this, Serbia has appropriated the mythology created by Tito's Yugoslavia and has used the myth of 'partisans' and their historic fight against the Germans as a basis for depicting the strength of the present army and its irregulars. This 'myth' of guerilla warfare has been used by various international bodies as one of the excuses for not engaging their troops in order to stop the Serbian invasion, first in Croatia and later in Bosnia and Herzegovina, as Owen Harries concludes:

Finally, in any effective military intervention, there would be a high likelihood of numerous casualties – both taken and inflicted. The terrain of most of Eastern Europe and Balkans, as well as the passionate hatred that often characterizes the region's quarrels, would not allow for military action that was both effective and cheap as the Persian Gulf War was . . . as far as the United States is concerned, there is a serious point to the pithy dictum coined by some military men: 'We do deserts. We don't do mountains and jungles.'

(Harries 1993: 46)

In contrast to Serbian nationalism, Croatian nationalism has been discouraged and branded as Nazism, creating the negative symbolic value of anything close to the expression of a Croatian national consciousness, especially after the popular revolt of 1971 – better known as the Croatian Spring (Tripalo 1990). Even the opera *Nikola Šubić-Zrinski* was seen as 'politically incorrect', and was not staged in Yugoslavia until the late 1980s although it was one of the most popular operas with Croatian audiences. The aria from the same opera titled *U Boj U Boj* (To Battle, to Battle) sung by the main character just as he embarks on his last battle with the Turks, has long been used by Croatian patriots worldwide. Since the time this opera acquired its 'politically unsuitable' status inside Yugoslavia (together with the Croatian national anthem), it has gained an outstanding cultural and symbolic value, especially among Croatians in diaspora. Together with other cultural texts that were perceived as nationalistic, this opera has played an important role in awakening the spirit of Croatian patriotism, a spirit which later turned into Croatian nationalism.

THE YUGOSLAV STATE AND THE CIRCULATION OF AUDIO VISUAL TEXTS

It is not within the scope of this study to give a comprehensive socio-historical political account of the break up of Yugoslavia. (Many others have done so, e.g. Thompson 1992, Magaš 1993.) My intention is only to provide a brief background to the changes that occurred in the Yugoslav community in Perth and elsewhere in Western Australia and which were a direct result of the changes in the homeland. Since the focus of this study remains the dynamics of the VCR and its use in the Croatian community, it is important to attend to the popular construction of Croatia and Croatian national identity through media such as VCR, including direct broadcast and satellite television.

Benedict Anderson (1983) has drawn attention to the connection between the rise of such cultural technologies as printing and the standardisation of vernacular languages in the creation of national consciousness, arguing that through these means people can: 'visualize in a general way the existence of thousands and thousands like themselves through print language' (*ibid.*: 77). If the printed word could achieve the degree of visualisation necessary for one to imagine onself as a part of a larger 'imagined community', the modes of electronic communication, involving the instantaneous delivery of images, supply the visual as immediate information and allow for the secondary meaning to develop almost at the same time. Furthermore, if visual technologies such as television are largely regarded as 'passive technologies', the VCR is regarded as 'an active technology' (Hanson 1987: 122–6) because the audience 'is making a conscious decision about controlling the information on the visual screen', thus turning the video screen into an active part of the process of communication. Thus if 'the context in which the technology is used, influences the levels of perception perspectives applicable' (*ibid.*: 126), the use of the VCR in a domestic setting in Croatian households at the time of the rise of Croatian nationalism in Perth requires closer attention. The choice of the participant-observation ethnographic research method has been explained in the Introduction and here I simply want to stress the importance of the 'family and friends' as a social unit and as a cultural space in which ideologies settle and in which the ensemble of ideals and images (in this case pertaining to national mythologies) operate on the most basic level of what Bourdieu (1977: 78) simply terms *habitus*.

The rapid penetration of the VCR into the Macedonian and Croatian communities and the subsequent development of an alternative community-based market for ethnic video has been described partly in Chapter 2. Nevertheless, it is important at this point in the discussion to return briefly to the development of that ethnic market, and outline the role of the Yugoslav state and its institutions in that development.

It has been argued (Letić 1989: 102–5) that migrants have a greater than usual need for information from the homeland they have left behind. Thus the traditional information media such as newspapers, radio and television, have different roles in the process of information dissemination in the migrant communities. Furthermore the importance of SBS-TV in Australia is not confined to the ethnic communities but is equally important to Australian Aborigines and other marginal audiences (O'Regan and Kolar-Panov 1993a, 1993b). In addition, SBS-TV involves a two-way process which makes the information about ethnic and other marginal communities accessible to a wider mainstream audience.

However, the position of migrant communities as marginal audiences in their relation to the mainstream media in general has made the role of the various homelands central to the supply and dissemination of information and entertainment. This has been especially true in Australia due to its geographical isolation prior to the development of technologies such as satellite communications, television, facsimile (fax) machines and the VCR which, once they became available, changed the communication landscape drastically, allowing the migrant communities to bypass easily 'official' channels of information (cf. White and White 1983).[8]

The largely centralised Yugoslav broadcasting system with its eight state-owned television stations (Golubović 1983) always rested uneasily with the republic-based (and republic-funded) migrant associations which were mainly responsible for the supply of information to the diaspora. An hourly mixture of news and variety programme produced by JRT (Jugoslavenska Radio Televizija) called *Naši Gradjani u Svijetu* (Our Citizens in the World) combined the peddling of propaganda documentaries about the success of self-management in Yugoslavia with supplying the various television stations with carefully selected films and children's programmes. In addition to the official programme and film exchange, officials and representatives in diplomatic missions and cultural centres disseminated print and visual information targeting various cultural institutions such as libraries, universities, or film institutes. What was left over was available for use in the ethnic clubs.

The geographical isolation of Australia and the composition of the migrant population from Yugoslavia in Australia, which was largely of Croatian and Macedonian descent, saw the two largest Yugoslav migrant associations in the homeland, the *Matica Iseljenika Hrvatske* (Croatian Migrant Association) and *Makedonska Matica Na Iselenicite* (Macedonian Migrant Association), taking most of the responsibility for forming and retaining cultural, and particularly symbolic, ties with their diasporas. The migrant associations, in addition to publishing monthly journals describing the lifestyles of the migrants all around the world, occasionally published monographs or biographies of and by prominent or famous migrants and often organised tours by popular singers and personalities from the cultural scene in their respective republics.

With the changing political climate in the SFRJ and the increased push for unitarism and Jugoslavism after the 'Croatian Spring' of 1971 (Tripalo 1990), the migrant associations increasingly came into conflict with the federal institutions (such as the Ministry for Foreign Affairs) and had uneasy relations with officialdom. These strained relations led to migrant associations being infiltrated and administrated by more 'politically suitable' personnel, bringing their informal association with the so-called 'extremist' migrant organizations to an effective end.

When, in 1977, the centralised JRT in Belgrade started to produce video cassettes for migrants, in co-operation with all television centres in Yugoslavia, it did so only when the content of such videos was approved by a watchdog committee overseeing the 'planning, production and distribution' of approximately ten videos a year (Letić 1989: 165–6). The video cassettes, destined to be shown mainly in ethnic clubs overseas, contained approximately thirty hours of a variety of television programmes from all Yugoslav television stations, containing a selection of programmes approved by the above-mentioned committee. The videos were oriented mainly towards entertainment and were not intended for information dissemination.

The total number of video cassettes sent to Yugoslav diplomatic missions and cultural centres is estimated at somewhere between thirty and fifty a year (*ibid.*: 166). These videos were still expensive, hence the small numbers, and their impact could be seen to be negligible. Based on personal experience, I can argue that such videos seldom seemed to reach the diaspora and were mostly used for the purposes of private enjoyment by officials of the diplomatic missions and their friends. One of the reasons for this was that in traditional migrant European countries, such as Sweden and Germany, the majority of ethnic clubs in the late 1970s and early 1980s still 'did not own a video cassette recorder' (*ibid.*). Because of the limited number of available video tapes, and because the technology of the VCR was still beyond the reach of all but the most affluent, we cannot talk of the influence these video tapes might have had on the ethnic audiences.

The relatively high cost of production and the limited availability of the hardware to migrant organisations might be the reason why the Yugoslav government did not take the opportunity to use VCR technology for the purpose of reaching large audiences in its diaspora. The other reason might be found in the socio-political reality of the slow disintegration of the SFRJ that set in after the death of Josip Broz Tito (cf. Magaš 1993: xii). The decentralisation process that led to the total disintegration of the Yugoslav federation greatly influenced the activities of different national migrant associations, which started organising communication and information channels outside the protective umbrella of the centralised watchdog bodies in Belgrade, and showed an increased tendency towards bypassing the official (diplomatic and other) channels used until then for communication with the diaspora.

As a result of the lack of federal funding and the relatively limited republic-based budgets available to the migrant associations, such organisations constantly struggled to meet even the basic needs of the diaspora for communication with the homeland. Thus the availability of the VCR as an ideal information and communication technology and its relatively fast penetration of ethnic households was not followed by an increased production of video tapes in the various homelands. This was compounded by the increasingly impoverished state of the SFRJ in the 1980s. Standards were at levels that did not allow the acquisition of new technologies by its population or even by its institutions, at least not at a rate of acquisition comparable to the more affluent countries such as Australia, Canada or Germany in which the majority of the diaspora from the SFRJ was living.

The inability of the Yugoslav state to establish an official and controlled flow of information and entertainment through the use of video technology was one of the factors responsible for the development of informal and often semi-legal individual and community-based production and distribution channels for ethnic video. The other reason behind the development of such informal channels is inherent in the technology and was discussed earlier.[9] I have described briefly the viewing of a melodramatic series from RTV Zagreb (*Velo Misto*) in the Yugoslav Club of Western Australia in Perth. However, I have not indicated the source of these videos, which constituted part of the informal video-distribution channels being formed at that time. At first the suppliers and distributors of ethnic video were mainly relatives and officials of migrant associations who travelled frequently and had open channels of communication with various migrant organisations at home and in the diaspora. These individuals not only served as a means of distribution, but often entered into private partnerships with small ethnic businesses (or individuals) in Australia. Because I have only limited access to data regarding such partnerships (which I suspect were illegal or semi-legal), the following account is based on confidential interviews with persons involved, who were often extremely reluctant to disclose information concerning the number of video tapes sold or rented, and the profit obtained. Basically, what I was interested in was the content of such videos and once that was understood by the participants, I gained their confidence, however limited, though I was still dependent on their willingness to volunteer information.

This reluctance to disclose information was understandable because the majority of the video tapes (apart from the family album ones) were pirated from broadcast television, and even though Yugoslavia was not a signatory to the international copyright law at that time, Australia was (O'Regan 1991; cf. Ganley and Ganley 1987: 80–94). This meant that the copies of such tapes, which were reproduced in Australia came under existing copyright laws as well as, most probably, being subject to some form of sales tax. In order to bypass the existing laws, such private ventures were mainly kept secret. The hunger for videos, especially from Macedonia, was of such proportions that the Macedonian State Broadcasting Service, TV Skopje, attempted in 1985 to enter a formal agreement for the production and distribution of TV Skopje programmes with a Sydney-based ethnic business. This failed, mainly because the same business already had a 'gentlemen's agreement' with one of the top executives from TV Skopje, who provided the video distributor in Sydney with advance copies of the most popular programmes produced for and by TV Skopje, often even before such programmes were broadcast in Macedonia. For example, the extremely popular New Year's Eve programme containing a variety of songs and entertainment was available on video tape in time for the Christmas holidays in Australia before it was shown in Macedonia. Such video tapes were often very expensive and sold for over a hundred dollars each. They were available only through tight and secure personal communication channels, endowing their owner with symbolic capital *par excellence* and thus raising the social status of the person in the ethnic community.

The 'official' channels for the exchange of television programmes between SBS and Macedonian Television were opened only at times when there was a favourable political climate for it, and the programmes contained the usual state-based television programming exchange offers for children's programmes, tourist propaganda spots and limited drama and film.

Some of the titles in these offers have been shown on SBS, but all the Macedonian Television programmes broadcast on Australian television since 1990 would not significantly add to the hours of pirated programmes available on the shelves (or in the drawers) of private video libraries of an average Macedonian migrant family in Perth, in 1991.

However, the production and distribution of Croatian video tapes in Western Australia is a completely different story. At first it was extremely difficult to obtain any information about the sources of the video tapes I watched with the family and friends of the principal informants to this study. My questions were always answered with either 'I got it from a friend' or 'It was sent to me by someone from home'. This ambiguity about sources was due to the existing divisions in the Croatian community, and even though the expression of national sentiment and identity was increasingly welcomed in Croatia itself, the diaspora remained suspicious and retained a certain fear, amounting almost to a phobia, towards an outsider, especially if that person had connections with the Yugoslav state or its institutions. It was only when the ethnic press, such as *Hrvatski Vjesnik* (Croatian Herald), started to advertise video tapes originally produced by IVS (International Video Studios – a Swiss-based organisation that rented technology, the equipment and the know-how to anyone prepared to pay for it), that I was able to trace some points of origin to the videos circulating in the Croatian community. The IVS videos which were advertised contained mainly popular music or tourist propaganda types of tapes and much later videos of popular song festivals, such as the Split Festival.[10]

Besides the production of video tapes by IVS and later by independent producers in Croatia, the majority of the video tapes were still the product of the same practice of pirating television programmes from broadcast television, in the case of the Croatian community mainly from TV Zagreb and later HTV (Hrvatska Televizija – Croatian Television). The distribution channels for such videos were well guarded and I suspect that the practice of pirating television programmes had been established longer and more solidly than in the Macedonian community. For example, the last episode of the popular melodramatic series *Velo Misto*, (discussed in chapter 2, pp. 55–6; see also note 9, p. 229) was available in Perth almost at the same time as it was broadcast in Croatia. It was stressed to me on several occasions that most of the pirated broadcast television programmes were taped off-air by private citizens and tracing such production and distribution was quite impossible, as well as time-consuming and costly. My own findings show this to be a reasonable assumption.

The availability of more affordable video technology, such as the camcorder, coincided with the increased moves towards democracy in Croatia itself. The large number of video tapes I watched in the Croatian community were tapes produced by video enthusiasts who had often had their first chance to visit Croatia thanks to the more relaxed (or confused) policies towards political migrants by the disintegrating Yugoslav state. One such video tape documented the re-erection of the Ban Jelačić (Viceroy Jelačić) monument in the main square in Zagreb, from where it had been removed by the Communist regime in 1947 in complete secrecy, and has remained a very touchy issue ever since. The campaign for the re-erection of the Ban Jelačić monument is often taken as the first public display of nationalistically coloured sentiment by the Croatian people and the monument itself has gained even more symbolic value than it possessed initially (Macan 1990: 16–17).

Before describing the occasion of the viewing of the Ban Jelačić tape (I call it that, in the absence of a title), I would like to draw to a conclusion the background description to the production and distribution of the ethnic video tapes which will be described or analysed later in the text.

I have already described the production and distribution of video tapes which I classify as video letters and video albums (and sometimes family albums) and I will return to that classification as necessary. However, a new type of video tape can be fitted broadly into the category of the family album, since it serves the same purpose of recording an event pertinent to the history of a family (or its members) in more than one way – either re-evoking personal memories of the event, or as a record of the general history of its time. The video tapes I am describing are tapes which record various events and functions in the Croatian community in Perth and elsewhere. I have watched tapes that contained similar sequences such as dinner dances or celebrations of Croatian Independence Day celebrations in Toronto, Canada.

Such video tapes were different in several ways from what are usually termed 'home movies' (Levy and Gunter 1988). The first point of difference was that the tapes were produced professionally, in Perth at least, by two young cameramen of Croatian descent working for Perth-based commercial television stations. The young men ran a side-line of taping significant events in the Croatian community, and distributing them privately through community channels. They were usually thirty-minute tapes, with the longest I know of running for just over an hour. They sold usually for 25–30 dollars.

The interesting detail in the business venture of the two young cameramen was that other video tapes produced either by International Video Studios (which incidentally always had a copyright warning on them) or from any other sources, were freely retaped (pirated) by the members of the Croatian community – so much so that sometimes the copies we watched were losing colour and had very poor sound. In the best case if the tape was purchased 'for a good cause', the cost would be shared between two or three families. While there was no guilt whatsoever involved in retaping such tapes and even no awareness of copyright breach, the video tapes produced by the above-mentioned pair were largely purchased without question, with a comment such as 'Let the poor lads make a buck'. This shows the high degree of solidarity existing between the members of the Croatian community, the same solidarity that has raised over 3 million dollars to finance the election campaign of the HDZ in Croatia.[11]

ETHNICITY BEGINS AT HOME

The disturbances staged in Krajina by the Serbian minority well before the first Croatian democratic elections in 1990 caught the world press unprepared. Just like the British press later when the war started (Magaš 1993: 302), the Australian media resorted to simplistic stereotypes in reporting events in Yugoslavia. This was not at all difficult since the well-organised centralised propaganda machine operating from Belgrade (capital of both Serbia and Yugoslavia) enjoyed a good reputation mainly because of the Yugoslav press agency, Tanjug. Tanjug was for a long time a press agency which had access to information both from 'behind the Iron Curtain' and from other non-Western countries, due to Yugoslavia's involvement in the non-aligned movement. It was often quoted by Western media as 'reliable' and 'unbiased'. This reputation was strong enough to legitimise the organised 'hate campaigns' first against the Albanians in Kosova (*ibid.*: 15–48) and later against Croatia's movement towards democracy. As the popularity of the HDZ grew, so did the Belgrade-inspired paranoia and 'hate campaigns'. Even if the HDZ of the late 1980s advocated moderately nationalistic policies, it was labelled 'fascist' and 'ustaša', in the best cases 'extremist and dangerous'. It is not surprising that the word 'ustaša' had such an impact, not only on audiences in Yugoslavia but on audiences worldwide. The reason for such an avalanche of negative connotation can be explained very easily inside the simple semiotic connotative model.

Umberto Eco (1990a: 29) argues that 'There is a phenomenon of connotation when sign function (Expression plus Content) becomes in turn the expression of further content.' Just as with Eco's example of the word 'pig', the word 'ustaša' has negative semantic markers. In this case they are based on the most commonly used first (literal) meaning of 'ustaša equals Croatian fascist' (Glenny 1992: 147; Thompson 1992: 259). The negative semantic markers belonging to the word 'fascist' also affect the word 'Croatian' because of the culturally recorded connotations of the word ustaša which must always be used in context. In contrast to this, the word 'četnik', which is the Serbian equivalent of ustaša, has lost its initial meaning and has acquired the meaning of 'Serbian guerilla fighter', thus having both positive and negative semantic markers, leaving open for negotiation its culturally recorded connotations, mainly according to its use in a context. Even if part of the Serbian army and irregulars openly use the name četnik and display the original četnik insignia, the world media still refer to četniks as 'Serbian irregulars'. It has also been shown that they have committed atrocities in this war comparable to the ones committed by četniks during the Second World War (see *Helsinki Watch Report* 1992).

Besides my having to deal with the negative mythology around Croatian nationalism, the negative image of the HDZ was further compounded by an 'oversight' in the policy-making in the new Croatian constitution of 1990 which was later amended, but the damage had already been done. The policy concerned the autonomy of the Serbs in Croatia, limiting that autonomy and denying them the right of nationhood and hence equating them with other ethnic or national minorities. On the basis of this mistake the Serbs in Croatia (Krajina) declared independence in August 1990 (Magaš 1993: 285), forming the first Republic of Krajina. The second and third Krajinas would be formed later, in Croatian Slavonia and in Bosnia respectively. By the formation of Srpska Krajina, Croatia was effectively split into two, making it increasingly difficult to communicate between the two parts.[12]

After repeated unrest and increased disruption of road communications between Croatia's north and south (often referred to as 'Balvan Revolucija' – The Log Revolution – since the Serbs used to cut trees and place them as road blocks in order to disrupt traffic in the mainly mountainous terrain), the Croatian community in Perth started to seek additional information about events in the homeland. At this time the Australian media carried only limited news coverage of 'events'. Audiences of Croatian descent, especially the ones who had relatives living in the areas close to the unrest, increasingly showed changes in their viewing and listening habits, and to a lesser degree in their reading habits. The 'family and friends' unit I will refer to from now on became the site of my research from that time.

It was not only by choice that I limited my work to a smaller audience, but it was rather by the set of socio-historical circumstances and my position in those circumstances, which in this case was determined more than anything else by my ethnicity. The fact that I was perceived as in the same position as my audience, away from the homeland, with family 'over there' at a time when war was knocking on their door, was another condition which brought me closer to the Croatian community. The concern for our loved ones and our country created a bond between myself as a researcher and 'my' audience, a bond which was of such a nature that it is often difficult to distinguish (or single out) my own voice from the multiplicity of voices originating from the audience. Thus for the most part I will be using 'we' as a reference, only distinguishing between myself and the audience with the first-person 'I' when I want to differentiate myself and the audience, either for analytical or descriptive purposes.

I have known the principal informant family since 1984 and was considered by them a family friend, trustworthy and always welcomed. When I returned to Australia to continue my research (without my family, on my own) the M.M's had taken upon themselves to 'take care of me', offering 'a family away from family' in order to make it easier for me to be alone.[13] Such support was and is very common in the close-knit ethnic communities, who offer emotional and often material support for newcomers. It has been described by most of the researchers into ethnic communities in Australia (e.g. P. Hill 1989; Bottomley 1992). From the very inception of this research, I made a point of explaining to the M.M. family the goals and purposes of the study I was undertaking, but their understanding of 'what I do' was, and remains, sketchy, mainly confined to my interest in the videos and other information from and about Croatia. I did not insist on explaining my research in detail because it was easier to take up a position of participant observer and to ask questions before, during and after the viewing of videos from the position of a member of the audience. This space was generously provided initially by the M.M. family and later by others through their accepting me as 'one of them'. Thus in the position of an insider in the group of family and friends, I was able to have access to information that would otherwise have been coloured by the audience's awareness of my presence as a researcher. However, the marginal position members of the audience ascribed to themselves in connection with my scholarly work surfaced from time to time. I shall describe such an occasion.

When the article 'Radio and civil war in Yugoslavia' was published in

Media Information Australia, (Kolar-Panov and Miller 1991) I brought photocopies of it to the audience in order to show, to some extent, what I was doing. The general reaction at first was that they could not possibly understand it, since it 'had too many big words'. Moreover I was immediately scorned for using the name of Yugoslavia, which by this time was considered at least bad manners in Croatian circles. The second objection was to the use of the term 'civil war'. It came from M.M.'s husband (R.M.), who was genuinely surprised by our use of 'civil war'. He explained to me he did not expect 'that' since I surely knew that the war was only on Croatian territory, and it was clearly an aggression. I attempted to justify the use of such a title with the explanation that Croatia was not recognised by the world at the time the article was written, and the momentary tension was eased, but not before I was warned 'not to show the article to anyone from the Croatian Club' since 'they would not understand why the title'. I was asked to explain what the article was about, and since the members of the audience we quoted in the text were present, the quotations were the best way to engage them with the explanation. They found pleasure in the recognition of their own utterances and this produced a further discussion on the role of Pierre Vickary (the ABC's European correspondent) in reporting the war, which in turn triggered off a general discussion on the ways in which Australian radio and television report the war in Yugoslavia. This started one of many endless debates with agreement only on the 'fact' that Croatia did not seem to have friends, apart, perhaps, from Germany. The article was soon forgotten as the audience continued to discuss the most recent events, and questioned the absence of Pierre Vickary from the airwaves.

For the next two years I often spent weekends and weeks at a time with M.M.'s family, and observed and recorded changes in their media behaviour from their quest for more information about the war through outrage and sadness at the destruction, and finally to a point of fatigue and a form of resignation that had set in towards the time I had to finalise my fieldwork in early 1993. I was at first interested only in continuing my inquiry into VCR dynamics, but an increased cross-referencing of media, mainly with radio and the ethnic press such as *Hrvatski Vjesnik* (Croatian Herald) created a unique media landscape or mediascape which in turn shaped discourses around VCR viewing.

The principal informant family in this study consisted of two households until September 1991, when the eldest daughter of M.M. returned from Yugoslavia and moved into the house next door to her parents. Thus three generations of one family lived next door to each other in the Perth suburb of Spearwood. The suburb has a large population of migrants, especially Italians and 'Slavs'. The Slav migrants are mainly from Croatia, specifically from the Dalmatian coast, and even though the upward mobility of the second and third generation has brought about a large exodus from the suburb, with urban sprawl replacing the market gardens with family homes, a large number of migrants who settled in Spearwood on their arrival have chosen to stay either in their old homes or in one of the new developments in the area. All of this means that most of the participants in this research were either within walking distance of my principal informants' home or just a very short drive from it, allowing them to come at short notice if a new video was available. The centrality of their home, which was situated straight across from the Spearwood Dalmatinac Club, meant also that at the time when the Yugoslav community was still united, people often stopped by to visit the M.M. household on their way to or from the club. However, at the time that the main body of data for this research was collected, the division in the community was already visible, and the upstairs terrace of the same house served as a sort of 'lookout' for identifying those who were still attending the Spearwood Dalmatinac Club functions and thus perceived as remaining loyal to the Yugoslav idea.

Many marriages and friendships were broken because of the widening gap in the community caused by the political fragmentation in Yugoslavia. The nuclear M.M. family consisted of five members. The husband, R.M., in his early forties, is a roofer with his own business, who came to Australia with his parents when he was 15. The wife, M.M., a housemaker, had been a trained nurse in Yugoslavia, but came to Australia soon after graduating from nursing, and has not worked in her profession since she married soon after her arrival. She has held occasional positions, from working in a factory to cleaning and catering jobs. Their proficiency in English consisted of a functional vocabulary, with self-taught literacy skills. This was mainly the result of the Australian government policies towards migrants which had a distinct lack of support structures, especially programmes for Teaching English as a Second Language (TESL). Besides the Dictation Test which ensured that all NES migrants had at least some knowledge of English, there was no other incentive for them to develop their language skills (Bungey 1993). Furthermore, community support structures meant that the migrants could work and live in the community, communicating in their mother tongue most of their lives. Neither R.M. nor M.M. attended any ESL classes until I coerced the wife to attend some adult literacy classes, which she reluctantly did for six months, but still claims that she is 'too old to study'.

The three children were K. 19, S. 16, and M. 10 years old when I started my research in early 1990. They were all born in Australia. The two elder children are girls, and the youngest a boy. At the start of my study, the eldest daughter was studying in Zagreb (Croatia), and had married a Croatian there. Upon their arrival in Australia in September 1991, they moved into the house next door, and now have two sons.

The third household of this family-and-friends group are the husband's parents, both in their early seventies, pensioners, who live apart from the family. Their knowledge of English is very poor with the wife (I refer to her as the grandmother) having difficulty understanding anything but the simplest of everyday communications.

This extended family is well known and well liked in the community, and most often referred to as 'hardworking and honest'. It has an extended circle of friends, not only in the two Croatian (earlier Slav) communities but also in the Italian community in Perth, to which the husband and his father have been linked through the traditional South European base for his trade in the building industry.

The generational range provided by this extended family unit allowed access to intergenerational audience dynamics of which I would otherwise not have been aware. Their friendship and their acceptance of myself as 'one of them' removed to a certain degree the barrier that would have been put in place if I had came to their home as an 'educated outsider' looking for information about their viewing habits. Nevertheless, the one barrier that did influence my research was the difference in our cultural, educational and symbolic capital or, perhaps, simply my own awareness of it. This difference often worked in my favour, since the men treated me as an equal, often discussing politics with me, and even more often seeking information about the events that were unfolding in Yugoslavia. The women, on the other hand, ignored or rejected the barrier that could have been created from this position of knowledge-power – and initially often sought advice on personal matters. I believe that the last barriers of my social status were broken when I showed a genuine interest in and knowledge of the daytime soap opera, *The Young and the Restless*, which I used to watch while living in Canada, and I easily picked up the plot ten years later in Australia. Actually my first observation of a major change in their viewing patterns and VCR dynamics occurred when M.M. declared one day that she was not taping *The Young and the Restless* any more. Two years later, when fatigue and despair set into the community due to the ongoing war in former Yugoslavia, M.M. started to watch the soap opera again, and the gathering of family and friends returned to patterns similar to the ones I had noticed before the war, with the men on one side and the women on the other.

I shall not enter into a close description of the friends of the family or for that matter the extended family living outside these three households because of the large number of people in that circle, anywhere from 50 to100. However, there were 5 to10 families who were the most frequent visitors, as well as aunts and cousins and other distant relatives, and I will give demographic specifics, were necessary, in the description and analysis of the particular VCR viewing sessions.

THE HOLY ICONS IN RED, WHITE AND BLUE

The get-togethers and 'video news' sessions referring to the tapes that contained information about what were at first political situations, and later war reportage mainly taped off broadcast television, had by now become a ritual in M.M.'s family room, but they started with the election campaign by the HDZ (Magaš 1993: 254–9). This party's desire to enlist the diaspora led to a number of politicians visiting Perth and bringing with them posters, post-cards, stickers, badges and the other knick-knacks that are a usual part of election campaigns. Glenny (1992: 92) calls this 'Croat triumphalism in the form of flags, symbols and songs'. All of the paraphernalia of the campaign were in three symbolic colours, red, white and blue (see discussion later). The most powerful of these symbols were the flag and the coat of arms that replaced the Communist star on the 'old' flag ('old' as in Socialist Republic of Croatia), but the flag and the replacement of the star with the traditional chequerboard was seen as anti-Yugoslav and fascist since a similar flag was used by the NDH. (The paranoia over the threat of a revival of fascism was understandable since the existing 'Yugoslav national spirit' left little ambiguity concerning the existence of the NDH.) Thus, the candidates for the first free election in Croatia were not welcome in any other ethnic clubs but the Croatian ones, which until then had been labelled extremist.

The migrants from Croatia, especially those who had relatives still living in Yugoslavia, showed an increased interest in political developments in the homeland and started to attend the meetings that were held in the Croatian Club in East Fremantle. The change in loyalties was in full swing and for the benefit of those who still did not feel comfortable visiting the Croatian Club, such election rallies and speeches were readily recorded on video. The M.M. family still held respect in both communities, and the 'Slav oriented' Croats would often come to their home to watch the video tapes of such election rallies. On the occasions of such viewings there was often more than surprise at the display of what were considered 'ustaša' symbols, and it did not help that the Croatian Club kept the photograph of the NDH leader, Ante Pavelić, often side by side with the new flag and the photograph of the then leader of the HDZ, Dr Franjo Tudjman (now president of Croatia). The outrage felt by some members of the audience over such an open display of nationalistic feelings was more than disgust. Arguments broke out often and lifelong friendships ended there and then. There were a lot of migrants in the 'Slav' community who considered the red star in the Croatian flag not as a sign of Communism, but rather as a symbol of victory over Nazism. Most of the 'Slav' families had a strong pride in the partisan background of their parents or relatives, and viewed Dr Tudjman as legitimising the ustaša position. They could not be convinced otherwise despite the well-known fact that Dr Tudjman was a general in Tito's partisan army and was purged later for his political views. Even if the HDZ was not a fascist party, the Slav members of the audience believed it to be so. The subsequent election of the HDZ as the first democratic government in Croatia (April 1990) with Dr Franjo Tudjman as president saw the final division of the Yugoslav community, with no option left for the ones who either would not declare their loyalty to the new Croatian Republic or stayed loyal to the idea of Yugo-slavism. Choices had to be made, and I made the obvious one, staying with the M.M. family and friends, even though my personal stance often was very different to the general euphoria that had taken over the community.

REBUILDING THE NATION

The dominant discourses of nation-building see the nation as an expression of an innate and age old ethno-cultural identity (or *ethnie*, to use A.D. Smith's term (1988)). This 'primordialist' view is well presented in studies of nationalism and ethnicity (Smith 1988, 1991; Armstrong 1982), and is pre-sumed as self-evident in various nationalist ideologies and strategies of nation-building. The alternative 'constructivist' approach to problems of ethnic fragmentation emphasises ethnicity and the nation as constructed socially through the manipulation of historically derived symbolism and signs (Anderson 1983; Gellner 1983; and Hobsbawm 1983, 1990). 'Con-structivists' ask how this articulates with élite strategies of popular mobilisa-tion. Eric Hobsbawm (1983, 1990) proposes that nations are created, not born, but he recognises the need for certain conditions under which nations can be created, such as those concerning language, ethnicity, religion, 'holy icons' as well as traces of collective consciousness of belonging or having belonged to some kind of political entity in the past. This he calls 'proto-nationalism'. But nationhood is also based on a sense of common history in which the history of common sufferings is a potent binding myth. Along with other myths listed by Smith (1988: 192), this myth can be seen as a part of the primordial identity, which can be proven by evidence found through-out the recorded history of nations. In the case of Croatia as addressed here, a primordialist national strategy was developed by the HDZ, but this strat-egy could only be successful if there was a collective cultural memory to sustain it. Thus the success of the Croatian claim on its diaspora is a result of the use of an artful combination of primordialist–constructivist strat-egies. This combination has (re)produced (or re-invented, in Hobsbawm's terms) the myths of Croatia which were claimed to be lost in recent history.

The word 'Fatherland' or 'Motherland', with connotations of the 'his-toric' land, the often elusive 'homeland', the 'cradle' of the nation, or the 'holy ground', is the most powerful reference to the site where all historic memories and associations reside. It is a place where heroes of the nation fought, sages ruled, and its rivers, coasts, lakes and mountains are sacred places of veneration and exaltation. Thus identification with a certain terri-tory exists inside all ideologies of the modern state. When Croatian people looked for their right to self-determination, within the democratic move-ments in Eastern Europe, they had to deal with not only the political and military boundaries set by the modern Yugoslav state (SFRJ), but also the idea of Yugoslavism which had been present for over a century (see Dedijer *et al.* 1974) and which had a strong influence on the formation of the national consciousness of all Yugoslav people. Thus, Croatia within its modern borders established in 1945 as an image of homeland was more acceptable to the as yet 'unconvinced' ones (referring here to the Slavs) than any claim on the territories which have been lost during the long history of foreign rule over the Balkans (cf. Lederer 1963). Nevertheless, a small number of right-wing Croatians have long harboured hopes of regaining that territory, and had formed a political party that, even if it had no chance in the first elections, gathered some followers, especially among the Croatian migrants of more right-wing orientation. The display of the NDH insignia, especially the infamous 'U' for 'ustaša', has done a great deal of harm to Croatia's image.[14] This was a time of great changes in Europe and daily reporting on neo-Nazi organisations in Germany and elsewhere were part of the media's 'everyday diet'. Thus any publicity and support given to such political parties was always blown up out of proportion.

Candidates for different political parties in Croatia toured the globe in search of support in the Croatian diaspora. They concentrated especially on Australia, Canada, the United States, and the European countries such as Germany and Sweden, which all had large numbers of migrants and temporary workers from Croatia. The most powerful party, the HDZ, enlisted artists, academics and other popular personalities to carry the message 'for democratic Croatia' across the world. For example, during the Christmas holidays 1989–90, Perth was visited by the chancellor of Zagreb University as well as by a group of the most popular singers and groups of pop musicians. All of them were there on behalf of the HDZ in order to enlist popular support, raise funds and, finally, enlist the vote of Croatians in the diaspora. All of them sang the Croatian anthem, wore T-shirts with the Croatian flag and coat of arms, and sold books on Croatian history together with the audio and video cassettes of the latest nationalistic songs, and it seemed that the Croatian community could not get enough of it. The members of the Croatian community jumped at every opportunity of learning the 'truth' about their homeland, in the hope of finding or confirming their cultural identity. By the end of the election campaign, most of the Croatian homes I visited owned at least one Croatian coat of arms and numerous everyday items with Croatian insignia, of which the most interesting was a square fruit cake with the Croatian coat of arms in the middle and red and blue decorations around the edges. The cake was acquired by the proud owner for 700 dollars at a fundraising auction for the HDZ. The proliferation of items for everyday use had all the characteristics of the marketing hype surrounding Hollywood blockbusters such as *Batman* or *Jurassic Park* or popular cartoons such as *Teenage Mutant Ninja Turtles*. I was constantly reminded of the latter since the son of the M.M. family 'sported' the Croatian flag, the Croatian emblem and posters of Batman and the Teenage Mutant Ninja Turtles, all side by side on the walls of his room. As the boy grew out of the cartoon phase and became interested in cars, the posters of Batman and Teenage Mutant Ninja Turtles had gone. The Croatian flag and the coat of arms remained, somewhat out of place alongside the photographs of vintage cars.

Another indication of the reinvention of Croatian national identity was found in the content of the video tapes that circulated in the Croatian community. The symbiosis of popular television culture and political power was most powerfully brought home for the first time in Croatia during the celebrations marking the re-erection of the monument of Ban Jelačić in the main square of the Croatian capital, Zagreb. The campaign calling for the re-erection of the monument is often seen as one of the first signs of the re-emergence of Croatian nationalism, and has been used very successfully by the HDZ for increasing its popularity (see Macan 1990). Thompson (1992) writes about the historical figure of Ban Jelačić and the campaign around him:

> Jelačić's reputation is a neat instance of nationalist revisionism and of the Croats' ambiguous ties to Austria-Hungary, although he preferred to rescue the dynastic state than to support the Croatian revolution, and, although he was distinctly pro-Yugoslav, Jelačić has been sanctified by Croat separatists.
>
> (*ibid.*: 255)

But it was exactly this ambiguity about his importance to the Croatian nation that made him an ideal transitional hero. His monument was removed by the Communist government after the Second World War in spite of the fact that he was not part of the 'shameful history' of the NDH or party to collaboration with Germany. This fact justified the claim of the Right, that the Yugoslav state was hostile to Croatians and Croatian culture in general, and not only due to the NDH's collaboration with Nazis. The celebrations surrounding the re-erection of the monument were preceded by an air of expectation artificially inflated by the daily countdown, 'progress reports' and extensive media attention to the people responsible for the preservation of the original monument in the basement of an academic institution.

I spent what I now think of as a 'video weekend' in the M.M. household watching mainly video tapes of news programmes taped off Zagreb television with a mixed audience at different times, when we were offered an unexpected 'treat' by a visitor who had just returned from a visit to Croatia. He was visiting the M.M. family in order to deliver letters, video letters and gifts from the family 'back home'. The visitor was not a regular member of the family and circle of friends around the M.M. household. Among other things he brought a new video tape, which was a combination of video-letter messages and taped off-air mainly news programmes sent to M.M. by her sister, and that was the tape we were watching. The conversation was at first concentrated on inquiries into the well-being of family and friends in Croatia and later shifted to the inevitable political discussion. When the highly edited version of the story behind the Ban Jelačić monument and the official version of the celebrations around it started to be shown (as taped from that evening's 'direct' broadcast from Ban Jelačić Square), the visitor protested, saying:

> V.(A): It was not like that, I was there, and I taped it with my camera. What you see is only a small part, how much can you fit into an hour in a TV show of the celebrations that went on all day and all night.

His words caught the attention of all of us in the audience and before he could escape from us, a promise to come 'tomorrow' and show us 'his' tape, was solicited.

THE BAN JELAČIĆ TAPE

While in Yugoslavia itself, Croatians, like Macedonians, Slovenians, Albanians and Bosnians, have all chosen between patriotism towards the Yugoslav state and nationalism by electing their democratic governments from the most nationalistically oriented parties, the Croatians in diaspora were still divided at the time when M.M. family and friends gathered to watch the three-hour tape showing the celebrations around the re-erection of the Ban Jelačić monument in Zagreb. The audience present at the showing of this tape was mixed. Most of the members belonged to the Croatian community, with only one person of a strong Yugoslav conviction who left rather abruptly after a heated argument with the rest regarding the origin of the Croatian coat of arms. The confusion surrounding the debate about the origin of this coat of arms and its use by the pro-fascist NDH was often the reason for misunderstandings between the Croatian and Slav members of the community.[15] I was often summoned to resolve such confusions. But not this time. The visitor who had brought the tape we were watching interrupted the argument and said:

> V.(A): While I was at home we saw on television a documentary programme which showed that the Croatian coat of arms dates far, far back, at least to King Krešimir who lived in the eleventh century. And it was always the symbol of Croatia. At home everyone is talking about it, they cannot agree which colour, red or white, should be the first of the twenty-five fields in the chequerboard. I don't see the point, but they are still debating about it.

It was obvious that a very awkward situation had been created by the accusations voiced by the 'Slav' member of the audience who after this got up, gathered her two children and left with the words:

V.(B): I am really disappointed in all of you, especially you [talking to me]. Can't you see that all of this is going to lead to nothing good? All those people are crazy, first electing that lunatic, Tudjman, and now wanting to separate from Yugoslavia. It will lead to nothing good.

There was silence for a few seconds after the 'Slav' viewer (B) left, but the tape was rewound to the beginning and M.M. commented:

Good [with reference to her leaving]. Now we can watch the tape in peace.

The tape itself was a unique document of the view through one person's video camera eye, of the 'hype' and staging of the re-erection of the Ban Jelačić monument. I will give only a short description of the content here, since I did not have the chance to view the tape again, and I was trying to record as much of the audience reaction as possible during the viewing. The lights in the living room were left on, and the viewing was often interrupted by comments and questions to the visitor/author. The lights would usually have been turned off when the audience watched a tape whose content required uninterrupted attention, such as in the case of viewing the documentary film on Stjepan Radić (described in chapter 5) or when watching a film or drama series pirated from Zagreb Television. However, the tapes of popular songs, or family-album-type tapes were usually watched with the lights on, thus inviting comments and allowing the audience to interact.

The tape started with frames of close-ups of portraits of Ban Jelačić and his family. V.(A) explained that he had been visiting an exhibition depicting the life of Ban Jelačić, but was interrupted with an exclamation from the audience *Evo ga*! (Here he is) when the next frame showed a motorcade carrying the monument itself on one of the vehicles. The motorcade was reminiscent of sports parades with trucks decorated with flowers in red, white and blue and with endless rows of flags, with important-looking officials sitting and standing in their cars or on the top of the trucks. They were not 'floats' in the true sense, since the trucks were carrying parts of the monument, but the air of festivity was present. We could not see the band since the camera rested mainly on the monument itself or on the decorations. The story about the removal of the monument from the main square was retold by V.(A), who indicated that 'it was removed by the Communist regime in 1947'. There was a short discussion over this issue, since the members of the audience disagreed with him on the date. This in turn triggered a general discussion about the Communists banning everything that had any 'Croatianness' in it. The motorcade reached its destination and we could see a mass of people congregated on the main square obviously waiting for the motorcade. I had noticed the date on the screen in the right-hand corner as 10 September 1990, which was six days before the official ceremony (the official ceremony was on 16 September). The camera zoomed in on an Australian flag, then on a Canadian flag and back, and we could hear V.(A) talking to someone in one of the Dalmatian dialects (from one of the islands in the Adriatic – Korčula), exchanging impressions and experiences of the day. Apparently it was 'a fellow Australian' who just like V.(A) had come to visit Croatia for the first time in forty years, and was excited and full of joy about it. The conversation on screen was barely audible due to the background noise of singing and shouting. The words of the song *Ustani Bane* (Rise O Viceroy – a song which was blacklisted by the Yugoslav regime) filled the room suddenly and most of the audience in the living room started to sing as the dusk was falling in real time. The images were fading on the screen and the sudden burst of searchlights pointed at the monument, which was now half hidden by the supporting structures, surprised us all.

The very next frame was of a visit to the cemetery – not just any cemetery, as was explained to us by V.(A), but the one built for the thousands of Croatian victims of the post-Second World War massacre by Communists, of soldiers of the NDH and civilians alike. The story of Bleiburg was to fill the newspapers and to get considerable media attention in Croatia, and some of the media campaign had reached Australia, but most of the members of the audience were not sure about 'what really happened' mainly because the 'after the war death camps' and their victims inhabited the blurry space between myth and reality. The post-war massacres were used by both Serbians and Croatians to vilify the enemy, and I will discuss them in chapter 5 (Prcela and Guldescu 1970; Omračanin 1975; Nikolić 1988).

At this point in the viewing I became aware of what was happening to my audience. The video tape was only a trigger for discussion and explicit explanations that were given during the screening by V.(A) only raised more questions and induced further debate. There were eleven people in the room (counting myself) and it appeared that they were all talking at the same time. It was obvious that this was very different from other video and television viewing. The question of Bleiburg had only amplified the already heated debate. V.(A) was answering numerous questions, two teenagers stopped by on their way out to ask for some money from their father, M.M. brought in the coffee and cakes, all with the discussion going on. It was obvious that the myths around the massacre had influenced the debate, with one of the members of the audience quoting 200,000 Croatians being killed. Although the number of victims (as with other Second World War massacres) will probably never be known, V.(A) announced that:

> V.(A): The Croatian parliament [in 1990] invited foreign experts to join the commission in order to launch an inquiry into the massacres, for the first time after the war.

The elderly man in the audience who until now had sat quietly without joining the discussion said softly:

V.(C): Yeah . . . they need foreigners to find out the truth . . . they still don't believe us, do they?

I seized the moment and asked him, 'Who are *they*?' He looked up, surprised by the question, and answered:

V.(C): Don't you read the papers or watch television, child? . . . The whole world is against Croatia.

Unfortunately I was not able to continue the conversation since the part showing the official opening was starting to play on the television screen. When someone from the audience asked him if this was taped from television, V.(A) boasted that he had got a 'real good' spot for taping it, since he knew 'some guys' from Croatian Television (HTV).

We had seen some parts of the official celebration of the reinstallation of the monument earlier on one of the tapes M.M.'s sister had sent, taped off television, but for the next two hours the audience sat only making occasional comments. The lights were switched off. The audience was watching carefully, first the opening speeches by the mayor of the City of Zagreb and later the very, very long speech by Dr Franjo Tudjman, president of Croatia. The speeches were followed by a very well staged summary of the history of the Croatian people in 'seven scenes' from the time of the first Croatian kings until Ban Jelačić's reign. Each of the scenes consisted of a recitation of poetry and a musical composition, mainly from the repertoire of the most famous Croatian poets, writers and composers, depicting some aspect of the struggle for independence for Croatia. Out of these all except one were unknown to the audience – as they revealed in the discussion afterwards. The only one known to the audience was the last act of the opera *Nikola Šubić-Zrinski* which contained the popular aria, *U boj, U boj* (To Battle, to Battle), described earlier in this chapter, pp. 96–7 (see also note 6, p. 231). Towards the end of the official celebrations a certain degree of boredom set in, perhaps caused by the monotonous tone of theatrical diction adopted by the announcer, but most probably due to the fact that the music was unknown to the audience. The end of the opening ceremony signalled the start of the *narodno veselje* (mass celebration) as was indicated by V.(A). Until the end of the tape V.(A) and his video camera documented some interesting parts of the celebration, first on the main square and later inside the popular restaurants and 'watering holes' around the town. Endless unknown faces shouted into the camera 'Long live Croatia', 'God and Croatia', 'Long live Ban Jelačić' and everything and anything else, including some obscenities aimed at the former Communists and the Serbs. After the tape had finished, we all had coffee in the kitchen, and the 'young ones' (four teenage boys) moved into the living room to watch a rented video tape; once again that living room could have belonged to any Australian home.

The subsequent conversation about the tape revolved around the speech

117

that President Tudjman delivered at the opening ceremony. It was interesting that the audience remembered the part of his speech where he glorified the history of Croatian fighting for 'freedom and independence' and called on the unity of 'brother and sister Croatians from all around the world'. He openly stated that Croatians were ready to 'fight for freedom and lay their lives on the altar of Croatia', alluding to the troubles that were already starting in the Serb-populated regions of Croatia. More than one member of the audience pointed out how 'handsome he, the president, is' and 'how well he speaks'.

My own thoughts were occupied only with the flashes of another 'leader' calling for the unity of a nation, and the tragedy that swept Europe and the world as a result of it. There were flash-reminders of Adolph Hitler's tragically effective appeals to the German masses in the name of the nation (the *Volk* or the state or *Deutschland*).[16] This image was to haunt me every time I heard another political speech or proclamation, which, before I would usually have dismissed as propaganda. But I have seen how the audience in M.M.'s living room reacted time and time again to similar speeches, and understood that the appeals of the political leaders to a sense of nationality, of brotherhood and sisterhood, to their common ancestry and most of all to the sense of shared blood or consanguinity represented most powerful tools in the hands of Croatian leaders. And they have used those tools to solicit popular support, just as other national leaders would.

A transformation was taking place in that living room. The use of familiar metaphors was magically transforming the distant homeland into Motherland, the ancestral land, land of our fathers, sacred soil where our fathers died, the cradle of the nation (Smith 1991: 28–9, 93–5) and most commonly, but most powerfully, *Dom* (Home). A spiritual bond between the diaspora, the Croatian homeland and the territory of Croatia was being formed. The appeals in the speeches were made through and to the emotions, no space for reason was left. Gone were the initial arguments over the political speeches that we watched on the video tapes earlier. Speeches were now constructing a rationale for seeking independence from the 'relative economic deprivation due to the exploitation of the Croatian economy by the federal government' (my personal favourite), to the more sophisticated internal colonialism argument which always involved the question of the suppression and the imposition of language. Emerging in the audience that night was a creation of a hate–love continuum. It only reminded me of the countless senseless and fanatical sacrifices which have been made in the name of a nation or a homeland in the past. I left my audience in a celebratory mood but I was overcome by fear.

Some time later, on the day before Christmas Eve 1990, I was sitting in another living room watching television. It was the eve of the Croatian parliament's vote on the new constitution. This time I was with a childhood friend in Zagreb, Croatia. Apart from the 20,000 kilometres difference and the winter outside, the mood of that audience watching the direct broadcast from the Croatian Parliament was not much different from the mood of the audience in Perth. We listened to President Tudjman delivering a speech on this occasion, a speech which was laden with the same phrases, metaphors and calls on Croatian brothers and sisters. After I left, on my way home I had to cross the main square, the Ban Jelačić Square. I looked up at the monument of a horseman and noticed that the laser beam that was extending his sword on the opening night (that we had watched on the video tape described earlier) was gone, but the spotlights were still there, as were the holographic images of the Croatian flag and the Croatian coat of arms in its revised version. It was cold and late, but there was a crowd around the monument, and I could see that people were lighting candles in silence.

It was the first day of my return home after more than ten months (ten months in which the whole world had changed, including my home town). The Christmas Bazaar was still open, but instead of the traditional red and green colours of Christmas, everything was red, white and blue. New calendars displayed the flag, there were countless copies of the coat of arms, plasticised sheets of music with the words of the Croatian anthem, *Lijepa Naša Domovina* (Our Beautiful Homeland), and of course photographs of President Tudjman, all lying side by side with miniature flags, key rings, coffee mugs and scarves. These were all adorned by one or all of the Croatian insignia. The stalls were well lit and the mixture of traditional Croatian Christmas music plus *Rudolph the Red Nosed Reindeer* could be heard. A few years earlier, tapes and records of Christmas music were a rarity at the New Year's Bazaar (as it was then called).

Just a year later, in December 1991, the celebratory mood of 1990 had vanished. There was a smaller crowd lighting candles around the Ban Jelačić monument. This time the candles were lit not in celebration of democracy and of the rebirth of nation. Each and every candle under that monument stood for one of the dead or missing Croatians who voluntarily or accidentally had 'laid down their life on the altar of their Mother Croatia' (an expression used frequently in the Croatian media when reporting the casualties on the Croatian side).

FROM ETHNICITY TO NATION

According to Philip Schlesinger (1991: 177) 'The relationship between the present of a national collectivity and its past' is partly an imaginary one 'mediated by the continual, selective reconstruction of "traditions" and "social memory".' In the absence of cultural and educational institutions in the diaspora which could bring about the 'deep adjustments in the relationship between polity and culture' (Gellner 1983: 35), which was already happening in Croatia itself, Croatian audiences (in Perth) relied on the Australian media institutions and on the VCR to provide them with the basic capacity to negotiate their cultural (and national) identity at a time of drastic changes in their country of origin.

Taking into consideration the particular construction of ethnic cultural identity inside Australian multicultural society (see Birch 1989: 183–220), I shall argue that 'migrant' and 'ethnic' are 'elastic concepts', just like 'the people' or 'the working class' described by Pierre Bourdieu (1991: 90–1), as owing 'their political virtues to the fact that one can extend the referent at will' and 'manipulate its extensions in order to adjust it to their interest'. Thus the nation-building process of social and cultural interchange within and across the Croatian nation in the homeland and the diaspora relied on that 'elasticity' of Croatian ethnic identity for popular support, first during the democratic changes and quest for self-determination and later during the ensuing war.

First of all, the Croatian diaspora (just like the Croatians in the homeland) had to 'recompose their boundaries' (Schlesinger 1991: 153). They had to differentiate themselves from the 'other' groups in the Yugoslav community in particular and in Australia in general. For this to happen it was necessary to 'recodify' their 'social memory' (ibid.: 141). The fragmentary nature of the information received made the effects of the successful 'recodification' in the homeland equally fragmentary, but no less influential. What it meant was that the final negotiation for meaning was taking place most often on the 'secondary level of meaning-making' during discussion, talks and gossip (Fiske 1987: 77–80), thus allowing the existing mythologies to mix freely with the content of the cultural text, in this case videos.

In order to gain some understanding of the processes involved in the negotiation of the rise of Croatian nationalism and other changes taking place in Croatia, and the influences it might have on the Croatian audiences I was researching, I have narrowed my study by focusing on the audience of 'M.M.'s family and friends'.

Other media researchers, especially David Morley (1980, 1986, 1991, 1992), James Lull (1980, 1988, 1990) and Roger Silverstone (1990, 1991) have all used families or households as the site for ethnographic media research, but it was David Morley who argued that:

> [T]he sitting-room is exactly where we need to start from, if we finally want to understand the constitutive dynamics of abstractions such as 'the community' or 'the nation'. This is especially so, if we are concerned with the role of communications in the continuous formation, sustenance, recreation and transformation of these entities.
>
> (Morley 1992: 283)

Morley also examines the 'interfacing' of the public and private in the living room, concluding that because the experience created 'is neither public nor 'private', the 'public' is 'domesticated' (ibid.). Thus it is socialised as such. It could be said, then, that the kinship-like ties that had already existed in the

Croatian community in Perth grew stronger through the socialised and private perception of what it entailed to be Croatian.

It was also in M.M.'s home that I first noticed a gradual but significant change in the viewing patterns and habits of the family and their friends. For example, 'watching the news' always meant watching SBS evening news at 6.30 p.m., while 'listening to news' meant listening to Croatian radio broadcasts on multicultural radio (now 6EBA-FM). The most noticeable changes started at the time of the fall of Communism and the increased media coverage of Eastern Europe. At first the audience started to listen to ABC (on 6WF station in Perth) and Radio National (6WN), and watch the local ABC evening news, then gradually started to notice current-affairs programmes, such as *Dateline* on SBS and *Lateline* on ABC, which in turn altered the viewing of other popular programmes.

There was also an increased flow of video tapes from the homeland which contained a large proportion of information programmes mainly taped off television news and current affairs, which of course gave extensive coverage to the first democratic elections in Croatia. This provided the audience with first-hand knowledge of the candidates and when some of the political leaders visited Australia (including Perth) on their fundraising rallies, they were already known to the audience. Effectively this was a 'television election' through the medium of the VCR (cf. Morley 1992: 286 citing Pateman).

Video tapes such as the celebrations of the 'return' of the Ban Jelačić monument to the main square in Zagreb recreated in M.M.'s living room the celebratory spirit of Croatian independence, and allowed the audience present to feel a part of the Croatian nation, at least for the time of the viewing.

In the next chapter, I follow up the changes in television viewing patterns as well as the change in VCR dynamics in the same family and circle of friends, and attempt to show how it influenced the day-to-day functioning of the family in the light of the increasing ethnic tensions in the homeland (then still within Yugoslavia).

5

EXCUSE ME WHAT IS
GENOCIDE?

Contemporary viewers of Music Television (MTV) have grown used to the multi-sensory space created by images fitting together in a dream-like or psychedelic manner. One short segment of one of the self-edited video tapes circulating in the Croatian community in Perth was of this type. A well-known popular singer performs on the stage, the Croatian political leaders are seen in the foreground, with crowds holding signs and banners in the background. First we recognise the Croatian anthem, then an old man's voice, untrained and shaky, joins in with the *a capella* singing; finally a crystal-clear baritone takes over, bursting into passionate song. Next come the official speeches interrupted by folk dancing, some popular Croatian music, speeches again, and an excerpt from Ivan Zajc's opera, *Nikola Šubić-Zrinjski*, symbolising the centuries of the Croatian struggle for freedom, followed by more speeches, more music, and so on . . . we are watching a video tape of the celebration surrounding impending Croatian independence, in the wake of the first democratic elections (in 1990).

It is through video tapes like this one that we are able to 'see' what is happening in Croatia, and the images of the celebratory mood of the population made visible on the screen validate the reality of Croatian freedom in a digestible, 'ready to wear' format. The ideology of Croatian nationalism which legitimates as 'good' and correct anything that is Croatian, is internalised into the cultural milieu of audiences in Australia as an ingrained 'common sense' that is next to impossible to challenge.[1] One of the most powerful characteristics of the VCR is its ability to bring together through the homogenising tendency of 'ethnicity' (or nation) so many different fragments of the Croatian diaspora across Australia and around the world. This kind of fragmented video tape, in which the discursive co-ordinates of élite cultural practices are not detached from the folk and popular, functions as an instrument for national unification on all fronts: in the Croatian homeland itself and its diaspora worldwide.

Through the representational practices made possible by advances in VCR technology, the Croatian leaders have found an ideal medium for reassuring the Croatian diaspora that whatever might be happening in Croatia

– the threat of civil war, unemployment, ethnic unrest and violence, collapse of the economy – it is not really so. National unity is presented to us packaged in fragments and is claimed to represent the 'reality' of the Croatian nation unified under a new flag, ready and willing to fight for democracy and independence.

As the viewing continues the remote control 'zaps' and 'zips' through the 'boring' parts of the political speeches. It switches backwards and forwards to performances of folk groups or popular music performers. Sometimes the tape is 'freeze framed', stopping for a second in sudden recognition of a face of someone one thinks might be a relative or acquaintance – the recognition is erroneous, but weren't the political leaders mentioning something about the atrocities the Serbs carried out during and before the Second World War? Let's listen – rewind the tape. Yes. What emerges is this sweeping picture of the Croatian nation endangered by Serbs. This fact strongly emerges from a mixture of broadcast television and home-video segments as presented on this tape. At one point there is a dramatic reading of a poem, 'To our Homeland' (Našoj Domovini), written by an anonymous Croatian emigré to America. The broken English-Croatian language of a peasant-poet read out and canonised by a contemporary theatrical star. Without any sign of warning, sepia-coloured images from the newsreel footage of the archive film that captured the shooting of the Croatian Parliamentarian and the Leader of the Croatian Peasant Party HSS (Hrvatska Seljačka Stranka) in the Yugoslav Parliament between the two wars in 1928. The 'dominant theme' and the 'invariant motif' of the video we are watching is sealed now.[2]

The video tape we have been watching with family and friends in the M.M. home is only one of many that circulate in the community at this time. The video tapes provide the community with the kind of shared political and cultural happening we have grown accustomed to from news and current affairs programmes on broadcast television. But these tapes are different since the genres of news, as information, and music videos, as entertainment, are combined, with one exceptional ingredient, and that is that the viewer is now editor and appears to be in control. What started as entertainment with politics, is now politics through entertainment.

The changes in the viewing habits of Croatian audiences described in the previous chapter (and developed in later chapters) include the replacement of the mainly entertainment videos by documentaries, historical and non-fiction video tapes composed often as ad hoc collages of news items (pirated from television) and a blend of popular music and political speeches, with an occasional item from what is still considered 'high culture', such as opera excerpts. A casual viewer, confronted for the first time with home-produced and home-edited video tapes, may be surprised at not finding in such videos anything worth watching, and would most certainly find it strange in form and content. However, the seemingly non-narrative structure of the video creates narratives through the video–viewer and viewer–viewer relationship creating meaning as it unfolds, relying mainly on the popular memory of the audience as well as on cross-referencing and intertextuality with other cultural texts and other media. Members of the ethnic audience often depend on the video tapes sent from Croatia not only for information but also for entertainment. The VCR is thus used as a form of 'surrogate for social and political memory' (Bromley 1988: 13).

There is a difference between historical documentaries or scripted historical dramas for television and these fragmented video tapes. Documentaries and dramas (as well as feature films) usually strive towards 'accurate' historical reconstruction either through the use of archive footage or through historical reconstruction of sets, costumes and a highly professional repertoire of camera-work and montage (Nichols 1991). The producers of historical documentaries, dramas and films mobilise every resource available, from art forms to the latest technology, in order to recreate the history and authentic 'feel' of the historical period. In contrast, the home-edited videos are inscribed with a blend of the editors' personal memory at a level of cultural signification with an insistence on particular symbolic and discursive forms. The texture, the blurring, the fuzziness – which most of the time are the results of the tape being a second- or third- or even a fifth-generation product – only reinforce the qualities of authenticity that are attributed to such tapes by the ethnic audience. It could be argued, then, that the fragmented irrational visual imagery of the tapes circulating in the Croatian community creates their narrative structure exactly through that fragmentation. The meaning is created from clusters of signifiers by means of repetition, redundancy and discontinuity.

As the political and ethnic tension grew inside Yugoslavia and the Australian media began to refer to the possibility of 'Yugoslavia sliding towards civil war' (cf. Magaš 1993: 260–302), the ethnic audiences in Perth grew ever more restless, searching for every bit of information about 'what is really happening'. They increasingly monitored all media, television, radio and newspapers for news; there was an increase in dialling for the Croatian news in Melbourne. Such telephone news, which was in Croatian, was taped most of the time and often shared with friends – to escape the cost involved in the daily use of an interstate telephone number. The M.M. family for the first time since I had known them took out a daily subscription to *The West Australian*. Previously they had bought either *The West Australian* or the *Sunday Times* paper at the weekend for the 'classified ads' and the television guide. I also noticed the increased frequency with which I was summoned, often at very short notice, to watch a tape that was available 'only for that evening'. One of those occasions was an urgent call to come and view the tape on Stjepan Radić.

This was a preview for audiences interested in purchasing the tape from an unnamed distributor. On my arrival at M.M.'s home I was also offered for purchase a photograph in the form of a postcard issued on the occasion of the sixtieth anniversary of Stjepan Radić's death. 'It's for a good cause', I was told by M.M., and the price of 5 dollars a copy was not even questioned. Since Stjepan Radić died in 1928 and the documentary of his life (and death) was made in 1988, I had my suspicions that someone was cashing in on the increased anxiety of the Croatian population as well as on their 'hunger' for information. (I was to have similar doubts later as well.)

There was hardly time for me to sit down before the screening. M.M. explained:

> M.M.: Marija is coming to collect the tape in less than an hour. They want to see it tonight, but her husband is working late and there is a deadline for ordering them – if we want to buy the tape – by tomorrow morning when I have to return it.

With these words she pressed the start button.

HISTORY LESSONS THROUGH THE VCR

At this point in my research, the video tapes circulating in the community increasingly began to include representations of certain events in Croatian history to illustrate the quest for Croatian independence. Historical periods, events and heroes were presented by documentaries and video tapes containing fragments of special broadcasts of public performances such as concerts of popular and classical music alongside dramatised and restaged history. These 'texts' for learning Croatian history were made available through the Croatian television to audiences in the homeland. As these programmes were often taped off-air and, either coupled together with or enriched with other video material (from television or family albums), they found their way into the homes of Perth audiences. Even though an abundance of printed histories of Croatia, from glossy coffee-table editions to paperbacks and pamphlets, was increasingly available, the video tapes dealing with the history of the Croatian people were favoured above all other sources. Audio-visual representations, according to a member of the M.M. family-and-friends audience were 'more readily understood' since:

> V(A): The experience of history through visual form comes across as actual experience . . . It is not at all like learning history in school. It is just like experiencing it yourself. I just wish they [the Australian media] would show some of this stuff on television. . . . To see that Croatia is not all ustašas, that we had a history . . . I mean before that . . .

It was obvious from his words as well as from the comments from others that the negotiation of Croatian identity was now translated into a political theme. The new-found historical continuity of Croatian cultural identity as seen through its history and as offered by the new Croatian state also provided the Croatian Australians with a positive point of identification. This was in contrast to the negative connotations of being Croatian which had dominated both the diaspora and the Australian popular discourse in the past.

The documentary on the life and death of Stjepan Radić was one of the most frequently watched and quoted video tapes in the community for a long time. Stjepan Radić was the leader of the Croatian Peasant Party and is regarded as one of the fathers of Croatian nationhood (Mužić 1990). The documentary claimed to be 'the first documentary ever made' on the topic. It strove to give an impression of objectivity in its presentation of historical facts. The well-substantiated narrative was in the form of a biography. Following Bill Nichols' (1991: 34–5) documentary classification, we could classify it as being in 'the expository mode'. It used text superimposed on image, voice-over and music all at once. This expository style was reinforced by the sepia-coloured archive footage and the photographic stills. Both were used to establish and maintain the rhetorical continuity offered as 'historical truth'. Since the mode of expository documentary 'frequently builds a sense of dramatic involvement around the need for a solution' (*ibid.*: 38), the 'solution' in this film is the independence of Croatia. The narrative suspense of Stjepan Radić's life and his tragic death not only offers a point of entry into the Croatian past, but also equates the quest for independence in the past with the Croatian quest for independence in the here and now.

The story of Stjepan Radić was also interesting to the audience because together with Ban Jelačić (described in the previous chapter), Radić represents 'the modern cult of a great man' which 'expresses our attachment to our nation' (Smith 1988: 193). Through the great heroes of intellect and culture such as Radić the need for 'national genius is fulfilled'. As such he was celebrated by the new Croatian state, and events commemorating the one hundred and twentieth anniversary of his birth preceded a comprehensive campaign for his rehabilitation from the relative obscurity assigned to him by the former Yugoslav regime. Thus the moral–emotional attitude of the audience towards Radić had been created by the positive image being promoted even before the documentary reached Perth on video tape. I watched this documentary on two occasions, first with the audience of M.M.'s family and friends in early 1991, when the warning signs of the war in Yugoslavia were already present. Much later I watched the video again as I embarked on writing the draft of this chapter from my notes. I borrowed the tape from M.M. (who had bought it and added it to her video library), and watched the tape in the privacy of the university's preview room. What follows is an account of both viewings.

The first viewing situation did not allow for the transcription and translation of the superimposed text. It led to only fragmentary information about the interpretative worlds of the audience, yet provided a valuable opportunity for understanding some of the audience's interpretative strategies for understanding Croatian history.

The tape captured the undivided interest of the audience, and I noticed a progressive abandonment of the parallel activities, such as chatting, that usually accompanied viewing of videos. I also noticed a lack of adequate knowledge of the places, historical facts and personal histories of the characters portrayed or mentioned, which resulted in a different articulation and understanding of the documentary by different members of the audience. The meanings grasped and agreed on later during the discussion were very different from what I expected. The members of the audience connected the content of this video to different episodes from Croatian history, mostly learned from other video tapes seen earlier. They also included in the reading of the documentary, an implicit meaning of dislike and disgust with the Serbs as a nation. This meaning had completely eluded me until pointed out by the audience.

Later, on the second viewing, I came to understand the mechanisms through which the negative meaning of Serbia was constructed. Similarly the reconstruction of the documentary by the retelling of the story allowed the audience to fully negotiate the meaning, not only because it allowed additional time for making intertextual connections, but also because during the viewing of video tapes the meaning-making remains tentative as we wait for the next frame. Thus the variation in my interpretation of the video tape did not depend only on the difference in the cultural and educational capital between the audience and myself, but was also a result of the difference in the social settings and the historical context in which the viewing took place. For example, my second viewing was taken out of the context of M.M.'s living room as well as taking place later, after the Serbian attacks on Slovenia and Croatia had already happened. After watching the tape for the second time, and reading the field notes and transcripts of the first viewing, I became aware that the documentary seemed to have exploited the detail and atmosphere, particularly in the funeral scenes, more successfully than any history book I have read. As I was attempting to analyse the video tape according to the choice and the presentation of the documentary material, the interpretation of its arrangement and the formal composition of the story, I realised that what I was doing was saturating the interpretation with my own cultural commentary based on a mixture of personal interpretation and scholarly discourse.

What resulted from the convergence of the notes on the first viewing and the transcription of the second viewing is accounted for below and I only hope that it may broadly fit into what John Fiske (1990) generously terms 'ethnosemiotics'.

I will pick up here where I left off at the beginning of this chapter with M.M. pressing the start button for the VCR. The other members of the audience are: three married couples, two men in their early forties and two women in their late thirties, and a retired couple in their early seventies who are parents of our host. They are my usual audience with the exception of the host's teenage daughter who was born in Australia but is fluent in both languages.

The music starts – surprisingly it is Mozart's *Requiem*. There is a still shot or a photograph of a dead man lying in a coffin. His arms are crossed over on his chest. Flowers and candles are all around. We have to assume that it is a photo of Stjepan Radić because of the title of the video, or perhaps some actually recognise him in an instance of intertextuality with his photo in the migrant journal.

We know he is dead because he is lying in state in a coffin, and the closed eyes, the crossed arms, flowers and candles around it are all culturally definable signs of death. This is so obvious that the audience did not pay any attention to the man himself but rather made comments like 'He was quite a young man.' The comment referred to his age and the text over the image which read:

Beta Film Presenting
Stjepan Radić 11.7.1871–8.8.1928

In the meantime I am nominated to read the text,[3] as the most literate in Croatian of the ten people in the room. The text over the first photograph changes and now we read:

This film has been produced in memory of and on the 60th anniversary of the death of the prominent Croatian politician and writer Stjepan Radić, the founder of the Croatian Peasant Party . . .

The three full stops at the end of the intertitle appear throughout the film and are signalling to the viewer that the story continues. This strategy is reminiscent of 'children's' story books of the kind in which the whole page is a scene from the story and the text at the bottom of the page always has three stops to signal to us that the story continues if we turn the page.

The page is turned and a sepia photograph of a young man in attire from the beginning of the century appears. The following intertitle is superimposed almost immediately:

His troubles started from his high school days when he was expelled from the seventh grade for his ideas concerning the existence of Croatian 'consciousness' . . .

The next frame shows what appears to be a student logbook with 'Index Lecionum' written at the top. We are given a few seconds to read the particulars on the documents. At this point I have to be reminded by the audience of my duty as narrator. The teenage daughter explains to her grandparents what the document was:

S.M.: It is something like a report card ... you know, to put in the grades you get in school.

The next text appears:

6 March 1893. He was expelled from the Law School, University of Zagreb and was sentenced to four months in jail for his attacks on the civil governor of Croatia Khuen Hedervary ...

The next document that is shown is some kind of student identity card. The text that appears immediately made reading the particulars extremely difficult. The grandfather insists on knowing what it says, but S.M. refuses to oblige this time.

In June 1895 he was sentenced to six months' imprisonment for burning the Hungarian flag on the occasion of the visit by HRH Franz Joseph to Zagreb ...

Such flag-burning necessarily brings to mind other instances of flag-burnings as instances of intertextual reference. For me it is the US flag, burning in Vietnam and Cambodia, and most recently the Yugoslav flag during the struggle for independence in Croatia.

The grandfather demands to know why they are burning the flag. This time his son answers impatiently:

M.R.: It was a long time ago and they wanted to separate from Hungary.

As he speaks he is looking for approval in my direction, while the grandfather nods his head, satisfied with the answer.

The close-up of the photograph from Radić's youth (the same one as before) appears and the text superimposed is:

In 1904 jointly with his brother he founds the Croatian Peasant Party ...

The music from Mozart's *Requiem* continues as sepia-coloured photographs are now replaced by the first monochrome documentary footage. The film shows, as we assume by the attire of people on screen, life in Croatia at that time. Crowds are assembled for what looks like a public meeting. The inter-title reads:

Croatian people saw in Stjepan Radić an ideal leader and an ideal representative of their ideals and he was well loved ...

The film continues, showing the welcoming committee and showing Radić with a woman (we assume it is his wife) – from the audience the grandmother asks: 'Is it his wife?'; no one answers as a comment is made on the national costumes worn by the crowd and a touch of nostalgia comes from the grandfather about all the 'people' wearing hats. (He meant 'all the men'. The Croatian plural noun *ljudi* means people but is often used colloquially to refer to men only.)

In my repeat viewing, I notice a large banner with 'Welcome' and the Croatian insignia. As the documentary footage of this public rally rolls on, the intertitles situate the event in time and space:

> This visit to Koprivnica [a small town in central Croatia] is typical of the welcome he received everywhere he went . . .

A seemingly endless procession of people on the screen passing by and attempting to touch Radić or shake his hand.

> The people following their leader . . .

The unnecessarily overt nature of the text in relation to the visual image does not bother other viewers but the blatancy of the statement reminded me of the popular demagogic tone of Nazism. I fight it off, but the negative taste stays with me from now on. The only comment in the living room, made by one of the younger women, was V.(A): 'You see how popular he was.'

The camera shows Radić speaking at a public rally. But he is voiceless. The music of Mozart's *Requiem* still provides the only sounds. Radić's voicelessness is significant. It is almost as if the meaning of it could be that even he warned the Croatian people not to enter into a joint state with the Serbs. But no one listened. Radić remains voiceless all through this video. I am not sure whether there is any documentary footage containing the sound of his voice, but where there is no such record, the usual practice is to have narration or voice-over.

No one in the audience finds this unusual and I do not raise the question but read on:

> All his ideas and plans he presented publicly . . .

A comment from the audience:

> R.M.: Yes, not like the bloody Serbs, who kept their plans a secret and they are destroying our country now.

Some other speakers are shown. They are also voiceless. No recognition of them is afforded by the audience. Audience members are engaged in 'Serb bashing' by now and the text I read out next goes by almost unnoticed:

> Other public figures and members of HSS [Croatian Peasant Party] from that region took part in speeches . . .

The film with speakers rolls on and the next intertitle appears as Mozart's *Requiem* intensifies. We don't know what Radić or his successors at the podium were talking about, but the intertitle clarifies that:

He believed that his and the Croatian cause would be victorious just by being just . . .

But this time the 'Croatian cause' and Radić's personal goals have become virtually interchangeable. I noticed this and I think the audience had too.

The montage process of the film is then 'laid bare' to the audience through a dissolve marking a shift as the screen changes by allowing the overlapping of the two shots. We are then introduced to a new atmosphere after the previous sunny shots of the political rally. We are now in a wintry fog or in the dusk, signalling a change in 'climate' and auguring an unpleasant development.[4] A pain of nostalgic recognition of the street I lived on with my grandmother hits me every time, but for anyone who does not know that it is Zagreb, for the viewer who has no recognition or personal knowledge, only the foggy atmosphere would be of any significance. I read out again:

> The speech you are about to hear was delivered by Stjepan Radić at the fatal sitting of the Peoples Council in Zagreb and warned of the future rule of the Serbian bourgeoisie . . .

The presentation of everyday life in Zagreb continues for a few seconds as the text appears:

> Zagreb, in those days . . .

At this point the music stops and an educated male voice reads the speech mentioned above. A 'hush . . . hush' goes on among viewers in the living room in anticipation.[5]

An open market in snow is shown. Peasant women offering their goods for sale are shown. It is Zagreb's main market and those who know Zagreb well would recognise it as such, and for a moment I am transported home. The monochrome and fuzzy images 'readily lend themselves to a licensed nostalgia . . . the idealizing of the past is given a powerful impulse by the styles and the solemn faces looking [and] golden ages are inscribed even in the weather' (Holland 1991: 91). The fact that my nostalgia is now a 'licensed nostalgia' doesn't make the pain go away but rather intensifies it with each frame, bringing back more recognition, more memories. I am wondering if any members of the small audience have experienced the same nostalgic feeling, but the answer would be 'No' since they indicated in the discussion after viewing that they have no more powerful memories of Zagreb than a passing recognition of the images. They all come from parts of the Adriatic Coast and some of them have never visited Zagreb. In this instance my viewing is very different from that of my audience.

The words of Radić's speech, beautifully articulated by the narrator, only partly reach my consciousness while the pain of nostalgia remains. As for the rest of the audience, they hungrily seize on each word, while the narrator in the name of Radić speaks:

a better future
that everyone is a Croatian enemy
the war did not teach us
against the centralised state
against the Serbian dynasty.

These phrases are remembered and then repeated by members of the audience after viewing.

Radić's photograph as a grown man is inserted in the middle of the speech as the voice-over calls the impending unification 'the biggest mistake of the Croatian people' and accuses the then present government of presenting the Croatian people with a *fait accompli*.

There are more shots of Zagreb. (The pain of not being there becomes unbearable.)

The speech goes on warning against a coalition with Serbs. As frame after frame evokes more memories, there is a shot of the cable car and the medieval tower of Lotršćak, a tower which is one of the most powerful icons of my home town. Icon after icon, symbol after symbol, the clock on the tower showing twenty minutes to twelve – there is still time ... for what – the narrator's voice, with beautiful diction, speaks of the conspiracy against the Croatian people and finally the words 'Long live Croatia' with the simultaneous appearance of Radić's photograph.

As soon as the narration is over, Mozart's *Requiem* resumes. There is a clear change of atmosphere in the room. The members of the audience start talking again. Someone repeats 'Long live Croatia'. The new context of what appears to be a parliament is on the screen. The conversation stops and I am called upon once again to read the text:

The Parliament in Belgrade has been a constant place of fighting for the rights of Croatian and other people for their rights inside the Hegemonic State of Greater Serbia . . .

The phrase 'Hegemonic State of Greater Serbia' is used today often in a derogatory sense and there are sounds of approval from the audience. The shots of Parliament fade as the same photograph of Radić as a mature man appears. The intertitle over the photo reads:

Stjepan Radić was the most persistent opponent of the Serbian Hegemonic State : . . .

After the text vanishes, the photograph lingers. This gives us time to absorb it, remember it. The shots of the Parliament reappear but this time it is not an orderly picture of delegates sitting in their seats. It appears to be disorderly. Something is about to happen. The stage is being set for the next text:

20 June 1928. The Court's (secret) agent and representative of the radical party, Puniša Račić, assassinated in the Belgrade Parliament the representatives of the HSS [Croatian Peasant Party] Pavao Radić and Djuro Basaricek and fatally wounded Stjepan Radić . . .

The newsreel stops rolling and on the still shot of the Parliament a text appears:

The Croatian representatives were shot because they wanted social justice and national freedom, naively hoping that they would achieve their aim with help from the dynasty of Karadjordjević . . .

The intertitle on the still shot of the Parliament stays on for what feels a long time. It appears designed to make a lasting impression on the audience. I catch fragments of two conversations. The one between the two younger men:

R.M.: Fools, how could they think that the Serbs would do anything for Croatians – except perhaps to kill them . . .

and the other between the two younger women:

M.M.: Pavao Radić was his brother – imagine losing two sons at the same time . . .
V.(A): Your cousin showed us some books written by his brother . . . They must have been a smart family.

It appears that the audience is occupied with the interpretation of the assassination and with linking it to the present situation. Anxiety about the tense situation in Croatian areas inhabited by Serbs is voiced by R.M. and instances of violence already taking place are recounted. The older couple is silent, and the teenage girl (S.M) leaves the room obviously thinking that this is the end to the video. (Or perhaps she was bored?)

However, the documentary film of the arrival back home in Zagreb of the convalescing Radić forms the background to the following text:

Almost the entire population of Zagreb welcomed the convalescing Stjepan Radić home . . .

The viewers in the room continue their conversation, at the same time attempting to find Radić among the images on screen, while I watch in recognition every shot of the railway station that I know so well. But I don't look for the image of Radić as the nostalgic pain takes hold of me again imagining all the happy 'hellos', and all the sad 'goodbyes' of my past on that same railway station. I am haunted with the reappearance of faces not belonging to this video but to my own past, and I ask myself: are the others who have watched this documentary in Croatia (and beyond) also haunted by memories as I am? Do these images affect me more because I am alone and away from home?

There is an excited exclamation from the grandfather as he recognises Radić disembarking from the train, walking away and climbing up into a waiting car. I am again reminded to read along. A photograph appears of what looks like a hospital bed – we recognise Radić sitting on the bed, and the same woman from a shot at the beginning of the film sitting on the other bed holding flowers. The grandmother comments 'It *is* his wife.' She is satisfied that this fact is now established. The intertitle reads on:

> Stjepan Radić spent his last days at home dreaming the same dreams that were the cause for the turbulent path of his life which was filled with fighting, jails and arguments, but also filled with the unconditional love of the Croatian people for their leader . . .

Mozart's *Requiem* plays on. No participant in the audience notices the discrepancy between the texts of the intertitle and the photograph. The text states that he spent his time at home, the photo clearly shows a hospital room. This did not seem to bother the audience, and I did not want to interfere and point out this discrepancy to them. What has captured the interest of the audience are the photographs and the footage of what appears to be a home movie. The last photograph of Radić, his wife and two small children solicits a few comments:

> V.(B): Did he have children?
> M.M.: I did not know he had children . . .
> V.(B): Perhaps these are not his kids . . .

And they turn towards me with the question in their eyes. I don't know the answer. Luckily I am saved by the next close-up. It is of his dead body and the intertitle:

> Stjepan Radić died on 8th of August 1928 . . .

The music stops for a brief moment. When it restarts it is louder and sounds more dramatic. We are shown Zagreb in mourning, the camera capturing black flags in evidence. I get a gentle nudge in my ribs reminding me that it is time to become the narrator again.

> The entire city of Zagreb was filled with black flags, the people were protesting against the violence of the hegemonic Serbian regime . . .

We are once again transported to the main railway station (interestingly enough it does not have the effect that it had on me earlier). People are crowded in trains, some of them crying, lots of people carrying Croatian flags, obviously coming to Radić's funeral:

> Masses of people were coming to Zagreb from everywhere to bid farewell to their leader . . .

Mozart's *Requiem* sounds even more dramatic as a shot of old Ban Jelačić Square appears.

An exclamation from a member of the audience:

V.(C): The horse is turned the other way . . .

For a moment we don't know what he is talking about. The knowledge of the other text showing the re-erection of the momument comes through in this instance of intertextuality. I restrain myself from explaining sarcastically that when the monument was erected originally, the enemy was coming from the north-west. (It was the Austro-Hungarian Empire.) Today the enemy is coming from the south-east. The only comment on his exclamation comes from M.M: 'It does not matter which way he is turned as long as he is there.' (I have asked several members of the audience if they noticed that the monument was turned 'the other way', but no one seemed to care very much, so I dismissed the fact of Ban Jelačić facing 'the other way' as my own mania for detail.)

The crowd on the screen forms a procession as the sounds of the *Requiem* intensify. As the funeral procession moves on through the streets of Zagreb a succession of short texts appears on screen:

The sad procession started from his home . . .

This intertitle was superimposed on the shot of the coffin carried by young men and surrounded by mourners. The interesting detail here is that, while most of the intertitles were superimposed over the middle of screen, this text was in a position that is usually occupied by subtitles, leaving the coffin and the faces of the mourners clearly visible to the audience.

The procession continues and I recognise the streets. The audience in the living room, obviously overcome by memories (of intertextuality) of other funerals, perhaps of a loved one, is silent. A boys' choir is singing in the next frame; however, we don't hear their voices but the voices of the unseen choir from Mozart's *Requiem*. It is an eerie feeling as the gestures of the conductor to the boys' choir almost coincide with Mozart's music.

The text continues:

The commemoration was held in front of the Croatian Peasant Party's headquarters . . . and again speeches were delivered by the most distinguished public figures . . .

The speakers come and go but we do not hear them, instead the 'Benedictus' from Mozart's *Requiem* is in full progress.

The next intertitle is over the moving images of the procession and it appears when they reach Ban Jelačić Square:

The procession crossing Jelačić Square . . .

The seemingly endless funeral procession with more frequent close-ups of wreaths and flowers, the local band, all somehow fit the rhythm of the *Requiem*. Suddenly the camera singles out a woman holding a sleeping child. Mother and child are surrounded by a crowd and the expression on her face is one of grief and weariness. The intertitle over this image reads:

In spite of the unbearable heat there was not a single person who did not want to pay a last tribute to Stjepan Radić . . .

Again there are close-up shots of wreaths. The camera tracks one in the form of the well-known Croatian coat of arms. There is an exclamation of recognition from the audience in the living room. I recognise the beginning of the front walls, known as 'the Arcades' of Mirogoj, the most famous part of the Zagreb cemetery. Only dignitaries and gentry are buried there.

The next intertitle reads:

The most beautiful cemetery, Mirogoj, was too small to accommodate the whole funeral procession which stretched from the railway station throughout the city streets to the Arcades of the Cemetery . . .

I think to myself: ' – which is quite long if we know that from the cemetery to the railway station is approximately 10 kilometres'. The film continues showing the details of the funeral procession inside the cemetery. Another close-up of the wreath in the form of the Croatian coat of arms, a close-up of the Croatian flag, a close-up of the grieving widow helped by friends, people crying, his coffin approaching the grave. A comment from the audience: M.M: 'I feel like crying myself' – obviously the power of intertextual linking with one's own memory of deaths is too much.

Now we see the grave with no people around. It is full of flowers and with the monument to Radić just as I remember it. Back in the preview room, I remember the many occasions I laid flowers at Radić's grave, as it used to be a gathering place for students in the 1960s during the student uprising. The next intertitle appears across the screen:

To this very day Stjepan Radić's grave is never without flowers and candles and the flame of those candles is the flame of the continuing memory of love of each and every new generation in order to maintain the ideals of Stjepan Radić, one of the finest sons of Croatia.

The still shot of his grave fades and a photographic representation of his life begins. The sepia coloured photographs are followed by the finale to Mozart's *Requiem*, as an inventory of 'images to remember' rolls on:

the photo of him as a young man
a family snapshot with a wife and son
Radić as a mature man
the same ID card as at the beginning of the film
a group photograph

Radić as an older man
a photo of a page of his handwriting
Radić at a rally
people waiting in front of his home for the start of the funeral
procession
his last photograph
Radić lying in the coffin
the photo of his grave as before.

The credits roll

Producer: Josip Horvat

Music by: W.A. Mozart

Zagreb 1988

and finally the *Requiem* stops.

There are no other credits: None for editing, none for research. We don't know to whom the well-educated voice that read the speech belongs. It is almost as if the producer does not want us to know. There seems to be a desire to leave the images as they were and have the speech belong just to Radić. We don't know who the musicians or the orchestra or the conductor or the choir are. Perhaps the voiceless boys' choir and the soundless musicians in the funeral procession are the ones we are supposed to remember. The historical past has achieved more of a presence through not having the usual credit sequence.

There was a discussion among the audience after the end of the video. The grandparents had left and only the three couples remained. After quizzing me on some historical points relating to the period presented in the film, they lapsed into a mixture of 'Serb bashing' and retelling the old myths of the massacres by Serbs in Croatia (from the earlier wars this century).

I was curious about whether Mozart's *Requiem* affected the others in the audience as it had affected me, and when I asked the small group one of the women V.(C) replied with the question: 'What is a Requiem?' Her husband V.(D), who holds himself as being more educated and informed than the rest, replied: 'It is a sort of mass for the dead', adding the derogatory 'You dummy'. The only reaction from his wife was: 'No wonder it sounded so sad.' The others paid no attention to this domestic scene. The previous conversation continued, with an occasional exchange of angry glances between the couple who shared this exchange.

As for this 'would-be media ethnographer', the only sensible thing to do was not to ask any more questions but to go home to make sense out of the half-legible notes taken during the showing of the video.

Almost a year elapsed between the first viewing of the video and the second viewing in the preview room. On that occasions the memories that were triggered by the video itself tangled with the memories of the reactions and comments by the members of the audience on the first viewing. The images of the audience were so strong that I could even remember the clothes the women were wearing. Maybe because:

> [P]oints of stability and anchored meaning (however temporarily) are to be found not in the text itself, but in its reading by a socially and historically situated viewer. Such a meaning is, of course, not fixed in a universal, empirical reality but in the social situation of the viewer. Different readings may stabilize texts differently and momentarily. But they do achieve moments of stability, moments of meaning.
>
> (Fiske 1987: 117)

The film about Radić is clearly the product of a skilful montage of newsreel footage, photographs, family movies, documents and music. Sergei Eisenstein (1986: 34), in 'Word and image', argues that the strength of montage is in the fact that 'it includes in the creative process the emotions and the mind of the spectator'. We can apply this conclusion here since the same images that were 'created by the author were recreated by the spectator' (*ibid.*: 35) as they also became the 'flesh of the flesh of the spectator's risen image'. Not only has the author created meaning here but so too has the creating spectator (*ibid.*: 36).

Sitting in the university preview room with a notepad on my knees, a pen in one hand and a remote control in the other, I am in total control, (or so I think). I carefully note what is going on on the television screen, stop, review, fast forward, copy down the intertitles superimposed on the photograph and the live footage. Doing all of this reminds me of the collection and juxtaposition of the selected memories of my childhood: of the cold Sunday afternoons when my grandmother would make us watch some 'family history' (recorded on home movies) before she would show us some old Disney cartoons on her 16 mm projector. The monochrome and sepia images of the video I am watching are so similar to the images that smiled and looked at myself and a group of bemused neighbourhood children on those winter afternoons with my grandmother. I realise that my appreciation of the narrative structure of those videos for me depends on those images and their combination with other images distant or more recent, all of which heighten an awareness of the emotions involved. Any meaning that I will ascribe to this video will depend on this interpretation and it will depend not only on the further content of the video, but will depend on the evoked memories and forgotten images called to life by intertextual interaction – by the instances of recognition of the image or sound, their aggregation and juxtaposition – just as the pictures of hopelessness, of the ethnic hatred, the war and destruction of life and property surface every time I start working on this book, bringing sometimes unbearable emotional pain. Am I an exception here? I don't think so.

AN ATTEMPT AT ANALYSIS

The sepia-coloured photograph, the black and white footage of film and the decision to omit direct narration or voice-over, the montage of the same photographs at the beginning and at the end, are all part of the specific narrative structure which allows the viewer to read the images as a unified and coherent story. There was no narrator in the usual sense for the screening of the 'Radić video'. However, in the conditions of a family living room, the one who is thought of as the 'most learned' will assume the role of the narrator and will read out loud the titles superimposed on the film. The role of this narrator is even more complex than reading the text. The role is similar to that of the story-tellers in oral cultures, and not too different from the narratorial voice in written tales. Walter Benjamin (1992: 87) writes: 'The storyteller takes what he tells from experience – his own or that reported by others. And he in turn makes it the experience of those who are listening to his tale.' Even though Benjamin writes about literary texts and the 'birthplace of the novel', video, just like any other cultural text, carries information 'incommensurable to extremes in the representation of human life' (*ibid.*). What we have to recognise here is the mobility of the boundaries between genres and the complexity of the relations that arise from this mobility. I was quick to define the video in question as 'documentary fiction', but as I progressed in my analysis I realised that it was not so much concerned with the documentation of the past as it was with an interpretation of the relationship between the past and the present of the Croatian people. Its purpose was to provide a new 'historical truth' and prove that if the Serbian and Croatian people couldn't live together then, they can't live together now.

The producer did not include a narrator (or a voice-over) whose role would be to function as an interpreter and could therefore interfere with the presentation of historical documentation. So too the individual viewer was intended to be the only channel through which the facts presented in this film could be re-imagined. Obviously it does not function as intended in the above described viewings. The self-appointed narrators or the narrators appointed by the audience in the living room changed the narrative structure as intended by the author. The above description of one such viewing session where I was appointed to read the text shows that the narrator outside of the video can find her- himself directly in the line of questions which the dual emotional experience of the viewers evokes.

Let me explain this duality further. It lies, I think, in the intended feeling of authenticity of the events presented and their direct ideological link to the struggle of the Croatian people today. Thus, in creating the documentary the film-maker created the narrative structure by juxtaposing the events happening in the 1920s with the 'real life' experiences of the audience today. He skilfully directed the audience towards the boundary where past and present intersect, setting up and emphasising the tension between the recent events in Croatia and the historical struggle for independence through this fragmented tribute to Stjepan Radić. It is significant that the speech by Radić heard on the tape was published in the migrant journal, *Nova Matica* (1991), and the article features a photograph very similar to (if not the same as) one of the photographs of Radić in the film. But the speech that is read out by a well-modulated educated male voice has been shortened considerably, perhaps to fit to the length of the documentary. The parts chosen to be presented were those where there was a very strong denunciation of the Yugoslav idea and warnings against Serbs. This indicates the purposeful omission of the rest of the speech. This proved very powerful, since the audience made very clear sense out of the documentary, showing increased animosity toward Serbs and once again reiterating that it was a mistake to make any alliance with Serbia, just as Radić had demonstrated.

What we were presented with was not a tribute to Radić, but a form of testimony to the sufferings of all Croatian people over the past sixty years. This was realised through the incorporation into this film of elements from other genres, such as home movies, photographs and official documents added to the documentary footage and old newsreels. The educated male voice reading out the speech is suddenly expanded and transformed into a metaphor representing all the silent voices we don't know about, representing the struggle of entire generations. The most expressive construction that outlines in advance the outcome of the narrative is not the first shot of a dead man, but it is rather the choice of music – Mozart's *Requiem*. Thus the sepia-coloured photos and the film footage play the role of 'syntactical phrase and the music has the role of rhythmical articulation' (Eisenstein 1986: 53). The role of music in this case becomes clear because we as audience, 'while hearing music, visualise some sort of plastic images, vague or clear, concrete or abstract, but somehow peculiarly related and corresponding to our own *perceptions* of the given music' (*ibid.*: 129).

In contrast to my audience, I noticed the use of Mozart's *Requiem* and found it significant to the documentary itself. As I had previous knowledge of Mozart's life, I knew that the *Requiem* was left unfinished and I also knew details of his short and tragic life. The points of comparison and intertextuality are obvious, and designed to be so for audiences like myself. The *Requiem* might have the meaning, as one of the participants explained to his wife, of 'a sort of mass for the dead', but it also has the meaning of an unfinished work – like the unfinished struggle of the Croatian people for independence.

THE SOUND OF DRUMS

The familiar sounds of the song dedicated to the newly formed Croatian guards (*Hrvatska garda*, then a Croatian paramilitary organisation) greeted me on my arrival at M.M.'s house on the occasion of yet another video-viewing session. The VCR in the living room was on, showing the changing of the guards in front of the Croatian Parliament edited to correspond with the drum beats of the song.

The changing of the guard ceremony is another example of the 'reinvention of Croatia'. The troops in the Hapsburg Dynasty military look-alike uniform marching in front of the Croatian Parliament are a pure invention of the choreographers employed to design the ceremony. The ceremony of the changing of the guards is a direct copy of the changing of the guards in front of Buckingham Palace in London, aiming to accentuate the 'age old' existence of the Croatians in terms of royalty and traditions.[6] Without the war and its attendant nationalistic fervour, such ceremonies would be ridiculed as silly. Yet this ceremony in front of the Croatian Parliament has been accepted by the Croatian diaspora without any questioning of its genuine 'traditional value'. In Croatia itself it caused controversy only in intellectual circles and only for a very short time.

There was no one in the living room except M.M.'s teenage son and his friend. They were imitating the highly ceremonial steps of the guard at the same time as attempting to hit each other on the head in order to mimic the drummer. The playful atmosphere reminded me of times not so long ago when the VCR was playing for hours at a time with no one watching – just a background of popular Croatian music as everyone went about their household chores.

The music videos of Croatian popular music were the most popular video genre especially before the further development of VCR technology which brought video cameras and editing equipment within everyone's range which in turn allowed an increase in recording and viewing of family albums and video letters. The video tapes of popular music were usually watched with some attention for the first time only. On subsequent runnings the tapes would be treated just like radio, with household members going about their usual business and paying little attention to the screen.

When tapes of popular festivals and concerts reached the community from the homeland it was often an excuse for a dinner party or at the very least for an afternoon or morning coffee with honorary guests present not in person but on tape. A new video tape of popular music was also the only occasion that I have seen M.M. bringing her ironing from the sewing room down to the living room, an honour normally reserved only for the daytime soap, *The Young and the Restless*.

Popular music from the homeland has played a large part in the lives of the Croatian ethnic community just as it has been significant to the Macedonian community (as described in chapter 2; pp. 70–1). Gillian Bottomley (1992: 71–88) examines the importance of dance and music to the Greek migrants in Australia. She suggests that 'dance can be used in the maintenance of cultural hegemony' (*ibid.*: 77). However, even though the large social functions with their inevitable dancing provided opportunities for the members of the Croatian community to 'show off' or to display symbols of their social status (*ibid.*: 80), the role of the music and popular songs of the Croatian community was more significant than the dance itself. The traditional (and specific) gender roles and social customs and traditions pertaining to Greek dancing (as described by Bottomley) are sometimes mirrored in mutated, borrowed forms in dance-related etiquette in the Macedonian community which has appropriated and internalised a large number of Greek traditions by virtue of inhabitating the same geopolitical space. But dancing in the Croatian community was different, it meant two things: first, folk dances in one of the numerous folkloric ensembles; and second, a form of ballroom dancing to the beat of the Croatian popular and new composed folk music.[7]

Jacques Attali (1985: 6) has proposed that 'more than colour and forms, it is sounds and their arrangements that fashion societies'. Since most of the members of the Croatian community originated in Dalmatia, the Adriatic Coast or its islands, the music they brought with them to Australia was based on the sounds of the Mediterranean – the sound of the sea, the sound of cicadas in the pine trees and harmonising a capella voices occasionally joined with the strings of a mandolin or a guitar. Thus sounds of the homeland formed a particularly vibrant part of the collective consciousness of Croatian migrants since it is music which in the collective memory 'allows those who hear it to record their own personalized specified, modelled, meanings, affirmed in time with the beat' (*ibid.*: 19). Of course there is also an influence of other European musical traditions, those from Italy being especially noticeable. The geographical proximity, similarity of lifestyles and, above all, the long history of Italian domination over the coastal part of Croatia have left a permanent influence on Croatian culture. Thus popular forms of music resemble very much the popular form of Italian canzone, or canzonetta, the form popularised by the oldest and most popular Italian music festival, the Festival of San Remo.[8]

However, the forms of popular music most favoured by the Croatian VCR audiences described here on several occasions came under a broad category which I call new composed folk music (NFM).

NFM AND ETHNIC REVIVAL

New composed folk music is an urban phenomenon, a bricolage of traditional folk music and repetitive folk tunes enriched by the rhythms and motifs of contemporary popular music such as rock, reggae, and so on. NFM has been described as the yearnings of modern urban man, who has not completely adapted to urban life, for the musical expression that will describe that struggle. However, music like other cultural forms easily becomes a political resource and tool for political differentiation under specific circumstances, and in that process those cultural forms and values are transformed into political symbols (Brass 1991: 13–15).

Before the war in Croatia and Bosnia, most of the popular songs in the Perth Croatian community relied on their simulation of the beguiling yarns of stories and myths, the kind of village and family myths that are embellished and retold across a kitchen table late at night after returning home from yet another function in the local ethnic club, a fundraising dinner or a dinner dance. As a result of the war and ensuing ethnic hatred a lot of NFM sought to mobilise the ethnic group against its rivals by promoting the congruence of a multiplicity of Croatian (or Serbian) cultural symbols in order to argue that members of one ethnic group are different from the other. But the songs of one of the most popular artists, Dražen Žanko, seem to work more by reinforcing the emotional turmoil caused by the more intimate personal conflicts of being away from the home. These songs often have a propensity towards melancholy. They contain compassionate testimony to lives shattered by migration. Most of the time they are hauntingly effective, but at the same time there is a relentless sameness about them that eventually wears the listener down. Of course, the songs are also mass-produced items since their primary purpose is to be sold.

Such songs have a simple structure which could even be seen as formulaic. It is: tradition + popular culture + melancholy + nostalgia. As with most popular culture today, there is a large and successful industry in and around marketing NFM. In its turn NFM exploits the invariant themes of simple binary oppositions such as: myth–locality; myth–family; urban–rural; popular–traditional; and industrial–organic. As these binary pairs are not specific only to the diaspora, such music is often popular with large especially rural, segments of the population in Croatia itself. By the same token they are frowned upon by intellectuals as 'kitsch'.[9]

NFM's lyrics are descriptive of either village or traditional urban life which is seen by ethnic audiences as life 'back home'. Sometimes the music is set to the words of well-known poems dealing with the same themes. The identification of the audience with NFM occurs on two levels. First, there is an easy identification achieved by the recognisability of the musical scores; and second, the text is readily understood and most often tied to visual presentation of the narrative if the song is in the form of a video-spot. (The form of the NFM video-spot usually consists of a complete narrative with beginning and end in contrast to the popular MTV style video-spots.)

The repertoire of different NFM singers and groups is closely linked with and often based on, the assumed notion of 'what the audience likes' – resulting in the number of similar and often seemingly identical musical scores. This shows a high degree of commercialisation associated with ethnic markets created by the policies of multiculturalism in Australia which encourage symbolic ethnicity (cf. Bottomley 1992: 84–8).

The success of NFM in the Croatian diaspora can also be seen as a part of a wider socio-cultural change in Croatia itself, representing the movement from villages to cities or migration to other countries and the active phase of a transformation of folk music into forms accepted by the rural and urban population alike.

The representation and the construction of the 'everyday' by NFM utilises folk tradition as much as popular forms such as rock and reggae, and this also makes it acceptable to the different generations of ethnic audiences. Part of the popularity of NFM could also be ascribed to performers such as Dražen Žanko who easily transforms from a 'yuppie' to a prodigal son returning home to the village, or becomes a passionate player of traditional games at the village fair. (I am referring here to the ease with which Žanko transforms in his video-spots.) The multiple roles played by Žanko in his highly successful video-spots are further reinforced by his carefully groomed image of a 'stable family man'. The notion of a 'tidy' family life is reinforced by the appearance of his wife, his children and his parents in his videos. This knowledge is accessible to us only if we have access to the community communication channels. Such is also the case with the significance of the abandoned limestone house which often serves as a background shot – it is actually the house he was born in. All these elements are important to the audience members, who often comment on the inclusion of his family as representing the importance of kinship ties. Moreover, the traditional (thus 'high') moral values of society represented by Žanko are in sharp contrast to the rather flamboyant and often negative images of drug–sex–alcohol abusing rock stars of today. This makes NFM music more desirable as an influence on the migrant children and NFM stars more appropriate as role models.

The second generation of Croatian migrant youth born in Australia has embraced NFM with the same zeal as their parents but they hesitate to admit it outside the community circles. This is symptomatic of second-generation migrants who often openly denounce their cultural heritage in order to 'fit in' to Australian society. However, as the ethnic revival entered its second phase of open ethno-nationalism, young Croatians increasingly sought the company of other Croatians in the community by consolidating the foundations of social interaction on the basis of ethnic identity. Such groups of young people did not exclude other Australians, except of course Australians of Serbian descent. Inside such groups NFM was often played side by side with other popular music from MTV, and the Australian friends of M.M.'s daughter showed recognition of the most popular tunes, some even managing to sing a few lines of Žanko's song *Od Stoljeća Sedmog* (From the Seventh Century).

Dražen Žanko's highly successful video clips re-imagine the traditional way of life and often defy the individualistic orientation of postmodern self-oriented society, idealising the simplicity of 'life left behind' (which makes him acceptable to the older audiences). On the other hand, his well-known business sense and presentation of himself outside the NFM music scene presents a form of acceptable symbolic ethnicity for the younger generation.[10]

For example, the discussion with the mixed audience of Australian and Croatian youth after watching Žanko's video-spot *Konoba* (*konoba* is a wine cellar which is often restored as a type of family 'drinking hole') has shown that even if the song is a type of 'drinking song' it does not have the negative connotations which alcohol and drinking for drinking's sake would often have in Australian society. Or as one Australian viewer put it:

> V.: It is not like getting 'pissed', not at all, there you go to meet with friends and have a good time, you don't have to get drunk.

The rest of the conversation was structured around the fact that mostly men congregate in *konoba* (a drinking hole in coastal Croatia). This to me sounded like a reproduction of the stereotyped image of a 'Dalmatian man' who proves his manhood by drinking his first glass with his father in *konoba*. Perhaps this neutralises any negative connotations that consuming alcohol might have.[11]

In contrast to performers like Žanko who are equally popular in their homeland and the diaspora, there is a large number of singers and other media personalities who keep their careers alive by performing (and selling videos) almost exclusively to and in the diaspora. Such artists and groups regularly tour Australia (and Canada) and most often recycle their old hits. These are popular with the older generation and do not attract a following among second-generation migrants.

The increased politicisation of popular culture within the Croatian ethnic revival has also witnessed the re-emergence of the half-forgotten popular-music performers who had their careers cut short by their undesirable political activities during the socialist (Yugoslav) regime. The newly formed Croatian government, under the guise of 'giving them a second chance', sponsored and encouraged the restoration of their careers. In doing so they enlisted the services of such singers for the 'cause'. One such singer was Vice Vukov.

Vukov was a talented singer with a large following and a promising career when he was sentenced and jailed for his political activities during the 'Croatian Spring' in 1972. After his release from jail, he was forbidden to perform anywhere in Yugoslavia and, effectively, throughout the world (as rumour has it) since he was not issued with a passport. After almost 20 years of absence, Vukov first started to tour the Croatian communities in the diaspora. Finally, with the formation of the Independent Croatian State, he reappeared in his 'full glory', participating in concerts endorsing the HDZ (the Croatian Democratic Party) in Croatia itself and all around the world. His legend was kept alive in the Croatian diaspora due to the fact that his music was banned by the Communist state. Consequently he acquired mythic status through the constant reproduction of the 'banned' songs mainly on audio tapes produced (and often re-mixed) in Germany or Canada. In this case the legend was re-exported from the diaspora to the homeland.

The following is the record of an occasion of viewing a video tape called *Šibenik: The Wounded Town* – which is actually a tape of a 'Band Aid' style concert in Šibenik (a Croatian coastal town) for Šibenik, produced by IVS. An interesting point here is that a tourist-propaganda tape of Šibenik was produced and marketed by IVS in 1987. The two tapes are often sold together. Our expectations were that the second tape *Šibenik: the Wounded Town* would show the effects of the war since it was distributed after the first Serbian shells fell on Šibenik. However, what we saw instead was a concert with some recital of poetry. The only sign of the war was a hole from a mortar shell through the roof of the famous Šibenik Cathedral.[12]

The M.M.'s audience of family and friends was quite large, fourteen people altogether. The conversation recorded and translated below is between four women whom I have labelled viewers A, B, C and D.

> V.(A): He dyes his hair. It is his hair? . . . Yes, he just dyes it.
>
> V.(C): He's got so fat. But you can't see it when he buttons up his jacket.
>
> V.(D): He was not allowed to sing for seventeen years.
>
> V.(C): My cousin [in Yugoslavia] had his tapes in his car and when the police stopped him they confiscated them.
>
> V.(B): I heard him sing on the [ethnic] radio the other day.
>
> V.(C): We were not allowed to listen to his music . . . Yes, my other cousin even gave his son the name Vice . . .
>
> V.(B): Did you copy this tape? I would like to have it . . .
>
> V.(C): Aha.
>
> V.(D): I called Marija A. to come and see it, then I have to return it. Did you know that Vice is Marija's cousin . . .?

M.M.'s son enters the room asking something – no one pays attention – conversation continues.

> V.(A): When was he in Perth last time?
>
> V.(C): When he was in Perth in 1968 he stayed a couple of months, I had my photo taken with him – I wonder where that photograph is. [To her husband] Ray, wasn't he in Perth 3 to 4 years ago? Yes, I think he was . . .
>
> V.(A): Did you go to his concert then?
>
> V.(C): No, I did not. He was here with Maruška Šinković [female performer].

Attention to what is happening on the tape is only partial. Attention focuses when someone starts talking or reading poetry. The songs are listened to only with half-interest and the conversation flows freely.

V.(B): What did he say . . .? [Asking about the poem being read.]

V.(A): That the stone can be (smashed) cracked but not killed . . .

V.(B): [thinking] Smashed but not killed . . . powerful.

V.(C): What does he mean by not killed? Of course you can't kill the stone. It is not alive . . .

V.(D): It is a sort of metaphor for Šibenik . . .

V.(A): What did he say? I understand Šibenik [negotiating the meaning], this is a tape for *Šibenik: The Wounded Town* [examining the video-tape cover].

V.(C): You are looking at the wrong cassette cover . . . [talking to me] What are you writing again? You are always writing something, listen to the music . . .

I answer: 'I am writing about this tape . . . and the importance of this type of music for the preservation of Croatian culture.'

V.(C): [not allowing me to finish] Then you absolutely must see the tape about Osijek [another Croatian city under siege at that time] – I borrowed it from the priest, but Mile took it to retape it . . . [changing subjects]. You see [pointing to the screen]. They [Serbs] even destroyed our cemeteries . . . only the Catholic graves . . . [Mišo Kovač singing].

V.(A): Why the cemetery? They are all dead . . .

V.(C): Ah, they bombed it from the air . . .

V.(A): Oh my God . . .

The song that is shown is entitled: *The Graves will Never Forgive You* and the video camera lingers on one desecrated grave after another, allowing the viewer to read the mainly Croatian names.

V.(A): [reacting to the pictures of the destroyed graveyard] My God, but you see Mišo [the performer] is one of them. He is an Orthodox . . . He is not a Catholic.

V.(D): Yes, and last year during the election he publicly said that he will leave Croatia if it goes independent . . .

V.(C): And he is here now . . . performing for Croatia . . .

V.(B): Perhaps he is a spy . . .

The above conversation still shows the usual VCR audience dynamics, concerned as it is with the private life and gossip around the singers just as much as with the consequences of the war already raging in Croatia. However, the conversation after the tape was finished showed increased anxiety mainly due to the lack of information about the 'real' situation. At about this time the Australian television was showing mainly news from Croatia in what was perceived to be a watered-down form. Consequently the audience increasingly turned to radio, especially seeking out the reports by Pierre

Vickary on ABC Radio (Kolar-Panov and Miller 1991). The fear and the anxiety created by the increased difficulty of contacting friends and relatives in the homeland only facilitated the creation of a large number of popular narratives and emerging myths about atrocities perpetrated by Serbs. Increasingly it became more and more difficult to distinguish between myth and reality.

HISSING THE VILLAIN

The West Australian version of ABC television *News* (7.00 p.m.) showed the first massacred bodies from the unnamed Croatian village on 18 October 1991. Peter Holland (the news-reader) introduced it with the warning that 'the following scenes might be disturbing to some viewers'. He also noted that the news item was 'an amateur video tape filmed by the local village video shop owner' who 'until now used to film local weddings'. The tape showed the bodies of twenty-four people, mainly old, shot either from above or behind, all massacred and beyond recognition. Some bodies were huddled together 'as if embracing in death' as a member of the audience noticed.

This was the only time to my knowledge that the ABC showed material concerning the war in Croatia (or Bosnia for that matter) identified as an amateur video tape. The impact of this screening was more far-reaching than anyone in the ABC realised. Thereafter only news footage presented by accredited reporters was considered acceptable, since both sides in the conflict were known to fabricate 'amateur' video tapes. (Later on, scenes from the war in Bosnia shot by accredited media people contained similar scenes.) The Croatian audiences who by now were monitoring all television news with special emphasis on the SBS and ABC because of their international orientation taped the news item and it was reshown endlessly, that is, until the first video tapes with similar scenes from the war in Croatia started to arrive.

Even if tapes showing 'ceremonies of reconciliation' and what was most often the re-opening of mass graves from the Second World War were frequently viewed by the audience, such as the skeletons unearthed in Bleiburg or old photographs showing mutilated bodies, the audience was not too disturbed by them. This was because they realised that this had happened forty-five or fifty years ago.[13]

The representational ingenuity of the propaganda machines on both sides, Serbian and Croatian, which presented pseudo-historical facts of various massacres either by četniks or ustašas or Communists, was peculiar to the 'hate campaigns' and had only one aim: the vilification of the enemy (cf. Meeuwis 1993). And often this was understood by the audience, especially at the time when the euphoria of Croatian independence was clouded by the signs of the impending war. But it was only at times such as a showing on SBS-TV of a Belgrade-produced documentary depicting the Croatian massacre of 'Serbs, Jews and gypsies' in the infamous concentration camp of Jasenovac, that the audience was mobilised. I have not seen the documentary since M.M.'s son taped over it accidentally. But a distressed phone call by M.M. late the same evening pointed out that the narrator in the documentary kept referring to the Croatian people as genocidal, and repeated that Croatians perpetrated genocide on Serbians before, during and after the Second World War. This apparently caused considerable protest in the audience of friends with whom she was watching the tape.

I listened to M.M., patiently thinking to myself that SBS had probably shown the documentary as an illustration of the most recent news from Croatia. The news was all about the increased exodus of the Serbian population from Croatian areas mainly in provincial Slavonia (north-eastern Croatia). The tape was most probably among many similar ones distributed by the then still Yugoslav federal government agencies, and the sole purpose of distribution of such tapes was to represent the Croatian progress towards democracy and quest for independence as a revival of Nazism. (Such powerful propaganda had its effects. Long after its democratic elections Croatia was referred to as a 'break-away republic'. Due to its international recognition and the war in Bosnia, Croatia has also often been pointed out as the reason for the break-up of Yugoslavia.) SBS-TV credibility suffered at this point. It had taken sides and constructed an Australian ethnic community as 'genocidal'. SBS-TV has been careful thereafter to screen French or British documentaries (but never German!) on the Yugoslav crisis. But the damage had already been done. The Croatian ethnic community felt betrayed by what had been seen as 'their television station' until now.

Mainstream (Australian) audiences used this and similar retellings of the Second World War massacres, anchoring the fallacy of 'centuries' long tribal hatred between Serbs and Croats'. Croatian and Serbian ethnic audiences saw them as one more reason for distrusting each other. Most ominous were the doubts about the validity of the Communist fight for freedom in Yugoslavia by Tito's partisans. Increasingly the legitimacy of the partisans was questioned by the diaspora, such that people who fought in the war and had been proud of it until now, were ready to denounce their past in the light of new revelations of Communist massacres. This could be seen as a side-effect of the 'hate campaigns'.[14]

The fragments of these 'hate campaigns' that reached Western Australia were sufficient to weave a longer narrative of the 'Serbs as animals'. In the absence of the full story it was left to popular myth-making to fill in the gaps. After retelling the content of the documentary on Jasenovac, M.M. continued to fill me in on the latest unrest in Krajina (a Serb-populated region in the north-west of Croatia). She was worried because it was getting too close to the coastal town where her parents lived. Without finishing the story, she asked suddenly:

> You will think that I am really dumb, but could you please explain to me what is a genocide?

I was caught off guard, being in the listening mode as I made notes, and for a moment could not answer. This was interpreted by M.M. as hesitation and she added:

> The word has been used so often lately both on television and in newspapers, and I have to confess it is the first time I have come across it. . .

I had to reassure her that she was not 'dumb', and that the word would not be used in the context of everyday life, at least not often. After I had explained the meaning to her (in Croatian) and illustrated it with the genocide of Jewish people, she said:

> I do understand that. But I still don't understand what connection genocide has with the Croatian people as we are today.

In just a matter of weeks she would know all too well. And the world would embrace the more descriptive and euphemistic term for genocide: ethnic cleansing.[15]

6

ETHNIC CLEANSING, PLASTIC BAGS AND THROWAWAY PEOPLE

There was an unpleasant sense of intimacy brought about by the close-up style with which the camera lingering indiscriminately on the bodies of the victims examined the wounds in a depersonalised and dehumanised manner, stopping only when resting on the body itself, as if surprised to find a boundary and the limit to what it can explore and disclose.

As part of the audience I found myself harassed with bewilderment, apprehension, confusion and disquiet. The screening abruptly stopped, a man had fainted; and as a voice from somewhere in front of the hall announced that 'refreshments will be served now', the lights came on revealing the pale and tearful faces of the audience expressing the same harassment, bewilderment, apprehension, confusion and disquiet I was feeling. There were a few minutes of silence, with only the commotion at the back where some were attempting to comfort the man who had fainted.[1]

All this happened as we were sitting in the Croatian Hall in Fremantle, Western Australia, watching the first video tape of the war which was shown straight after the three 'heroes' of the Croatian community had talked to the audience about their visit and experiences in Croatia. The guests were: Father Brian Morisson, a well-known Catholic priest and charity worker who delivered to Croatia the first contingent of aid collected in Perth by Care Croatia; Paul Filing, Federal (Liberal) MP, the leader of Parliamentarians for Croatia, who was actively lobbying the Australian Federal Parliament for recognition of Croatia as an independent state; and Tony Ashby, the *West Australian* photo-journalist, who captured with his camera some of the most compelling scenes that we have seen from the war in Croatia (and later in Bosnia). The hall was packed and I estimated that there were at least 500 people present.

After their short reports on the success of their mission in delivering the aid containing medication and food donated by the community in Perth, all three guests expressed the hope that Croatia would be internationally recognised soon, which in turn would increase the chances of ending the conflict.

As an illustration of their reports a video tape was to be shown. The lights were turned off and the tape began with showing the most recent news, obviously taped off HTV (Croatian Television). Then, without warning, the camera started to follow an anonymous pair of hands measuring the wounds and the lens of the camera entered into disintegrating human flesh. This was interrupted by images of destruction of the countryside and bodies with slashed throats scattered all around and grass and soil saturated with blood. Then bodies naked and tagged lying on the cement tables and floor being washed – or rather hosed down – and revealing gaping wounds washed clean of mud and blood.

When Marshall Blonsky (1985: xivi) in his Introduction to *On Signs* argues that 'image power is to be exercised over our souls', he could be referring to this video tape but he is referring to the images of the mutilated bodies and souls in Susan Meiselas' (1985: 43–53) photographic essay, 'A portfolio on Central America'. Meiselas manages to sum up in twenty black and white photographs the whole history of violence and its consequences; the pain, despair and madness of war. The knowledge of those same signs of pain, despair and madness brought us instant recognition of the war when watching the video tapes of what was euphemistically called by the world press 'a civil war' or 'ethnic cleansing' on the territory of the former Yugoslavia.

But the scene that came to symbolise this war was not a scene of the death of a person, a human being, but rather the death of a car. This, one of the first frames showing the conflict in former Yugoslavia, was to become a symbol for this war, just as the pulling down of the Spirit of Democracy on Tienanmen Square in Beijing became a symbol of the students' movement for democracy in China (Wark 1990).[2] The shots of an army tank crushing a red Fiat 500, the penetrating sounds of the crashing and splintering, the rumbling and the falling of the collapsing car made us feel powerless to defend ourselves against the conquering violence of the tank on the screen; the tank, the symbolic instrument of the absolute claim for power, and a small red Fiat 500 the symbol of a humble victim. The feeling of helplessness was not a surprise, but we were all struck by the recognition of the scene, yet from some other time and other space. Perhaps it was only through intertextuality that we grounded our recognition of the crushing sounds of steel from all the war films, all the television dramas and series and most of all from all the newscasts of armed conflicts around the world.

This scene is usually replayed in any 'decent' documentary on the 'conflict in the Balkans' (with a comment: 'This is how it began . . .') but it does not lose the power to shock each and every time. What we do not find in these documentaries, and very seldom even in information programmes, are the scenes of death which freely circulate on pirated videos in the Croatian community of Western Australia.[3] They come without warning and they are obscene.

The tapes of death which circulate as 'information' in the community can be seen as obscene because:

Obscenity begins when there is no more spectacle, no more stage, no more theatre, no more illusion, when every-thing [sic] becomes immediately transparent, visible, exposed in the raw and inexorable light of information and communication.

(Baudrillard 1988: 21)

And 'obscenity is not confined to sexuality', what we have on these 'tapes of death' is 'the all-too-visible' and 'more visible-than-visible' (ibid.: 22).

The heroes on these tapes are not fictional characters in yet another violent film, they are anonymous witnesses of their own death. The visual language of these videos is the oxymoron – as a limit of expression, as a paradox of the logical connection between events, as an auto-da-fé of all slick expressions – in order to create the silence of horror, in the same way showing death, creating and re-evoking memories of dying in some other time, some other space and playing with its obscenity on the innermost fears of the audience.

This is a visual language of death marked by the 'keywords' which are the images of human carcasses devoured by pigs in the idyllic countryside of fields golden with ripened wheat, now splattered with blood. This is an example of what Michel de Certeau (1985: 143) calls 'the dispersal of narratives'. This is also a mixture of memories of childhood dreams of running through those golden wheat fields.[4] These flashes of childhood dreams mix freely with the flashes of other memories and slowly form into the sequences of the present yet unreal world of hatred, madmen and war, which makes it difficult to distinguish what we see on the screen from the memories of Salvador Dali's surrealist paintings.

Shots of destruction and screams evocative of nightmares (or perhaps from a film we saw recently) – and each and every one of us in the audience searches in the labyrinth of our consciousness, wanting to recognise or perhaps deny, or both at the same time. The audience is watching in disbelief and continues watching, waiting for something to happen . . . nothing happens. The camera follows the way in which death writes out the law of this war, of all wars, creating a new language for memory, a language whose function is an embrace of senseless death. We sit there as lost polyglots who have spoken a language we do not know.

It is almost impossible to identify signs which resemble the imaginary but depict the reality – because where is the line that separates our knowledge that we are human from the knowledge that we perform inhuman acts? Because 'inhumanity' is already a rejection of reality. It is quite difficult to identify any reality even in the video tapes we have watched, so many of which in a fragmented but powerful way depict prison camps, interviews with children who have been raped, beaten and exposed to every conceivable and even more inconceivable abuse, and then suddenly burst into a revolutionary song.[5]

We can speak here of an aesthetics of fragments, a kind of a chain reaction in which, as in the game of billiards, one image sets another in motion. As the camera looks at the naked trees of the continental European winter with the same intensity as it looks at the naked bodies laid out on the grey cement tables and on the dead grass around them, the nakedness of the trees and the deadness of the grass symbolise the cycle of the seasons, the regeneration of the earth, but in fact they are all one world of death – united in their utmost 'deadness' in their difference from one another by the eye of the camera, which finally rests for a moment on a wooden cross without an inscription. This nameless wooden cross returns all that we have seen to a kind of non-existence, creating a nostalgia-like feeling for identity, any identity, even if inscribed on the cross (creating cries for help – sobs in the audience), identity, which, if denied at this moment, will become repressed with too many scenes of death – too many anonymous bodies lying on the cement tables and dead grass – and will be washed away with the same green hoses that are flushing out the bodies and washing away the reality of dying. The streams of clear water entering the wounds and every other opening on the human bodies symbolically remove death and our responsibility for it. Water, a symbol of baptism, new beginnings and a symbol of a cleansed soul, cleansing, or as Baudrillard explains:

> Once everything will have been cleansed, once an end will have been put to all viral processes and to all social and bacillary contamination, then only the virus of sadness will remain, in this universe of deadly cleanliness and sophistication.
>
> (Baudrillard 1988: 38)

Perhaps it is what the euphemism of 'ethnic cleaning' or 'ethnic cleansing' means – just sadness.

WATCHING THE WAR UNFOLD

The 'Krajina' regions, first in Dalmatia and Lika, then in Banija and Slavonija and Baranja, had been under Serbian control since mid-August 1990, but Serbian insurgents took over the government of the self-proclaimed autonomous regions between June and August 1991, establishing an illegal government which was run parallel to the newly elected Croatian democratic government (Thompson 1992: 270–8; Magaš 1993: 283–5). Armed patrols were set up in the Krajina regions and the world media increasingly started to refer to the 'unrest' in Yugoslavia or the 'break-away republic of Croatia', showing columns of shoulder-to-shoulder refugees of Croatian civilians either exiled by Serbian militiamen or fleeing in fear from their villages. The Serbian militiamen, who were referred to as 'Serbian rebels' (by the world media), robbed and ransacked Croatian houses and abused and humiliated the Croatian population that remained behind. Shooting and killing were also reported.[6]

As the violence between the Serbian and Croatian populations in the Krajinas escalated, stories of harassment, disappearances and horror killings started to circulate in the Croatian community in Perth. Even before the Serbian aggression against Slovenia and Croatia on 26 June 1991, the audience I was working with started to consolidate and meet more often, either to watch video tapes that were still received regularly, or just to exchange information about 'news from home'.

M.M.'s family was at the centre of attention in this small community, since their older daughter was trapped in the southern Croatian port city of Split, too advanced in her pregnancy to undertake travel to Australia. As the tension in Yugoslavia mounted, M.M.'s family and friends gathered daily to watch news and to exchange information. Instead of the usual greeting of 'Hello' or 'How are you?', the first words exchanged were 'Any news?' or 'Have you heard the news?' or 'Have you seen?' The lives of the members of my audience changed drastically. Everything was scheduled around getting more information about the 'situation back home'.[7]

Watching and listening to the news or, for that matter, reading newspapers, had only one purpose: to get as much information as was possible about what was 'really happening' over there. The Australian media, including SBS, had suffered from an overload of news from Eastern Europe and the world in general. This was the time of the great change (if we recall), or as it was called then, the 'New World Order', a time of the demise of Communism, from the fall of the Berlin Wall to the army putsch against Mikhail Gorbachev in the former USSR. The events in Yugoslavia were reported among other world events and the reports were perceived by this audience as 'scant and inadequate'. In order to have a more complete overview of daily developments, all news programmes were monitored, radio included. A 92-year-old male member of the audience who was known to suffer from insomnia was supplied with a high quality short-wave receiver and he listened to all European radio stations: the BBC in Serbo-Croatian, the Deutsche Welle in German and Radio Moscow in Russian. He then reported to his son who would call friends and report on any new developments in Yugoslavia.[8]

The other members of the audience monitored ABC Radio and Radio National, while all television news programmes were recorded on VCR. If there was someone at home at the time when the news was broadcast, they had a duty to monitor the news and record only those segments that pertained to Yugoslavia. In this way we often ended up with an hour of video tape containing a selection of news from ITN (6.30 a.m.), American ABC (10.30 a.m.), Channel Seven *Eleven AM* morning programme (11.00 a.m.), and then the evening news from three commercial channels (Channel Ten at 5.00 p.m., and Channels Seven and Nine at 6.00 p.m.), at 6.30 p.m. SBS

World News and at 7.00 p.m. ABC *News*. The ABC's *Current Affairs*, *7.30 Report* and SBS's *Dateline* (7.00 p.m.) were also monitored, and the ABC's *Lateline* (10.30 p.m.) and the delayed telecast of the NBC *Today* show were becoming increasingly popular. The American news programmes we always watched with special attention since the audience believed that if there was a segment on Croatia included in the news, this could signal the interest of the US government. And the interest of the US government could signal a possible change in United States policy, and military intervention to stop the Serb aggression.

This type of condensed news from Yugoslavia was watched regularly by the audience, most often after dinner, in what was considered a prime time, thus affecting the viewership of prime time broadcast television. At first the films and television series were regularly time-shifted in order to be watched later, but this practice was soon abandoned since it was realised that they were not being watched at all because of the audience's total absorption with news or their lack of time (or both). The tapes of news were watched most often in a group and the time before and after viewing was used for an exchange of information from other sources. Such tapes were kept only for a few days and often passed from one household to another to enable everyone to see 'what was happening'. After some time it became evident that most of the television news came from one or two sources and that often what was seen on one station would be repeated by others, or even the same footage used as archive material or shown again a day later. There was increased dissatisfaction among audiences, both Croatian and Serbian, Croatian audiences accusing the Australian media of 'being influenced by the Serbian lobby' (comment from audience), especially with the sudden absence of the popular television personality Vladimir Lušić, who used to present the SBS multicultural current affairs programme, *Vox Populi*.[9] The protests of Serbian audiences against what they perceived as the Australian and world-media bias against Serbia were partially the result of the successful campaign by Milošević, who insisted that the whole world was against Serbia. As was pointed out in *The Economist* – 'Picking over the pieces of war' (1992: 55):

> Mr Milošević insists that his country is a victim of the world's plots and misunderstandings but even some Serb nationalists realize that the world's picture of a Serb patriot nowadays is of a vicious drunken killer.

As the world slowly understood that what was happening in former Yugoslavia was not the result of a 'centuries old ethnic hatred' (Magaš 1993: 310–16) but a hegemonic quest for power and later open aggression on the part of Serbia and the Yugoslav Federal Army, the peace movements and lobbying mainly by intellectuals from the West started to be organised. To no avail. Or as one of the members of the audience commented on seeing the news item referring to the latest petition for peace in Yugoslavia organised by a group of Nobel prize winners (see 'An appeal from 43 Nobel prize winners' 1992: 33–5):

V.(A): It is useless for all those 'smart' people to talk. While they talk Serbians kill. For every word another person is dead or injured or driven out from their village. It would be better if they gave us arms. Tanks. Then we can talk back to Serbians with the only language they know. The language of war.

The M.M. household became even more involved in the community information-exchange process when M.M. decided to join her daughter in Croatia to help her with the child's birth and hasten their evacuation to Australia. The regular group gathered every night at M.M.'s husband's place, bringing audio and video tapes of news, and video tapes received from Croatia. There was often a long discussion saturated with numerous popular narratives and emerging myths about the Serbian atrocities, usually washed down with a few bottles of wine. Very often R.M. would call his wife while the friends waited to hear the 'hottest' news.

When M.M. returned just a couple of days after the Serbian and Yugoslav army's (JNA – Jugoslovenska Narodna Armija) aggression on Slovenia and Croatia, she brought with her twelve three-hour-long video tapes containing mainly pirated programmes off HTV and only a few tapes with the family-album-type of material. I have heard of 'video binges' organised by younger members of the audience who rent 4 to 5 commercial video tapes from the video shop and then watch them all evening and most of the night. I have also witnessed extensive viewing of video tapes containing a mixture of entertainment and news or family-album material in the ethnic audience. But the extent to which this 'video binge' developed was something new. For the first week, people were coming in and out mainly to talk to M.M. about her experiences, and ending up staying for hours watching the tapes. After approximately a week M.M., tired from lack of sleep, confided to me that she had not even unpacked her suitcases, and in order to escape from the constant congregation of people in her home she started to lend the tapes out.[10]

In the meantime the war in Yugoslavia intensified. It was the most difficult period of my research. The war had broken out in my own country and all my family was 'back there'. I virtually moved in with M.M. and her family, who insisted on not letting me 'be alone in times like this'. I believe that hundreds of thousands of people of Croatian descent (as well as other Yugoslav nationalities) were glued to their radios and television sets unable to believe what they were seeing or hearing. Branka Magaš sitting in her London apartment writes:

As I write these lines the radio reports MIGs in action over Osijek, a city in north-eastern Croatia . . . Hard as I try, I am not yet ready to accept the break-up of Yugoslavia. Yes, the red star adorning the federal army uniform and the country's flag is now a cruel deception.

(1993: 304)

Magaš (*ibid.*) writes further on about her uncle who died in 1943 fighting with the partisans, wondering if the united fight for freedom has been forgotten so quickly. I could easily identify with these questions, since my father was wounded in 1944 fighting for his country – Yugoslavia. So could most of the members of my audience, since the majority of them have or had relatives who fought with the partisans. Everyone called us 'Yugonostalgics' (cf. Drakulić 1993) more or less derogatorily and I increasingly had to be on my guard not to express my grief for the disappearance of the life I had known.

However, it soon become clear that like many others, I had underestimated Serbian hegemonic aspirations and the scope of the Serbian campaign which successfully convinced first and foremost the Serbs and, I suspect (with regret), the rest of the world that Croats are ustašas, Moslems are 'fundamentalist', that Macedonians do not exist but are rather southern Serbs or Greeks, and finally that Slovenes are 'selfish exploiters of the Yugoslav South' (*ibid.*: 305). Only the Serbs could guarantee a 'stable Balkans' in the greater Serbia called Yugoslavia. While the audience cheered the final steps towards Croatian independence, I cried. I also cried when I watched new borders being erected between Croatia and Slovenia, knowing that it would never be the same again, and when I read the lines by Magaš (1993: 309) two years later (but written about the same time), I realised that there were others who cried on the 25 June 1991, knowing that they had no country with which to identify any more.

Later that year, in early December 1991, I was held on the Croatian border with Slovenia (just 20 kilometres from home) for four hours, taking shelter outside the improvised barracks housing the soldiers and border guards while waiting to be searched before being allowed to continue towards Zagreb. Yugoslavia had disintegrated, Croatia was at war, the flights to Zagreb had been suspended long ago and everyone took me for a lunatic for wanting to go home for Christmas.

I stood in the freezing rain on the Slovenian–Croatian border, the countries separated by only two simple white wooden ramps less than two metres apart, on the side where I was standing the green uniforms of the Slovenian border guards, and on the Croatian side the army fatigues of the Croatian Guard. In the middle, in 'no man's land', I saw groups of people huddled together just a few feet away. They were easily identified not only by the empty look in their eyes, but by the numerous packages they clung on to, mainly ordinary plastic shopping bags filled with all that remained of their worldly possessions.[11] They were the refugees of this war. They had nowhere to go. Slovenia had closed its borders, the refugees could enter only in transit, and only if they had a valid visa for a visit or stay in one of the countries of Western Europe. Until then, for me and my audience, the refugees had been only silhouettes of endless rows of poorly dressed people clutching their plastic bags and baggage of all sorts, riding on the backs of trucks or on horse-drawn carts, pushing bicycles or just walking along the road with heads bowed as in shame, children of all ages, the youngest ones often asleep in the arms of adults, old women trying to keep up the pace. This was one side of the face of war that we watched with the M.M. family and their audience of friends in Perth. Now it had become a reality.

M.M.'s daughter with her new-born baby and husband made it safely back to Australia on the very last flight from Split before the airport was closed (in September 1991). She was glad to be back and the endless stream of visitors to M.M.'s house started all over again. The young couple not only brought with them the first 'real images' of the war in Croatia on video tapes but also brought back stories of first-hand experiences, of spending nights and days in air-raid shelters, and the description of Split swelling with thousands of refugees. The young couple had lots of friends in the community and often visitors from the 'Slav' side of the Croatian community would meet with the Croatians. On such occasions the tension was almost unbearable, with the 'Slav' Croatians ready to start an argument in an attempt to prove that the war that was destroying the common 'homeland' was the result of the Croatian quest for independence.[12] As the war intensified and the first rumours, followed by images, of atrocities in Croatia reached Perth, a new 'breed' of video tapes emerged.

CONCENTRATED DOSES OF FEAR

The question of screen (television, video, film) violence and its effect on audiences has fuelled academic and public debates for decades. It is possible to find research carried out that yields results supporting any number of views from those linking screen violence to 'violent behaviour and delinquency' to suggestions that 'television was not a cause of violence, but, rather a contributing factor' (Morley 1992: 50), and to the extreme position that television is becoming a scapegoat for the social violence caused by 'poverty, abuse and sexual harassment in families and institutions' (Crompton 1993: 16). The issue remains controversial but attempts to show that it does have 'direct behavioural effects' on the audience are repeatedly made by researchers. The debates around issues of screen violence often escalate, especially at times when amendments and changes to existing censorship laws and regulations are proposed, such as the change, in 1993, in the television rating system in Australia. Helen Crompton (*The West Magazine*, 31 July 1993, p. 18) quotes a survey that 'discovered that about 65 per cent of people thought there *was* a link between violence in society and violence shown on television – despite the lack of evidence'.

Crompton interviewed 'academics and students' in order to present different perspectives on the questions formulated in the article, but what I found interesting and significant was that out of the three academics interviewed, *two* found reporting from the war in Croatia and Bosnia disturbing. The question asked by Crompton was:

> Question 5. Have you ever witnessed something violent on film that has affected you deeply?
>
> *(ibid.:* 16)

Peter Gibbon (associate lecturer in Psychology from Curtin University in Perth, Western Australia) answered:

> Fictional depictions of violence no longer have much of an impact on me (desensitisation?). However, many of the scenes of conflict in Yugoslavia have disturbed me because of the inhumanity, hatred and brutality to which they bear witness.
>
> *(ibid.)*

The other academic, John Hartley, well-known author and internationally recognised authority in the field of television theory and research (associate professor at Murdoch University and director of the Centre for Research and Communication at that time) was quoted in the article as stating that his 'daughters (all under six) are only bothered by advertising' since 'it gets in the way of the stories' (I assume that his daughters wouldn't watch news programmes containing violence). However, when presented with the same question quoted above (question 5) asking him to single out 'something violent that has affected him deeply', Hartley answered:

> Yes. Most recently the SBS presentation of Henrik Gorecki's *Third Symphony* intercut with war footage from Bosnia, Somalia, Nazi death camps and the like. The effect it had on me was not only emotional but also political.
>
> *(ibid.:* 17)

The significance of the two answers singling out the events in 'Yugoslavia' and 'Bosnia' as 'disturbing' and having an 'emotional and political effect' lies in the fact that both academics live and work in Perth, the very location of my audience research. We can presume that they have been exposed to the same media reporting from the war in Croatia and Bosnia, minus, of course, the video tapes described in this work which have circulated almost exclusively in the fragments of the former Yugoslav community. (I say 'almost' because occasionally friends and visitors from mainstream Australian society or other ethnic groups were present at the viewings.)

The question arising from the above is obvious: if the exposure to war

160

reporting from Croatia and Bosnia has such an effect on the members of the mainstream audience, what are the possible effects that a continuous exposure to the concentrated images of death and destruction could have on, the ethnic audiences? The question is almost impossible to answer, especially because the violence we were watching in M.M.'s living room (or in the Croatian Hall) was violence of a different kind. The new type (or new 'breed') of video tapes which started to appear more often in the community was similar to the tape described at the beginning of this chapter, that shown in the Croatian Hall which had to be interrupted. In these tapes there was no unfolding of the cause–effect linkage between sequences and events we have learned to expect from news and current affairs programmes (Hartley 1982; Jensen 1987; cf. Lewis 1991: 123–58). There were only recurrent images of destruction and death and an occasional interview with victims. There was often small artillery fire in the background, with distant sounds of explosions and sounds of combat woven into the strange textual logic of still-burning houses and eyewitness accounts of the few survivors weeping over the dead bodies of loved ones. These video tapes had no intention of establishing any relationship between us as viewers and characters and situations (Nichols 1991: 43). They were just there like silent witnesses to pain.

The cumulative effect of such images of emotional pain and violence presented in the nakedness of its silence, produced in audiences just that: silence. The audience which used to engage in commentary – if nothing else the usual 'Serb bashing', repeating for who knows which time all the popular myths around the war – on the occasions of such viewings kept silent. I noticed people frequently getting up and leaving the room: 'to get a drink', 'to go to the bathroom', 'to check on the baby', until finally the video would be stopped, usually with an excuse that there is another one 'which is really more interesting, and we should watch it since it has to be returned' or 'it was time for the news', which would be taped otherwise if we were watching a video tape. No one, including myself, was ready to admit that we were sickened by such tapes, that they disturbed us. Much later when I mentioned a particular tape to M.M. asking if I could borrow it for purposes of analysis, she confided that they don't retape such tapes, and that:

Such images of continuous death caused nightmares for weeks after viewing them. I couldn't sleep, all those dead people looking at me!

Her friend added:

V.(B): Imagine, people working all their lives, and then they come and burn down, destroy everything. Destroy what they can't steal. You remember [talking to me] when we watched the tape that showed us those houses in the village where Serbs had their war headquarters? They lived like animals. They ate, slept and defecated in the same room. Just like animals. ['They' of course being Serbs.]

She then went on to compare the images of clean-shaven Croatian soldiers seen marching to the music on the video-spot of the song *Croatian Guard*[13] with the bearded, drunken Serbian irregulars devouring lamb on a spit 'which they stole from the villagers'. (The latter was one of the favourite shots over the world media illustrating the siege of Sarajevo.) She obviously did not make any distinctions between genres, moving freely in what Fiske (1987: 84) refers to as 'extra generic' reference, between video-spots, news and popular mythology. I was talking to the group of women seated around the kitchen table without men present, and the women expressed their emotions more openly away from the men. M.M.'s mother-in-law added:

> V.(C): You remember when we watched the tape that showed us dead people that had been put into orange plastic bags, you know the kind that we use for rubbish from the garden? Those people, a number of them, were at least put in plastic bags. Perhaps the UN soldiers did that. But, anyway, I was praying all the time that they would not open any of those bags. Imagine if they opened them. Those people were dead over a year. At least they will be buried now. But if they had shown any opened bag I think I would have been sick in my stomach.

It was obvious from the announcement of the hostess that 'we should really have some coffee' and the change in the subject to the next fundraising dinner, that she felt uneasy about feelings expressed towards death and dying. But the conversation was continued as we drew up a plan for organising a charity foundation that would support the orphans left by the war.[14] I could sense a need in these women to find something positive to hold on to, to feel that something was being done, and 'since the rest of the world was just watching', as viewer (B) put it, 'we have to do something', of course to the extent which was achievable in such a small community. M.M. added:

> At least we *are* doing something, we collected another container of medications and surgical material, and we will send it soon. Now when the world is helping Bosnia, most of the aid is going there. They forget about Croatia, and we have all the refugees.

The conversation continued about the grim outlook of another winter and the hope that 'something would be done' before another cold European continental winter helped Serbs to kill off the people they had not killed or exiled so far.

The men came in from outside and, on hearing what we were talking about, one commented:

> V.(D): They are all afraid of the bloody Serbs. They think that Serbs are all heroes, like they were all Tito's partisans. They [the Americans] would have to do some real fighting, not like in Iraq where they fought with computers.

And then, pausing for a few seconds, added one of the most repeated clichés about this war:

> V.(D): Anyway, they have no interest. Croatia is not Kuwait, we don't
> have oil.

Unfortunately, I was leaving Perth for an extended period of time and did not have a chance to continue observing the effects of anger and outrage on Croatian audiences.[15] On my return from overseas, the invitations to view 'video tapes from home' came less frequently. Those invitations were replaced by an increased number of invitations to contribute to different charity drives, attend fundraising dinners and contribute to letter-writing campaigns. It was almost as if the audience was relieved at being so busy organising help for the homeland. Or perhaps just disillusionment and fatigue had set in.

It has been argued (Fiske 1987: 9) that inside the narrative structure of a televisual story where heroes are more attractive and more successful than villains, 'heroes and villains are equally likely to use violence and to initiate it'. However, in the end 'heroes are successful in their violence, whereas villains are finally not'. This could be applied to the storylines of most film and television productions depicting wars, especially the films dealing with the Second World War. The negative stereotyping of the Nazis and the celebration of the Allied victory is even more exaggerated in this direction in the post-war film production in former Yugoslavia[16] and the only experience of the war that the majority of M.M.'s audience of family and friends had as a point of reference (apart from a few veterans of the war) was from such films and current television reports. The most recent of the wars of global importance, the Gulf War (nintendo war, video-game war, virtual-reality war), had left little or no impact on the audience and the surgical precision of the 'smart bombs' which were shown worldwide, courtesy of CNN, only reinforced the belief in the strength, righteousness and swift effect of action by 'the West' in order to put in place anyone who might 'step out of line'. (For a language analysis of media reporting on the Gulf War, see Hodge and Kress 1993: 153–201. For different accounts see: Morrison 1992; Norris 1992; P.M. Taylor 1992.) When the world did not react according to these expectations, first in Croatia, and later in Bosnia, the narrative structure whereby the violence is a means for the heroes' victory was disrupted. Nevertheless, we still expected something to happen or, as it was put to me on numerous occasions by the audience I was researching: 'the world will not let this go on', 'something is going to be done', 'the world can't allow this to happen'. These statements were echoed by the journalists reporting the war, by intellectuals organising peace action groups and by most of the people I know. The assumption of the audience that 'something had to happen' was expressed in their feverish search for information of any kind, in almost obsessive expectations which were expressed by one of the members of the audience most clearly while explaining why he taped all the news programmes:

V.(E): Just at that time when I will not be watching the news the Americans will decide to intervene . . . because I wouldn't want to miss for anything in the world seeing the Serbian bastards being bombed and having a taste of their own medicine, just for that I am taping the news when we are not at home!

Behind this statement lies a desire to re-establish the equilibrium and to mend the disrupted narrative structure, just as much as any desire to end the war and to solve the conflict. Fiske (1987: 307) argues that 'The convention that every story must reach a point of closure is a case in point' and that 'The differences between news and fiction are only ones of modality. Both are discursive means of making meanings of social relations' (*ibid.*: 308).

In addition, of course, war is seen as the domain of men and as such demands closure. Moreover, it is necessary to 'impose a masculine closure and sense of achievement' and the above statement by the male member of the audience only proves the validity of Fiske's statement that news can be seen as a form of 'masculine soap opera' (*ibid.*).

These audience dynamics in meaning-making, together with the genuine desire for information about the unfolding events in the homeland, kept ethnic audiences watching, listening, reading, always searching for more, disregarding the fear, the horror and the disturbing scenes of excessive violence that had affected the two academics quoted above. And that 'more' was provided by that new 'breed' of video tapes which reached Perth in late 1991. As I have said, these tapes were different from any that I encountered in my research and I sought for their origin and some kind of explanation of their unedited images without commentary, or with only a very scant comment in order to help with the identification of destroyed villages and mutilated bodies. The images were often accompanied by music, which was a noticeable montage of sound often leaving a few seconds between the scores and sometimes repeating the same song more than once, as if the editor had run out of musical material.[17] The musical background to the images consisted of mainly popular music, most often newly composed war ballads and marches, sometimes using the Croatian anthem and the popularised musical scores from historical dramas and operas which could be linked to wars, battles or sacrifice for the homeland. Paul Virilio's definition of the revolutionary song as 'a kinetic energy that pushes the masses towards the battlefield' and his definition of the national anthem as 'only a road song, regulating the mechanics of the march' (1986: 21) are the most appropriate definitions of the music accompanying the images of the war on such video tapes.

The absence of any commentary (with the exception of a few interviews and the identification of destroyed villages and mutilated bodies) made the impact of such video tapes even more powerful. It could be argued that video tapes of this kind (I have no generic category by which to label them) utilised the advantage of the visual over the verbal, creating a special semiosic relationship in which the 'realism' in the visual code corresponds to the 'truth' in the verbal code (Hodge and Kress 1988: 130–1).[18] Thus a realistic visual representation of the destroyed countryside, desecrated graveyards and churches and the continuous flow of images of human remains is most likely to be seen as true.

In an attempt to find the sources of such videos, I have questioned most of the members of the community and always received the same answers. The first was: 'I got it from a friend' and the second was: 'I borrowed it from the parish priest.' I did not find anything unusual about the parish priest being the source for the video tapes, since by then the absence of official institutions (the Yugoslav Consulate was closed and Croatia was not yet recognised) meant that there was no official representative. The Croatian church in Perth had taken on the semi-official role of providing the only link with Croatia to the diaspora.

It was much later, in early 1993, that I met and interviewed the producer of Opuzen Television who was visiting Perth, and it was on that occasion that I learned the source of most of these very disturbing video tapes that were watched by the community. But before I describe the interview, I would like to include below the only explanation I could find for the origins of such unedited horror images at the time I watched them with the audience.

SATELLITE TELEVISION IN PERTH

The logical explanation (which turned out to be erroneous) about the origins of these horror video tapes offered itself very readily during my visit in late 1992 to Germany, where satellite television was going through a phase of massification. A Croatian couple who live in Germany and have relatives in Perth asked me if I would take a video tape back to Perth to their cousin, explaining that 'now that they could receive the HTV satellite programme they could tape the news and did not have to rely on their sources of news in Croatia'. Apparently the 'German connection' was the most reliable one for sending and receiving anything, from letters to food packages, to and from Croatia since the Croatian branch of the Catholic humanitarian organization Caritas owned trucks which ran on a regular route, Frankfurt–Zagreb, twice a week. The disrupted communications and inadequate postal services that have remained unreliable even until now saw the Caritas truck drivers accepting personal letters and packages to and from Croatia. Many amateur video tapes found their way out from the occupied territories courtesy of grass-roots charity workers. Some of them were used by the world's media, and a lot were viewed only by Croatian audiences.

I viewed one such tape received through German connections from

Sarajevo in the home of a Bosnian Muslim friend, and for the first time I noticed a computer-typed message at the beginning and end of the tape that was in three languages, French, German and English. The message was:

> Please re-tape and pass on this tape to your friends, so the world shall know how we suffer in Sarajevo.

The tape contained interviews with witnesses and victims of the atrocities and rapes, with interviewees talking directly into the camera showing what Nichols (1991: 44) characterises as 'a sense of partialness of situated presence and local knowledge'. The camera often moved away from the person interviewed and showed added footage of scenes of massacres and destruction of the city.

But clearly this was not one of the horror tapes that circulated in the Croatian audience.

After an extensive search for some explanation as to the origins and producers of those video tapes I thought I had found it when I came across an article in a British magazine catering to satellite 'buffs', entitled '*What Satellite TV*'.[19] In its October issue, Richard Dunnett (1992: 59–65) explains to the readers the advantages of a multi-satellite system and a 'motorized dish' and presents the following example:

> Multi-satellite television offers a wider window on the world. The recent broadcasts from Yugoslavia were subject to heavy censorship, with many of the world-exclusive reports on Sky News cut to prevent showing distressing scenes of war . . . Some of these were sent to the channels' editing suites by satellite and could be picked up unedited by motorized viewers tuned to Eutelsat 1F4. Scenes included people *with their heads blown off* [my emphasis] . . . The motorized dish has allowed viewers to watch the news from both sides. On Eutelsat 1F5 HTV has been reporting with a Croatian slant, but RTB on 1F4 gave access to the Serbian point of view.
>
> (*ibid.*: 61)

In the full-blown propaganda war and the beginning of the 'real' war between Yugoslavia's (or what used to be Yugoslavia's) first Radio Television Belgrade (RTB) now called Radio Television Serbia (RTS) and then Croatian television (HTV) purchased six hours of satellite broadcasting on the Eutelsat (from 6.00 p.m. to 12.00 p.m. Central European time). The 'footprint' of that satellite covers all of Europe, part of the Middle East and, most importantly, North America, where there is a large Croatian diaspora. It is not possible to receive a signal from it in Australia.

With the imposition of UN sanctions on Yugoslavia which included the termination of the JAT (Yugoslav Airlines) flights to Australia, travel in both directions was brought almost to a standstill, to say nothing of the near impossibility of travel inside the 'occupied territories' (the war zone).

Given these and the general difficulties over any form of communication, it was indeed surprising to find video tapes containing, among others, regular HTV programmes, most of the time less than a week old, circulating in the Croatian community in Perth. As I have described in Chapters 2 and 4 the Croatian ethnic audience, especially in a time of social and political change (and war), has actively sought alternative ways of obtaining information and entertainment from the homeland due to the scarcity of both in the Australian media (radio has a different dynamics – as described in Kolar-Panov and Miller (1991)). The development of solidarity and the cohesiveness of the Croatian diaspora all over the world and their increased communication has made it possible for pirated satellite programmes from HTV, RTB (RTS), SKY News, Channel 5, and CNN International (to list just a few) to enter the homes of the Croatian community in Perth, but it is my belief that a similar situation exists in the rest of Australia due to the conditions described above. Thus VCR, being easily accessible and also suitable for community use (when projected on a large screen), could be seen as changing the pattern of information dissemination regulated by the prevailing communication policy in Australia, to some extent bringing European satellite television programmes into Australia unofficially. TV Asia (on SKY Channel) and TCC (carrying Chinese news and other programmes from China, Hong Kong, Taiwan on ASTRA, 1B, 1A) and the availability of satellite technology for the general population (one could get a full ASTRA satellite system for approximately DM700 in Germany at that time) could bring to Australia's Indian, Chinese and other communities, in the form of a video tape, pirated satellite television which in Australia has not been made available mainly because of the protectionist policies of the Australian government (O'Regan 1993: 27–9). The video tapes, which were put together from fragments of different pirated satellite broadcasts, depended largely on the 'creativity' of those taping the programmes and the decisions were often made randomly. The tapes mainly consisted of various pieces of news and information concerning Croatia and it was often the case that news recorded from other than HTV got cut off in the middle. The lack of sophistication and the often poor quality of the tapes was seldom complained about since the importance of 'any news' for the audience took priority.

The consolidation of the Croatian community and the increased call on the diaspora by the government of the homeland had seen an increase in the quantity and later in the quality of such tapes reaching Perth. There was also an increasing tendency towards amateur editing of such video tapes. The English-language material, a summary of the world media reporting on Croatia, which is shown with Croatian subtitles in the daily information programme *Slikom na Sliku* (Picture on Picture or Image on Image) broadcast in the late evening on HTV (approximately 11.00 p.m.), and repeated on satellite HTV every afternoon, was often favoured. This programme is very popular in Croatia itself (still showing in mid-1996) where the freedom of the press is at least questionable (*Helsinki Watch Report* 1992: 299, 303) and any programme which shows news items concerning Croatia from foreign countries is welcome. The other feature of the programme is the regular interview with a person 'in focus' or 'in the news', and these interviews also serve as a contact between the government and the audience. However, besides the pirated tapes of HTV, there was a large number of tapes which at the time I thought could be recorded by television and satellite buffs, and together with the regular satellite broadcast contained the various 'news feeds' to home stations by the foreign journalists reporting from Yugoslavia. I thought these were news feeds mainly due to the fact that the video tapes often contained images without sound or with completely inadequate music which I thought was due to the practice by some television stations of broadcasting the image only and adding sound later, or broadcasting the sound on a different frequency. The audiences, who were used to watching structured television news, when presented with the unedited horrors of the war from news feeds containing footage recorded by amateurs after a massacre, often raised the question whether what we were seing on the Australian media showed only 'watered-down' versions. Most of the people watching the tapes (including myself at first) did not realise that the images of obscene death never made the news and have not been seen by television audiences anywhere. Without knowledge of the sources for the fragments of the video tapes, most of us assumed that the material came from HTV or related studios.

At the beginning of this chapter, I described a viewing session with a large audience in the Croatian Hall of a fragment of one such tape, which, with the precision of a coroner's report, described each victim, stating age and sex and included the size of the wound inflicted, the damage to the tissue, and so on. The screening of this video, as I described earlier, had to be stopped as a member of the audience fainted. I often ask how many similar ones still circulate in the community.

What I had not realised at the time of the screening, since the previous frame was a news item from HTV, was that it was indeed a copy of the coroner's report of the victims of the war in Croatia. This report had obviously been taken out of the archives and by chance or deliberately found its way to the video tape which was supposed to be a 'newsreel' tape of the first report from the war in Croatia. For a propaganda tape this was a very unusual way of presenting the war. The dominant ideology of Croatian nationalism, resting on the rejection or revival of other ideologies present in our collective and individual consciousness, and which was now knitting together the audience, was not present on the screen. But the iconography of Croatian flags, the Croatian coat of arms and the photograph of President Tudjman were all around us decorating the walls of the hall.

As I remember the video camera's menacing intrusion into human flesh, I seek out my own emotions realising that the fear I feel is the result of the convoluted play of all death and destruction I watched for over a year, sometimes day in, day out. The concentrated doses of death and death again (making by now no distinction between death of country and death of people) have caused more stress than I had realised, and as I lie awake night after night, the pair of anonymous hands measuring' gaping wounds, pigs devouring children's corpses and old people huddled together in their final embrace, appear out of the darkness of my room. The images of the 'silent witnesses of the war' joined together with other images that surrounded us, and the words of the clinical report for which even the sterile morgue of the popular American television drama *Quincy* did not prepare us, stating the age, sex, and the nature of the wounds, when joined, strung together with fragments of news, formed a powerful representation of the war. Thus the seemingly incomprehensible part of the video tape, the coroner's report, when presented as a part of a supposed 'newsreel' and framed by a news item from HTV, turned the disjointed images of death into something larger, into a very powerful cultural text.

Together with the tissue of contradictory stories about massacres that have been circulating in the Croatian community for some time, the video tape we watched that afternoon in the Croatian Hall in Fremantle will have displaced all the previous images of death for a long time. For those of us who watched it, those images will remain the dominant factor in the iconography of the war in Croatia.

OPUZEN TELEVISION IN PERTH

The first time I heard of Opuzen Television (OTV) was in late 1991 when M.M.'s elder daughter returned from Croatia. Some of the video tapes she brought contained a logo (in the upper right-hand corner of the screen) of OTV which I assumed belonged to the experimental Omladinska Televizija (Youth Television) from Zagreb (Croatia). Most of the OTV footage was popular musical scores and when I commented that the OTV I watched in Zagreb used to broadcast more satellite MTV and that I didn't recall seeing this much of popular Croatian video-spots, I was quickly corrected that *this* OTV was a local illegal television station operating only for some hours a day on a hijacked frequency, transmitting mainly to southern Croatia and eastern parts of Bosnia and Herzegovina.

However, OTV soon become more than a local television station providing the only television services to the parts of Croatia which were cut off from all communication with the outside world since most of the communication infrastructure was either destroyed or occupied by the Serbian forces as a first priority. Apparently the government in Zagreb, which exercised more or less power over the media in Croatia (*Helsinki Watch Report* 1992: 345–54) did not like OTV at all but had to tolerate it, since, with HTV buying time on the European satellite OTV, had taken to narrowcasting the news and current affair programmes, which, of course, was extremely significant for the Croatian government which could not organise broadcasting in the areas held by Serbs.

Part of the OTV's services 'for the Homeland' included packaging and delivering news to Perth Croatian, ethnic, radio programmes. It was not surprising, then, that when the executive producer and director of OTV (M.V.) came to Perth in early 1993, the Croatian community publicised his visit and used it to organise numerous fundraising functions where the guest of honour was M.V. I interviewed M.V. during his stay in Perth and it was during this interview that the complete picture of the origins – the production and distribution – of the horror video tapes discussed earlier emerged. The unstructured interview given by M.V. was more a monologue since I asked only a few questions in order to clarify some points. The interview was conducted at Murdoch University in a relaxed atmosphere.

It was interesting that M.V. did not want to talk about himself at all, which I found unusual for a television producer. The only time he became personal was when he described the death of his brother. A thin man, chain smoking and with sadness in his eyes, M.V. did not laugh or smile even once. The meaning lost in the description, transcription and the translation of the interview can never do justice to the intensity and the passion with which M.V. uttered every word. He paused often, to think or to light another cigarette and I did not interrupt the silence.

Finally the story behind OTV emerged and with it the origins of the horror tapes of war that were circulating in the Croatian community. I will attempt to put into chronological order the story of OTV, adhering to the information given to me in the interview which was very fragmented and mixed with descriptions of the war, the political situation and the functioning of the black market. Only when it is of special significance will I translate and quote M.V.

OTV started out as Video Klub Informatika, in Opuzen (Croatia), renting videos and providing video services for regular ceremonies like weddings, christenings and funerals. As the equipment for narrowcasting from satellite television became available, the Video Club started to re-transmit four channels (from the ASTRA satellite), to audiences that could be reached by a 10-watt transmitter. This sounds very similar to the usual practices of suburb-based cable television which was mushrooming in the countries which did not have any regulation and policies in place regarding satellite and cable television.[20] The ingenuity shown by the staff of OTV in hacking the Eurosport channel (turning it off and playing their own programme) was the only difference between OTV and dozens of similar installations in the area. At first they hacked the channel only after 9.00 p.m. twice a week, showing a programme entitled *Magazine* which was a mixture of music and human interest stories. However, by late 1990, the increased politicisation of everyday life saw OTV broadcasting election campaigns and talk shows concerned with the processes of the Croatian quest for democracy and the disintegration of Yugoslavia. With the ethnic unrest and finally war, OTV turned towards war reporting, producing some of the most compelling and disturbing images that have emerged from this war. In addition, as a service to HTV, OTV served as a transmitter for the area, transmitting the HTV's satellite programme, but continued to hack the Eurosport channel after 9.00 p.m. every day to broadcast their own productions. The first images of Dubrovnik in flames seen worldwide were the product of OTV and M.V. proudly stated that it was their footage that was seen for months on ITN, CNN and all European television stations. I asked him if they sold the footage to those stations and he was surprised by my question answering 'Surely not, we were guides to foreign correspondents and often did most of the on-spot filming, supplying them with footage without sound. We wanted the world to see what was happening.' M.V. indicated that a number of local cameramen were killed in their desire to 'show the truth' with the comment 'they just went too close, too close'.

OTV's crew was usually the first to enter every liberated village or town and as such was asked by the civil defence to do some intelligence in reporting enemy positions. As the story slowly unfolded, it turned out that at the start of the war M.V. and his chief cameraman were recruited by the Croatian government agencies to tape all the places liberated by the Croatian army and produce footage and accurate reports for archival purposes and perhaps future war-crime trials. Some of the footage was allowed to be shown on OTV as information for refugees and the rest of the population, or as information about the state of the war, but M.V. stated: 'I am sure that the Americans aboard their aircraft carriers in the Adriatic sea monitored our programmes very carefully.'

OTV was operated continuously, illegally transmitting from a makeshift studio in a one-bedroom fifth-floor apartment in Opuzen which served as an office, editing suite, newsroom and, often, lodging place for the crew. The headquarters of OTV also served as an oasis for radio amateurs working night and day to keep in touch by short-wave radio (the only available means of communication) with the Croatian and Bosnian territory occupied by Serbs. This fifth-floor makeshift studio was the source of the tapes that had such an impact on audiences in Perth and on myself. OTV crew frequently travelled to other parts of Croatia (then divided in two by Krajina) and M.V. told the story of how they hid their video equipment under mandarins in the back of the trucks, when posing as aid workers while crossing to Slavonia, in the fall of 1991, to capture on tape the battle for Vukovar. He said:

It was so strange, we were waiting to cross the bridge between Bosnia and Croatia. Life on the Bosnian side was still normal. The soldiers of JNA [Yugoslav army] were checking every vehicle for arms. We could hear the thunder of the battle from the other side. I was very nervous trying to hide it . . . when we crossed to the other side, there was only ordinary police, you know in the old blue uniforms. We couldn't distinguish if they were Croats or Serbs. My driver, fooled by the appearance of normality, said out loud 'I am sure glad that those bastards let us pass' talking to the policeman coming to check our documents. That was very close, but nothing happened. We unloaded the mandarins to people who needed medications, food and arms, but mandarins were the only thing we had to offer. It was a good harvest. We spent over a week in Slavonia and filmed such horrors that I would not like to show any of that on television. As a matter of fact not much of what we filmed could be shown on television.

At this point I interrupted, asking him if he was aware that some of the tapes showing video footage which he classified as 'not for television' were circulating in Perth. He sighed and added thoughtfully: 'I know. But our people have a right to know . . . they do have a right to know.'

I asked him how the distribution of tapes started in Australia and he told me that it started before the war, when people visiting Croatia brought back video tapes of the local OTV *Magazine* programmes. With the inception of the war he was approached by one of the leaders in the community to contribute to the Croatian radio programme on a weekly basis and later he was approached to provide some video information, and he started to send tapes. M.V. was very cautious with the information about those tapes, hiding the fact that he was most probably supplying footage never intended to be seen by a general audience, and was doing so either without the knowledge of his superiors or acting on some silent agreement. I asked him again, did he realise the effects of those tapes, to which he answered quietly:

I know. I have seen the fear and frozen expressions on the faces of the most seasoned soldiers who accompanied us on those missions when we recorded massacres. And I have experienced all the grief and pain when, on one of those missions, I found the dismembered parts of my younger brother whom I saw off to a patrol only that very morning. He complained to me again that morning that he did not have a uniform, but it was good that he did not have a uniform. That way I could recognise which parts of the bodies lying around us were his. By his shoes, his jumper, and his jeans. The only thought I had then was to collect all the parts of his body to be able to give him a decent Christian burial. I never did find all of one of his legs. You see, he stepped on a mine that those bastards [the Serbs] left behind when withdrawing from their positions.

There was a long period of silence, another cigarette, and I felt that I had intruded on something very private, not certain any more that I had any moral right to ask this man more about the OTV or production of video tapes, let alone to make any judgements, draw conclusions or even to present this interview as part of the current research. I questioned my position as a researcher and asked myself how should I know when to stop, when not to proceed and when to continue? Who sets the limits?[21]

7

MNEMOSYNE IN VCR

A tall, long-haired young man with an earring, dressed in a pink T-shirt and washed-out jeans, a sort of 'egoless' identity, one you would expect to see with a Nintendo glove and virtual-reality goggles, was singing the Croatian national anthem. There was nothing unusual about the audience sitting mainly on the floor of the middle-class suburban living room, the morning after the celebrations of the twenty-first birthday, watching the video of the 'party last night'. Nothing unusual; in fact, most of the young people were pale with visible signs of hangovers, but they were wearing white T-shirts with the Croatian emblem and 'Stop the War in Croatia' written across their chests. The young woman whose birthday had been celebrated[1] noticed my long glance over her T-shirt, and proudly ironed out the creases with the palm of her hand, asking me:

> V.(A): Do you like it? My aunt, who came for my birthday from Melbourne, brought me one as a present. The others she had for sale were sold in an instant. You see there are no adult sizes in Perth to buy. Just for kids. They are all sold out, but if you really want it, I can ask her to send you one . . .

What we see here is a public discursive performance, a public staging of the self that is part of the activation of a particular framework in which being 'a good Croatian' means displaying Croatian colours on every possible occasion.

Her words are uttered in broken Croatian, and I wonder what has happened to this young woman. Four years ago when I first met her she insisted that she was an 'Aussie'. V.(A) had always refused to admit to her Croatian heritage, spoke very little Croatian and was known to be a feverish fan of the West Coast Eagles and 'Aussie rules' football. This was indeed a change. The video tape of her birthday party which had been held the night before in the Croatian Club continued running but hardly anyone watched it. There were speeches, first in Croatian and then in English for the benefit of the English-speaking guests at the party. A strange hybrid of the celebration of the rite of passage, the twenty-first birthday, appropriated in countries like

Australia and Canada from colonial England, the British official drinking age of times past, symbol of maturity, and a totally alien symbol in Croatian culture. (In both Australia and Croatia the age of legal consent is 18.) The rite of passage taken from Australian culture was framed by Croatian nationalist songs. The words of 'For she's a jolly good fellow' mixed with the words to 'Stop the war in Croatia'.[2]

The home-video camera zooms in on the portrait of the Croatian president, Franjo Tudjman, the Croatian flag, the flower arrangements on the table in three colours, red, white and blue, the candles in the same colours and then a ceremony of the presentation of the symbolic key – key to adulthood: a seamless but eerie mixture of Croatian iconography and Australian rite of passage; the unceasing recurrence of the symbols belonging to some other place, some other culture, and the transfer of the meaning of those symbols into symbols of celebration and happiness.

What is made clear by the above brief description is how a degree of redefinition and transformation is required to fit that celebration of maturity to different, unfamiliar and new circumstances, first, to Australian culture, and secondly, to the new circumstances in the Croatian community, circumstances of cultural nationalism. The Australian rite of passage, it appears, must both stretch and adopt its form, and at the same time resist and retain its form allowing for the Croatian distinctiveness to participate in, but not change, the adopted Australian tradition. Without this dual ability this ritual of rite of passage would not survive as a cultural variant that can be re-enacted regardless of its translation into other cultural settings.

So far I have described video tapes containing image clusters ranging from horrific portrayals of mutilated bodies to exuberant cameos of enthusiastic politicians celebrating Croatian freedom, all of which served members of the Croatian community as a means for marking boundaries between self and other – the 'other' first and foremost being Serbia. Thus the video tape circulating in the Croatian community played an active and significant part in articulating national identity and difference sometimes to such a degree that emphasising one's 'Croatian-ness' became anxious and almost obsessive.

The tape I was watching that Sunday morning was not the first family-album tape I had seen of a birthday celebration or a wedding that had shown the importance of displaying the 'Croatian colours' as signs and symbols of celebration. With every festivity I witnessed in three years of fieldwork (1990–3), there was a renewed celebration of Croatian independence, of Croatian freedom. It was almost as if the symbols of independent Croatia had to be constantly negotiated and renegotiated in an attempt to make them socially as well as symbolically pertinent to the everyday life of the community, enriching the cultural capital and fostering the cultural competence of the audience in a way which is very close to the naturalising processes which made everything Croatian pleasurable and acceptable.

I would like to propose, then, that adopting certain of the cultural practices of Australian society and blending them with elements of the homeland (as in the instance of the twenty-first birthday celebration in the
Croatian Club) allowed the members of the community to exist in two
cultures simultaneously without the need for any explicit orientation towards one or the other. These 'displaced peoples and dislocated cultures and
fractured communities' have had to learn to live in that 'other place'
because:

> They have had to learn other skills, other lessons. They are products of
> the new diasporas which are forming across the world. They are ob-
> liged to inhabit at least two identities, at least two cultural languages,
> to negotiate and 'translate' between them . . . They are the products of
> cultures of hybridity.

(Hall 1993: 361-2)

What becomes significant here is the overlapping of two ideological fields in
which the ethnic identities and discourses through which they exist become
recognisable, arbitrary classifications of one generation, and these then
easily become inherent properties of reality even several generations later.
Traditions of the homeland mix freely (but not intentionally) with newly
acquired traditions essential for survival and the no less important signs of
progress of adapting to the 'new country'. Eventually this should lead to an
inevitable degree of acculturation and possible assimilation. However, as
Hall points out, the assimilation will never happen to some, since these 'new
diasporas':

> [b]ear the traces of particular cultures, traditions, languages, systems
> of belief, texts and histories which have shaped them. But they are also
> obliged to come to terms with, and to make something new of the
> cultures they inhabit, without simply assimilating to them. They are
> not and will never be unified culturally in the old sense, because they
> are inevitably the products of several interlocking histories and cul-
> tures, belonging at the same time to several 'homes' – and thus to no
> one particular home.

(ibid.: 362)

Indeed, social change always seems to be at odds with processes of assimilation. Processes of 'hybridisation' on the other hand articulate the mythological constructs from two (or more) cultures. Nevertheless, the seemingly
'spontaneous' production of the hybrid (ibid.) or 'creolised' culture (Lotman
1990: 142) is usually grounded in the cultural, ideological and political ideals
of the host country, and is never neutral. Given that social formations and
traditions usually differ, to impose a single ideal of society on cultures
whose traditions and histories differ would only create resistance. The larger
the cultural gap between the two cultures, the longer and more tenacious the

process of hybridisation becomes. Thus by allowing for changes to happen gradually, the cultural practices which are at odds with the cultural formations in which they operate often either pass into the realm of symbolic existence or become mythicised. The more ambiguous the cultural material transmitted to new generations and the more mundane the process through which it is transmitted (like the twenty-first birthday celebrations described above), the more tenacious the mythical constructions it permits. None the less, sudden changes in the functions of either homeland or host culture can cause temporary disturbances in the process.

As we followed the processes of Croatian nation-building on video tapes and other media in the diaspora, we recognised processes of ethnic identity formation as part of the larger process of cultural production through the ideologically justified institutional programmes of the new democratic Croatia. However, Croatian identity in the homeland and ethnic Croatian identity sustain a different presence in the cultural discourses within which they exist. This is because, inside the discourse of ethnicity, individuals experience the meaning and the value of Croatian national culture in ways that differ from 'non-ethnics' who are not only identified as the producers and 'owners' of the legitimated and homogenised Australian culture, but are placed in a different symbolic position in regard to the Croatians in the homeland.[3]

As the social world of Croatians in the diaspora is constantly shifting and re-forming under the influence of recent developments in Croatia, and as the availability of information and its speed of delivery confronts the audiences on a daily basis with the past and the present, new meanings are ascribed to old myths and new myths are created. Such confrontations of past, present and perhaps glimpses into the future create new struggles for cultural identity. We can see a moment in this struggle for that new identity in the video tape of the celebration of that twenty-first birthday as Australian-born children of Croatian parentage easily moved between symbols of Croatian ethnic nationalism and Australian popular culture and its practices. What we witnessed, captured on that video tape, was a functioning public identity, neither ethnic nor national.

This 'public' identity of second- and third-generation Croatians allows us to understand the way cultures merge and interlap within their boundaries. This interlapping of the cultural boundaries allows an existence of self inside more than one, national or cultural, semiosphere (Lotman 1990: 131–42). This is all the more permissible because Australia's official and popular nationalist ideologies are themselves 'multifaceted and fractured' (O'Regan 1993). By integrating the elements of Croatian nationalist fever into the Australian ritual of 'rites of passage', the processes by which ideologies are integrated into everyday life are rendered visible. Even though the creation of nationalist ideologies usually anticipates a larger project such as (re)-inventing a national culture, it is on the levels of integration into everyday life that a consciousness or perception of 'what it is to be Croatian' is ultimately tested.

THE (RE)CONSTRUCTION OF NATIONAL MYTHS

Immanuel Wallerstein (1991: 78) raises the question of labels, names and consequences which allocate people to categories such as race, nation and ethnicity not only for individual identity but also on the levels of political, social and cultural rights. He argues that, even though 'the three terms are used with incredible inconsistency', there is an indication that 'most users of the terms use them', all three of them, to indicate some persisting phenomenon which, by virtue of its continuity 'besides making [a] strong impact on individual behaviour' also 'offers a basis for making political claims' (*ibid.*). Thus, the label 'people' is said to be or act as it does because of either genetic characteristics, or its socio-political history or its 'traditional' norms and values (*ibid.*).

The 'Yugoslav' identity, which was so strong for over forty-five years (1945–91), insured social and cultural rights and had a strong impact on the lives of various nationalities and ethnic groups in the former Yugoslavia. Besides offering a basis for political claims, being Yugoslav meant being a part of a myth, a part of a dream of a peaceful coexistence between the people of the Balkans. Because of that, it is tempting to see a connection between the break-up of the former Yugoslavia, and the events that mark the crisis of Communism, and the death of Yugoslav leader Josip Broz Tito. Accordingly, and inside the theoretical framework, we can argue that, when the validity of a narrative with a determined hero in a straight logical plot was undermined and disrupted so were the socio-cultural rights and values of the Yugoslav 'people' subjected to that narrative. Thus the political events stemming from Tito's death are all about disillusion and defeat. Defeat of a dream of peaceful coexistence and a multi-ethnic state. It is perhaps symptomatic that the video narratives circulating in the Croatian community showed the break-down of a political order and social values as an end to the deceit and conspiracy against Croatia, and not as a part of a larger break-up of the world order. In addition the world media focused directly on the instability of 'the Balkans' and on the revival of 'age old ethnic hatred' exorcising all the past demons of betrayal and establishing powerful genres, formulas and narrative stereotypes which were easily acceptable, and have been called upon each and every time the 'conflict in the Balkans' is described or debated.

The absence of any support for Yugoslavia's meekly armed political and cultural pluralists from the centres of political power in the various republics led to the violent eruptions of ethnic unrest, fuelled by the deliberate diabolic campaigns of hatred under the guise of nation-building, and silenced the voices of dissent which were in opposition (cf. Magaš 1993: 195–

213). This led to the acceptance of staged paramilitary provocations by extremist Serbian groups armed by the JNA as a result of 'ethnic' tensions. The chain of unstoppable propaganda[4] which was aimed directly at the vulnerable cultural identity of the diaspora existing on the boundary of two societies (or semiospheres) was effective. The members of the community were convinced that in order to redefine their cultural identity they had to identify themselves along the new ethnic lines established by the distant centres of the semiospheres of Croatia or Serbia. The until then unacceptable solution, war, became acceptable. Through the reconstruction of archaic and heroic values of mythical images from the past of the various nationalities new (often competing) realities were forged. I have described earlier the way in which video tapes, some of which were themselves fragments of the government-controlled media manipulations of myths of hatred presented as from a distant past, generated new cultural texts in the forms of gossip and other popular narrative forms. What I have not pointed out is that all of the popular mythology was encouraged and reinforced from the centre (or from above), which in the name of freedom and racial and ethnic survival legitimised and inadvertently reinforced the ethnic division, spreading racism not only in the former Yugoslavia itself but also in the diaspora.

This was an easy task, since the powerful forces of Yugoslav unitarism which suffocated formations of separate national identities had negative effects on the different diasporas. This created a unique set of conditions, allowing the existence of two separate diasporas best exemplified by the legitimate and parallel existence of two Macedonian communities in contrast to the antagonistic existence of a Croatian and 'Slav' community. In the present conditions of war in the homeland, the Croatian diaspora was no longer content to build a new united, national identity but was antagonistic to Serbia as a nation (and later to the Muslims in Bosnia), using acts of war, destruction and violence itself to legitimise the Croatian nationalist ideologies and national culture.

At the very time when the Croatian homeland was making claims on its 'glorious past' in order to reinvent Croatia, the Croatian national 'temporal dimension of pastness' (Wallerstein 1991: 78) became a central issue in reclaiming the fragments of its nation outside the boundaries of the newly formed nation state, its diaspora. There appeared a desire among the community in Perth to conceive its nation's dignity along the lines of an ancient mythical genealogy, a desire to recount Croatian history as far back as possible. Video tapes addressing historical issues such as *The History of the Croatian People* (in two parts) or *The Treasures of Croatian Sacred Institutions* were produced by institutions of the newly formed Croatian government in an attempt to legitimise the social reality of Croatian separation from the former Yugoslavia.[5] This form of presentation of 'the temporal dimension of pastness' provided the Croatian diaspora with a link to certain metaphors and stereotypes needed for that cultural legitimation. It also allowed the Croatian community to consolidate along ethnic lines in a very short period, and by the time of the inception of the war in Croatia, the diaspora shared a common knowledge (however fragmented) of Croatian history which first and foremost painted the Serbs as the main enemy and a source of immediate danger to the Croatian nation. Even though Croatian history was mainly separate from the turbulent history of the Balkans in general (Kennan 1993),[6] it was the recent mythology concerning the creation of Yugoslavia, the Serbian abolition of the state, the reintroduction of the monarchy and, later, the massacres of the Second World War, as well as Serbian hegemony in modern Yugoslavia (SFRJ) that dominated most of the video material shown on the 'historical' tapes that were circulating in the community. The ethnic press, as well as special publications like *Two Thousand Years of Croatian Literacy* (Katičić and Novak 1989), also presented the community with the imagined and real Croatian cultural past, only reinforcing the already strong basis for the creation of national pride by offering positive points of identification to the members of the diaspora. Wallerstein (1991) describes the importance of pastness thus:

> Pastness is a mode by which persons are persuaded to act in the present in ways they might not otherwise act. Pastness is a tool persons use against each other. Pastness is a central element in the socialisation of individuals, in the maintenance of group solidarity, in the establishment of or challenge of social legitimation. Pastness therefore is pre-eminently a moral phenomenon, therefore a political phenomenon, always a contemporary phenomenon.
>
> (*ibid.*: 78)

We can view the newly found Croatian 'pastness' in the light of the creation of a popular mythology around the ethnic unrest and finally the war. Using the theoretical proposition of the economical logic of ricurso – that is, a renewal of human history through the reconstruction of archaic and heroic values – we can easily follow how across recursive spaces the nationalist ideologies of all nationalities (and minorities) involved in the conflict turned the unacceptable-inappropriate into the acceptable-appropriate, by creating a mytho-logic as described by Edmund Leach (1976) that does not disrupt discourse or even break the coherence out of which individuals are interpellated as Croats or Serbs. As Leach argues, it is that non-logicality that is an integral part of what he calls a 'mythical code'.

The representation of Croatian (or Serbian) cultural distinctiveness in the myth of either ethnic origin (Smith 1988: 200) and the new emerging myths from the war clearly point to the need of each ethnic group or nation to construct boundaries. Lotman's notion of a cultural boundary is extremely helpful in understanding the way in which the creation of new boundaries has affected the diaspora, since Lotman sees a cultural boundary as 'one of the primary mechanisms of semiotic individuation' because it 'can be defined as the outer limit of first person form' (1990: 131), and helps to turn cultural difference and tradition into a key symbolic element in the politics of cultural struggle in order to fix reality.[7]

For the present discussion, the politics of cultural struggle by the Croatian diaspora 'to fix the real' requires us to understand how the video representations first of material objects such as monuments, churches, and so on, that represented the pastness of Croatian people, accompanied by the mythological construction of heroic values, and later the endless repetition of accounts of their destruction, helped to produce 'a mirror-like relationship' (*ibid.*: 132) between the Serbian community and the Croatian, outraged and disgusted by their inhumanity and constant killing which justified vengeance and reprisals.

At the time of my research, these were the elements of the recreation – however fragmentary – of the 'common history' of Croatians that through video tapes transcended the constraints of the physical distance of the Perth-based diaspora from Croatia. This allowed the temporary subordination of other identities such as those based on gender, class or differences of cultural and educational capital.[8] The symbols of the new Croatian state became precious symbols of individual identity which were fetishised to the degree that they were even worn as items of clothing or jewellery and extensively used for adorning objects of everyday use.

If we interpret this everyday 'display of Croatian colours' in terms of Lotman's notion of a semiosphere and its boundary in their function as 'the primary mechanisms of semiotic individuation' (*ibid.*: 131), the use of Croatian insignia on items of clothing or other personal adornments could be seen as marking one's 'Croatianness' (Croatian identity) and at the same time building a boundary between the 'Croatian self' and others.[9] By constructing their cultural present from the cultural symbols of the past the community at first started to live *with* and soon lived *the* Croatian past as the present; or to paraphrase Wallerstein (1991: 78), the real past might be inscribed in stone but the social past was inscribed in the easily moulded clay of the present of the community.

If we accept Lotman's information model of centre and periphery and the dialogic principle involved in it which requires asymmetry and alternating directions of message flow (1990: 144–5), we can argue that the initial stages of the reconstruction of Croatian history in the diaspora presented a very one-sided flow of information, from the centre to the periphery, nicely exemplifying the structures and mechanisms of text production. This is what happened with the cultural texts which came to the diaspora (periphery) from Croatia (centre), and affected the production of all cultural texts in their relationship to the existing texts, on all levels, from genre to national culture. Lotman proposes the following pattern for generating of new cultural texts:

[T]he relative inertness of a structure is the result of a lull in the flow of texts arriving from structures variously associated with it which are in a state of activity. Next comes the stage of saturation: the language is mastered, the texts are adopted. The generator of texts is as a rule situated in the nuclear structure of the semiosphere while the receiver is on the periphery. When saturation reaches a certain limit, the receiving structure sets in motion internal mechanisms of text production. Its passive state changes to a state of alertness and it begins rapidly to produce new texts, bombarding other structures with them, including the structure that provoked it. We can describe this process as a change-over between centre and periphery.

(ibid.)

If we apply the above to the Croatian audiences, we can argue that the phase of 'the re-invention of Croatia' saw the constriction (but not closure) of permeable cultural boundaries between the ethnic community and the Australian centre, allowing only for a flow of information from the other semiosphere, the boundaries touching through a space occupied by the Croatian immigrants in relation to Australia, a space which served as a periphery to both semiospheres, the Australian and the Croatian. Thus, the diaspora as periphery turned towards the Croatian centre in the receiver mode accepting information, up to a point of saturation. Then it re-established the permeability on both sides and through the internal text-production mechanism, re-established both the asymmetry and the alternating directions of the message flow with both centres. In relation to the centre of the Australian semiosphere, the possibility of dialogue has been increased since the consolidation of the previously negatively perceived Croatian community allows for an exchange of information on different levels. To use the mother and child metaphor as proposed by Lotman (*ibid.*: 144), if we perceive Croatia as mother and the diaspora as child, the participants in the dialogue have just ceased to be completely dependent but have not yet quite wholly separated. Thus the social semiotic situation of the diaspora in relation to Croatia will change only if the Australian centre acknowledges a need for a dialogue and creates a favourable climate for the continuation of the processes involved in acculturation. This can be achieved, since Croatian ethnic identity which, as we have seen, turned into ethnic nationalism, exists outside the territorial boundaries of the Croatian state, as a fragment and only inside the 'interlap' of its semiosphere, and can just as easily revert back to an ethnic identity which also accommodates Australian national identity. Furthermore, the centrality of the issue of cultural identity to the current Australian debates (as well as to the local–global issues), the search for national identity and insistence on the creolisation or hybridisation of cultures allows us to claim an existence in more than one cultural space at a time. This in turn allows the functioning of the dual identity of Australian

Croatians in the cultural space created by the overlapping and touching boundaries of two semiospheres.

We have seen for a brief moment a simulation of the movement from the periphery towards the centre, towards the mother, towards Croatia. This represented a shift in the sequence of the stages of the reception process that cultures go through in order to accommodate their encounter with other cultures (which is described as falling into five stages by Lotman (1990: 146–7)). In the case of the Croatian diaspora, the ethnic revival and later the war displaced the, until then, standing superiority of the Australian culture and the Croatian culture acquired the dominant position normally ascribed to texts from 'outside' which usually retain their 'strangeness' (*ibid.*: 146) and are considered of higher value. This creates a paradox whereby the Croatian language and knowledge of Croatian culture and history occupy the position that should be ascribed to the English language and Australian culture displacing the 'uncultured' low-valued view of ethnic (Croatian) and allowing it to appropriate a place of preferred knowledge. In Bourdieu's (1991: 163–70) terms this change in the perception of the value of what is considered cultural and symbolic capital (which refers to a degree of accumulated prestige or honour or symbolic power, and is founded on a dialectic of knowledge and recognition), could be seen as an important point in the overall orientation of the diaspora towards the homeland, towards Croatia. Thus the more 'Croatianness' one displays – including the knowledge of Croatian history and language – the larger the amount of symbolic power one exercises.

At this point a kind of inversion of the (former) rules governing ethnic discourses in the Croatian community took place. Croatian symbolic ethnicity was always a part of multicultural life in Australia, addressed in both public and private spheres. The difference between being Croatian before the proclamation of Croatian independence in 1991, and being Croatian today, is a result of the legitimisation of the existence of Croatia as a separate country, separate from the former Yugoslavia. Before Croatian secession (from Yugoslavia) and the consequent war, there was an order to display Croatian culture and claims of cultural identity in the diaspora. On the private level this was locked into family and homes, on a public level it was displayed in marked, organised spaces such as ethnic clubs, while on the level of the wider Australian community it was displayed on special, but none the less marked, occasions of multicultural festivals. Such manifestations of ethnicity function on a 'decorative level of folkloric ethnic markers detached from substructures of real and agnostic difference', thus reproducing 'imaginary identities at the level of ethnic community' (Frow and Morris 1993: ix).

At times when the question of Croatian ethnicity entered the Australian political discourse it was almost always in a negative form: as a question of Croatian antagonism towards Yugoslavs and Serbs – if, of course, we overlook the limited positive discourses such as the question of electoral appeal which was strongest during the cold war climate of the 1950s and 1960s.

Once again, the ethnic club became a particularly interesting and powerful locus of cultural production. However, the striking preoccupation with renarrating and reconstructing the cultural past of Croatia, so obvious at the time of ethnic revival, was always present as a part of dissident discourses (cf. Bhabha 1990a; Hall 1993). But this kind of engagement with the past was not historically marked by forms of specialised knowledge. It was rather embedded in a mixture of domains of personal life histories and sometimes in collective history as carried by oral narratives. With the increased availability of new cultural technologies, including the VCR, it was easier to frame historical validity and offer specialised knowledge, and the personal and the national could be fused into a dynamic and powerful discourse of ethnic nationalism.

The impassioned and sometimes relentless preoccupation of the audiences with the 'news from home' that I have described earlier, and the endless retelling of stories heard or seen on video, produced a series of dominant and frequently recurring themes to the myths about war. By the time that the third winter was setting into continental Europe (1993) and hunger and everyday violence became the naturalised conditions of living in Bosnia and part of Croatia, the mythology about this war was deeply rooted.

Within the interpretative framework there are two approaches to myth that are relevant at this point. The first is a notion that the structure of myths and stories reveals the 'structure of meaning through which men [sic] give shape to their experience' (Geertz 1963: 312). Geertz focuses on the analysis of metaphors that create the interplay of discordant meanings (based on analogies between the real and the symbolic) in a higher unitary conceptual framework. Defining 'cultural ideology' as 'schematic images of social order' (ibid.: 218) and again as 'maps of problematic social reality and matrices for creation of collective conscience' (ibid.: 220), Geertz finds that myths and stories function to fill a vacuum, the information gap, between what our bodies tell us, and what we need to know to function.

The second approach, by Claude Lévi-Strauss (1963), describes myths as messages made up by symbols and signs seen as sets in binary opposition that create a pattern of meaning. The basic scheme in Lévi-Strauss's system can be reduced to paired opposites, binary elements derivable from each other by logical operations (inversion, transposition, substitution, etc.) The totality of forms makes up an ordered whole in which there is a limited number of systems made up of stock themes arranged in different patterns that constitute variant expressions of an underlying structure. And the best time to study the mythic map to the underlying structure of a culture is in a 'liminal zone' (Leach 1976; Turner 1974). A liminal zone is a marginal state that arises at the moment of change. For Lévi-Strauss (1963) moments of cultural change are windows for interpretation in which the repetition of myths makes the structure of the myth apparent. The elements of the myth (such as themes, scenes, acts or events) are organised both synchronically and diachronically, so that multiple versions of a myth can be compared both as syntagmatic linear chains of events (metonomycally as signs), and as paradigmatic linear chains frozen in time (metaphorically as symbols). According to this, a 'window' has been opened by the disintegration of the former Yugoslavia, revealing the underlying structure of the myths about 'the Balkans'. It should not surprise us then, that the stories and myths about the disintegration of the former Yugoslavia, and the war, are all reminiscent of the descriptions from 'The Report of Carnegie's Balkan Commission' and the quote below reads as a summary of the video tapes of the war circulating in the community, except for the fact that the Carnegie Report was written 80 years ago, in 1913:

> Villages were not just captured, they were in large part destroyed. The inhabitants were driven out (where they had not already fled), and their houses burned. Woe betide the man of military age, or the woman of 'enemy' national identity, who was found alive in the conquered village. Rape was ubiquitous, sometimes murderous. Victims, now wholly dispossessed and homeless, were obliged to take to the roads or the mountain trails by the thousands, in frantic search for the places where they could at least lay their heads. Great streams of pathetically suffering refugees could be seen on many of the roads of the peninsula. Little pity was shown for the sick and wounded. Prisoners of war, if not killed outright, were sometimes driven into outdoor compounds or ransacked buildings and left there to die of hunger and exposure.
>
> (Kennan 1993: 5)

The ethnic audiences I was working with, tired of and disillusioned with this *status quo*, slowly returned to some kind of normality in their everyday life. They resumed activities inside their ethnic clubs and returned to familiar patterns of social life which produced syncretic and ultimately creolised cultural forms and practices. Audience members immersed themselves in activities such as fundraising inside Australian-based charity organisations. The funds raised were nevertheless destined for Croatia. The public displays of Croatianness lost their novelty and slowly retreated into the private spheres of family and friends.

The temporary nature of this ethnic nationalism in the Croatian diaspora is neither new nor surprising, because 'a national culture is always "temporary"... whether antique or recent, its character and puissance are matters of historical plastic constructions, not cultural givens' (Fox 1990: 4). And it is obvious that the fragments of the Croatian diaspora were only following the historical changes taking place in the homeland.

Anderson (1983), Hobsbawm and Ranger (1983), Handler (1985) and others have all described and demonstrated how national traditions come to be invented and how these traditions serve to legitimise, idealise or even heroise the statehood. What makes the case of the reinvention of Croatia within the Croatian diaspora in Western Australia different, is the absence of (or at least weakened) direct influence of Croatian state institutions such as education or even Croatian media in the early stages, which created an ideal climate for the mythico-historical consruction of Croatia. And the VCR played a large part in it. However, the degree of Croatian integration into Australian society does not seem to have changed; what has changed is the foregrounding of the Croatian cultural identity, and its movement into a more public space, as a 'national' identity, an official nation that the Australian state has recognised (Birch 1989).

Thus the simulation of the movement towards the centre of the Croatian semiosphere that I have charted was a result of the historical change taking place in the homeland, while at the same time the position of the immigrants or the diaspora on the joint boundary or dual periphery did not change. What had changed was the flow of the dialogue. The almost total exclusion of exchange with the Australian centre followed by the one-sided flow of information from the Croatian centre has created the mirage of a movement that did not exist. The multilayered structures of the Croatian diaspora as a periphery retained the position they occupied earlier, becoming only more visible in their marginality.

The 'multicultural mayhem' (Sluga 1993: 90), which is a metaphor for the danger perceived by an Australian society engaged in the creation of 'an Australian national identity' and searching for an 'Australian cultural identity' (O'Regan 1993: 93–7) within the framework of a politics of multiculturalism or of unity in diversity, never happened. However, some find in the example of the disintegration of another culturally diverse country, the former Yugoslavia, much to fear, because the break-up of a multi-ethnic country such as Yugoslavia could 'be used by opportunists in Australia to represent all that is politically and culturally dangerous, not in politically contrived nationalism, but in the multicultural state' (Sluga 1993: 91). Perhaps because of this fear, the political stance of the Australian government towards the changes that were taking place in the former Yugoslav community was not always clear. Apart from the clichéd slogan of 'Don't bring your ethnic quarrels into Australia',[10] the community was more or less left to a process of self-regulation and coping with the change in the best way they knew how, leaving an open field for influences from other sources.

Working in the Croatian community for more than eight years gave me an opportunity to observe and record these mechanisms for coping, and to notice just how quickly the community took to the forms of cultural technology such as VCR, facsimile machines, e-mail, and so on. Immersing itself into the electronic-communication environment without hesitation and with very little difficulty, the Croatian audiences forged new and innovative information corridors.

I examine in Chapter 8 just how 'the boundaries of cultural spheres' which are 'defined by modern media' as 'relatively permeable' (Meyrowitz and Maguire 1993: 45) allowed cross-referencing in so far as the audience was aware of the variety of different media formats. But for now let us return once again and for the last time to my audience which crossed media boundaries with ease, allowing television and video imagery to blur the question of the public and private realms, if only for a limited time.

THE MEDIUM AS MASSAGE

Paul Jerome Croce (1993: 12–13) proposes that 'if mass culture in general brought distant people close, video almost made them seem palpable and real'. The intimate reality of the unedited videos of massacres, desecrated graves and destruction depended on that residual sense of the representation of reality ascribed to video, the video space and the referential space. Barthes (1982) has pointed to our identification of photographic and referential space as being reproduced in the still photograph. I would like to propose that this process acquires an enormously greater impact with the moving image reproducing *ad infinitum* the elements to construct myths and narratives about the war.

Thus the VCR, as well as being a powerful cultural technology, could be seen at the same time as a form of cultural text, mediating and translating the conditions of the war that was being fought in the distant homeland. Unlike the video tapes produced and distributed by the institutional organisations of society, which could be seen as constructs serving 'the prevailing system of social power' (Schiller 1973: 51), the narratives created from the archive videos of the Opuzen Television moved into the referential spaces provided for them by their forms isomorphic with the official discourse, but were perceived *not* as communication between centre and periphery. They have built their contextual spaces by equating the reality of the video space with referential space. The semiotic conditions made available by the two semiospheres (Australian and Croatian) which have provided the audiences with specific semiosic instruments for understanding the brutality of this war, created a semiotic climate that has favoured the mechanisms of meaning-making which belonged to the centre of the Croatian semiosphere.

Describing the influence of mass communication on American audiences, Croce accentuates the impact of the visual media reporting on the Vietnam War, arguing that 'video images sent more powerful messages about the conduct of America's longest war than all political pronouncements combined' (1993: 13) In the case of the Croatian audiences which watched the gradual break-up of Yugoslavia followed by the JNA and Serbian army invasion, first of Croatian land and later of Bosnia and Herzegovina, the agenda set by the Croatian centre and the clusters of video images from 'unofficial' sources set bluntly complacent standards for understanding the conflict based on the common ground of 'blaming the Serbs'. Everything Serbian (and consequently Yugoslav) was identified as hostile and unacceptable and the possibility of dialogue across that boundary (Serbia–Croatia) was closed off.

Between hostile cultures in general there is little common ground and no motive for communication. Therefore the cultural segments inside the former Yugoslav community had very little to do with each other and were not ready to listen to each other's points of view. The total breakdown of the Yugoslav community was not only the result of the polarisation of different ethnic groups but also a result of the cessation of all communication except, of course, occasional hostile outbursts, such as sports violence.[11] I have argued earlier that friendships were broken, mixed marriages began to fall apart, and there was an inflation of political rhetoric from the homeland which only further poisoned the well of sentiment towards compromise at any level.

Issues and political personalities of less or different importance to Australian society at large, such as the unity and functioning of the European Community, or the question of its presidency, became issues of central concern to the Croatian community in Perth. Names of presidents, prime ministers and foreign ministers to the European community became household items, acquiring the celebrity status of television or movie stars or rock musicians, bringing into migrant homes a new familiarity with European politics and an awareness of the power it could exercise to put an end to the war in its catastrophic unfolding. As cease-fires between the Serbs and Croats were signed and broken endlessly, the audience hung on every word uttered by the peace negotiators such as Lord Carrington, Cyrus Vance, Lord Owen, and so on. Consequently, they ascribed the failure to initiate peace not only to the impossibility of making any deals with the Serbs, but also to the personal histories of the peace negotiators. There was gossip circulating about their private conduct or their past: Lord Carrington was the most disliked and unpopular of all negotiators, sharing his negative image with the then US secretary of state, Lawrence Eagelberger, who regularly featured in the Croatian ethnic press in yet another 'scandalous' revelation of his private business dealings with the Serbs.[12]

The emphasis on the power of individuals to influence the outcome of the conflict and the constant address of the issue of peace conferences by the world media which created an illusion that 'something was being done' (Pearson 1993: 21) directed the audience's attention inward. For example, the naming of individuals responsible for war crimes by Helsinki Watch or Amnesty International was no more than 'pointing a finger at individuals rather than institutional power' which only for a moment distracted attention from the larger issues of the war and the institutional bases for it.[13]

According to the conventions of Australian television news reporting, where the quest for audience attention not only involves dramatisation of the story but also requires a dramatic resolution, the story of the fall of Vukovar was reported on a daily basis, almost as a dramatic serial. It has been argued that 'News stories . . . come and go in an unending procession' and that 'structural features of news organisations ensure that the choices provided to the audience remain standardised, highly circumscribed' (*ibid.*). Thus the story of the fall of Vukovar rested all along on the 'journalistic canon of objectivity' and was rhetorically linked to notions such as 'truth' (see Hartley 1992: 46–63). Night after night we were presented with reports from journalists risking their lives on the front lines (on both sides) to bring us the 'latest' on the human tragedy unfolding in that sleepy Slavonian town of Vukovar . . . Vukovar as it appears on the front page of the book *The Destruction of Yugoslavia: Tracking the Break-Up 1890–92* (Magaš 1993), in the photo of the destroyed front entrance to the railway station, and the Vukovar of my past with the heavenly shade of old oak trees on its boulevards in the lazy summer Sunday afternoons visiting friends and relatives. Driving, in the winter of 1992, on the straight stretch of what used to be the main highway from Zagreb to Belgrade, I notice that all the street and traffic signs indicating the way to Belgrade had been removed in Zagreb itself and along the highway, creating almost a 'twilight zone' effect when one drove towards the east or north-east. Then we suddenly reach a point where the wet and icy asphalt road disappears into the whiteness of the freshly fallen snow. There is no sign of life after that sudden strange, white boundary. The military policeman who suddenly appears instructs us that there is a detour, and I look long and hard into the strange whiteness of the Pannonian winter into nothingness. The nothingness in what used to be Vukovar.

Magaš describes the fall of Vukovar:

> The fall of the ruined Croatian town of Vukovar (once a town of some 50,000 inhabitants, 43 percent Croat, 37 percent Serb, 20 percent Hungarians and others), two days after its besiegers had solemnly signed yet another cease-fire agreement, brokered by Lord Carrington, stands as a stark monument to the inadequacy (or cynical complexity) of the outside world's response to the degradation of the Yugoslav crisis into war and barbarism.

> (Magaš 1993: 356)

Vukovar is a ghost city, a town that had its soul annihilated by the neglect of the world that failed to recognise the resurrection of the evil that spares nothing in its path. This is the reason why it is almost forgotten, replaced by Sarajevo as a symbol of urban destruction. Vukovar lies somewhere behind that white nothingness that I saw in the winter of 1992 at the imagined end of the highway that used to lead from Zagreb to Belgrade.

Yet for weeks before its fall we kept a vigil beside our radios and televi-

189

sions. For a long time we had known that we would not find much in the daily newspapers, but still kept looking hungrily in the pages containing what the audience characterised as 'yesterday's news'. When Vukovar fell on 18 November 1991 it was compared with Berlin, with Stalingrad. Or as Mark Thompson (1992: 297) puts it: 'Destruction was victory' for the Serbs who claimed that they had 'liberated it'. Western media reporters 'walked into the destroyed town together with the liberators', taking footage almost undisturbed by Serbian and JNA forces who with nauseating pleasure laid out long rows of bodies side by side on the slush of rich Slavonian earth and melting snow. The part of that footage showing a Serbian irregular in četnik uniform proudly poking three fingers into the eye of the camera[14] is immortalised on the video tape entitled *The History of the Croatian People*. This tape was produced not as a documentary of the war but as an official document representing Croatian history and aimed mainly at the diaspora.[15]

I have argued above that the reproduction of video images which equate the image space on the screen with reality, and occupy the referential space of the sign in meaning-making, often become solidified through the narratives of the myths about this war. Thus, the destruction of Vukovar which is a sad example of the 'scorched earth tactics' which Thompson (1992: 329) calls 'the Vukovar technique' is often recalled by and associated with the image of the Serbian irregular (četnik) peering into the camera, or as a member of the audience put it:

> V.(A): I remember the fall of Vukovar, but nothing seemed like it was happening for real until they showed that toothless četnik [the man had a front tooth missing] with bloodshot eyes, and the četnik insignia on his cap. He was a pure image of a devil, only the horns were missing . . . when he raised his three fingers you know . . . as their sign of victory I almost smashed the television set . . .

This description sounds like something straight out of an imaginary encyclopaedia of stereotypes listing villains from the Second World War, and I knew it very well. They had belonged until now to the representations often depicted in what I call 'partisan films' (Ostojić 1977) or to the tales told by my grandfather who had actually seen 'them'. Yet this figure of an unshaven, toothless četnik became a potent part of the iconography belonging to the end of twentieth-century history representing the disappearance of a whole town and most of its people.

The choice of this image by the authors of the video, *The History of the Croatian People*, shows a deliberate and skilled use of the archetypal image of the četnik as an illustration of the continuity of the suffering by Croatian people perpetrated by Serbian hegemonic desires for domination. Words in cases such as this are not necessary as the story is told by the četnik icon and the audience had a 'ready to wear meaning' presented to them and needed nothing else to make a link between Serbian forces and the dead city. The instant homogenous meaning available to the audience through a single image is an extremely potent point of identification of the fall of Vukovar with the Serbian irregulars and of the Serbian irregulars as četniks, giving rise to the meaning of all Serbs as 'unshaven, toothless, bloodthirsty creatures of the dark' (Morrow 1993: 72). Hegemony at work at its finest.

Thus it becomes obvious why that particular image of the 'toothless bearded četnik' was chosen by the authors of *The History of the Croatian People* as one of the opening shots for their video presentation of Croatian history. The shot also includes a full view of the Serbian nationalists' flag.

Most of the Croatian people, especially the ones in diaspora, would have no ascribed place of importance for Vukovar inside their collective consciousness, except if they possess individualised, personal memories. Vukovar, on the eastern border with Serbia in the prosperous, rich Slavonia, produced few émigrés. The abundance of the Pannonian plains removed the economic need for migration and, on the contrary, attracted internal migration within former Yugoslavia, and this was one of the reasons for its culturally mixed population. On the other hand, the provincial character of its existence as a periphery to the centre, Zagreb, the capital of Croatia (in fact it was closer to Belgrade than to Zagreb), made Vukovar fairly obscure in its cultural significance to Croatian nationalism. To everyone but the local population and a few art historians, Vukovar was just another small mid-European town which was put on the map of the world only at the very time of its destruction. 'There are many well documented massacres perpetrated by the Serbian forces during the conflict' writes Misha Glenny (1992: 123), but 'the levelling of a whole town, street by street, house by house, makes Vukovar the most flawed jewel in this crown of shame' (cf. *Helsinki Watch Report* 1992).[16] Although Vukovar will remain a symbol 'of a crime without parallel in post-war Europe' (Glenny 1992: 115),[17] in fact, it was the bombardment and the siege of another Croatian city at the very opposite, southern border with Montenegro that has outraged the world and mobilised public opinion.

ASSAULTING THE CITADEL

There is an inscription on the ancient walls surrounding the southern Croatian port of Dubrovnik. It reads: *Non bene pro toto libertas venditur auro* (Do not sell your liberty for all the gold of the world). Like Babylonian priests or Venetian merchants, the people of Dubrovnik and the city itself are mythical. And in the mythical world sacred objects handed down from generation to generation symbolise the continuation of life and culture. Thus the remains of things from the past become the monumental signs of power in the present. The world has reacted not to the siege of the city but to the possibility of the destruction of the historical memory inscribed in it.

Everything in Dubrovnik was coagulated from separate signs from pastness and cut loose from time and space, situating itself into a mythical world just like the Tower of Babel (which was built on the supposition that people can overlook and control the course of things). Dubrovnik has always remained outside the turbulent times and historical struggles between East and West that affected the great 'fault line' running through the Balkans. Like a citadel on its hilltop, Dubrovnik until now had been assaulted only by the sea (and occasional fire) which polished its steep limestone cliffs and the bricks and glazed tiles of the palaces, which all served as a symbol for the transience of culture, and which was now under the threat of destruction.

There was no warning for the scenes that came, no music, no narrator introducing the theme, just a sudden burst of particles of soil and rock, and then a brown mushroom-like cloud of smoke changing to dark grey, almost black. The sound of explosions and the thunder of a fighter aircraft, the camera pointed towards the sky exposing the dark shadow of the aeroplane over the telecommunications tower. I recognised the tower and the 'Imperial' fortress of Dubrovnik. We have seen the scene at least a dozen times during the past few months on television. Dubrovnik in flames. Fighter planes belonging to JNA (Jugoslovenska Narodna Armija – the Yugoslav People's Army) bombing Dubrovnik. The shock and disbelief of the world faced with the first pictures of Dubrovnik were such that those scenes of the bombardment were shown over and over again on television stations around the world.

Now we were watching them again on a tape that had exposed far more than any broadcast or current affairs programme was ready or able to air. We watched the planes flying in semi-circles around the communications tower and the hill above Dubrovnik, petrified when bombs fell from under the wings of the plane. A faint thundering noise and the planes disappeared from view. The screen went black and then fuzzy, just to allow the camera to show the clouds of smoke rising upwards. There was no commentary or any trace of the person who recorded it. Just a date in the right-hand corner of the screen (3.10.91).

The next frame was already an inventory of the damage. A camera moving amidst smoking or still burning houses, hotels, and then the devastation in the marina, yachts, fishing boats, all alike reduced to a spectacular inferno. Flames rising up among thick tree tops. Firemen dragging fire hoses, people running up and down the street. As the video chronicle of 'Dubrovnik at War' as I call this nameless tape rolled on, there was more of everything we had seen on similar tapes before. Destruction and sadness. People in quest of water, food; old people, children in shelters. Water and electricity supplies cut off. Funerals. But this was different, this was Dubrovnik.

Dubrovnik, besides being a tourist mecca, has always attracted filmmakers, photographers, reporters. The city itself, its architectural harmony, symbolised the Adriatic and Yugoslavia. My own experience was that nine times out of ten when I was asked abroad where I was from, my answer that I come from Yugoslavia was met by 'Oh, I know, Dubrovnik.'

On the evening when the first pictures of Dubrovnik in flames hit the Perth television stations, my telephone rang. It was an Australian friend, who was in tears calling to tell me that she had just seen on television the hotel complex in which we had stayed the previous year, being bombed and in flames. She could not get over it. The world was waking up to the fact that an act of aggression was taking place. Waking up with Dubrovnik in flames. And the world reacted with the words of hundreds of intellectuals who had visited the Inter University Centre for Graduate Studies (IUC), now in rubble, and hundreds of artists who had performed at the renowned Dubrovnik Summer Festival. Some of them, like Kathleen Wilkes, the president of the Executive Board of the IUC, or Bernard Kouchner, the French minister for Social Care, stayed in Dubrovnik and acted as live shields in using their access to world media and their international reputations to prevent Dubrovnik from further destruction (Obradović 1992). But the destruction that left the city more damaged than the 1667 earthquake had already been done.

Appeals to friends of Dubrovnik, to heads of states, to foreign ministers, to academic institutions, and so on were mass produced daily and sent by all means of communications. Concerts, charity balls, fundraising to restore Dubrovnik, were organised.[18]

Not even Vukovar, which was completely destroyed and turned into a ghost town and is comparable to the worst dreams of 'the day after', has aroused so much anger and disgust in the world as Dubrovnik has. For months we watched ambulances, hospitals, kindergartens, schools, old people's homes and urban and natural landscapes savagely destroyed in Vukovar. We watched the endless line of refugees exiled from their homes. We heard and sometimes saw foreign journalists targeted on purpose and killed, and everyone agreed on only one thing: 'sure it was a dirty war'. But we reacted when Dubrovnik was bombed (cf. Banac 1992: 41).

When the same guns of the same army that had caused over 300,000 people to flee their homes, left over 30,000 dead,[19] and occupied one third of Croatian territory finally turned Dubrovnik into their target, the world started to protest. On 19 September 1991 Pero Puljanić, the mayor of Dubrovnik, sent a general appeal to the world (reprinted in *Dubrovnik* 1992: 565–6). I will quote only one sentence out of that letter:

> At this very moment, Dubrovnik is, perhaps for the first time in its history, isolated by air, sea and land; the guns, cannons, rockets, etc. are turned against our Dubrovnik, which is your Dubrovnik too.
>
> (*Ibid.*: 566)

It is the last line of this appeal that explains the question repeatedly asked by members of the audience watching the video tape of destruction of Dubrovnik:

> V.(B): Why did they bomb Dubrovnik? It is not in the territory they claim as theirs. It does not even have any army or military barracks. Dubrovnik was always free, an independent open City. Why?

The answer is in their question. Dubrovnik, the City, is a symbol of freedom. As I watched the IUC's building destroyed, gutted, documents, books, the intellectual wealth of twenty years of IUC history half burned, it was not Dubrovnik itself that brought tears to my eyes. It was the flood of memories of a by now very distant 1971 when as a student I witnessed the creation of a dream, of a project which was going to unite the world in Dubrovnik. Now I was watching that dream destroyed, gutted by fire.[20] And, once again, I became aware of the difference of the reference points (between me and the audience) for the symbols we were watching being destroyed on the screen (on the difference between *immediate context* and *referential context* see Lull 1988: 18). I was crying for the destruction of the place that symbolised my youth and the intellectual fervour of that youth which energised my beliefs in the distant past of 1971. Other members of the audience reacted differently. One of the men commented on the devastation of the marina and the agony of the owners of all those fishing boats that were lost. The young daughter noticed the ecological catastrophe as the sea around Dubrovnik became polluted but everyone agreed that 'if the Serbs dared to bomb Dubrovnik they will dare to do anything and everything else that will serve their purposes'. The statement was made by one of the women and the rest of the audience just nodded silently.

CITY WITH A CAPITAL G

As long as I can remember when we used to refer to Dubrovnik we just said *Grad* (City) with a capital *G*. That capital letter *G* is an explanation of the question behind all those hundreds and thousands of 'why' and 'why Dubrovnik' (cf. Talbott 1991).

According to Lotman (1990: 191) 'In the system of culture's symbols, the city has an important place.' It is also a 'complex semiotic mechanism' (*ibid.*: 194) and 'like culture, is a mechanism which withstands time' (*ibid.*: 195). As cultural symbols have the ability to store up and condense cultural texts, and symbols as finalised texts exist on their own without necessarily being an element in a syntagmatic chain, cultural symbols also escape the anchorage to one synchronic section of a culture or they come from the past and pass into a future cutting across culture's synchronicity vertically (*ibid.*: 102–3).

Dubrovnik, the *Grad*, was (and even now remains) an important mechanism of Croatian cultural memory, and as such it could 'transfer texts, plot outlines and other semiotic formations from one level to another'. Since 'the national and area boundaries of culture are largely determined by a long-standing basic set of dominant symbols' (*ibid.*: 104), attacking and destroying Dubrovnik was an act of symbolic violence as much as an act of real violence.

For example, cutting off Dubrovnik's water supply had a dual effect. As in other cities under siege, it had been used as a weapon in a form of warfare which affected the citizens of Dubrovnik directly. But on the symbolic level it was felt as an act of symbolic violence by every person who had access to the knowledge that Dubrovnik was the first Croatian city to have running water as early as the fifteenth century.

For me personally, the siege of Dubrovnik is a symbol of the ineffectiveness of world diplomacy in preventing and stopping the war in Yugoslavia, a form of diplomacy which has obviously learned nothing from Dubrovnik's diplomatic tradition. Dubrovnik, an ideal embodiment of freedom, art and pleasure is what Lotman (1990: 192) characterises as 'at the same time an image of the heavenly city and a sacred place'. Thus Lotman's reference to 'the world turned upside down' could be used in referring to the ruined city and in the case of the *Grad* Dubrovnik it does have 'the frightening features of Breughel or Bosch' (*ibid.*: 193).

Dubrovnik's history is, like the histories of most cities (and almost anything and everything else), inseparable from its mythology. Myths and historical facts blend easily under the warmth of the Mediterranean sun. The myth of Dubrovnik was of a cultural treasure, since it was, after all, under the protection of the UN, as a treasure which was 'a minimum of matter and a maximum of soul' ('Dubrovnik U Ratu' 1992: 573). This myth was well known to the JNA generals and the aggressor who besieged and attacked it. By attacking Dubrovnik, they reached the last corners of the injured souls of the Croatian people. The appeals, the pledge of financial help to rebuild Dubrovnik might rebuild the walls of the old city, but as Nada Grejić sadly states:

> But the arches will be cast from concrete. The frames which we will cut with machines will not be the frames that were carved by Peter Andrijić. There will not be the stucco work which it seems was shelled yesterday in Gvozdarijev's 'Čajkovci' summerhouse and which was made by Marino Gropeli, the architect of Dubrovnik's Saïnt Vlaho. These walls will not be the same as were touched by Cvijeta Zuzorić, nor will the trees of the arboretum be those planted by Vito Guetić. Thus this crime perpetrated on the Dubrovnik region from Pelješac to Vitaljina is immense and unforgivable.
>
> (Grejić 1992: 574)

Allow me to return to the audience with whom I was watching the tape of the siege of Dubrovnik on that Friday night. To the members of the audience who had visited Dubrovnik at one time or another, as tourists, most of the names and architectural icons that Nada Grejić (*ibid.*) mentioned wouldn't mean much. But the broken stones of the city's walls, the flames engulfing houses are not the broken stones and fire of Dubrovnik only. They are symbols of the aggression and, as one member of the audience remarked (quoted earlier) 'If they dared to bomb Dubrovnik there is no telling what they [the Serbs] will do next.' Thus the bombing and the siege of Dubrovnik represents an interruption of the existence of Dubrovnik and *Grad*, as well as an interruption of our imaginary past. Because Dubrovnik as a symbol of City has the capacity to allow us to see and remember the quality of imagined life in it at all times (Lynch 1960).

Dubrovnik is not a 'corporate citadel' (Soja 1989: 122). It is rather an epitome of civilisation and the locus of European art and culture, fascinating because of its 'wholeness' and, according to Michel de Certeau (1984: 92), there is a pleasure in the totalising effect of the City. Thus, shaped by the discursive practices of generations of its inhabitants and visitors, even if described by tourist brochures as a 'hotel city', Dubrovnik is quite the opposite of Fredric Jameson's (1984: 80–90) city, which is a 'postmodern hyperspace' of the Bonaventure Hotel, vertiginous and reflective. Thus the cognitive mapping of Dubrovnik comes easily to us, unlike the 'alienated' space of Jameson's city in which people are unable to map their minds, their own position or even the city itself as urban totality.

With Dubrovnik the sense of a place which we remember, and can associate with its mental map, is the sense of the pleasure of its totality. That is why the pain of the destruction of that pleasure of totality by seeing it bombed is far more than symbolic. It is a very real pain.

IRA INITIUM INSANIE

The Latin proverb attributed to Cicero describes more than adequately the processes of the creation of madness and hatred in former Yugoslavia which have reversed completely the dreams for future existence of any 'Nation of South Slavs' (dreams which Rebecca West finely captured in *Black Lamb and Grey Falcon*, (1943)). The struggles of different national and ethnic groups to free themselves from the constraints of the Yugoslav State produced uneven political movements at a time when the rest of Eastern Europe was looking towards democracy as the only solution. These struggles were based on quite different and diverse interpretations of their so-called common or shared past experiences inside the former Yugoslav State, which often involved a sense of extreme oppression. Before the war the cultural struggles inside Yugoslavia provided the raw material for the creation and maintenance of competing subnationalities (in contrast to Yugoslav nationality) and minority identities which finally created conditions of 'permanent madness' (Glenny 1992: 128).

The aggressive Serbian machinery of death and violence that we encountered on a daily basis from newspapers and from mainstream and
ethnic media was often directly and immediately transformed into the everyday discourse about the war by siphoning off the intensity of a violent
event. But the video tapes from Opuzen television naturalised the violence
because of their non-narrative structures. Furthermore, the brutality of the
images had an autonomous power to identify with the main theme by completely incorporating the video images into the already existing discourses of
all wars, and the prevailing discourse of this war included the insane hatred,
scenes of horrific orgies of death, which the world media qualified as 'setting
new standards for horror' (*60 Minutes*, 1 August 1993).

The 'incredible and inconceivable forces that have sprung from primordial
darkness' (see Djilas 1993: 5) were seen as being behind the conflict, and the
voices of reason such as, for example, Andre Glucksmann's, were easily
displaced and lost inside the already functioning discourses of 'the madmen
and the war'. Glucksmann often spoke out against Europe's and the world's
inability to stop the bloodshed, and among other things warned: 'What is
happening in Bosnia is not some age-old Balkan quarrel. It's our future. It is
post-Communism's political AIDS – a dangerous virus, a mutant strain that
will catch on in the rest of our continent if we don't do something' (quoted
by Krushelnycky and Moutet 1993: 1).The viral metaphor has been used
very often in reference to this war (see Morley and Robins 1995: 142–6), but
the political AIDS metaphor used by Glucksmann and connotating incur-
ability is by far the strongest.

COPING WITH THE INFORMATION OVERLOAD

When I wrote this, the war in Croatia and Bosnia and Herzegovina was still
going on. What first appeared as the senseless destruction of the urban and
natural environment has turned out to be the systematic destruction of sites
which evidence any culture, religion or human life in general. The destruction was being carried out not only to erase the possible evidence of who
these lands once belonged to and were inhabited by (Croatians, Muslims
and Serbs) but also to destroy the mnemonic markers as reminders of the past
for those who survived, including the diasporic fragments of those nations
all around the world. The Croatian audiences in Perth, just like anybody
else who had not witnessed or experienced this war at first hand, found
it difficult to understand that the war was 'really happening', let alone to
understand the meaning of what appeared to be such senseless destruction.

It was almost impossible to cope with all the information that was by now
flooding into the community. Although an investigation of the psychological
aftermath of seeing so much violence on video tapes and television is
beyond the scope of this research, it was obvious that the audience was
fatigued. Anxiety, depression and frequent nightmares were described to me

on several occasions by audience members. These could be seen at the very least as an indirect consequence of the strain put on the diaspora by its voluntary and imposed involvement in the war.

I had made a decision to discontinue my fieldwork, even though the war was far from over and an interesting new polarisation was emerging between the Muslims and Croats in Bosnia and Herzegovina (see Frost 1993: 2). But I had to slowly remove myself from the community in order to finalise my writing, and also because the repeated viewings of death and violence had affected me personally. I started to have frequent nightmares and difficulty in concentrating, and I suffered from prolonged fatigue and recurring headaches. It was impossible for me to separate my research from my private life, not only because it was linked to my personal situation directly, but because the potency of the repetition of the iconography linking the war to, for example, music was so powerful that I carried it with me all the time. I used to love Albinoni's *Adagio*, but I cannot listen to it any more without visualising the lonely cellist, Vedran Smailović, sitting in his concert attire surrounded by the graves of killed civilians in Sarajevo. Smailović issued a worldwide appeal at the beginning of the siege of Sarajevo to cellists to play Albinoni's *Adagio* at noon (of a certain day) in protest over the war. I have not heard of any response to his appeal. Nevertheless, the *Adagio* is off limits for me, at least for a while.[21]

As a result of my increasing inability to deal with the imagery of death within an academic discourse, what follows is a somewhat incomplete and fragmented report of what was to be my last 'official' participation in the viewing of a video tape with my audience. (I specify 'official' since there were occasions when I watched videos with my audience right up until when I was due to leave Australia, but I did not take field notes and have only included a few key observations as a part of this book.)

I was invited to watch the video tape of the destruction of sacred (religious) institutions in Croatia, and as I walked in I could hear a voice in Croatian:

> The warriors who want to destroy the temples of God, do not simply want to conquer the land and gain its riches. They want to kill the entire nation by erasing its centuries-long memories by mortifying its spirit, by tearing its heart out . . .

The rest of the sentence was cut off by the hostess who clicked the stop command in order to greet me. After the usual greetings I was seated and it was explained that what they were watching was a video tape of the destruction and damage to sacred institutions in Croatia. A male member of the audience remarked:

V.(C): They also kill priests and everybody who is Catholic. I heard the

story that they ask you to cross yourself before they execute you.
With three fingers like an orthodox . . .

'They', of course, were the Serbs and the story was an old one belonging to
the negative mythology of the religious wars.

The sombre male voice with an educated, somewhat artificial diction,
which I had heard when I walked in, continued to comment, identifying and
naming churches, chapels, mosques and cemeteries, some still thick with
smoke, others standing ruined and ghostly in the nakedness of their destruction. Later in conversation, it was revealed that most, if not all, the mentioned names were unfamiliar to the audience. But the voice of the narrator
continued:

> This is a war that is an attempt to create greater Serbia. And to achieve
> that the četniks have to erase every trace of Croatian and Catholic
> elements and create Serbian areas. The barbarians understand that the
> cultural and religious monuments which are made equally from love
> and stone, tenderness and iron, are all symbols of a nation unique and
> original. What kind of people therefore are those who destroy the very
> history of Croatia. The answer is: the same enemy which makes no
> difference between soldiers and civilians and kills in cold blood, and
> whose primary aim is to annihilate.

This was more like it. The audience livened up, the comment was noted
and the tape rewound and the sequence played again in order to ensure
understanding. Later on the comment was discussed and retold endlessly,
interwoven with examples from popular mythology. I was told again the
story of how the JNA and četniks left bodies putrifying for weeks before
allowing the UN or Red Cross to collect the corpses. The story of how
četniks from all around Serbia terrorised a group of old people in a village is
a variant of the story written by Glenny who asks:

> What solace is left to the families of the twenty-four aged people in
> Vocin and Hum, two harmless villages in Western Slavonia, who were
> slaughtered by the retreating četnik monsters, determined to leave a
> trail of scorched humanity in their wake?
>
> (Glenny 1992: 124)

Old people unable to leave or refusing to leave the territory which was in the
path of the Serbs and JNA were often victims. Since most of the members
of my audience still had ageing relatives, often parents, in Croatia, there was
often a sigh of relief when their village or their town 'did not make the
news'. There were eleven people in the room that night, eight adults and
three children (teenagers).

It is Friday night and the young ones are getting ready to go out. The four
couples are my usual informants, assembled there tonight to watch two

video tapes they have borrowed from someone who brought them from Melbourne. They have already watched most of the first tape, the end of which I have seen on my arrival. As I am staying for the weekend, it is (again) suggested that I see the rest of the tape later so we can proceed with viewing the other one. Coffee and cake are brought out and the conversation continues. They are talking about the damage to historical monuments and sacred objects in Šibenik which is the home of one of the members of the audience. Since I am being quizzed on my knowledge of some churches that we had just seen destroyed, I manage to write down only snippets of conversation between two women:

> V.(A): Angie's brother was killed near Šibenik – he was only eighteen ... She is out of her mind ... You know her parents are over there. She couldn't go to the funeral ... I am sure that her parents are not able to cope ... They have lost that lovely house Angie and Tom built for them up in the hills. It is pure luck that they have evacuated from there when ordered ...
>
> V.(B): Talking about evacuation ... Have you heard of Željko's grandmother?

Željko is M.M.'s son-in-law, and his grandmother stayed all alone in a small village when the rest of the population was evacuated. She refused to leave and no one has heard from her for over four months. She is 82 years old and the fear is that she might be dead. (We heard about the old woman after that. Apparently the soldiers from the UN Nigerian battalion took her food up in the hills to a shack in what used to be the family's vineyard. She had no electricity or water, and no one knows how she survived those two last winters all alone.)

> M.M.: [answers] No, we have not heard anything. It is so unbelievable. The village is just a few kilometres from Šibenik and I cannot believe that no one can go and check out if she is alive ...

Her husband interrupts:

> R.M.: How can you say a stupid thing like that. It is war. No one is going to risk their lives to look for an old woman. The village is in the middle of Serb-conquered territory ... Haven't you watched the tape? They destroy everything ... They leave death and destruction after them ... Didn't you see just now? ... The Serbian aggressor does not distinguish between historically precious churches or monuments and simple villages or even cemeteries. They destroy everything ... So if you don't want to be killed you run, flee, abandon and save your life ... The foolish old woman ...

This rebuke made everyone start to talk at once. An argument developed as to whether one should stay and defend one's home or simply flee in the face

200

of the Serbs and most probably be killed or, in the best scenario, be taken prisoner and raped. At about this time stories of rape and torture started to circulate in the community. They became international news on 29 July 1992 when the first images of concentration camps and stories of rape camps started to circulate in the world media (see Knightley 1993).

But the community in Perth had already seen it all. The Opuzen TV tapes and the propaganda tape produced by HTV had shown us more than the world audiences will ever have a chance to see. As we watched the UN soldiers discovering mass graves full of massacred civilians or the images of desecrated churches, or deserted farms and villages littered with animal corpses, often side by side with human bodies, as we watched one after the other towns becoming ghost towns whose inhabitants had been killed or intimidated into leaving, we learned new words and new meanings such as 'urbanocide', 'culturocide' and the most utilised euphemism for genocide – 'ethnic cleansing'.

The next tape we watched was no exception. It was produced by *Krščan-ska Sadašnjost* (Christian Reality) and the first frame was the figure of Zagreb's archbishop Cardinal Franjo Kuharić who was standing underneath a bullet-riddled statue of Jesus on the outskirts of the village of Farkašić, 50 kilometres from Zagreb, which is now lying in Serb-occupied territory. This bullet-riddled crucifix often appears as a symbol of the war together with the small red Fiat crushed by a tank or the cathedral tower in Šibenik with the grenade hole through it. The propaganda purposes of assembling such video tapes which connect the destruction of human life and the cultural and natural environment are obvious and are aimed at promoting the necessity for sacrifice, boosting morale and bringing the nation together, and, of course, are aimed at the vilification of the enemy. However, the recurring images of the red Fiat crushed by the Yugoslav army tank or of the consequences of the shelling of Dubrovnik strengthen the 'reality effect' (Nichols 1991: 41) and anchor the meanings of such videos to the struggle for freedom in Croatia.

I draw this conclusion partly from my own emotions and meaning-making. For example, the emotional geography of the space which I associate with each and every building that I see damaged in Dubrovnik allows me to understand how parts of the audience watching the destruction of villages and towns 20,000 kilometres away felt personally challenged. It is because part of our own sense of identity was not only challenged but destroyed together with Vukovar, Jajce, Goražde, Kijevo and numerous other places which, even if we have not lived in or visited them personally, we have all known through someone who 'came from there'.

The video camera does not restrain itself in exploring and then reproducing what we accept as a representation of reality later, on VCRs in our living rooms. It appears to know no boundaries. The camera is the first audience to the stories told directly into its lens like the one told by the parish priest from Kijevo which was, as explained to me by a member of the audience, the first Croatian village to 'be erased from the face of the earth'.

After identifying himself as the parish priest Father Mate Gverić, he proceeded with the story. As there is no person visible behind the camera, the priest is the only one talking into the lens to the imagined audience:

> On Monday, 26 August 1991 . . . my parishioners and I were hiding in the mountains all day. As we were leaving our village the night before we saw it all in flames. A Yugoslav army tank was approaching our church and fired at least four cannon shells into it. The church was already totally demolished, but more than a hundred various projectiles were launched during the period of occupation . . . [a long pause] Serbian reservists and četniks were throwing hand grenades into the burning houses. As if that was not enough, they were jumping off the tanks, entering houses, barns and stables, making sure that everything was destroyed and set on fire . . . [the camera moves around the countryside.] It was an act of ritual destruction, a satanic ritual. We (the villagers and I) were hiding in the hills, but even there we were attacked at random, they knew that we were there, and they tried to kill us with mortar shells and cluster bombs.

As he spoke, his eyes were filled with tears and the camera moved away for an instant to show us the ruins of the church and Kijevo itself, revealing the presence of someone else behind it.

Video tapes that contained such material, mainly involving monologues spoken straight into the camera put, the audience in the position of an 'ideal observer' (Nichols 1991: 43). A certain dynamic of empathic identification sets in, which in the case of the audience and myself was further emphasised by the personal losses already inflicted upon us in the course of the war. The inflammatory and emotional intensity of these compilations defies analysis and leaves the audiences to negotiate the meaning through their emotional aftermath, when the images seen at such showings start to haunt us in our dreams and nightmares.

And I ask today the question Anton Barac asked in 1943, while writing his *Sloboda Šutnje* (The Freedom to be Silent):

> Witnessing all the destruction and demolition which in times of great conflagrations one encounters at every step, there is full psychological justification for the question which rises from the intimate depths of an intellectual: In this breakdown of spiritual and material values, against the death of millions and the disappearance of entire nations, what is the sense of this scribbling?
>
> (quoted in Katičić and Novak 1989: 171)

8

BRIDGES AND BOUNDARIES

Standing in a small crowded café in Wiesbaden, Germany on 5 February 1993 I was waiting to meet the two Caritas truck drivers[1] who were supposed to arrive from the Bosnian city of Mostar and bring me the video tape I was to take back to Perth, Western Australia. The cold early twilight of the late afternoon could not penetrate the windowless space, thick with cigarette smoke and the air of sadness. Had it not been for the German advertisements for numerous brands of beer hanging side by side with the Croatian coat of arms, Croatian flag and enlarged photographs of the Croatian cities of Dubrovnik and Zagreb, this café could have been in any country or even on any planet in the universe. It existed as the space where 'people in the diaspora' Those 'lonely gatherings of scattered people', bring their myths, fantasies and experiences.[2]

Bhabha (1984, 1990a) also points out that times and places of gatherings (like this café) exist everywhere because hybridity of the colonised and the diasporic is not a state of comfortable multicultural pluralism or gradual synthesis, but is marked by asymmetry and by the edgy coexistence of incommensurable experiences and often by the unpredictable incursion of the uncanny. Bhabha knows this well because:

> I have lived that moment of the scattering of the people that in other times and other places, in the nations of others becomes a time of gathering. Gatherings of exiles and émigrés and refugees; gatherings on the edge of 'foreign cultures'; gatherings at the frontiers; gatherings in the ghettos or cafés of city centres; gatherings in the half-life, half-light of foreign tongues, or in the uncanny fluency of another's language; gathering the signs of approval and acceptance, degrees, discourses, disciplines; gathering the memories of underdevelopment, of other worlds lived retrospectively; gathering the past in ritual and revival; gathering the present.
>
> (Bhabha 1990a: 291)

The two truck drivers arrive, young men with two days' growth, eyes swollen and red from sleepless nights and non-stop driving. A small group of people encircles them immediately. Questions are asked in low voices. Small packages and envelopes change hands. My younger brother approaches them, there is a short exchange of inaudible (to me) words. The men look in my direction, as I am the only woman in the room beside the two waitresses busy serving espressos and capuccinos. As I stand there, conscious of my visibility, I want to tell all these people that it is OK, that I am one of them, that I belong to the same wounded universe they come from. But instead I just keep standing there silent.

After a short exchange with the two men, my brother returns with a small envelope and a video tape. I do not insist on talking to them. According to the unwritten law among the refugees, they should address me first. This is because the space of vulnerable visibility that refugees inhabit is also a space of extremes and instability, and the boundary of that space between them as 'other', and the German (host) society, suddenly becomes the boundary separating me as the 'other' from the group in that café. The moment of self-consciousness of my own existence as the 'other' is asserted only by the self-consciousness of estrangement and a displaced desire to be somewhere else, anywhere, just not in this place of cool *Angst* of loneliness.

My brother tells me that both of the drivers are returning to the front lines after a few days' rest. Driving Caritas trucks is considered a sort of 'shore leave' for Croatian soldiers. (Upon my return to Australia I was to learn that one of the drivers was killed just a few days after our silent meeting in Wiesbaden, leaving a wife and three children somewhere in a refugee camp.) I look around once more, noticing in the half-light the tired faces of these 'people of Pagus' (*ibid.*: 315) who, like Marx's 'reserve army of migrant labour', are part of the new subclass of displaced people and refugees from the former Yugoslavia (and other countries of former East Europe). They have joined the scattered people from the Third World in their quest for entry to and work permits in Europe, or at least refugee status. And I ask silently whether they will all become 'Nietzsche's mobile army of metaphors, metonyms and anthropomorphisms' (*ibid.*).

Ready to leave, my brother takes my arm and leads me through the crowded café towards the door. One of the young men steps out of the group, comes towards us, extends his hand towards me and says a simple: *Hvala* (Thank you). As we walk out to the street, still alive with late shoppers, I can feel the firm grasp of the young man's hand and see the trust in his glance when for a split second our eyes meet in the act of the conspiratorial handshake. For the first time in my life (and after thinking of myself for three years as being part of the ethnic audience), I feel completely a part of them, people of a shadowy existence, the diaspora.

I was reminded again of this incident and the video tape I brought to Perth by a friend in late 1993 when she called to tell me that the Mostar Bridge 'was gone'. (The Mostar Bridge was a bridge dating from the sixteenth century, built by the Turks. It had always symbolised the meeting of

East and West – the Ottoman Empire and Europe.) In a tearful voice my friend said:

> M.B.V.: The bridge is gone . . . but we will build other ones. What we cannot replace is people . . . You remember the video tape you brought earlier this year from Mostar. The woman who sent it, she was killed . . .

I did not record the conversation, nor do I recall any of it after those words. I hardly heard the rest of what she said. All I could think of was the fading memory of a young woman dressing a small child, trying to get her to 'say "Hello" to your auntie'. I never saw the rest of that video tape. I am deeply ashamed of my curiosity to see it, rationalised by 'I should know what is on that video tape, if I carry it into another country.' When I turned the VCR on and saw the first frames showing a tiny living room with a young woman attempting to dress a small child, trying to get her to wave into the camera and say something, I turned it off immediately, feeling guilty about intruding into someone else's private life. It was the same shame and guilt I felt when I interviewed M.V. (the producer of OTV), a feeling of uninvited and unwelcome entrance into someone else's soul, like peeping through the windows of strangers as one passes along an empty street. This intrusion is different from what ethnographers feel when they are drawn into the spaces of human life where they 'might really prefer not to go at all' and where 'once there they don't know how to go about getting out except through writing' (Scheper-Hughes 1992: xii). It was different to the extent that I had a choice. It was the same choice that my audiences had all along: simply push the 'stop' button on the remote control for the VCR.

The reason why I never saw the rest of that tape with the family in Perth was that the Muslim community (from former Yugoslavia) in Perth closed its doors to outsiders. My only access to that community was the friend who called to tell me about 'the fall of the Mostar Bridge'.

Bridges, like no other structures built by people, symbolise meeting. Meetings of river banks, mountains, cities, but above all meetings of peoples, of cultures. I saw the empty space where the Mostar Bridge used to stand on the television news (ABC *International News*, 11 November 1993) that very night when my friend called and I was still in a state of shock over the death of a bridge. The Mostar Bridge had numerous narratives built around it, from horrific accounts of Turkish slaughter of the gentile population by beheading them and then throwing them from the bridge into the river, to more poetic stories of how it was built with egg whites and goats' hair.[3] It does not matter which of these narratives I heard so often from my friend (who had built the replica of the bridge as the entrance gate to her house in Floreat Park, Perth), these narratives now only signify what no longer is. Yet they still evoke memories of what was or what people continue to imagine to have taken place in that space, that empty space that stares at us from a full colour-page photograph in the issue of *Time* magazine (22 November 1993, pp. 34–5). On the same pages Frederick Painton writes about the destruction of this cultural icon, quoting a local Bosnian radio journalist Omer Vatric: 'The bridge was like a rainbow giving hope to the possibility that both sides could still live together one day' (Painton 1993: 35).

The daily encounter with scenes of dead bodies and burned villages by now appeared only on the shallow horizons of my consciousness, in which only timeless signs meet the necessary condition for the synchronisation of the past and the present, allowing emotion to enter the memory of my own existence. I eventually tried to 'distance' myself from the death and the war I was watching with my audiences, always returning to the safe haven of academia. But the audiences I was leaving behind had no such escape. They lived with the visions of suffering and endless destruction day in, day out, until every form of violence became a routinised part of their understanding of the conditions of war. The destruction of the Mostar Bridge was no exception. It was only another casualty of the war, and another disturbance in the 'iconic continuum' (Lotman 1990: 203) of my audiences. But for me and my artist friend it meant something much more. The empty space in which the bridge once (not so long ago) used to stand has become a triumphal sign of the destruction this war is leaving behind. The emptiness of the space was infused with meanings, like an empty stage that retains the autonomy of souls of the past existences of all the actors that have ever crossed it. Framing the emptiness that the bridge left were the half-destroyed buildings, dwellings of the human souls that were now crowding inside the space left by the bridge. There, inside that emptiness, a window has been projected, offering us a glimpse of the future, a future that belongs to that empty space which simultaneously reveals itself for what it is and what it is not.

The disappearance of the Mostar Bridge will for certain be inscribed in the history of what is already known as the 'Third Balkan War' (Glenny 1992). But the origins and the reasons behind the war will be lost in the rationalisations about its past, and in the memory of the people remembering it will become distanced events, perhaps preserved in fragments in the electronic (and digital) writing on the video tapes. However, the fatefulness of the reality preserved on those tapes already reveals itself more like a murmur than a message. This war as a media project is so different from the 'mini series of the Gulf War' (De Landa 1993: 84). In this age of referential cultural products this war could be seen as a 'horrific sequel to the Gulf massacre' (Morley and Robins 1995: 142) but like many other sequels it has been turned into a plotless narrative, like a long-running drama serial whose writers don't quite know how to finish it off. While the viewing public waits only for an end, it is often forgotten that dying in its stark reality still goes on out there.

In time, the audiences I was working with started to return to mending their lives in terms of an acceptable symbolic ethnicity. Their 'Croatianness' provided them not only with new forms of association, new friends and new identities, but also locked them inside a tighter structure from which there were fewer visible ways out. My personal relationships with the different audiences from the former Yugoslav community were eroded as the country fell apart. If the war created new relationships with the Croatian audience, my old friends from the Serbian community were the first to denounce my constant presence amongst the Croatian community and reacted by limiting my access to any information – but volunteered propaganda from their press releases.[4]

In regard to the Muslim community, they remained 'willing informants' for a long time, but became increasingly suspicious of outsiders (including myself) with the arrival of the first refugees from the Serbian detention camps in Perth. Towards the end of this study, Western Australia had already accommodated sixteen Muslim families from Bosnia, under its special refugee programme.[5] Only a dear old friend, an artist with a free spirit, remained in touch. My friend (M.B.V.) is a Bosnian Muslim married to a Croat, but she has always considered herself Yugoslav. She disregarded my work in the Croatian community and put our friendship first. Or, as she has put it:

> I am like a bird whose wings have been clipped. There is a door left ajar . . . I can see through that crack. On one side of that door are my people, dying and suffering endlessly. On the other side is the world. You are on the other side of that door, with the rest of the world watching through the door left ajar. I am caught right between in that space, neither here nor there. It is you who comes to me, I cannot move from my position. What is even worse, I can't go to my people either.

With Croatian audiences it was different. If I expected them to be my informants, they expected me to help 'the Croatian cause'. I functioned as an intermediary who could help expedite projects such as, at first, composing letters for letter-writing campaigns for the international recognition of Croatia, and later helping to organise charity drives and functions. The dual position I had been occupying started to become transparent. I was a stranger and friend at the same time, often shocked by the recognition that I understood lives so very different to my own. As I moved sometimes uneasily from the third-person narrator to first-person participant in the video viewing sessions, I was aware of my own functioning in what Geertz (1988: 117) has called the 'mutually interfering' relationships with my audience, as I now existed on the same margins as my audience of the cultural semiospheres of Australian and Croatian societies. This schizophrenic existence increasingly started to put constraints on the amount of my involvement in the Croatian community. They in turn started to be suspicious about the

absence of nationalistic fever in my stance, and started to question my loyalty to 'the Croatian cause'. After finishing my fieldwork in early 1993, I
distanced myself somewhat from the wider community and stayed in touch
only with the principal informant group of M.M.'s family and friends. This
was partly to allow time for writing as I realised that the data I had collected
had grown far beyond manageability, but I distanced myself also because I
increasingly disagreed with some of the policies and actions of the Croatian
government towards the war in Bosnia and Herzegovina.[6] I did not want to
be put into the position of lying to people who regarded me as one of their
own. Like any other 'modern nomad' (Clifford 1992), I knew that I had
exhausted this time and place, which was closing its welcome on my intrusion into it. This was the moment for departure (not closure, since a closure
was not possible at this time).

As I was leaving, I dismissed my experience of feeling a part of the diaspora in the wintry coldness of a Croatian café in Germany as a part of the
'rags and patches of everyday life' (Bhabha 1990a: 298) of a modern nomad.
Nevertheless, in their liminality, these elements allowed my perplexed existence between two continents to reveal itself and I was left with a question:
do I belong to a category of people that I had never perceived myself to be a
part of, the kind of creatures that Bhabha (*ibid.*: 293) calls 'a tribe of inter-
preters' whose 'metaphoric movement requires a kind of 'doubleness' in
writing'?

DIASPORAS: A (GLOBAL) LOCALITY OF SELF-
PERCEPTION

Ien Ang defines diasporas as: 'commonly understood as transnational, spatially and temporally sprawling sociocultural formations of people, creating
imagined communities whose blurred and fluctuating boundaries are sustained by real and/or symbolic ties to some original "homeland"' (Ang
1992/1993: 6). The Macedonian and Croatian communities described
throughout the present work are no exception and are created and sustained
by the same 'symbolic ties' to their homelands. Just how strong those 'symbolic ties' were, was shown at the time of the war in the homeland when the
ethnic communities from former Yugoslavia created new boundaries
between old allies. While the war raged in Croatia, the Croatian community
closed its ranks inside its boundaries, realising the historical necessity for the
same consolidation as the one embedded in the conflict developing in former
Yugoslavia. (And, I believe, the same was true for the Serbian and Muslim
Bosnian population.)

The 'transnational' character of the diaspora and its embeddedness in a
common history has informed my main arguments. The 'complex positioning' of the Croatian community in Perth between the host and homeland
cultures during the civil unrest and war in that homeland (as I have de-

scribed it), also shows attempts on the part of the community to balance their everyday life between their existence in Australia and their loyalty to Croatia, because:

> [A] critical cultural politics of diaspora should privilege neither host country nor (real or imaginary) homeland, but precisely keep a creative tension between 'where you're from' and 'where you're at'.
>
> (*ibid.*: 13)

This study has shown that such 'creative tension' can be arrested for short periods of time in order to accommodate changes in that 'homeland'. And this will delay considerably the productivity of the 'in-between-ness' (*ibid.*) and the proposed hybrid (Hall 1993) or creolised (Lotman 1990) cultural forms that should be born out of a diaspora's 'productive syncretism' (Ang 1992/1993: 13).

Moreover, the diverse and heterogeneous diasporic identifications are already existing and functioning worldwide (cf. Boyarin 1991). They are extremely fragmented, and already part of the 'postmodern ethnicity' which requires constant '(re-)invention' and '(re)negotiation' of cultural identity. I suspect that this is not a specific condition to being a part of the diaspora, and that the '(re-)invention 'and '(re)negotiation' of cultural self is not characteristic only of people identified as diaspora but of all people inhabiting this 'mixed-up, interdependent, mobile and volatile postmodern world' (Ang 1992/1993: 14).

The electronic and digital revolutions that have changed the meaning of communication are at the forefront of this volatility of postmodernity. If we agree that every communication technology is also a cultural technology, than cultural technologies, and especially the visual media, which are also technologies of self, provide us with an instantaneous source of mirroring 'the self or the other' (see Gutman 1988; C. Taylor 1989). These are powerful agents in the formation, (re-)invention or (re)negotiation not only of individual cultural identity, but also in the formation of collective attitudes, values and aspirations, constantly reshaping and transforming the collective consciousness of cultural groups. For example, I have shown in this study that the VCR has fostered the creation of 'ethnic revival' (Smith 1981), creating at first 'militant separatist nationalism' in an otherwise peaceful ethnic community in Perth, and later caused encapsulation and ethno-phobia under the pressure of the virulent propaganda from 'back home'.

It might be too speculative to link the 'encapsulation' of ethnic communities and the heightened awareness of cultural identities of diasporas around the world to the development of technology. But it is an increasing possibility that the domestic VCR (as part of a larger communication and media development) has not only greatly influenced the collapse of the meaning of cultural identity under globalisation but has also contributed to the formation of cultural identities fuelled by the desire for a sense of continuity (or belonging). This need for continuity is based on 'shared memories and common destiny' with 'others [just] like us' (Smith 1990: 179), and creates global diasporas that function on local levels. This creates an alternative to the increasingly powerful call for the 'globalisation' of culture which Smith (*ibid.*) sees as 'essentially memoryless'. This is not so with ethnic communities that are based on continuity of shared memories and the shared pull of symbols, stories and myths, all of which can be easily accessed because modern and postmodern technology allow for instant communication and access to information worldwide.

In contrast to the inability of the global communications networks to create a global culture along the lines of the formula 'culture follows structure' (*ibid.*), a potential for the (re)negotiation of the multiplicity of cultural identities has been created. And as we have seen in this study, these are often appropriated for nationalist projects. The information circulating in the Croatian and Serbian community prior to the break-up of Yugoslavia was aimed directly towards re-creation of Serbian and Croatian cultural identity. As the tension grew in former Yugoslavia, the content of information changed towards the creation of ethno-national identity, positioning, more and more, the Serbian and Croatian identity as antagonistic towards each other. All of this was presented through video tapes containing a mixture of information, entertainment and often family-album inserts, and the underlying propaganda was well hidden. In addition there was a proliferation of 'historic tapes' aimed towards establishing the 'historicity' of the Serbian and Croatian nations. These most frequently draw their power not from sober historical assessment, but 'from the way events, heroes and landscapes have been woven by myth, memory and symbol into the popular consciousness' (*ibid.*: 182).

I have noted earlier the eagerness with which the Croatian and Macedonian communities in Western Australia embraced VCR for the purpose of consolidating the same 'events, heroes and landscapes woven by myth and memory' that Smith (*ibid.*) sees as so important in the development of popular consciousness. We have also seen how the video tapes circulating in the Croatian community became the precious veils for the symbolic representation of Croatian history, legitimising Croatia's quest for independence from Yugoslavia and offering at the same time historicity to the 'people without history' (Wolf 1982). This provided grounds for distinguishing the Croatian diaspora from the larger Western Australian Yugoslav community. And it served to define the boundary between cultural self and the other in relation to the creation of the Croatian state.

Given this, I would like to propose that no form of cultural activity in the late twentieth century so clearly displays the globalisation–localisation dichotomy of postmodern culture in terms of its use of electronic media and communication as does the use of the VCR. Even though electronic communications encompass such diverse aspects as transborder (transcontinental interplanet) data flows, owing their existence to the Internet and computers, satellites and other technological advances, the VCR is still the most accessible and therefore most popular means of communication in diaspora, second perhaps only to the telephone.[7]

FAILING TO ARTICULATE MICRO- AND MACRO-: DOES IT REALLY MATTER?

It has often been argued that the media in general, and television in particular, have far-reaching effects on the minds of individuals, and therefore influence the actual political and cultural dynamics of societies worldwide (e.g. Mattelart, Delacourt and Mattelart 1984; Schlesinger 1991).[8] In addition the new 'image spaces' (Morley and Robins 1995) created by the complex interaction of the postmodern media have displaced the past metaphor of television that was suggesting uniformity of delivery. Today, television as a part of the complex multimedia system suggests a new kind of relationship between a lot of different media that all relate to some kind of structure (private or state), and are compressing the traditional structure of time and space, creating fundamental changes in the relations between private and public and between local and global. In such a media climate, it is also more difficult to control information flow and the potential impact of new technologies is subject to a wide range of debates, from scholarly to governmental. Debates about 'cultural imperialism' (H. Schiller 1991) are gaining currency (especially in Europe), 'as it has often been assumed . . . that the integrity and continued existence of communities and their political institutions depends crucially on their communication sovereignty' (Morley and Robins 1995: 44). This in turn justifies the claims that media are at the forefront of globalisation processes with their influence on the development and continuation of the national and cultural identity.

Joshua Meyrowitz and John Maguire (1993: 41–9) in the recent debates about the influence of the media on society in the United States go so far as to propose that 'shared experiences through television have encouraged minorities to demand equal rights and treatment' (*ibid.*: 43). However, their argument is with regard to television programmes which target different ethnic groups, such as the Spanish-language television, that actually isolate people, undercutting the traditional identity and displacing the 'old local subcultures'. The result, they claim, is the eroding of differences, for example, between the diverse Hispanic groups, which results in a tendency to project an artificial 'Hispanic national identity' (*ibid.*: 44). The trend of American media towards a greater homogenisation on the one hand and a greater fragmentation on the other is supported by their assertion that 'traditional groups are bypassed in both directions; individuals experience more diversity and choice, while traditional group cultures are overlapping, losing identity and blurring into each other' (*ibid.*).

This might be the case in the United States where the 'melting pot' is still bubbling in a 'chaotic and unfathomable way', (*ibid.*: 48), but Meyrowitz and Maguire draw their conclusions on the basis of years of research on and observation about the development and influences of media on American society, where cable television, public broadcasting as well as various forms of 'narrowcasting' have been present since the mid-1970s. Given the different media environment in Australia, it is difficult to compare their findings with any available research on the Australian media regarding ethnic communities, simply because satellite television and some forms of narrowcasting (cable, pay TV) are still 'on hold' in Australia (with the exception of various Aboriginal narrowcasting as described by Eric Michaels and the first ethnic cable television in Melbourne, *Tele Italia*). It is because of this absence of television delivery outside the television networks that VCR penetration patterns and the dynamics of its use are so distinctive in Australia. This has created a mediascape specific to Australia which makes any comparison with media influences in other developed countries next to impossible. Such is a case with any attempt at comparison with the European 'image spaces'. For example, when Morley and Robins (1995) examine the transformation of information and communication media and the restructuring of 'information and image spaces' through the emergence of global media markets, and the relationship between global and local media, they accentuate that 'the issue is not one of global or local media, but of how global and local are articulated' (*ibid.*: 2). However, their discussion is about Europe, European identities and European culture in relation to the 'new global landscape' (*ibid.*: 10–26). The Australian mediascape is very different from the European one even though some concerns driving Australian media spaces are the same as or similar to those discussed by Morley and Robins, especially the issues relating to the development of new media technologies and markets which 'seem to make a mockery of borders and frontiers' (*ibid.*). But in contrast to the real borders of the European kaleidoscope of nation states, Australian borders are discursive borders, and are created by questions of relationship to the 'other' (Said 1978), and such borders are more difficult to cross, overcome or make a mockery of than the state borders of the European Union (EU). Thus it is for the reasons behind the uniqueness of the Australia's mediascape that the articulation of local and global media in the Australian context is very difficult. And it is for the same reasons that the desired macro-level of analysis as proposed by Morley (1992: 288) is difficult to put into perspective, let alone to articulate with the micro-levels of analysis according to which the investigation into ethnic video and its use was carried out in this research.

This study has concentrated on the construction of discourses around ethnic (national) and cultural identities on the micro-level, observing and recording the dynamics of VCR as cultural technology at the domestic and community level. Following the mobilisation of the VCR as a communication and cultural technology to be used for the maintenance and repair of their cultural identities in Macedonian and Croatian migrant families in Perth, and bearing witness to the extent of the influence of the VCR on the re-creation of Croatian national identity for the Croatian community during the civil unrest and war in the homeland, I was barely able to cast these within the wider context of 'global/local dynamics' (*ibid.*: 289). This was only accomplished through those avenues available and permitted to me by my 'nomadic' existence, that is, travelling between the Croatian homeland and its diaspora in Western Australia.[9] Thus the required 'grounding in theory' (*ibid.*) was not achieved, mainly because the war in Croatia and Bosnia created new environments, both discursive and real-life, and my fieldwork and the descriptive results of it sometimes transcend acceptable theoretical categories and often refuse to comply with norms of analysis.

GLOBALISATION AND ETHNIC POLARISATION: THE CONTEXT

Since the first signs of the demise of Communism in the late 1980s and the fall of the Berlin Wall, emerging nationalist and ethnic divisions have been seen by the conventional wisdom of the West as home-spun philosophies of the former Eastern bloc and the Third World. They are seen as part and parcel of their struggle for survival. In the meantime, a resurgence of academic interest in the formation and re-formation of cultural identities through ethnic identification has hastened the collapse of the meanings of oriental, post-colonial, post-cold-war and other metaphorical characterisations of 'otherness' and 'difference' (cf. Bhabha 1990a). It has also seen the appropriation of some 'real' categories, for example immigrant or migrant, into the new acceptable monolithic 'other': the ethnic (the current vogue is also a collective other: the diaspora).

To illustrate the above I will give an example how the phrase 'ethnic style' was appropriated for a 'non-Western' style of interior decoration. The December (1993) issue of the Australian *Elle* in its Christmas book review carried the following description:

> 'Ethnic Style. From Mexico to the Mediterranean' by Miranda Innes 'As far from the slick design of the Eighties as possible, 'Ethnic Style' encompasses the tradition of non-Western cultures. Vibrant, inspirational interiors (Conran Octopus, Hardcover, \$45).'
>
> (*Elle* 1993: 18)

Even though the 'Ethnic Style' is still in inverted commas, the above shows an increased acceptance of ethnic as non-Western, thus exotic, replacing 'oriental' in the discourse of everyday life such as that of interior design.

This acceptance of ethnic as the universal, non-Western 'other' adds to the already existing monochromatic representation of black and white polarisation that characterises the media reports of political and other crises, or the position the good against the evil.[10] First, it was Communist against non-Communist, later, all the struggles and ills of the emerging, struggling 'would-be democracies' of the former Eastern bloc countries were brought into another simplified frame of ethnic and religious polarisation, or the even simpler notion of a 'collision of cultures' (i.e. the localised wars in the former USSR). Thus those initial generic (Western European) ideologies of nationalism which resulted in an emphasis on homogeneity as stability against the reality of heterogeneity (Armstrong 1982) are no longer valid or acceptable in the light of the rising nationalisms around the world.

The former Yugoslavia is no exception. First the civil unrest and later the war were addressed in the same manner, including the consistent and constant equation of all problems with geographically bound territories (see Mlinar 1992a). This only seemed to reinforce the arguments of some theorists of nationalism (i.e. Gellner 1983; Smith 1988; Hobsbawn 1990) that an implicit interpretation of ethnicity is largely a matter of territorial belonging. The disintegration of Yugoslavia and the war enacted there are also seen as a result of a failure of 'ethnic homogenization under Communist rule [and a failure] to deliver on its promise of common proletarian culture or transnational identity' (Bugajski 1993: 31). This in turn raises alarm in nation states formed by and from diverse ethnic communities such as Canada or Australia. There the fear is of a 'multicultural mayhem' which would be a danger to the proposed cultural pluralism, or as it is called in Australia 'multicultural policy'. As has already been mentioned, Glenda Sluga (1993: 91) warned of the danger that the conflict in the former Yugoslavia could be used by opportunists in Australia to represent all that is politically and culturally dangerous. This is not as in politically contrived nationalisms, but in the multicultural state. Similarly, Stuart Hall asserts:

> Lest we think that this kind of ethnic absolutism is restricted to the Balkans – which Western Europeans have always thought unfit to govern themselves – we must remember that versions of it are alive and well in the old 'modern' nation states, especially in the wake of the multicultural diversity which the dislocations of globalization are pushing along.

(Hall 1993: 356)

This fear of a revival of nationalism (always in its connotations of the ugliness of Hitler's Germany) is based on the remote possibility of ethnic consciousness rising beyond the desired 'symbolic' level of ethnic identification, or 'symbolic ethnicity' (Krizek and Stempien 1990), which is frequently addressed as 'standardised diversity' (Meyrowitz and Maguire 1993) or 'prescribed "otherness"' (Ang 1992/1993: 12).

The fear may be real, but it may also be misdirected. What has happened and is happening in Eastern Europe (especially in the former Yugoslavia) is the result of historically specific and unique conditions related to the evaporation of the one-party system of state (without provision of any other workable system), which has opened the floodgates for a revival of ethnic consciousness and a resurgence of national and all other kinds of self-assertion. The search for new cultural identities that would replace the state-provided and institutionally embedded identities based on either 'proletarian' or other potential collective points of identification, is still going on. Lacking direction and leadership and locked into the larger search for postmodern identity these people turn towards re-discovering their cultural past, and once they have accessed it they turn it into their cultural present and future. Or as Hall puts it:

> [M]any of the new nationalisms are busy trying, often on the basis of extremely dubious myths of origin and other spurious claims, to produce a purified 'folk' and to play the highly dangerous game of 'ethnic cleansing' – to use the *charming phrase* [my emphasis] which the Serbs have returned to the postmodern vocabulary. Here, real dislocated histories and hybridized ethnicities of Europe, which have been made and remade across the tortured and violent history of Europe's march to modernity are subsumed by some essentialist conception of national identity, by the surreptitious return to tradition – often of the 'invented' kind, as Hobsbawm and Ranger define it – which recasts cultural identity as an unfolding essence, moving apparently without change, from past to future.
>
> (Hall 1993: 356)

And it is the media, especially the audio-visual media, which by providing an instantaneous source of referential points, emerge at the forefront of the process of self-assertion, individual and collective.[11]

The globalisation of the media flow and the 'democratic' revolutions in the former Communist countries have coincided with the internationalisation (in ownership) of the large media production companies, for example: Sony buying MGM, Rupert Murdoch establishing SKY Satellite Network and buying FOX (but flopping with Asian STAR satellite channel) and so on. However, the American entertainment industry is still the most productive and most successful in the world.[12] It rests on its film and television production backed up by the production and promotion of popular culture consumer items by the same multinationals that are involved in the manufacture and sale of media technology and equipment (cf. O'Regan 1992). Since the fundamental law of commercial success for media products is that they be designed to appeal to the largest possible audience, the opening of the former Eastern bloc for the uninhibited flow, of not only consumer items but also information products, turned out to be an added bonus in the victory of democracy over Communism.

There is an almost insatiable hunger for American entertainment in the countries that have recently joined in the consumption of Western (read American) popular culture. The endless reruns of television series, soap operas and old movies is not a characteristic only of broadcast television services of the former Eastern Europe. (Most of the television stations find the new television productions too expensive, and opt to buy the cheaper, older television shows and films.) Old films and serials largely occupy the schedules of the satellite television programmes available on ASTRA and other European satellite systems which can be received in the northern hemisphere (cf. Schröder 1992). However, the channels of satellite television that are still not encrypted or scrambled are channels that carry the reruns of such 1960s and 1970s shows as *Bonanza, The Brady Bunch* or *Remington Steele*. The encrypted or scrambled movie channels such as SKY Movies provide a fare of newer releases of feature films, and often offer a 'free access' to a 'classic movie' channel with every subscription. There is an increase in the number of satellite television channels based in south-east Europe and they all carry endless reruns of American movies and television series.[13] Since the influence of the ever-growing number of satellite television channels is yet to be researched, it will suffice to say that VCRs and satellite television equipment are still regarded as status symbols in most of the countries of the former Communist bloc.[14]

The importance of the free flow of American and other Western television programmes worldwide cannot be exaggerated (cf. Schou 1992). The newly democratised countries of the former Eastern bloc are passing through a stage of accelerated acculturation into the television culture of the West through watching the endless reruns of mainly American programmes (as old as the early 1960s such as *Father Knows Best* and the original *Star Trek*), which in their time influenced the formation of a distinct 'public', later called 'popular culture' in America (Meyrowitz and Maguire 1993). The audiences of the former monolithic 'other' (the Communists) *vis-à-vis* the source of these programmes (the United States) are quickly learning the language and vocabulary that it took the West at least fifty years to create, absorbing the imagined and simulated realities that they rightly perceive as being deliberately denied them for so long. (The next *Star Trek* convention to be held in Bucharest or Moscow – why not?)

In the meantime, broadcast television in these countries, for example in the states of the former Yugoslavia, is still largely regulated by the state. The state does this in the hope that it will retain the same homogenising and thus hegemonic power over its audiences that the centralised former Yugoslav Television system used to exert (see Golubović 1983). Even though the television service was among the first institutions of the newly formed nation states (of Slovenia, Croatia, Serbia, Macedonia, Bosnia and Herzegovina) to be renamed and reconstituted as national television (e.g. TV Zagreb, now HTV, or RTV Skopje, now MTV – Macedonian TV), the model of centralised broadcasting and television as an instrument and mouthpiece for the current political systems has been largely followed, not only in Yugoslavia but in most of the countries of Eastern Europe. The isolated and largely unsuccessful attempts to create a commercial television in Croatia could be seen as due as much to insufficient capital investment and know-how as to lack of audience interest. While the insufficient capital investment is a direct result of the war as well as the large competition for foreign aid and investment, with other countries from the former Eastern bloc the lack of audience interest is most probably caused by the ready availability of access to satellite television, which is still largely unregulated by the state.

I have inadequate evidence to permit any further assertions about the influence of the 'free flow of information' caused by the demise of communism and the impact that it has on the audiences in Croatia. But what I can argue in the case of HTV is that it is the old mass-élite dichotomy that becomes evident once again in HTV's retention of the state-owned and state-regulated television format. Let me explain. Apart from furthering the ideological and political goals of the national party in power (HDZ), it is the higher-income, educated stratum of Croatian society (the one not so affected by the war) that tends to be more sensitive to the creation of television with a high degree of local (Croatian) flavour, searching for inspiration in the history of Croatian culture and insisting on a localised agenda. Those concerned with the health and viability of the new-found (and largely re-invented) Croatian national culture are the middle and highbrow audiences of the upper-class cosmopolitans who are already literate in the cosmopolitan global culture, but look towards the local for the cultural future of Croatia, eager to foster and reinforce the nationalist ideologies of the present.

For the rest of the population, the one that strongly upholds the democratic right to the freedom of information and full access to its global flow, there are two options left. The first one is to gain access to satellite television. Indeed the satellite television craze is endemic in Croatia – despite the fact that Italian and Austrian television have been present in Croatia for as long as twenty years, being able to be 'picked up' by powerful television antennae (due to their close geographic proximity). The second option is the use of VCR. By putting the two technologies together, the VCR and the satellite dish, localised (and mainly illegal) 'cable' television circuits are built. Thus not only individuals but also suburbs and whole previously geographically isolated areas have established a form of 'narrowcasting' satellite television through an unauthorised reception of the satellite television channels, many of which are meant to be available to bona fide subscribers.[15]

The result of all this is a change not only in the mediascape of Croatia but what it entails. There was a strange, almost surreal mixture of broadcast television (3 channels) bringing to audiences reports from the war and concerns about the economy and other institutional functions of the Croatian state (including live broadcasts of sessions of the Croatian Parliament) enriched with reports about the state of the war as reported on CNN and SKY News or BBC.

This exposure to global electronic offerings created a situation in which it was extremely, and increasingly, difficult to comprehend the reality of the tragic war unfolding on the doorsteps of, and in, Croatia, making the war often appear distant and almost unreal. The conditions of the war which directly or indirectly affected everyone in Croatia were effectively masked on two levels: first by the concerns and priorities of HTV (broadcast television) and other Croatian media to promote Croatian culture and the 'Croatian cause' – meaning that news and other information seen as unfavourable to the state or politically incorrect were often withheld from the Croatian audiences (thus affecting the freedom of the press). The second level on which the war often got subordinated was in ordinary people's pursuit of everyday life influenced by approximately the same concerns as those of the rest of recession-ridden Europe (provided there are no air-raid warnings or direct shelling, of course).

As for the concentrated doses of war reporting which we saw functioning via VCR in the diaspora, they were non-existent in such condensed and vile forms in Croatia, but were part of the regular news and current affair programmes on HTV. On the other hand, the enhanced war propaganda that existed at the inception of the war has taken on a much more subdued form, allowing the population (or at least those who have the means) to resume a form of everyday life – although that too is of course dictated by the unfolding of the war itself. But watching the war from 'afar' (as in my case), it was always surprising to find that, in spite of the war, life goes on.

THE STRANGE CASE OF *SANTA BARBARA*

Thus, after finishing my fieldwork with Croatian audiences in Perth and witnessing the ways in which the Croatian community lived day in, day out with the horrors of the war (brought to them on video tapes) and organised their entire lives around the unfolding of the war in the homeland (even if only for a short period), I was angry, disappointed but not in the least surprised, that on a 'Christmas holiday home' in 1992 most of the people I visited wanted to talk not about the war, but either about leaving the country or about the American soap opera *Santa Barbara*, currently running on HTV. (This soap is one of the longest-running ones in the United States and is shown worldwide.) Most of those talking about the soap presumed that, coming from Australia, I should have an advanced knowledge of the unfolding plot, and inquired about the outcome of several parallel stories told in the television serial. I soon learned that it was not wise to visit friends in Zagreb between 6.30 p.m. and 7.00 p.m., since *Santa Barbara* had similar effects on Croatian audiences to those described in the substantial body of work on soap operas (of which Ien Ang's *Watching Dallas*, (1985) is perhaps the best known; see also e.g. Brundson 1981; Hobson 1982). For example, the previous night's development of the story was discussed at the work place, on streets, or in the queues for refugee cheques. The print media in Croatia went so far that in the middle of war reporting, concerns with black markets, international news and sports, the weekly *Globus*, (a Croatian independent publication with a large readership) featured a two-page photo-strip spread in its television-guide showing a day-to-day summary of *Santa Barbara*'s unfolding plots, just in case one missed an episode. I was to learn in late 1993, from M.M.'s cousin who came to visit Australia from the Dalmatian port-city of Split, that *Santa Barbara* was just as popular there. Moreover, a popular revolt was caused when electricity cuts (which were frequent during the war) prevented part of the population from watching *Santa Barbara*. Under the pressure of public demand, broadcasts of *Santa Barbara* were delayed usually until late evening (with different times for different regions) in order to accommodate the electricity cuts and allow the audiences to watch the programme in spite of them.

The multiple and contradictory social realities of Croatia today make it feel like a place where almost anything is acceptable. Everyday life was seemingly normal, but to me, in late 1992, it appeared to exist only in the negative. It was not only the fact that *Santa Barbara* was more important than Sarajevo: I understood later that it was the routinisation of death and dying that was so terrifying. Having a dinner with my family in Zagreb while the television news showed bodies with plucked-out eyes and gaping wounds lying in ditches while soldiers stood over them with still warm guns in their hands, was not quite the same as watching videos of similar scenes in Perth in Australia. In Zagreb we were only 20 kilometres from the front line. In Perth the contradiction of normality that the community was functioning in by taking part in day-to-day living was somehow acceptable and understandable. After all, we were 20,000 kilometres away from it all. Here, at home, it was like an aberration. Everyone was expected to return to normative peacetime sobriety and function like members of civil society, while just on the outskirts of the town the war was raging on.

While the social and personal spaces of the Croatian community in Perth were filled with rumours of 'yet another atrocity' or whisperings of 'so and so' losing a member of family 'at home', my family and friends at home appeared to be concerned with the imaginary financial losses and love affairs of the fictional family which is the main focus of *Santa Barbara*. After my initial feelings of outrage and anger it became obvious that the routinised manner of acceptance of the war (and the restructuring of everyday life that came with it) was only part of an anxious and ontological insecurity about possible identification with the people whose lives and deaths were featuring on HTV day in day, out, in the hope that 'It will not happen to us.'[16]

It is evident, then, that the remoteness, a distance both geographical and cultural, of the Croatian diaspora in Perth from everyday life in Croatia produced a very different and unique condition for following the changes in the homeland, mainly through the VCR. It is also obvious that the conditions of available mediascape in Croatia itself are determined by the potent forces of the globalised mediascape modified by the local conditions under which the local/global operates (see Morley 1992: 270–89). These conditions have given rise to an information climate in Croatia that is not very different from the rest of Europe, even though the conditions of other facets of everyday living are very different indeed. I have shown earlier that, while other electronic and digital media such as computers (where computer-generated graphics can be manipulated to generate any desired symbol) are conceived and understood as such, as abstract computer-generated symbols, with VCR it is different, because 'video can act immediately on the objects and people around us', providing us with symbols which are the result of 'direct intervention in life' and video – like photography – offers more than just an inert facsimile of the object (Armes 1988: 213). It reactivates the image and sound, every time we turn the VCR on, reproducing the reality captured *ad infinitum*.

For the audiences in this research, this in turn had both domestic and international implications, since the domestic is allowed to become trans-national by the circulation of the video tapes taped from HTV in the Croatian diaspora worldwide, making the local available globally, while the global in Croatia itself has become part of the accepted conditions of everyday life. Thus the use of VCR in Perth, Western Australia can be seen as essentially transnational in character, and yet its users have little percep-tion of its 'international' functions, in so far as the institutionalised voices of power from Croatian political centres are confused with the video tapes such as those from Opuzen TV or even with the family-album type videos.

Let me explain. A clear distinction needs to be made here between the *transnational* flow of information (information and entertainment) crossing national boundaries without the canonisation of official trade and foreign policies of the countries in question and the *international* flow of informa-tion. This is information which is seen as institutionally correct and is cre-ated by the 'legitimate' media, usually representing the official stances of the respective governments towards each other. For example, the information about the war in Croatia and Bosnia as seen on television (or time-shifted and seen on VCR) was usually perceived by Croatian audiences in Perth as expressing the official line of the Australian government towards the war and Croatia. Thus the television news and current affairs programmes as well as documentaries broadcast on Australian television, especially on ABC and on SBS, were perceived as 'approved' voices. This was in contrast to the *transnational* information obtained from the video tapes, which, because they owed so much to the 'truth value' of the VCR, were perceived as representing the 'real' situation in the homeland. There is an immense difference between these two categories, which has a localising, ghettoising and disempowering effect on the ethnic community itself, members of which often argue that 'the Australian media are biased against Croatians'. (It should be noted that Serbs and Greeks and others also think the media are biased against *them*.)

However, what is seen on broadcast television in Australia belongs to the larger global (public) discourse of international television. It does not necessarily include the view of the Australian government, but often reflects the views of the American or British governments respectively, depending on which world news service has been tapped into (e.g. ITN, WTN, CNN, BBC, ABC-US). Because of the comparatively negligible reporting by Australian foreign correspondents and documentary producers on issues other than 'immediate war reporting' and an occasional 'human interest story', the Australian media have relied almost exclusively on the purchase of packaged news from international news corporations, thus allowing the voices heard and belonging to America or Britain to be equated with the Australian stance towards the unfolding war. It is no surprise that all the communities formed from the former Yugoslav community tend to consider the Australian media (in reporting on former Yugoslavia), as one of my informants put it, as 'impotent'. Consequently the use of the VCR has enabled the 'Croatian' to function as 'local' in Australia, at first causing crises in the cultural identity formation and later resulting in a restructuration of the Croatian diaspora in Australia.

From the perspectives of the issues addressed in this study, the most intriguing aspect of the local–global dichotomy and the reliance of ethnic audiences on the VCR for information from their homeland is their hunger for information about the international stance towards the ongoing war and possible solutions to it. This was sought from Australian broadcast television (and print media) and also from the delayed telecasts of the American news and current affairs of the American Broadcasting Corporation (ABC-US) and NBC networks. It showed an awareness among the ethnic audience of the existing – or ascribed – sources of globalised power. And these sources of power were often seen as beyond the reach of the community, given its localised and polarised existence within the multicultural Australian society. There is also an awareness of the existence of an ethnic cultural self functioning inside the globalised culture; a form of 'postmodern ethnicity' (Ang 1992/1993: 14). Perhaps this helps explain how the disastrous effects of ethnic polarisation which are most often seen as the cause of the monstrous and horrific war in former Yugoslavia have had a limited effect on its diasporas in Australia. However, the ethnic polarisation inside the former Yugoslav community in Western Australia (and Australia overall) has had its impacts and effects – they are simply different and separate from those of the homeland.

The reasons behind this difference are in the specific ethnic audience dynamics which could be seen as a result of: first, the balanced and seem-ingly uncommitted (and often distanced) approach by the Australian media towards the reporting of the war from Croatia and Bosnia, which has cre-ated a media climate allowing for an unobstructed flow of information through unofficial channels providing the community with desired informa-tion. Second, the almost complete ignorance on the part of Australian in-stitutions about the circulation of the largely illegal video tapes was taken as an attitude of tolerance, allowing communities to carry out internal restruc-turation more or less undisturbed and with minimal interference from state institutions. And third, the timid and unadventurous habits of the com-mercial television networks catering to the parochial tastes of 'imagined' mainstream audiences created a space inside which ethnic video could operate undisturbed and unchallenged. These three strategies prevented the possible explosive polarisation of ethnic groups from former Yugoslavia in Australia from happening (beyond isolated violent incidents).

A strategically acceptable and useful outlet for ethnic tensions has been tolerated on the radio-waves, especially within the ethnic radio station broadcasting in Croatian, Serbian and Macedonian. Coming under a pan-ethnic umbrella (of Australian multicultural policies) these could easily be policed. Tensions could also be kept at bay by endless civil law suits filed constantly against each other. Still, the impact of what is available 'on air' has determined how much information was sought from the sources outside the available media and information systems in Australia.

It is also important to note that the most feverish hunt for information by Croatian audiences took place when official relationships on insti-tutional levels were absent. This was the stage when Australia had not yet recognised the Croatian state officially, and had largely given up on the existing relations with the disintegrating and corrupt Yugoslav state. At this time the Australian media were locked into the uneasy task of presenting the official US or European Community (now European Union) line, and this rested uneasily with Croatian audiences. This was also the time of a major shift in the viewing habits of the Croatian audience. They turned towards an almost total substitution of broadcast programmes with video tapes from home and time-shifted selection of news from Australian television.

MAKING IT OFFICIAL

In this study we have caught glimpses of an ethnic audience embedded in a host culture which seems to have responded with calculated ambivalence towards the restructuring of segments of its population along polarised ethnic lines imported from the respective homelands. In the process another, sometimes publicly submerged, side of Australian multicultural policy sur-faced: namely, that this was a policy just as much aimed at managing interethnic conflict as it was at smoothing the connection between the ethnic culture and the host Australian culture.

Under such conditions of ambivalence, direct propaganda from Croatia and Serbia was permitted to circulate freely in their diasporas, leaving the diasporas to negotiate their future existence within the diverse Australian society, but using the information corridors provided outside that same society. To an extent this effectively quarantined the ethnic conflict. If this tended to infantalise the communities as being 'at it again', it also benefited each in that the Australian state and public did not have to choose between either (Croat or Serb); to declare one the victim and the other the aggressor. Given the ongoing nature of the war in Croatia and Bosnia, and Australian incapacity to influence the conduct of the war and peace negotiations, this was doubly propitious for these communities. The apparent Australian indifference as to victim or assailant opened the space for lobbying for and obtaining Croatian, Serbian and Muslim intakes as part of Australia's humanitarian and refugee programme. Soon, Australia's refugee and humanitarian intakes became dominated by people from the former Yugoslavia, replacing the dominance for the last fifteen years of the intake of Indo-Chinese refugees.

In the meantime, once official diplomatic ties with Croatia were established, international relations between the two countries have allowed the creation of an official Australian stance towards Croatia. This allowed the revival of patterns of information dissemination which accord primarily with the mutual interests of the governments involved, not only in fostering good international relations, but also in strengthening economic and cultural ties. The continuous tendency to overlook the use of VCR for providing information (and entertainment) from illegal or semi-legal sources could always be seen as more or less calculated non-interference with the transfer of information. This stems from a deeply ingrained terror of interference with freedom of speech as a basic human right, enabling Australia to sustain its reputation as a 'human rights champion'. In this process, breaches of international copyright laws continue to be easily overlooked. In the Croatian case these will be enforced in Australia only when there is Croatian and Croatian–Australian business pressure for them to be so, thus following a pattern representative of other (e.g. Italian) Australian ethnic communities; there will be a gradual move from informal and semi-legal markets and cultural structures towards more transparent and formal business and culture interconnections between diaspora and homeland and between ethnic community and host society, with this transition being managed largely according to the community/diaspora/homeland's own timetable.

The effectiveness of Australian policies – or absence of policies – regarding the supply of information to the Croatian diaspora during the war in their homeland, whether accidental or intentional, does not make them less transparent. Many influential Australians were concerned, and this was evident in the behaviour of individual politicians such as Paul Filing, MP, who actively engaged with the interests of their constituents in supporting the ideological drive and concerns of – in this instance – the Croatian community, at a time when the official stance of the Australian government was largely non-committal (Filing 1991).

Nevertheless, the major consequences of the naturalisation of the newly found ethnic cultural identities will surface in all their ugliness at times when, inevitably, a disagreement occurs on any level, domestic or communal, between friends or between communities. The newly produced and already deeply set ethnic differentiation is more likely than not to influence the future smooth development of harmonious living within the policy of 'unity in diversity'. It will do so on the most basic individual levels, and the formerly accepted intermarriages, business associations and simple friendships between, for example, Serbs and Croats are now seen as completely unacceptable. Australian multicultural policy becomes in this context a coercive instrument stipulating minimal levels of courtesy and comportment towards hated 'others' pushing for some self-regulated limits to the public and interpersonal expression of inter-ethnic division.

Such a situation is not new to Australia. The larger history of the world with its wars, famines and migration movements has helped to shape Australia's past and future. Every war in Europe and in Asia (thinking here mostly about the two World Wars, and the wars in Vietnam and Cambodia) has directly brought waves of refugees and migrants to Australia. As a consequence of this, Australia is made up of numerous ethnic fragments and this is a direct result of Australia being one of the few remaining countries seen traditionally as 'migrant countries'. (The others are Canada and to some extent the United States.) Under such conditions each of the new wave of migrants carries with them recent cultural memories different from those functioning in the fragments of the same nations already in Australia. As a result tensions and rivalries emerge not only between 'traditional' rival groups such as Serbs and Croats, but also among the groups of the same ethnic origin. The emerging situation of renewed interest and constant pressure on Australia, not only from former Yugoslavia but from all the 'trouble spots' (such as the countries of former Eastern Europe and Pakistan, China, India, etc.) suggests an emerging situation comparable only to the late 1940s. Then, as now, intercommunal frictions and antagonisms ran deep, encouraging the development of encapsulated communities. At the same time, Australia offers an alternative solution to encapsulation, a possibility to escape from ethnicity into a mainstream of emergent Australian national identity and culture.

Just as some second-generation Croats, Serbs, Macedonians and others opted out of the close ties with the core of their ethnic communities, so will others. By emphasising their Australian identity and lifestyles and by marrying outside the community of their ancestors, such people are becoming the foundation of a new and emerging postmodern national identity which allows for simultaneous existence of both an ethnic and an Australian self. This is partly made possible by the technological developments of information networks providing a media and information climate favouring the ways which allow for the simultaneous existence of self as Croatian or Macedonian in Australia; as well as always remaining negotiable for becoming someone or something else.

THERE IS NO REWIND BUTTON
ON THE BETAMAX OF LIFE

The above dictum is attributed to Nam Jun Paik, the well-known Korean video artist who bought the first commercially available video cassette recorder in New York in 1965. It is more than appropriate as a form of non-conclusion to this work, since like a video viewer with a remote control in hand, I have been moving backwards and forwards in search of some answers. This has resulted in a somewhat convoluted description of equally convoluted research. And I can only hope that in this study I have managed to claim a speaking position not only for myself but more importantly for all those who were, like me, watching from afar the 'world they knew' falling apart.[17]

NOTES

1 A SILENT REVOLUTION

1 'Video cassette recorder' and 'VCR' and 'video cassette' and 'video tape' are used interchangeably throughout this work. The term 'videographic apparatus' is taken from Lili Berko (1989) and refers to all technological advances introduced such as modem, etc.

2 The point of entry into public use by VCR is debatable. For example: Stuart Marshall (1979: 109) in 'Video: technology and practice' writes: 'In 1965 the Sony Corporation released the portapak – a portable camera/recorder unit – into the consumer market. The Korean artist Nam Jun Paik purchased the first machine available in New York. This date has come to figure strongly in any history of the artist's use of video and the reasons for its celebration are fairly obvious.' Other authors like Aaron Foisi Nmungwun (1989) indicate 1962 as the year in which a 'portable video tape recording machine' was introduced (*ibid.*: 187). Others like Eugene Secunda (1990) take the date of public introduction of VCR as far back as 'April, 12 1956' (*ibid.*: 9).

3 Amateur film cameras with 8 mm and super 8 film were available in the late 1970s and early 1980s but their uptake was limited.

4 Nmungwun (1989: 269) shows that 'three out of four home VCR buyers choose VHS' over other types of video hardware. He also includes in his book a useful glossary of terminology regarding VCR technology (*ibid.*: 264–9).

5 It was Eric Michaels who contributed most to the understanding of the uses of television and video by Australian Aborigines. A partial guide to his work can be found in: 'Eric Michaels: a practical guide to his written work', *Continuum* 3,2 (1990: 226–8). The guide was compiled by Jay Ruby and Tom O'Regan. Articles by Jay Ruby (*ibid.*: 32–52), Ron Burnett (*ibid.*: 119–39) and especially by Tom O'Regan (1990) represent discussions of Michaels' work that are relevant to this work.

6 Since this was written the Canadian Broadcasting Corporation (CBC) has created an official Inuit television via satellite which will broadcast both in English and in Inuit languages.

7 This is also changing, i.e. the Hong Kong based STAR satellite channel is now available in Malaysia. The Malay government sees this 'as a danger of Westernisation', but can do little or nothing about already existing satellite dishes that crowd the Malay skylines.

8 Nmungwun (1989) has given a useful comparative overview of the available video technology up to 1989. However, the international markets are flooded with 'new' improved and even 'simpler' video equipment almost on a daily basis. There has

also been a proliferation of very inexpensive pre-recorded video tapes for some time now, all of which might make the concerns of video research in the 1980s appear archaic.

9 For example, social historians like Paddy Scannell and David Cardiff (1991) have attempted to show the importance of media technologies in the process of 'putting the nation together', supporting their proposals through an investigation of BBC policy and programming rather than of audiences' reception of the programmes. This perhaps accounts for their overestimation of the national unity of Great Britain (e.g. Irish, Welsh, Scottish, etc.).

10 Eco's formulation is distinct from a psychological theory of selective perception, where each individual is seen to be making his or her private readings.

11 Paul Virilio in his *Speed and Politics* (1986) and in his joint work with Sylvere Lotringer *Pure War* (1983) examines the relationship technology–time–speed–war. But it was not possible to apply their theoretical proposals in this discussion since it was effectively hijacked by the real war in the former Yugoslavia.

12 I use Lili Berko's (1989) term 'videographic apparatus' frequently and at times differently, thus not always acknowledging its source.

13 The newest 'fad' in the United States is the production of television shows based on 'documenting' the lives and problems of young people randomly housed together.

14 Thirty foreign journalists had been killed and fifty-six wounded in the war in the former Yugoslavia by the end of 1992.

15 Geoffrey Batchen (1993: 83), outlining the capacity of optical technology, cites Oliver Wendell Holmes (1859), 'The stereoscope and the stereograph', and describes the stereograph as (re)producing different spaces which the observer simultaneously inhabits in 'a dream-like exaltation in which we seem to leave the body behind us and sail away into one strange scene after another, like dis-embodied spirits'.

16 There is a proliferation of accounts (written and other) regarding the demise of the USSR and Communism and the resulting raging conflicts in the former USSR and in former Yugoslavia. Friends and colleagues aware of the area of my research used to overwhelm me with references to new books and articles regarding the topic, on a daily basis. I will mention but one book on the USSR which I had time to engage with. It is a collection of essays edited by Alexander J. Motyl (1992) titled *The Post-Soviet Nations: Perspectives on the Demise of the USSR* which proved to be somewhat of a disappointment since it is not at all about 'Post-Soviet Nations' but rather offers a perspective of the late Gorbachev era. The body of works on the former Yugoslavia is more relevant to this work and I will refer to them in the text.

17 There is a large body of literature on nationalism in German that I am not familiar with. In addition, the revival of interest by academia in issues of ethnicity, race and nationalism has produced a vast number of re-examination of relevant theor-ies, producing some interesting if not always new proposals. Julia Kristeva's (1993) *Nations without Nationalism* addresses the question from quite another perspec-tive, that of psychoanalysis and linguistics. Kristeva writes about people's feeling of 'otherness' or 'strangeness'. She argues that when people are confronted with an environment different from their own they tend to withdraw into the familiar – into their ethnic identity. In this way nationalism forms a 'defensive hatred'. Kris-teva at the end of this very personal work appeals for a cosmopolitanism which would transcend today's virulent forms of nationalism. I deeply regret the fact that I had no access to this book earlier, and also regret that I have to relegate an account of her work to a note.

18 Clifford Geertz's (1973: 147) conclusions on the cultural production of religious traditions of Java might seem far removed from a discussion of the formation of ethnic identity, but more recent arguments on the formation of cultural identity in diaspora such as by Ien Ang (1992/1993), in which she addresses the cultural production of Chinese diaspora as 'productive syncretism' (*ibid.*: 13), bear a resemblance to Geertz's 'balanced syncretism' in more than one way.

19 This classification is based on an early version of the unpublished paper 'Marginal audiences' (1991), that was written jointly with Tom O'Regan. Part of that paper was later incorporated as a chapter in *Australian Television Culture* (O'Regan 1993) under the title 'SBS-television: a television service' (O'Regan and Kolar-Panov 1993b).

20 For a full discussion of those changes see David Morley and Kevin Robins, *Spaces of Identity: Global Media, Electronic Landscapes and Cultural Boundaries* (1995).

2 THE CULTURAL FUNCTIONS OF VIDEO

1 The number of NES population estimated at 5 per cent is debatable, since the NES and NESB population is sometimes shown together in official records. Thus the figure above includes only non-Australian born NES population. For further information on Australia, see Ian Castles (1988) *Overseas Born Australians* and various reports such as 'Ethnicity-related Data for Local Government Areas in Western Australia' (1988). For demographic information on Yugoslav migrants see Pink (1992).

2 There is a difference between NES and NESB audiences. NES refers to non-English-speaking born, population as used in Australian official statistical records. For the purposes of clarity, I will use NES for non-English-speaking born, category and NESB for non-English speaking-background, people, which includes several generations of migrants who identify themselves as such. It is interesting to note that Western Australia had a larger population of NES-born migrants (7.4 per cent) than other Australian states. See Australian Bureau of Immigration Research (1986a), *Community Profiles: Non-English Speaking Born*.

3 I am drawing here mainly on personal experience, since I either was present at such negotiation in the role of interpreter, or have translated official documents regarding cultural exchanges between the former Yugoslavia and countries such as Australia, Canada, the United States, etc.

4 The statistics on refugee intake in Australia indicate a drastic shift as to the country of origin. For example in 1990–1 the number of refugees from former Yugoslavia was *zero (0)* or *0.0*, in 1991–2 it was already 337 or 4.7 per cent (of total refugee intake to Australia), while in 1992–3 it was already 3,133 or 28.6 per cent of the total intake. It is by far the greatest intake, comparable only to the number of refugees from Vietnam in 1990–1, which was 3,136. (*Immigration Update June Quarter 1993*, Australian Bureau of Immigration and Population Research 1993: 29).

5 Jurij Lotman (1990) uses the term 'creolised' for cultures changed under conditions arising from their encounter with and influences from other cultures. However, Umberto Eco in his Introduction to Lotman (1990b: xii) signals the interchangeability of the terms 'hybrid' and 'creolisation'. Or as Eco puts it: 'Lotman understood clearly that the multiplicity in codes in a given culture gives rise to contrast and hybrids, or "creolization"'.

6 On the demographic composition of these suburbs see *Perth Social Atlas* (ABS 1993).

7 Carnarvon is a small farming community in the northern part of Western Aus-

tralia with a total population of 6,336. There is no available official data on the background of population as regarding Yugoslavia the number given by ABS Census (1986) is under the category of 'Southern European' and is 189 persons, which is 4.7 per cent of population. However, this number is misleading since there are Australian-born members of the Yugoslav community who would declare themselves under the category of Australian. I was a frequent and welcome guest among the large (in Carnarvon terms) 'Slav' population (read Croatian) between 1984 and 1988. On the occasion of my visits it was considered a special treat to organise 'video evenings' with the screening of variety video tapes from our common homeland, under the assumption that my nostalgia was comparable to theirs. The data on Carnarvon used throughout this work belong to an abandoned research project, which after it was compiled was shelved. This was due to the content which included some criticisms of the cultural policies of the Yugoslav state regarding the diaspora. This was not allowed at the time concerned (1986), since my official position as a senior diplomat's wife required uncompromised loyalty to the Yugoslav state which my husband was representing.

8　I call such tapes 'video albums' since their function and content is similar but not the same as photo albums. The descriptions given by Patricia Holland (1991) of the social functions of snapshots and photo albums are closest to the intended meaning of my term 'video album'.

9　After the unmatched popularity of the series *Moje Malo Misto*, the sequel *Velo Misto* was used to accentuate the role of 'brotherhood and unity' basing it on the introduction of positive characters in the serial. These were of different nationalities (different from Croatian) and often dominated some episodes in the roles of partisans who freed the city of Split from its Nazi occupiers.

10　For the organisation and functioning of Yugoslav Radio Television – JRT – and its state and regional centres, see Tomislav Golubović (1983).

11　Since this was written, Macedonia has been involved in a dispute about its name and is often referred to as Former Yugoslav Republic of Macedonia (FYROM), see Loring M. Danforth: 'Nationalist conflicts in a transnational world: Greeks and Macedonians at the conference for security and co-operation in Europe' (1995).

12　The term 'video letter' has been utilised by others, e.g. Tom O'Regan (1990: 82). However, it has not been defined. Video letters as used here signifies a video tape which is a mixture of a personal letter and snapshots with the added effect of an oral communication. This form of personal communication is partly comparable to the video-phone with the exception that the immediacy of the telephone is not present. Science fiction (novels and films) has utilised this form, first by descriptions of either video letters left by the deceased as messages to friends and family or as audio-visual history of whole civilisations. Whichever is the case, the fascination with audio-visual communication remains, as shown by film and television productions which nowadays inevitably include some form of reference to video.

13　For the influence of the Macedonian Orthodox Church as a guardian of Macedonian culture, see Done Ilievski (1973) *The Macedonian Orthodox Church*.

14　I am grateful to my friend, Mr Sam Christie, for allowing me to include this account of his experience.

15　The average income of the Yugoslav population is shown by ABS Census (1986) as higher than the average Australian income. But the purchase of such equipment as video cameras and VCRs usually made a dent in the family budget of migrants.

16　These are well-organised summer schools and language seminars run by both the *Matica Iseljenika Hrvatske* (Croatian Migrant Association) and the *Makedonska Matica Na Iselenicite* (Macedonian Migrant Association). These summer schools and seminars are funded by the respective governments.

17 This lack of of exchange of Greek films and videos in the wider Macedonian community is most probably due to the fact that any display of 'Greekness' among Macedonians in Perth is still regarded as 'being a traitor' to one's own heritage.

18 This estimate is taken from unofficial statistics of the communities themselves. There is hardly any specific demographic or other statistical data from official sources outside the all-inclusive category of 'Yugoslav' migrant which effectively excludes most Aegean Macedonians and part of the population declaring themselves as Croatian. Since the official records rely for their data on country of birth, people of Macedonian and Croatian descent born elsewhere are also left out.

19 At approximately the same time, with increased activity on the part of the Croatian government led to the Croatian immigrants being referred to as 'diaspora'. This might be only a shift reflecting the changes in terms of reference worldwide, but I interpret this shift as giving more importance to Croatians living outside Croatia in order to solicit their support.

20 Aleksandar Aleksiev (1976: 13) argues that Kostadin is afraid because he has seen men like his father leaving the village and simply never returning home, dying in an unknown land.

21 There are discussions among literary historians about the authenticity of Panov's songs in the play but this is not our concern here.

22 Tome Sazdov (1987: 18), in the conclusion to his discussion of the history of the Macedonian folk lyric, concludes with regret that there has not been 'enough work done' such as 'scholarly analysis of Macedonian folk poetry', and that it still lacks 'detailed and specialized studies'. I would add that there is an equal absence of research on the influence of folk songs and folk music especially in the form of 'video spots' and their influence on the development and maintenance of culture, especially in terms of fragments of ethnic culture worldwide or research on ethnic migrant fragments as (marginal) specific audiences.

3 CLAIMING A CULTURAL SPACE

1 Most of the chronological data for this account of the history of ethnic clubs are from non-classified reports to the former Ministry for Foreign Affairs of former Yugoslavia; however, the discussion is based on my own experiences, and countless informal gatherings in these clubs.

2 These numbers were provided at a meeting with the Carnarvon Yugoslav Club officials. The Yugoslav community in Carnarvon is of extreme importance to this study since the seeds of my interest in the relationship of technology, especially VCR and satellite technology, were sown in the fertile soil of the Gascoyne estuary.

3 The formation and the development of Macedonian clubs and societies, together with strategies to preserve Macedonian culture have been described by Peter Hill (1989) in his account of the Macedonian ethnic community in Australia. This is an important bibliographic source for the present work, particularly since Professor Hill is a native of Perth, Western Australia.

4 There is a large body of literature on the Croatian independent state (NDH) which is often contradictory since it was mainly informed by the Croatian diaspora defending its position or by Serbian writers attacking it, and the rest of the accounts are based on the official stance of the SFRJ.

5 I do not refer to anyone in particular, but rather to the fact that every historian and scholar of nationalism has touched upon the Balkans as a possible trouble point, which was of course justified given the history of the region, hence the term 'Balkanisation'.

6 Up to 213,000 Macedonians were exiled from the Aegean part of Macedonia at this time. The number of 213,000 is quoted by Stardelov, Grozdanov and Ristovski (eds) (1993: 82) from 'Protoporos', *Organo Tu K.K. Makedonias*, 15.V.1946.

4 RE-INVENTING CROATIA

1 For example, Branka Magaš (1993: 314) writes: 'Over the past few years, the Serbian propaganda machine has been trying to create the impression that Serbs were the chief victims of the war and that 700,000 of them were killed by Ustasha [*sic*] concentration camp at Jasenovac (Croatia) alone.' I would like to note that not only the different governments (e.g. Serb, Croatian, etc.) and their spokespeople fabricate numbers, but also respected foreign analysts such as Gregory Copley (the editor-in-chief of *Defense and Foreign Affairs Strategic Policy*) have put out reports that are biased and often based on less than reliable sources (see Copley 1992). In contrast to more sophisticated publications, Serbian publications such as M. Starčević and N. Petković (1991) *Hrvatska '91: Nasiljem i zločinom protiv prava* (Croatia '91: With Violence and Crime Against Rights) are obvious propaganda since they were published by the Military Publishing Centre in Belgrade.

2 Vladimir Propp (1984: 5) observes that: 'Under socialism, folklore loses its specific features as a product of lower strata, since in a socialist society there are neither upper nor lower strata, just people. Folklore indeed becomes *national* property.'

3 Smith (1988: 27) writes: 'In Yugoslavia, the old enmity between Orthodox Serbs and Catholic Croats is, in practice, one of religious community, since language differences are very slight; for all practical purposes, Serbo-Croat represents a unified language which affords no basis for two nationalisms'.

4 I hope the reader will forgive me for adapting or parodying the Latin proverb *Ubi pedes ibi patria*, but I have done so since it seems most appropriate for translation of the Serbian slogan *Gdje Su Srbi Tu Je Srbia* which is translated as 'Where the Serbs are, there is a Serbia'.

5 The propaganda myths these arguments relied on were examined in a report of an independent commission of inquiry established by the Union for Yugoslav Democratic Initiative Belgrade 1990. The report was titled: *Kosovski Čvor: Drešiti Ili Seći?* ('Kosovo Knot: to Undo or to Cut?').

6 The opera was composed by the Croatian composer Ivan Zajc in 1876, in the aftermath of the 'Illyirian revival' (1835–48). See Katičić and Novak (1989: 125–39).

7 I also recall in our literature course in high school memorising lines from Petar Petrović Njegoš, 1952, *Gorski Vijenac* 'The Mountain Wreath', a nineteenth-century poem which proclaims the expulsion and the massacre of Turks as a national duty.

8 The Croatian government, aware of the Australian media situation, has opened a home page and now, in late 1995, has a web site on the World-Wide-Web on the Internet. Besides general information on Croatia there is a daily updated 'News from Croatia', both in Croatian and in English. It will be interesting to see just how much this Internet service will be used by the Croatian diaspora.

9 David Morley (1992: 202) argues that meanings of both texts and technologies should be 'understood as emergent properties of contextualized audience practices'. This is also applicable to VCR.

10 The Split Festival is an annual musical event held in the Dalmatian (Croatian) port-city of Split. Because of its immense popularity in the diaspora the performers often tour the Croatian diasporas, in Australia and Canada and repeat the entire programme of the festival for the audiences abroad. The advertising

sections of *Hrvatski Vjesnik* (Croatian Herald) are the main source of information about both such tours and the availability of new audio-visual products from Croatia.

11 The sum of 3 million dollars is for Australia only, and was quoted to me by the current president of the HDZ in Perth. Even if it sounds an overestimate, my estimate (based on adding up some figures from *Hrvatski Vjesnik* (Croatian Herald)) is that it might be very near to the actual amount.

12 Since this study was completed the war in former Yugoslavia appears to be coming to an end (at least on paper). The Dayton Agreement is maintaining a fragile peace (Joffe 1995: 68). The first and second Krajinas are again under Croatian control. The 'Krajina' in Bosnia is now known as 'Republika Srpska' and is incorporated into Bosnia and Herzegovina, but still aspires towards annexation to Serbia.

13 I will use initials for the principal informants and not full names in order to fulfil the promised confidentiality agreement with my audience. For other viewers quoted in the text I will use V and (A), (B), (C) and so on in the order in which they spoke.

14 The new coat of arms has attached to the base of red and white chequerboard the miniature coat of arms of all the Croatian provinces, while the old one bears at its top a royal crown with the letter 'U' for 'ustaša'. This letter was the cause of a lot of misconceptions about the Croatian 'democratic movement' and caused endless debates in the audiences I was researching, since it was used by the NDH between 1941 and 1945.

15 For the origins of the Croatian coat of arms, see: Eterovich (1978) *Croatian and Dalmatian Coats of Arms*, or more recently Grakalić, (1990) *Hrvatski Grb* (Croatian Coat of Arms).

16 See Adolph Hitler (1992: 595) *Mein Kampf* who wrote: 'We [are] able to imagine a state only to be the living organism of a *Volk*.'

5 EXCUSE ME WHAT IS GENOCIDE?

1 I am using 'common sense' in a Gramscian sense (see Gramsci 1971: 323–36).

2 I have examined the questions of invariant motif and dominant theme in detail in 'The poetic world of Ivan Generalić' (Kolar-Panov 1989).

3 Texts were in Croatian. All translations of text and comments are mine if not indicated otherwise.

4 Radić's comment that the Croatians were embarking on the unification with Serbia 'like drunken geese in a fog' is well known and often cited. Mark Thompson has paraphrased it and used it as the title of the chapter on Croatia in his book, *A Paper House: The Ending of Yugoslavia* (1992). Ch 8: 'The drunken geese of Croatia'.

5 There is a full transcript of the speech in the archives of the Croatian Academy of Arts and Sciences in Zagreb. It does not seem necessary to translate and include it in the text at this point.

6 David Cannadine (1983) has also shown how much of the British 'tradition' surrounding the British monarchy is a recent invention, which only indicates the high success of such campaigns to 'invent tradition'.

7 There have been a number of folklore concerts in Perth, and the children from the Croatian and Macedonian communities were expected to attend folk-dancing lessons, just as they were expected to attend language classes.

8 Michael O'Toole has noticed the resemblance of Croatian popular music to 'Eurovision Song Contest' entries, which is perhaps very accurate since Italy was a frequent winner of that contest. Yugoslavia – unlike other socialist countries of

Eastern Europe – enthusiastically joined in from the earliest days of that contest. So has Croatia after international recognition.

9 There was a large controversy around the song 'Danke Deutschland' (Thank you Germany) which was broadcast on radio and television across Croatia, on 15 January 1991, in the light of Germany's recognition of Croatian independence. As a result of the heated debate the song was taken off the airways, but it was to spark the debate around the role of popular music for some time to come.

10 I have met Žanko on several occasions, and he appears to be a shrewd business-man who manages his own career and writes most of his own songs.

11 These negative connotations appear from the media health campaigns on drinking and driving, which implicitly promote alcohol consumption as a social pathology of the mainstream community. This in turn sits side by side with the excessive use of alcohol by young people as part of the adolescent rites of passage. This in turn obscures the remarkable similarities between Croatian drinking customs and those of the broader Australian community where father–son dynamics often include the same.

12 Šibenik Cathedral is considered one of the art treasures of Croatia. It was built in Gothic and Renaissance styles. The roof was a masterpeice built by the well-known Renaissance sculptor and architect, Juraj Dalmatinac.

13 The opening of mass graves by both sides, Croatian and Serbian, for 'reconcili-ation purposes' avoided open propaganda and has been described by others (such as Glenny 1992 and Thompson 1992). I don't find it necessary to describe it here.

14 I did not realise just how ferociously effective the 'campaigns' were in Yugoslavia until I went home for Christmas that year. Tito and his memory had become *persona non grata* in Croatia and Serbia.

15 I quote the *Helsinki Watch Report* (1992: 2) on genocide: 'Under Article I of the Genocide Convention, the parties undertake "to prevent" and "to punish" acts of genocide. Article II provides that genocide consists of acts committed "with intent to destroy, in whole or in part, a national, ethnical, racial or religious group as such". It specifies that the means by which genocide is carried out includes "killing members of the group". Article VIII authorises the United Nations to take ap-propriate action "for the prevention and suppression of acts of genocide"'. No further comment is necessary.

6 ETHNIC CLEANSING, PLASTIC BAGS AND THROWAWAY PEOPLE

1 Later I found out that the man who had fainted was a friend and a regular member of my audience. We never mentioned that incident, as fainting was not considered 'manly', and I have refrained from asking him any questions.

2 McKenzie Wark (1990: 39) writes: 'Meanwhile, in the West, the possibility of seeing, recording and remembering these events opened up by the satellite broad-cast has become more than that; it has become a duty. Already the Spirit of Democracy statute has become an international emblem.'

3 Similar video tapes circulate in the Serbian community. However, such of these tapes as I have had a chance to view were all professionally produced as propa-ganda tapes by Serbian Television. Due to my limited access to the Serbian com-munity I do not have sufficient evidence to make any further comments.

4 Michel de Certeau (1985: 144) argues that 'what is memorable is what we can dream about a site' and 'to employ space, therefore, is to repeat the joyous and silent experiences of childhood'.

5 As Paul Virilio (1986: 21) wrote: 'The revolutionary song is a kinetic energy that pushes the masses toward the battlefield, the kind of assault that Shakespeare had already described as "Death Killing Death".'

6 Helsinki Watch has extensively reported on such incidents in its reports; see for example 'Appendix C Helsinki Watch Report on Human Rights Abuses in the Croatian Conflict, September 1991' in *Helsinki Watch Report: War Crimes in Bosnia-Hercegovina* (Helsinki Watch 1992: 23–274). The report contains eyewitness accounts as well as descriptions of summary executions, disappearances, arbitrary detention and forcible dispatch of inhabitants from what Croatia refers to as 'occupied regions', but what are more often known as Serbian enclaves or Krajinas.

7 The audience still used 'back home' or 'homeland' instead of Croatia, not being used to referring freely to home as Croatia. This was the result of the negative connotations of the name I have described earlier. However, they gradually started to correct each other, and when one said 'homeland', one would be corrected with: 'You mean Croatia.' This showed a conscious effort on the part of the community to accept Croatian independence as reality.

8 The political and historical unfolding of events at that time has been recorded superbly by Branka Magaš (1993) in her book *The Destruction of Yugoslavia: Tracking the Break-Up, 1980–92*. A more descriptive and journalistic assessment of the disintegration of Yugoslavia is given by Misha Glenny (1992) and Mark Thompson (1992). A review of all three books was written by Glenda Sluga in *The Independent* (October 1993: 90–1). I shall not give a historical account of events described by the three above-mentioned authors, but will rather refer to their work when appropriate, since much of my own position is similar to that of Magaš and Thompson.

9 For a full description of the background to Lušić's dismissal see 'SBS-TV: a television service' (O'Regan and Kolar-Panov 1993b: 164–6).

10 M.M. did not like to lend her video tapes. She was very possessive and proud of her first-hand knowledge of the situation in Croatia which could be seen in Bourdieu's (1991: 163–71) terms as a claim on symbolic power and he argues that symbols of power are merely objectified symbolic capital (cf. Bottomley 1992: 13).

11 Plastic shopping bags, a throw-away item of consumer society, became a potent symbol of the exile, regardless of the nationality of the refugees from former Yugoslavia. See UNHCR publication *Refugees* (December 1992) which contains descriptions of the plight of such refugees and the increased difficulties encountered in accommodating the ever-increasing numbers of refugees from former Yugoslavia.

12 This hypothesis is often repeated worldwide, not only by politicians justifying non-intervention, but also by the world media. For discussion of some reasons behind non-intervention in the conflict, see Owen Harries (1993) 'The collapse of "The West"'.

13 The song *Hrvatska Garda* (Croatian Guard) is one of the first military folk songs which I call New Composed Folk Music (NFM) and is very popular with Croatian audiences in Perth. Regarding the image of Serbian irregulars, see the excellent essay by Lance Morrow (1993) 'A moral mystery: Serbian self pity'.

14 The plan was carried out later, when the Australian-Croatian Women's Association of Western Australia (ACWA) organised several charity balls in order to raise funds for orphans left behind by Croatian soldiers killed in the war.

15 The conversation I am referring to was recorded in June 1992.

16 There is an extensive body of work on Yugoslav cinema, especially the post-Second World War productions in Serbo-Croatian: see the collection of articles edited by Stevo Ostojić (1977) *Rat, Revolucija, Ekran* (War, Revolution, Screen).

17 It was revealed later in the research that the producers of the video tapes indeed used music as a powerful background for the scenes of destruction. To quote the producer of Opuzen Television (OTV): 'We would play *Čavoglave* (the most popular song by the rock singer Thompson) sometimes fifty to sixty times a night just to keep up morale.' Marko Perković-Thompson is a popular rock singer who caused a controversy with his hit song *Čavoglave* (see Ivanišević 1992: 19; Kuzmanović 1992: 26). The producer was describing the OTV direct broadcasts for audiences in Croatian, but the tapes we were watching were often put together from fragments of such broadcasts. I discuss this later in this chapter.

18 Bob Hodge and Gunther Kress (1988: 130) argue the correspondence of verbal and visual codes as showing 'the higher status of television news coverage over that of newspapers'. See also Kress and Hodge (1993: 167).

19 *What Satellite TV* is a monthly publication which besides satellite television programmes contains a mixture of information and advertising for satellite television.

20 Studies on satellite television are just emerging as I write this. For example, see Peter Larsen (1992) 'More than just images: the whole picture News in the multi-channel universe', for a study of the Norwegian mediascape.

21 Kevin Robins in 'Haunted screen' (1994) says about screen violence: 'The screen is a powerful metaphor for our times: it symbolizes how we exist in the world, our contradictory condition of engagement and disengagement. Increasingly, we confront moral issues through the screen, and the screen confronts us with increasing numbers of moral dilemmas. At the same time, however, it screens us from those dilemmas: it is through the screen that we disavow or deny our human implication in moral realities . . . But, how do we learn to live with this violence? To ask this question is to consider the mechanisms through which we manage to screen ourselves from evil' (*ibid.*: 309).

7 MNEMOSYNE IN VCR

1 V.(A) is M.M.'s god-daughter. Her parents were regular members of M.M.'s family and friends audience.

2 The song by Tomislav Ivčić, 'Stop the War in Croatia' was written in the expectation of a response similar to 'Live Aid' concerts heard round the world (see Nichols 1991: 11–12). The video version of the song was included in many of the video tapes we were watching. However, the song's audio tape has caused 'a storm' in Australia over its sale in Brashs, the chain of record shops, when the chairman of the Serbian National Council of Victoria, Peter Zukanović, issued an open threat against Brashs in order to stop its sale. The tape was taken off the shelves, but it was sold through community channels, raising over $100,000 through the sale of over 50,000 tapes (see C. Evans 1992).

3 I am first and foremost referring to the Australian perception of 'non-ethnic', which is still sometimes a puzzle to me.

4 The analysis of 'hate' campaigns and the propaganda war before and after the outbreak of the war in former Yugoslavia were just starting to be published as I finished my research. See, for example, Meeuwis (1993) 'Nationalist ideology in news reporting on the Yugoslav crisis: a pragmatic analysis'. However, the direct propaganda material in the form of not only video tapes but also publications such as Starčević and Petrović (1991) *Hrvatska 91* (Croatia 91) was present in the diaspora all along.

5 Such tapes were advertised in the migrant publication *Nova Matica*, and were sold semi-legally through the usual community channels described in Chapter 2.

6 The reference here is to the 'Introduction to the new edition of a report from the Carnegie Endowment for International Peace'. The report is written by George F. Kennan. The full title is *The Other Balkan War: A 1913 Carnegie Endowment Inquiry in Retrospect, Reflections on the Present Conflict.* The Introduction was reprinted in *The New York Review of Books* (11, 13: pp. 3–7) on 15 July 1993, but it is important to note that the same introduction was translated and published in Croatia in *Globus* (a weekly semi-tabloid) on 17 September 1993 as a feature article, with the addition of a series of most compelling photographs of atrocities from the present conflict together with archival photographs from the First and Second World Wars.

7 See Clifford Geertz (1973: 142–69) on logico-meaningful integration. For example, in logico-meaningful integration one has unity of style whereas in casual-functional integration one has unity of parts such as 'an element in a reverberating causal ring' which 'keeps the system going' (*ibid.*: 145).

8 Jurij Lotman (1990: 139) describes the notion of collective personality as lying behind the idea of the blood feud 'according to which the whole clan of the murderer is perceived to be responsible'. I draw an analogy here with the Croatian perception of Serbs (or the Serbian perception of Croatians).

9 Jurij Lotman (1990: 138) argues that 'The notion of personality is only identified with a physical individual in certain cultural and semiotic conditions. Otherwise it may be a group, it may or may not include property, it may be associated with a certain social, religious or moral position. The boundary of the personality is a semiotic boundary.' Lotman (1990: 138) also mentions a boundary between the living and the dead. This notion of boundary originates from Plato and has been analysed by Jacques Derrida (1981: 108–109) who in *Disseminations* writes: 'The boundary (between inside and outside, living and nonliving) separates not only speech from writing but also memory as an unveiling (re-)producing a presence from re-memoration as the mere repetition of a monument; truth as distinct from its sign, being as distinct from types. The 'outside' does not begin at the point where what we now call the psychic and physical meet, but at the point where the *mnémé*, instead of being present to itself in its life as a movement of truth, is supplanted by the archive, evicted by a sign of re-memoration or of com-memoration. The space of writing, space as writing, is opened up in the violent movement of this surrogation, in the difference between *mnémé* and *hypomnésis*. The outside is already *within* the work of memory. The evil slips in within the relation of memory to itself, in the general organization of the mnesic activity.'

10 Ivan Erceg, the president of the Yugoslav Clubs and Community Associations in Western Australia, wrote to Graeme Campbell, MP on 3 September 1991 appealing to the government to deal severely 'with any nation trying to run their politics in Australia' and expressing loyalty to Australia in the following words: 'By becoming Australian citizens we have sworn allegiance to Australia, our new, adoptive homeland which we love, respect and are loyal to as well. This means that we DO NOT WANT TO TRANSFER to Australia political differences which in our old country – Yugoslavia – have led to the tragic events in recent months.'

I quote in full the response from Graeme Campbell, MP:

Dear Member,
I have long held a view that migrants coming to this country should not bring the problems of their home countries with them and that their attempts to do so will not be tolerated by the Australian people.
I have a high regard for the Yugoslav community in W.A. as I've always felt

they adapt well to Australian culture and have a genuine commitment to this country. For this reason I have taken the liberty of circulating to you a copy of a letter from the president of the Yugoslav Clubs and Community Associations of W.A. and I know that the views expressed in this letter to be overwhelmingly the majority views of the communities.

Yours sincerely,

Graeme Campbell, MP

Member for Kalgoorlie

11 October 1991

11 The sports violence, especially at soccer matches between Croatian and Serbian clubs, was negligible in Perth, amounting to an occasional burning of a flag or a fist fight. However, in Melbourne it was of such ferocity that at one stage in late 1991 spectators were forbidden and the soccer matches between some ethnic clubs were played to empty stands. It is interesting to note that the worst incident in Perth took place at a soccer match between Spearwood Dalmatinac and North Perth Croatia and not between Serbian and Croatian clubs (Spearwood Dalmatinac is still considered a Yugoslav club, but has been registered as a Croatian club since 1991).

12 The Croatian press in Croatia itself also had a 'field day' with Lawrence Eagelberger, who was known to have business dealings with the Yugoslav car industry. This only reinforced the popular mythology around the UN inaction in preventing Serbian aggression.

13 I do not dispute the importance and the necessity of such reports; quite the contrary, I just notice the minimal effect they have today.

14 The symbol of three fingers has a double meaning – it is with three fingers that the Serbian Orthodox cross themselves, but it also represents the sign for victory, like Sir Winston Churchill's well-known two-fingered sign of V. See an excellent essay by Lance Morrow (1993) 'A moral mystery: Serbian self pity'.

15 *The History of the Croatian People* is produced by HTV (Croatian Television) and is available in both Croatian and English. The production of HTV's monthly information videos *Mjesečni Slikopis* (Monthly Video) is also aimed at the diaspora. It is interesting to note that under the wave of Croatian national revival there is a movement for the purification of the Croatian language, as well as the construction of new words and expressions in order to replace those perceived as 'foreign'. *Slikopis* is a descriptive compound word for video. It is compounded from the word *Slika* for image or picture and the root of the word to write, *pis-ati*.

16 Vukovar remains a wasteland with minimal habitation, and still represents a shameful question for all of us.

17 Perhaps the end to the Bosnian war and the as yet unknown crimes committed there will enable the well-documented massacres in Vukovar to gain the attention of the world again, but for the sake of the present discussion I will use Misha Glenny's (1992) qualification of the destruction of Vukovar.

18 For example, Gerard Davies (1993: 12) in 'Dubrovnik turns back on war to rebuild' writes about 'symbolically selling off the famous red roof tiles to Americans at US$10 ($14.70) a tile' and that so far the 'Buy a brick for Dubrovnik' campaign has raised US$35,000.

19 These are numbers given by the world media at the time of the siege of Vukovar, October–November 1991.

20 The IUC Centre was partly rebuilt and reopened as a Medjunarodno Središte Hrvatskih Sveučilišta Hrvatske (International Croatian University Centre) on 1 October 1993.

21 The photograph of Smailović was also printed in the UNHCR publication

Refugees (April 1993: 7). He used to play day after day all around Sarajevo in defiance of the danger from mortar shells and snipers and in protest at the war. I should also note that, in spite of my inquiries, I could not get any information about his subsequent whereabouts.

8 BRIDGES AND BOUNDARIES

1 I was in Wiesbaden, Germany, visiting my father and brother, who are involved in grass-roots humanitarian relief organisations.
2 Homi K. Bhabha (1990a: 292) draws our attention to Fredric Jameson invoking something similar to Edward Said's 'textual object itself' which for Jameson is a notion of 'situational consciousness or national allegory', 'where the telling of the individual story and the individual experience cannot but ultimately involve the whole laborious telling of the collectivity itself'.
3 This story was picked up by Frederick Painton (1993: 35) who also quotes Jerry Hulme, head of UNHCR office in Medjugorje and who carried the sad news back to his staff, as saying: 'We have 12 Croats, 12 Muslims and 1 Serb, and I had 25 people in my office in tears.'
4 There was a public forum held at Murdoch University (Perth, Western Australia) on 'The Rape of Bosnia and Herzegovina' (18 June 1993). This caused protests from the Serbian community in Perth and all over Australia. For some time after the e-mail of the speakers was jammed by Serbian propaganda.
5 There is no breakdown by nationalities of the refugees from the former Yugoslavia in ABS records. However, as of June 1993 there were 3,133 people (from the former Yugoslavia) shown as admitted under the category of 'refugees and special assistance arrivals'. See *Immigration update* by the Australian Bureau of Immigration and Population Research (June Quarter 1993: 29).
6 By this time the conflict between Croats and Muslims had flared up, and the world media focus moved from 'ethnic cleansing' by Serbs to a more interesting 'three-way civil war'.
7 The combination of video + telephone = videophone is gaining in popularity and will most probably take over some functions of the telephone, but I believe that it will never replace the use of the VCR. Also, some authors like Hart Cohen (1993: 105–19) in 'Margins at the centre', have argued that satellites are so far the most influential cultural technology.
8 From works on cultural imperialism such as by Mattelart, Delacourt and Mattelart (1984) *International Image Markets*, through arguments about Americanisation of world culture (see Tomlinson 1991) to the latest release of data from research on virtual reality (*ABC News* 7 December 1992) which claims that virtual reality harms the eyesight of young children – the visual media have always attracted a large amount of adverse research leading to the development of popular mythology around it. This mythology is helped along with 'television about television' type programmes, such as American *Entertainment Tonight* and its imitators (e.g. CNN's *Showbusiness*, and the Australian *TV, TV – ABC*).
9 See Homi K. Bhabha's (1990a) excellent essay 'DissemiNation: time narrative and the margins of the modern nation' – on the identity formation of travelling intellectuals. See also James Clifford (1992: 96–112) 'Travelling cultures'.
10 For example Chris McGreal (*Guardian Weekly*, 3 October 1993: 4), describing the civil war in Zaire writes in the manner habitual to journalists attempting to describe one of the many conflicts around the world: 'It was straightforward "ethnic cleansing" fuelled by ancient prejudices and modern political motives.' This shows that the so-called Third World is seen on the same terms.

11 For example, Boris Yeltsin's struggle to stay in power has included the control of Moscow television station as one of the focal points.

12 The globalisation of communication was initially fostered from the 'global' (Western) centres of capital and reached the former East with the aim of whetting the appetite for the consumer culture of the affluent West. Obvious examples of this are the showing of *Dynasty* or *Dallas* in the former USSR. See Angela Spindler-Brown (1988) *Red Tape*.

13 For a full rundown of various satellite television channels and the content of their programme see publications such as *What Satellite TV.*

14 Since this was written the number of satellite television channels in Europe has grown, accommodating the new breed of European broadcasting, such as Euronews – broadcasting in all EU languages on different tone frequencies.

15 This is a practice exercised in many other countries, for example India. Another example is China which has banned the use of private satellites for television reception – it will be interesting to see how this will affect the use of the VCR as a substitute for it.

16 The cartoon on the front cover of David Morley's (1992) *Television, Audiences and Cultural Studies* sums this up nicely.

17 Perhaps I should explain. As I am a product of a mixed marriage between a Hungarian Jew and a Croatian Catholic, former Yugoslavia always provided me with relative safety. Now, with its destruction, I will, like many others, remain a traveller in space and in time. Thus the pain, grief and sadness that surface from time to time and throughout this book belong to a personal anguish: anguish derived from irreplaceable losses of family members and friends and the loss of a country.

BIBLIOGRAPHY

Adorno, T. and Horkheimer, M. (1977) 'The culture industry: enlightenment as mass deception', in J. Curran, M. Gurevitch and J. Woollacott (eds), *Mass Communication and Society*, London: Edward Arnold, pp. 349–83.

Albarran, A.B. and Umphrey, D. (1993) 'An examination of television motivations and program preferences by Hispanics, blacks and whites', *Journal of Broadcasting and Electronic Media* 37, 1: 95–103.

Aleksiev, A. (1976) *Osnovopoložnici na makedonskata dramska literatura* (Founding Fathers of Macedonian Theatrical Literature), Skopje: Kultura.

Alexander, A., Morgan, M. and Harris, C. (1990) 'Adolescents, VCR, and the family environment', *Communication Research* 17, 1.1: 83–106.

Allcock, J.B. (1989) 'In the praise of chauvinism: rhetorics of nationalism in Yugoslav politics', *Third World Quarterly* 10, 4: 208–21.

Althusser, L. (1984) *Essays on Ideology*, London: Verso.

Alvarado, M. (ed.) (1988) *Video World-Wide: An International Study*, UNESCO, London: John Libbey.

Alvarado, M. and Davis, J. (1988) 'United Kingdom', in M. Alvarado (ed.), *Video World-Wide: An International Study*, UNESCO, London: John Libbey, pp. 9–28.

An Appeal from 43 Nobel Prize Winners (1992) 'Peace in Croatia', *Vjesnik hrvatske akademije znanosti i umjetnosti* 1, 1–2: 33–5.

Anderson, B. (1983) *Imagined Communities: Reflections on the Origin and Spread of Nationalism*, London: Verso.

Andonov, V. (1973) *Makedoncite vo Avstralia* (The Macedonians in Australia), Skopje: Kultura.

Andonov-Poljanski, H. (1973) *Goce Delčev: His Life and Times*, trans. A. Guzelova, Skopje: Misla.

Ang, I. (1985) *Watching Dallas: Soap Opera and the Melodramatic Imagination*, London: Methuen.

—— (1989) 'Wanted audiences: on the politics of empirical audience studies', in E. Seiter, H. Borchers, G. Kreutzner and E.M. Warth (eds), *Remote Control: Television, Audiences and Cultural Power*, London: Routledge, pp. 96–115.

—— (1990) 'Ethnography and radical contextualism in audience studies', paper presented at an international conference 'Towards a Comprehensive Theory of Audience', Urbana, Champaign: University of Illinois.

—— (1991) *Desperately Seeking the Audience*, London: Routledge.

—— (1992) 'Living room wars: new technologies, audience measurement and the tactics of television consumption', in R. Silverstone and E. Hirsch (eds), *Consuming Technologies*, London: Routledge, pp. 131–45.

—— (1992/1993) 'Migrations of Chineseness', *SPAN* 34–5: 3–15.

240

Ang, I. and Morley, D. (1989) 'Mayonnaise culture and other European follies', *Cultural Studies* 3, 2: 133–44.

Archer, M.S. (1988) *Culture and Agency: The Place of Culture in Social Theory*, Cambridge: Cambridge University Press.

Arena, F. (1985) 'The ethnic media: issues and problems: a consumer's point of view', in I.H. Burnley, S. Encel and G. McCall (eds), *Immigration and Ethnicity in the 1980s*, Melbourne: Longman Cheshire, pp. 95–9.

Armes, R. (1988) *On Video*, London: Routledge.

Armstrong, J. (1982) *Nations before Nationalism*, Chapel Hill, NC: University of North Carolina Press.

Arnheim, R. (1969) *Visual Thinking*, Berkeley and Los Angeles: University of California Press.

—— (1974) *Art and Visual Perception: A Psychology of the Creative Eye*, Berkeley and Los Angeles: University of California Press.

Ashbolt, A. (1985) 'Radio and television services for migrants: problems and prospects', in I.H. Burnley, S. Encel and G. McCall (eds), *Immigration and Ethnicity in the 1980s*, Melbourne: Longman Cheshire, pp. 104–10.

Atkinson, P. (1990) *The Ethnographic Imagination: Textual Constructions of Reality*, London: Routledge.

Attali, J. (1985) *Noise: The Political Economy of Music*, Manchester: Manchester University Press.

Attallah, P. (1991) 'Trends and developments in Canadian television', *Media Information Australia* 62: 51–9.

Australian Bureau of Immigration and Population Research (1993a) *Immigration Update June Quarter 1993*, Canberra: AGPS.

Australian Bureau of Immigration and Population Research (1993b) *Immigration Update: Settler Arrivals 1991–92, Statistical Report 8*, Canberra: AGPS.

Australian Bureau of Immigration Research (1986a) *Community Profiles: Non-English Speaking Born*, Canberra: AGPS.

—— (1986b) *Community Profiles: Yugoslavia Born*, Canberra: AGPS.

Australian Bureau of Statistics (1986) *Census of Population and Housing*, Canberra: AGPS.

—— (1993) *Perth Social Atlas: 1991 Census of Population and Housing*, Canberra: ABS.

Australian Department of Communications (1986) *Satellite Broadcasting: Answers to the Questions Most Asked*, Canberra: AGPS.

Australian Department of Immigration (1992) *Directory of Ethnic Community Organisations in Australia*, Canberra: AGPS.

Australian Ministry of Foreign Affairs (1988) *Annual Report*, Canberra: AGPS.

Babić, S., Finka, B. and Moguš, M. (eds) (1994) *Hrvatski pravopis* (Croatian Grammar), Zagreb: Školska Knjiga.

Bachelard, G. (1969) *The Poetics of Space*, trans. M. Jolas, Boston: Beacon Press.

Bailey, J.J. (1980) 'The road to ethnic television? Key dates and references', *Media Information Australia* 15: 12–14.

Bakhtin, M. (1968) *Rabelais and His World*, Cambridge, Mass.: MIT Press.

—— (1981) *The Dialogic Imagination*, Austin, Tex.: University of Texas Press.

Bal, M. (1985) *Narratology: Introduction to the Theory of Narrative*, trans. C. van Boheemen, Toronto: University of Toronto Press.

Ballibar, E. and Wallerstein, I. (1991) *Race, Nation, Class: Ambigous Identities*, London: Verso.

Banac, I. (1984) *The National Question of Yugoslavia: Origins, History, Politics*, Ithaca, NY: Cornell University Press.

—— (1992) 'Dubrovnik i Vukovar' (Dubrovnik and Vukovar), *Dubrovnik* 3, 2–3: 41–6.

Barr, T. (1985) *The Electronic Estate: New Communications Media and Australia*, Ringwood, Vic.: Penguin Books.

Barthes, R. (1969) *Elements of Semiology*, trans. A. Lavers and C. Smith, London: Jonathan Cape.

—— (1973) *Mythologies*, trans. A. Lavers, London: Paladin.

—— (1977) *Image–Music–Text*, trans. S. Heath, Glasgow: Fontana.

—— (1982) *Camera Lucida*, trans. R. Howard, New York: Fontana.

Batchen, G. (1993) 'Enslaved sovereign, observed spectator', *Continuum* 6, 2: 80–94.

Bateson, J. (1990) 'Australian turnoff video', *The Australian Financial Review*, 22 May, p. 26.

Baudrillard, J. (1981) *For a Critique of the Political Economy of the Sign*, trans. and introd. C. Levin, St Louis, Mo.: Telos Press.

—— (1983a) *Simulations*, trans. P. Foss, P. Patton and P. Beitchman, New York: Semiotext(e).

—— (1983b) *In the Shadow of the Silent Majorities or the End of the Social and Other Essays*, trans. P. Foss, J. Johnston and P. Patton, New York: Semiotext(e).

—— (1988) *The Ecstasy of Communication*, trans. B. and C. Schutze, New York: Semiotext(e).

—— (1990) *Fatal Strategies*, trans. P. Beitchman and W.G.J. Niesluchowski, New York: Semiotext(e) and Pluto.

Bausinger, H. (1990) *Folk Culture in a World of Technology*, trans. E. Dettmar, Bloomington, Ind.: Indiana University Press.

—— (1984) 'Media, technology and daily life', *Media, Culture and Society* 6, 4: 343–51.

Beljo, A. *et al.* (eds) (1992) *Great Serbia: From Ideology to Aggression*, Zagreb: Croatian Information Centre.

Beloff, H. (1985) *Camera Culture*, Oxford: Basil Blackwell.

Benjamin, W. (1992) *Illuminations,* trans. H. Zohn, London: Fontana Press.

Berger, J. (1972) *Ways of Seeing*, Harmondsworth: Penguin.

—— (1980) *About Looking*, New York: Pantheon Books.

Berko, L. (1989) 'Video: in search of a discourse', *Quarterly Review of Film Studies* 10, 4: 289–307.

Bernstein, B. (1971) *Class, Codes and Control*, vol.1, London: Routledge and Kegan Paul.

Betts, K. (1991) 'Australia's distorted immigration policy', in D. Goodman, J. O'Hearn and C. Wallace-Crabbe (eds), *Multicultural Australia: The Challenges of Change*, Newman, Vic.: Scribe, pp. 149–77.

Bhabha, H.K. (1984) 'Representation and the colonial text: a critical exploration of some forms of mimeticism', in Frank Gloversmith (ed.), *The Theory of Reading*, Brighton: Harvester, pp. 93–122.

—— (1990a) 'DissemiNation: time, narrative, and the margins of the modern nation', in H.K. Bhabha (ed.), *Nation and Narration*, London: Routledge, pp. 291–322.

—— (ed.) (1990b) *Nation and Narration*, London: Routledge.

Bilandžić, D. *et al.* (1991) *Croatia Between War and Independence*, Zagreb: University of Zagreb.

Birch, A.H. (1989) 'National integration in Australia' in A. H. Birch, *Nationalism and National Integration*, London: Unwin Hyman, pp. 193–220.

Blonsky, M. (1985) 'Introduction: the agony of semiotics', in M. Blonsky (ed.), *On Signs*, Oxford: Basil Blackwell, pp. xiii–li.

Bogišić, R. (1992) 'Hrvatski kulturni subjekt' (Croatian Cultural Subject), *Vjesnik hrvatske akademije znanosti i umjetnosti* 1, 3–4: 44–6.

Bottomley, G. (1992) *From Another Place: Migration and the Politics of Culture*, Cambridge: Cambridge University Press.

Bourdieu, P. (1977) *Outline of a Theory of Practice*, Cambridge: Cambridge University Press.

—— (1980) 'The aristocracy of culture', *Media, Culture, and Society* 2, 3: 225–54.

—— (1984) *Distinction: A Social Critique of the Judgement of Taste*, trans. R. Nice, Cambridge, Mass.: Harvard University Press.

—— (1990) *In Other Words: Essays towards a Reflexive Sociology*, Cambridge: Polity Press.

—— (1991) *Language and Symbolic Power*, trans. G. Raymond and M. Adamson, Cambridge: Polity Press.

—— (1993) *The Field of Cultural Production: Essays on Art and Literature*, ed. and introd. R. Johnson, Cambridge: Polity Press.

Boyarin, J. (1991) *Polish Jews in Paris: The Ethnography of Memory*, Indianopolis: Indiana University Press.

—— (1992) *Storm from Paradise: The Politics of Jewish Memory*, Minneapolis: University of Minnesota Press.

Boyd, D.A. (1989) 'The videocassette recorder in the USSR and Soviet-bloc countries', in M.R. Levy (ed.), *The VCR Age: Home Video and Mass Communications*, Newbury Park, Calif.: Sage, pp. 252–70.

—— (1990) 'Electronic media and national disintegration: the Lebanese experience with unofficial broadcasting', paper presented at an International Communication Association Annual Conference (ICAAC), Dublin.

Boyd, D.A. and Adwan, N. (1988) 'The Gulf states Jordan and Egypt', in M. Alvarado (ed.), *Video World-Wide: An International Study*, UNESCO, London: John Libbey, pp. 159–80.

Boyd, D.A., Lent, J.A. and Straubhaar, J.D. (1989) *Video Cassette Recorders in the Third World*, New York: Longman.

Brass, P.R. (1991) *Ethnicity and Nationalism: Theory and Comparison*, New Delhi: Sage.

Brennan, T. (1990) 'The national longing for form', in H.K. Bhabha (ed.), *Nation and Narration*, London: Routledge, pp. 44–70.

Bromley, R. (1988) *Lost Narratives: Popular Fictions, Politics and Recent History*, London: Routledge.

Brown, A. (1986) *Commercial Media in Australia*, St Lucia: University of Queensland Press.

Brown, D. (1989) 'Ethnic revival: perspectives on state and society', *Third World Quarterly* 11, 4: 1–17.

Brunsdon, C. (1981) '"Crossroads": notes on soap opera', *Screen* 22.4: 32–7.

—— (1989) 'Text and audience', in E. Seiter, H. Borchers, G. Kreutzner and E.M. Warth (eds), *Remote Control: Television, Audiences and Cultural Power*, London: Routledge, pp. 116–229.

—— (1991) 'Satellite dishes and the landscapes of taste', *New Formations* 15: 23–42.

Brunsdon, C. and Morley, D. (1978) *Everyday Television: 'Nationwide'*, London: British Film Institute.

Bryson, L. and Encel, S. (eds) (1984) *Australian Society*, 4th edn, Melbourne: Longman Cheshire.

Bugajski, J. (1993) 'The contours of ethnic politics in Eastern Europe', *Balkan Forum* 1, 3: 19–34.

Bungey, L.J. (1993) "A study of the fate and future of languages other than English in Western Australian schools', Ph.D. thesis, Murdoch University.

Burgmann, V. and Lee, J. (1988) *Constructing a Culture: A People's History of Australia Since 1788*, Australia: McPhee Gribble/Penguin Books.

Burnett, R. (1993) 'Camera lucida: Roland Barthes, Jean-Paul Sartre and the photographic image', *Continuum* 6, 2: 5–24.

Cannadine, D. (1983) 'The context, performance and meaning of ritual: the British monarchy and the "Invention of Tradition", *c.* 1820–1977' in E. Hobsbawm and T. Ranger (eds), *The Invention of Tradition*, Cambridge: Cambridge University Press, pp. 101–64.

Cardiff, D. and Scannell, P. (1987) 'Broadcasting and national unity', in J. Curran, A. Smith and P. Wingate (eds), *Impacts and Influences: Essays on Media Power in the Twentieth Century*, London: Methuen, pp. 157–73.

Carey, J.W. (1972) 'Harold Adams Innis and Marshall McLuhan', in R. Rosenthal *et al.* (eds), *McLuhan: Pro and Con*, Baltimore: Pelican, pp. 270–308.

—— (1981) 'Culture, geography and communications: the work of Harold Innis in an American context', in W. Melody and L. Salter (eds), *Communication and Dependency: The Tradition of H.A. Innis*, Norwood, NJ: Ablex Publishing Corporation, pp. 73–91.

—— (1989) *Communication As Culture: Essays on Media and Society*, London: Unwin Hyman Ltd.

Carter, F.W. (ed.) (1977) *An Historical Geography of the Balkans*, London: Academic Press.

Castles I. (1988) *Overseas Born Australians*, Canberra: Australian Bureau of Statistics.

Castles, S. *et al.* (1988) *Mistaken Identity: Multiculturalism and the Demise of Nationalism in Australia*, Sydney: Pluto Press.

Castles, S., Booth, H. and Wallace, T. (1986) *Here for Good: Western Europe's New Ethnic Minorities*, London: Pluto Press.

Chambers, I. (1990) *Border Dialogues: Journeys in Postmodernity*, London: Routledge.

Chaney, D. (1986) 'The symbolic form of ritual in mass communication', in P. Golding, G. Murdock and P. Schlesinger (eds), *Communicating Politics: Mass Communications and the Political Process,* Leicester: Leicester University Press, pp. 115–32.

Chliand, G. (ed.) (1989) *Minority Peoples in the Age of Nation–States*, London: Pluto Press.

Clay, J.W. (1989) 'Epilogue: the ethnic future of nations', *Third World Quarterly* 11, 4: 223–33.

Clifford, J. (1980) 'Fieldwork, reciprocity, and the making of ethnographic texts', *Man* 15: 518–32.

—— (1983) 'On ethnographic authority', *Representations* 1, 2: 118–46.

—— (1986) 'Introduction: partial truths', in J. Clifford and G.E. Marcus (eds), *Writing Culture: The Poetics and Politics of Ethnography*, Berkeley and Los Angeles: University of California Press, pp. 1–26.

—— (1988) *The Predicament of Culture: Twentieth Century Ethnography, Literature and Art*, Cambridge, Mass.: Harvard University Press.

—— (1992) 'Travelling Cultures', in L. Grossberg, C. Nelson and P. Treichler (eds), *Cultural Studies*, New York: Routledge, pp. 96–112.

Clifford, J. and Marcus, G.E. (eds), (1986) *Writing Culture: The Poetics and Politics of Ethnography*, Berkeley and Los Angeles: University of California Press.

Clyne, M. (1991) *Community Languages: The Australian Experience*, Cambridge: Cambridge University Press.

Cohen, A., Levy, M.R. and Golden, K. (1988) 'Children's uses and gratifications of home VCRs: evolution and revolution', *Communication Research* 15, 6: 772–80.

Cohen, H. (1993) 'Margins in the centre: Innis' concept of bias and the development of Aboriginal media', *Continuum* 7, 1: 105–20.

Coleman, A.D. (1979) *Light Readings: A Photography Critic's Writings 1968–1978*, Oxford: Oxford University Press.

Collins, R. (1990) *Satellite Television in Western Europe*, London: John Libbey.

Commission of Inquiry (1990) *The Report: Kosovski čvor: drešiti ili seći?* (Kosovo Knot: To Undo or to Cut?), Belgrade: The Union for Yugoslav Democratic Initiative.

Connor, W. (1993) 'Beyond reason: the nature of the ethnonational blood', *Ethnic and Racial Studies* 16, 3: 373–89.

Connor Report (1985), also known as Committee of Review of the Special Broadcasting Service, *Serving Multicultural Australia: The Role of Broadcasting*, Part 1, Canberra: AGPS.

Constitution of the Republic of Macedonia (1991) trans P. Marsh-Stefanovska, Skopje: Government Publications.

Copley, G. (ed.) (1992) 'Hiding genocide', *Defense and Foreign Affairs Strategic Policy*, 31 December, pp. 4–19.

Corner, J. (1991) 'Meaning, genre and context: the problematics of "public knowledge" in the new audience studies', in J. Curran and M. Gurevitch (eds), *Mass Media and Society*, London: Edward Arnold, pp. 267–84.

Couprie, E. and Olsson, H. (1987) *Freedom of Communication Under the Law: Case Studies in Nine Countries*, Media Monograph No. 9, The European Institute for the Media, Manchester: University of Manchester.

Court, D. and Maddox, G. (1989) *The Home Video Industry*, (A report for the Australian Film Commission), Sydney: AFC.

—— (1992) *The Home Video Industry in Australia*, (A report for the Australian Film Commission), Sydney: AFC.

Craig, G. (1993) 'Looking twice: thoughts on the practice of photo-journalism', *Australian Journalism Review* 15, 1: 103–15.

Croce, P.J. (1993) 'Erosion of mass culture', *Society* 30, 5: 11–16.

Crompton, H. (1993) 'Screen violence', *The West Magazine* (Perth, Western Australia) 31 July, pp. 15–18.

Cubitt, S. (1991) *Timeshift: On Video Culture*, London: Routledge.

Czekanowska-Kuklinska, A. (1986) 'Folk music as viewed from the perspective of its social conditionings and functions', in *Special Edition of the Academy of Arts and Sciences of Bosnia and Hercegovina*, Sarajevo: Academy of Arts and Sciences of Bosnia and Hercegovina, 16: 62–77.

Dahlgren, P. (1988) 'What's the meaning of this? Viewers' plural sense-making of TV-news', *Media, Culture and Society* 10, 3: 285–301.

Danforth, L.M. (1995) 'National conflicts in a transnational world: Greeks and Macedonians at the Conference for Security and Cooperation in Europe', *Balkan Forum*, 3, 2: 49–82.

Davies, G. (1993) 'Dubrovnik turns back on war to rebuild', *The Weekend Australian*, 10–11 July, p. 12.

de Certeau, M. (1984) *The Practice of Everyday Life*, Berkeley and Los Angeles: University of California Press.

—— (1985) 'Practices of space', in M. Blonsky (ed.), *On Signs*, Oxford: Basil Blackwell, pp. 122–45.

de Fleur, M.L. and Ball-Rokeach, S. (1989) *Theories of Mass Communication*, 5th edn, London: Longman.

de Landa, M. (1993) 'The machines take over', *Wired*, Premiere Issue: 84.

de Sola Pool, I. (1984) *Technologies of Freedom*, Cambridge, Mass.: The Belknap Press of Harvard University Press.

Dedijer, V. *et al.* (1974) *History of Yugoslavia*, New York: McGraw-Hill.

Derrida, J. (1974) *Of Grammatology*, trans. G. Spivak, Baltimore: Johns Hopkins University Press.
—— (1981) *Dissemination*, trans. B. Johnson, Chicago: University of Chicago Press.
de Saussure, F. (1966) *Course in General Linguistics*, trans. W. Baskin, New York: McGraw Hill.
Deutsch, K.W. (1966) *Nationalism and Social Communication*, 2nd edn, New York: MIT Press.
—— (1969) *Nationalism and its Alternatives*, New York: Knopf.
Djilas, M. (1993) 'Separated but together', *Balkan Forum* 1, 3: 5–8.
Dobrow, J.R. (1989) 'Away from the mainstream? VCRs and ethnic identity', in M.R. Levy (ed.), *The VCR Age: Home Video and Mass Communication*, Newbury Park, Calif.: Sage, pp. 193–208.
—— (ed.) (1990) *Social and Cultural Aspects of VCR Use*, Hillsdale, NJ: Lawrence Erlbaum Associates.
Drakulić, S. (1993) *The Balkan Express: Fragments from the Other Side of War*, New York: W.W. Norton and Company.
Drummond, P. and Paterson, R. (eds) (1986) *Television in Transition*, London: British Film Institute.
—— (eds), (1988) *Television and its Audiences: International Research Perspectives*, London: British Film Institute.
'Dubrovnik u ratu' (Dubrovnik in War) (1992) *Dubrovnik* 3, 2–3: 565, 573.
Dunnett, R. (1992) 'The wider word', *What Satellite TV*, October: 59–63.
Dyson, K., Humphreys, P., Negrine, R. and Simon, J.P. (1988) *Broadcasting and New Media Policies in Western Europe*, London: Routledge.
Džinić, F. (1988) 'Yugoslavia', in M.Alvarado (ed.), *Video World-Wide: An International Study*, UNESCO, London: John Libbey, pp. 211–22.
Eagle, H. (1976) 'The semiotics of the cinema: Lotman and Metz', *Dispositio Revista Hispanica de Semiotica Literaria: Soviet Semiotics of Culture*, Special Issue 3: 303–14.
Eagleton, T. (1976) *Criticism and Ideology*, London: New Left Books.
Eco, U. (1972) 'Towards a semiotic inquiry into the television message', *Working Papers in Cultural Studies* 3: 103–21.
—— (1976) *A Theory of Semiotics*, Bloomington, Ind.: Indiana University Press.
—— (1979) *The Role of the Reader*, Bloomington, Ind.: Indiana University Press.
—— (1984) *Semiotics and the Philosophy of Language*, London: Macmillan.
—— (1990a) *The Limits of Interpretation*, Bloomington, Ind.: Indiana University Press.
—— (1990b) 'Introduction' to J. Lotman *Universe of the Mind: A Semiotic Theory of Culture*, trans. A. Shukman, Bloomington, Ind.: Indiana University Press.
—— (1992) 'Overinterpreting texts', in *Interpretation and Overinterpretation*, Cambridge: Cambridge University Press, pp. 45–66.
Eisenstein, S. (1986) *The Film Sense*, trans. and ed. J. Leyda, London: Faber and Faber Ltd.
Ellis, J. (1982) *Visible Fictions: Cinema, Television, Video*, London: Routledge and Kegan Paul.
Enninger, W. (1988) 'The social construction of past, present and future in the written and oral texts of the Old Order Amish', in F. Poyatos (ed.), *Literary Anthropology*, Amsterdam: John Benjamins Publishing Company, pp. 195–256.
Eterovich, A. (1978) *Croatian and Dalmatian Coats of Arms*, Palo Alto, Calif.: Ragusan Press.
Evans, C. (1992) 'Peace song sales raise $100.000 for aid fund', *Hrvatski vjesnik* (Croatian Herald), 10 April, p. 15.

Evans, H. (1989) 'Achieving a qualitative diversity of choice in Australian television', *Media Information Australia* 53: 37–42.

Fabian, J. (1983) *Time and the Other: How Anthropology Makes Its Object*, New York: Columbia University Press.

Fairclough, N. (1992) *Language and Power*, 5th edn, London: Longman.

Featherstone, M. (1990) 'Perspectives on consumer culture', *Sociology* 24.1: 5–22.

—— (1991) *Consumer Culture and Postmodernism*, London: Sage.

Ferguson, M. (1990) 'Electronic media and the redefining of time and space', in M. Ferguson (ed.), *Public Communication*, London: Sage, pp. 152–72.

Filing, P. (1991) Media release, 13 November.

Fischer, M.J. (1986) 'Ethnicity and postmodern arts of memory', in J. Clifford and G.E. Marcus (eds), *Writing Culture: The Poetics and Politics of Ethnography*, Berkeley and Los Angeles: University of California Press, pp. 194–233.

Fiske, J. (1986) 'Television polysemy and popularity', *Critical Studies in Mass Communication* 3, 4: 392–408.

—— (1987) *Television Culture*, London: Methuen.

—— (1989a) *Understanding Popular Culture*, Boston: Unwin Hyman.

—— (1989b) *Reading the Popular*, Boston: Unwin Hyman.

—— (1990) 'Ethnosemiotics: some personal and theoretical reflections', *Cultural Studies* 4, 1: 85–99.

—— (1992) 'Audiencing: a cultural studies approach to watching television', *Poetics* 21, 4: 345–60.

Fiske, J. and Hartley, J. (1978) *Reading Television*, London: Methuen.

Fiske, J., Hodge, B. and Turner, G. (1988) *Myths of Oz: Reading Australian Popular Culture*, Sydney: Allen and Unwin.

Foretić, V. (1990) *Povijest Dubrovnika do 1808* (History of Dubrovnik to 1808), vol. 1–2, Zagreb: Nakladni Zavod Matice Hrvatske.

Foucault, M. (1972) *The Archaeology of Knowledge*, trans. A.M. Sheridan Smith, London: Tavistock.

—— (1975) *The Birth of the Clinic: An Archeology of Medical Perception*, trans. A.M. Sheridan Smith, New York: Vintage/Random House.

—— (1977) *Discipline and Punish*, trans. A. Sheridan, London: Allen Lane.

—— (1980) *The History of Sexuality*, vol. 1, trans. R. Hurley, New York: Vintage/Random House.

—— (1982) 'The subject and power', in H. Dryfus and P. Rabinow (eds), *Michel Foucault: Beyond Structuralism and Hermeneutics*, Chicago: Chicago University Press, pp. 208–226.

Fowler, R. *et al.* (1979) *Language and Control*, London: Routledge and Kegan Paul.

Fox, R.G. (1990a) 'Introduction', in R.G. Fox (ed.), *Nationalist Ideologies and the Production of National Cultures*, Washington: American Anthropological Association, pp. 1–14.

—— (1990b) 'Hindu nationalism in the making, or the rise of the Hindian', in R.G. Fox (ed.), *Nationalist Ideologies and the Production of National Cultures*, Washington: American Anthropological Association, pp. 63–80.

Fraser, M. (1981) *Multiculturalism: Australia's Unique Achievement*, Canberra: AGPS.

Frost, B. (1993) 'Croats join drive to rid Bosnia of Muslims', *The Australian*, 2 March, p. 10.

Frow, J. and Morris, M. (1993) 'Introduction', in J. Frow and M. Morris (eds), *Australian Cultural Studies: A Reader*, St. Leonards: Allen and Unwin, pp. vii–xxii.

Ganley, G.D. and Ganley, O.H. (1987) *Global Political Fallout: The VCR's First Decade*, Cambridge, Mass.: Harvard University, Center for Information Policy Research.

Gasparov, B. (1976) 'Some descriptive problems of musical semantics', *Dispositio Revista Hispanica de Semiotica Literaria: Soviet Semiotics of Culture*, Special Issue 3: 247–62.

Geake, E. (1993a) 'The electronic arm of the law', *New Scientist*, 8 May, pp. 19–20.

—— (1993b) 'Tiny brother is watching you', *New Scientist*, 8 May, pp. 21–3.

Geertz, C. (1963) *The Interpretation of Cultures*, New York: Basic Books.

—— (1973) *The Interpretation of Cultures: Selected Essays*, New York: Basic Books.

—— (1988) *Works and Lives: The Anthropologist as Author*, Cambridge: Polity Press.

Gellner, E. (1983) *Nations and Nationalism*, Oxford: Basil Blackwell.

Gewehr, W.M. (1967) *The Rise of Nationalism in the Balkans, 1800–1930*, United States: Archon Books.

Giddens, A. (1979) *Central Problems in Social Theory: Action, Structure and Contradiction in Social Analysis*, London: Macmillan.

—— (1981) *A Contemporary Critique of Historical Materialism*, London: Macmillan.

—— (1984) *The Constitution of Society: Outline of the Theory of Structuration*, Cambridge: Polity Press.

—— (1990) *The Consequences of Modernity*, Cambridge: Polity Press.

Gillespie, M. (1989) 'Technology and tradition: audio-visual culture among South Asian families in West London', *Cultural Studies* 3, 2: 226–39.

Glenny, M. (1992) *The Fall of Yugoslavia: The Third Balkan War*, Harmondsworth: Penguin Books.

Goldberg, V. (1991) *The Power of Photography: How Photographs Changed Our Lives*, New York: Abbeville Press.

Golubović, T. (1983) 'Television as an integration factor in Yugoslavia', *EBU Review, Programmes, Administration, Law* 34, 4: 17–22.

Grakalić, M. (1990) *Hrvatski grb* (Croatian coat of arms), Zagreb: Nakladni Zavod Matice Hrvatske.

Gramsci, A. (1971) *Selections from the Prison Notebooks of Antonio Gramsci*, trans. and ed. Q. Hoare and G. Nowel-Smith, London: Lawrence and Wishart.

Gray, A. (1987) 'Behind closed doors: video recorders in the home', in H. Baehr and G. Dyer (eds), *Boxed In: Women and Television*, London: Pandora Press, pp. 38–54.

—— (1988) 'Reading the readings: a working paper', paper presented to the Third International Television Studies Conference, London.

—— (1992) *Video Playtime: The Gendering of a Leisure Technology*, London: Routledge.

Grejić, N. (1992) 'Apeli i izjave za spas Dubrovnika' (Appeals and declarations for preservation of Dubrovnik), *Dubrovnik* 3, 2–3: 574.

Grossberg, L. (1983) 'Cultural studies revisited and revised', in M.S. Ander (ed.), *Communications in Transition*, New York: Praeger, pp. 39–70.

Grossberg, L., Nelson, C. and Treichler, P. (eds), (1992) *Cultural Studies*, New York/ London: Routledge

Gumpert, G. (1987) 'Talking to someone who isn't there or sex and the single phone', in *Talking Tombstones and Other Tales of the Media Age*, New York: Oxford University Press, pp. 121–39.

Gutman, H. (1988) 'Rousseau's confessions: a technology of the self', in L. Martin, H. Gutman and P. Huton (eds), *Technologies of the Self: A Seminar with Michel Foucault*, London: Tavistock, pp. 99–120.

Gutmann, J. (1977) 'Megapolis and antipolis: the telephone and the structure of the city', in I. de Sola Pool (ed.), *The Social Impact of the Telephone*, Cambridge, Mass.: MIT Press, pp. 303–17.

Hall, S. (1980) 'Encoding/decoding in television discourse', in S. Hall, D. Hobson, A.

248

Lowe and P. Willis (eds), *Culture, Media, Language*, London: Hutchinson, pp. 128–38.

—— (1982) 'The rediscovery of ideology', in M. Gurevitch *et al.* (eds), *Culture, Society and the Media*, London: Methuen, pp. 56–90.

—— (1987) 'Minimal selves', in *Identity: The Real Me*, ICA Documents 6, London: Institute of Contemporary Arts, pp. 44–6.

—— (1993) 'Culture, community, nation', *Cultural Studies* 7, 3: 349–63.

Halle, M. *et al.* (eds) (1984) *Semiotics: Semiotics and the History of Culture*, Ann Arbor: University of Michigan.

Halliday, M.A.K. (1979) *Language as Social Semiotic*, London: Edward Arnold.

Hammersley, M. and Atkinson, P. (1983) *Ethnography: Principles in Practice*, London: Tavistock.

Handler, R. (1985) 'On dialogue and deconstructive analysis: problems in narrating nationalism and ethnicity', *Journal of Anthropological Research* 41, 2: 171–82.

Hanhardt, J.G. (ed.) (1986) *Video Culture: A Critical Investigation*, Layton, Ut.: Peregrine Smith Books.

Hanson, J. (1987) *Understanding Video: Applications, Impact and Theory*, Newbury Park, Calif.: Sage.

Harland, M.C. (1986) 'Technological nationalism', *Canadian Journal of Political and Social Theory* 10, 1–2: 196–221.

Harries, O. (1993) 'The collapse of the "The West"', *Foreign Affairs* 72, 4: 41–53.

Hartley, J. (1982) *Understanding News*, London: Methuen.

—— (1987) 'Invisible fictions: television audiences, paedocracy, pleasure', *Textual Practice* 1, 2: 121–38.

—— (1992) *Tele-ology: Studies in Television*, London and New York: Routledge.

Hawkes, T. (1977) *Structuralism and Semiotics*, London: Methuen.

Hayes, C. (1960) *Nationalism: A Religion*, New York: Macmillan.

Hebdige, D. (1988) *Hiding in the Light: On Images and Things*, London: Routledge.

Hechter, M. (1975) *Internal Colonialism: The Celtic Fringe in British National Development, 1536–1966*, London: Routledge and Kegan Paul.

Hefer, S. (1959) *Croatian Struggle for Freedom and Statehood*, trans. A. Ilić, Buenos Aires: Croatian Information Service.

Heinz, W. (1988) *Indigenous Populations, Ethnic Minorities and Human Rights*, Berlin: Quorum Verlag.

Helsinki Watch (1992) *Helsinki Watch Report: War Crimes in Bosnia-Herzegovina*, New York: Human Rights Watch.

Henke, L.L. and Donohue, T.R. (1989) 'Functional displacement of traditional television viewing by VCR owners', *Journal of Advertising Research* 29.2: 18–23.

Henningham, J. (ed.) (1991) *Institutions in Australian Society*, St Lucia: University of Queensland.

Herzfeld, M. (1987) *Anthropology Through the Looking-Glass: Critical Ethnography in the Margins of Europe*, Cambridge: Cambridge University Press.

Hill, P. (1989) *The Macedonians in Australia*, Carlisle, Wash.: Hesperian Press.

Hill, S. (1988) *The Tragedy of Technology: Human Liberation Versus Domination in the Late Twentieth Century*, London: Pluto Press.

Hitler, A. (1992) *Mein Kampf*, trans. R.Manheim, London: Pimlico.

Hobsbawm, E. (1983) 'Inventing traditions', in E. Hobsbawm and T. Ranger (eds), *The Invention of Tradition*, Cambridge: Cambridge University Press, pp. 1–14.

—— (1990) *Nations and Nationalism since 1780: Programme, Myth, Reality*, Cambridge: Cambridge University Press.

Hobsbawm, E. and Ranger, T. (eds) (1983) *The Invention of Tradition*, Cambridge: Cambridge University Press.

Hobson, D. (1978) 'Housewives: isolation as oppression', in Women's Studies Group CCCS (eds), *Women Take Issue: Aspects of Women's Subordination*, London: Hutchinson, pp. 79–95.

—— (1982) *Crossroads: The Drama of a Soap Opera*, London: Methuen.

Hodge, B. and Tripp, D. (1986) *Children and Television: A Semiotic Approach*, Cambridge: Polity Press.

Hodge, R. and Kress, G. (1988) *Social Semiotics*, Cambridge: Polity Press.

—— (1993) *Language as Ideology*, 2nd edn, London: Routledge and Kegan Paul.

Holland, P. (1991) 'Introduction: History, memory and the family album', in J. Spence and P. Holland (eds), *Family Snaps*, London: Virago Press, pp. 1–14.

Hollins, T. (1984) *Beyond Broadcasting into the Cable Age*, London: British Film Institute, Broadcasting Research Unit.

Horowitz, D. (1985) *Ethnic Groups in Conflict*, Berkeley and Los Angeles: University of California Press.

Hristov, A. (1971) *The Creation of Macedonian Statehood, 1893–1945*, trans. B. Meares, Skopje: Kultura.

Hroch, M. (1985) *Social Preconditions of National Revival in Europe*, Cambridge: Cambridge University Press.

Ilievski, D. (1973) *The Macedonian Orthodox Church: The Road to Independence*, trans. J.M. Leech, Skopje: Macedonian Review Editions.

International Recognition of the Republic of Macedonia (1992) *Balkan Forum* 1, 1: 161–218.

Ivanišević, I. (1992) 'Bojovnik i trubadur' (Warrior and troubadour), *Nedjeljna Dalmacija*, 16 January, p. 19.

Ivanov, V.V. and Toporov, V.M. (1976) 'The invariant and transformations in folklore texts', trans. N. Fowler, *Dispositio Revista Hispanica de Semiotica Literaria: Soviet Semiotics of Culture*, Special Issue 3: 263–70.

Iyer, P. (1988) *Video Night in Kathmandu: And Other Reports from the not-so-Far-East*, London: Bloomsbury.

Jakobson, R. (1971) 'On the relation between visual and auditory signs', *Selected Writings* II, The Hague: Mouton.

Jameson, F. (1984) 'Postmodernism, or the cultural logic of late capitalism', *New Left Review* 146: 53–93.

Jankowski, N.W. (1991) 'Qualitative research and community media', in K.B. Jensen and N.W. Jankowski (eds), *A Handbook of Qualitative Methodologies for Mass Communication Research*, London: Routledge, pp. 163–74.

Jarratt, P. (1988) 'Captives of the VCR: how we became a couch potato culture', *The Bulletin*, 16 August, pp. 50–8.

Jauss, H. (1982) *Toward an Aesthetic of Reception*, trans. T. Bahti, Minneapolis: University of Minnesota Press.

Jayyusi, L. (1993) 'The reflexive nexus: photo-practice and natural history', *Continuum* 6, 2: 25–52.

Jenkins, H. (1992) *Textual Poachers: Television Fans and Participatory Culture*, New York: Routledge.

Jensen, K.B. (1987) 'News as ideology: economic statistics and political ritual in television network news', *Journal of Communication* 37, 1: 8–27.

—— (1991) 'Reception analysis: mass communication as the social production of meaning', in K.B. Jensen and N.W. Jankowski (eds), *A Handbook of Qualitative Methodologies for Mass Communication Research*, London: Routledge, pp. 135–48.

Jensen, K.B. and Jankowski, N.W. (eds) (1991) *A Handbook of Qualitative Methodologies for Mass Communication Research*, London: Routledge.

BIBLIOGRAPHY

Joffe, J. (1995) 'Europe's bitter Bosnia lesson', *Time*, 11 December, p. 68.
Johnstone, M. (1984) 'The photographs of Larry Burrows: human qualities in a documentary', in D. Featherstone (ed.), *Observations: Essays on Documentary Photography*, California: The Friends of Photography, pp. 93–102.
Kamper, D. and Wolf, C. (eds) (1989) *Looking Back on the End of the World*, trans. D. Antal, New York: Semiotext(e).
Kapferer, B. (1988) *Legends of People, Myths and State*, Washington: Smithsonian Institution Press.
Kaplan, E.A. (ed.) (1983) *Regarding Television. Critical Approaches – An Anthology*, Frederick, MD: University Publications of America.
Katičić, R. and Novak, S.P. (1989) *Two Thousand Years of Writing in Croatia*, trans. S. Bićanić and S. Bašić, Zagreb: Sveučilišna naklada Liber and MGC.
Katz, E. and Liebes, T. (1985) 'Mutual aid in the decoding of "Dallas": preliminary notes from a cross-cultural study', in P. Drummond and R. Paterson (eds), *Television in Transition: Papers from the 1st International Television Studies Conference*, London: British Film Institute, pp. 187–98.
Kennan, G.F. (1993) 'The Balkan crisis – 1913 and 1993', *The New York Review* 11, 13: 3–7.
Klaić, V. (1980) *Povijest Hrvata* (History of Croatian People), Zagreb: Nakladni Zavod Matice Hrvatske.
Knightley, P. (1993) 'Women in the war zone', *The Independent*, October: 10–16.
Kohn, H. (1944) *The Idea of Nationalism*, New York: Macmillan.
Kolar-Panov, D. (1989) 'The poetic world of Ivan Generalić', Honours thesis, Murdoch University, Perth, Western Australia.
Kolar-Panov, D. and Miller, T. (1991) 'Radio and civil war in Yugoslavia', *Media Information Australia* 62: 74–7.
Koneski, B. (1949) *Macedonian 19th Century Textbooks: A Contribution to the History of Macedonian Renaissance*, Skopje: Historical Library.
Kristeva, J. (1993) *Nations Without Nationalism*, New York: Columbia University Press.
Krizek, R.L. and Stempien, D. (1990) 'Networks and practiced culture: the maintenance of symbolic ethnicity among the Phoenix Irish', paper presented to the International Communication Association Annual Conference (ICAAC), Dublin, Ireland.
Krizman, B. (1980) *Pavelić izmedju Hitlera i Mussolinija* (Pavelić between Hitler and Mussolini), Zagreb: Globus.
Krushelnycky, A. and Moutet, A.E. (1993) 'Bosnia betrayed', *The European*, 28 May, pp. 8–9.
Kulchyski, P. (1989) 'The postmodern and the paleolithic: notes on technology and native community in the Far North', *Canadian Journal of Political and Social Theory* 13, 3: 49–62.
Kuzmanović, J. (1992) 'Pjesma olovnog vojnika' (The song of a tin soldier), *Nedjeljna Dalmacija*, 23 April, p. 26.
Lange, A. and Renaud, J.L. (1989) *The Future of the European Audio-Visual Industry*, Manchester: European Institute for the Media.
Larsen, P. (1992) 'More than just images: the whole picture News in the multi-channel universe', in M. Skovmand and K.C. Schrøder (eds), *Media Cultures: Reappraising Transnational Media*, London: Routledge, pp. 124–41.
Lazarov, R. (1995) 'The Albanians in Macedonia: co–citizenship or . . . ?', *Balkan Forum* 3, 2: 19–48.
Leach, E.R. (1976) *Culture and Communication*, Cambridge: Cambridge University Press.

251

Lederer, I.J. (1963) *Yugoslavia at the Paris Conference*, New Haven: Yale University Press.

Lee, A. (1993) 'VCR: angel or devil', student essay for 'Media Audiences' course, Murdoch University, Perth, Western Australia.

Letić, F. (1989) *Društveni život vanjskih migranata* (Social Life of Immigrants), Zagreb: NIRO Radničke Novine.

Letica, S. (ed.) (1990) *Croatia 1990*, Zagreb: Presidency of the Republic of Croatia.

Lévi-Strauss, C. (1963) 'The structural study of myth', in *Structural Anthropology*, vol. 1, New York: Basic Books, pp. 206–31.

—— (1970) *The Raw and the Cooked*, London: Jonathan Cape.

Levy, M.R. (1989) 'Why VCRs aren't pop-up toasters: issues in home video research', in M.R. Levy (ed.), *The VCR Age: Home Video and Mass Communication*, Newbury Park, CA: Sage, pp. 9–20.

—— (ed.) (1989) *The VCR Age: Home Video and Mass Communication*, Newbury Park, CA: Sage.

Levy, M.R. and Gunter, B. (1988) *Home Video and the Changing Nature of the Television Audience*, London: John Libbey.

Lewinski, J. (1978) *The Camera at War: War Photography from 1848 to the Present Day*, Great Britain: W. and J. Mackay Ltd.

Lewis, J. (1985) 'Decoding television news', in P. Drummond and R. Paterson (eds), *Television in Transition: Papers from the 1st International Television Studies Conference*, London: British Film Institute, pp. 205–34.

—— (1991) *The Ideological Octopus: An Exploration of Television and its Audience*, New York: Routledge.

Liakos, A. (1993) 'The Balkan crisis and nationalism', *Balkan Forum* 1, 2: 69–88.

Liebes, T. (1984) 'Ethnocriticism: Israelis of Moroccan ethnicity negotiate the meaning of "Dallas"', *Studies in Visual Communication* 10.3: 46–72.

Liebes, T. and Katz, E. (1990) *The Export of Meaning: Cross-Cultural Readings of 'Dallas'*, New York: Oxford University Press.

Lindlof, T. (ed.) (1987) *Natural Audiences: Qualitative Research and Media Uses and Effects*, Norwood, NJ: Ablex Publishing Company.

Livingstone, S.M. (1990) 'Personal construction of domestic technologies: Gender relations and family dynamics', paper presented at an International Communication Association Annual Conference (ICAAC), Dublin.

Lotman, J.M. (1976a) 'Culture and information', *Dispositio Revista Hispanica de Semiotica Literaria: Soviet Semiotics of Culture*, Special Issue 3: 213–15.

—— (1976b) *Semiotics of Cinema*, trans. M.E. Suino, Ann Arbor: Michigan Slavic Publications.

—— (1990) *Universe of the Mind: A Semiotic Theory of Culture*, trans. A. Shukman, Bloomington, Ind.: Indiana University Press.

Lotman, J.M. and Piatigorsky, A.M. (1978) 'Text and function', trans. A. Shukman, *New Literary History* 9, 2: 233–44.

Lotman, J.M. and Uspensky, B.A. (1978a) 'On the semiotics mechanism of culture', *New Literary History* 9, 2: 211–32.

—— (1978b) 'Text and function', *New Literary History* 9, 2: 233–44.

Lotman, J.M. and Uspenskij, B.A. (1984) *The Semiotics of Russian Culture*, Ann Arbor: University of Michigan.

Lull, J. (1980) 'The social uses of television', *Human Communications Research* 6, 3: 198–209.

—— (ed.) (1988) *World Families Watch Television*, London: Sage.

—— (1990) *Inside Family Viewing: Ethnographic Research on Television's Audiences*, London: Routledge.

Lyall, K. (1993) 'Home is where the hurt is', *Time*, 27 December, pp. 26–30.

Lynch, K. (1960) *The Image of the City*, Cambridge, Mass.: MIT Press.

Macan, T. (1990) 'U podnožju Jelačićeva spomenika' (Beneath the Jelačić monument), *Nova Matica* 1–2: 16–7.

McAdams, C.M. (1992) *Croatia: Myth and Reality*, Arcadia, CA: Croatian Information Service.

MacCannell, D. and MacCannell, J. (1982) 'Ethnosemiotics: beyond structural anthropology', in D. MacCannell and J. MacCannell, *The Time of the Sign: A Semiotic Interpretation of Modern Culture,* Bloomington, Indiana: Indiana University Press.

McFarlane, B. (1988) *Yugoslavia: Politics, Economics and Society*, London: Pinter Publishers.

McGann, T. (1993) 'Players group to build a place in fast changing global media', *The Weekend Australian*, 10–11 July, pp. 29, 31.

McGreal, C. (1993) 'Zaire buries victims of hatred and expediency', *Guardian Weekly*, 3 October, p. 4.

McLuhan, M. (1964) *Understanding Media: The Extensions of Man*, 2nd edn, New York: New American Library.

McLuhan, M. and Powers, B.R. (1989) *The Global Village*, Oxford: Oxford University Press.

McNeil, W.H. (1985) *Polyethnicity and National Unity in World History*, Toronto: University of Toronto Press.

Madden, K. (1990) 'The Inuit Broadcasting Corporation: developing video to sustain cultural integrity', paper presented at an International Communications Association Annual Conference (ICAAC), Dublin.

Magaš, B. (1993) *The Destruction of Yugoslavia: Tracking the Break-up 1980–92*, London: Verso.

Marcus, G.E. (1986) 'Contemporary problems of ethnography in the modern World System', in J. Clifford and G.E. Marcus (eds), *Writing Culture,* Berkeley and Los Angeles: University of California Press, pp. 165–93.

Marcus, G.E. and Fischer, M. (1986) *Anthropology as Cultural Critique: An Experimental Moment in the Human Sciences*, Chicago: University of Chicago Press.

Marks, L.U. (1992) 'The language of terrorism', *Framework* 38–9: 64–73.

Marshall, S. (1979) 'Video: technology and practice', *Screen* 5: 109–19.

Martin, J. (1965) *Refugee Settlers: A Study of Displaced Persons in Australia*, Canberra: Australian National University Press.

—— (1978) *The Migrant Presence*, Sydney: Allen and Unwin.

Martis, N.K. (1984) *The Falsification of Macedonian History*, trans. J.P. Smith, Athens: Ikaros Publishing Co.

Mattelart, A., Delacourt, X. and Mattelart, M. (1984) *International Image Markets: In Search for Alternative Perspective*, trans. D. Buxton, London: Routledge.

Meeuwis, M. (1993) 'Nationalist ideology in news reporting on the Yugoslav crisis: a pragmatic analysis', *Journal of Pragmatics* 20, 217–37.

Meiselas, S. (1985) 'A portfolio on Central America', in M. Blonsky (ed.), *On Signs*, Oxford: Basil Blackwell, pp. 43–53.

Meyrowitz, J. (1985) 'Lowering the political hero to our level: a case study in changing authority', in *No Sense of Place*, New York: Oxford University Press, pp. 268–304.

Meyrowitz, J. and Maguire, J. (1993) 'Media, place and multiculturalism', *Society* 30, 5: 41–8.

Michaels, E. (1985) 'Constraints on knowledge in an economy of oral information', *Current Anthropology* 26, 4: 505–10.

—— (1987) *For a Cultural Future: Frances Jupurrurla Makes TV at Yuendumu*, Sydney: Artspace, Art and Criticism Monograph Series 3.

—— (1988) 'Para-ethnography', *Art and Text* 30: 42–51.

—— (1990) 'A model of teleported text', *Continuum* 3, 2: 8–31.

Miller, T. (1992) 'Video truth: Rodney King and the reading of character', *FilmNews* 22, 4: 5.

Mlinar, Z. (1992a) 'Individuation and globalization: the transformation of territorial social organization' in Z. Mlinar (ed.), *Globalization and Territorial Identities*, Aldershot: Avebury, pp. 15–34.

—— (ed.) (1992b) *Globalization and Territorial Identities*, Aldershot: Avebury.

Mojsov, L. (1979) *The Macedonian Historical Themes*, Belgrade: Jugoslovenska Stvarnost, Medjunarodna Politika.

Molnar, H. (1990) 'The broadcasting for remote areas community scheme: small vs big media', *Media Information Australia* 58: 147–54.

Moran, A. and O'Regan, T. (eds) (1989) *Australian Screen*, Ringwood: Penguin.

Morgan, M. *et al.* (1990) 'Adolescents, VCRs, and the family environment', *Communication Research* 17, 1: 83–106.

Morley, D. (1980) *The 'Nationwide' Audience: Structure and Decoding*, London: British Film Institute.

—— (1981) 'The "Nationwide" audience: a critical postscript', *Screen Education* 39: 3–14.

—— (1986) *Family Television: Cultural Power and Domestic Leisure*, London: Routledge.

—— (1988) 'Domestic relations: the framework of family viewing in Great Britain', in J. Lull (ed.), *World Families watch Television*, London: Sage, pp. 22–48.

—— (1989) 'Changing paradigms in audience studies', in E. Seiter, H. Borchers, G. Kreutzner and E.M. Wanth (eds), *Remote Control: Television Audiences, and Cultural Power*, London: Routledge, pp. 16–43.

—— (1991) 'Where the global meets the local: notes from the sitting room', *Screen* 32, 1: 1–15.

—— (1992) *Television, Audiences and Cultural Studies*, London: Routledge.

Morley, D. and Robins, K. (1989) 'Spaces of identity: communications technologies and reconfiguration of Europe', *Screen* 30, 4: 10–34.

—— (1995) *Spaces of Identity: Global Media, Electronic Landscapes and Cultural Boundaries*, London and New York: Routledge.

Morley, D. and Silverstone, R. (1991) 'Communication and context: ethnographic perspectives on the media audience', in K.B. Jensen and N.W. Jankowski (eds), *A Handbook of Qualitative Methodologies for Mass Communication Research*, London: Routledge, pp. 149–62.

Morris, M. (1990) 'Banality in cultural studies', in P. Mellencamp (ed.), *Logics of Television: Essays in Cultural Criticism*, Bloomington, Indiana: Indiana University Press, pp. 14–43.

Morrison, D. E. (1992) *Television and the Gulf War*, London: John Libbey.

Morrow, L. (1993) 'A moral mystery: Serbian self-pity', *Time*, 12 April, p. 72.

Motyl, A.J. (ed.) (1992) *The Post-Soviet Nations: Perspectives on the Demise of the USSR*, New York: Columbia University Press.

Moyal, A. (1989) 'Women and technology: a case study of the telephone in Australia', *Media Information Australia* 54: 57–60.

—— (1992) 'The gendered use of the telephone: an Australian case study', *Media, Culture and Society* 14, 1: 51–72.

Muecke, S. (1985) 'Scribes', *Meridian* 4, 1: 41–8.

Mukarovsky, J. (1978) *Structure, Sign, and Function: Selected Essays*, trans. and ed. J. Burbank and P. Steiner, New Haven: Yale University Press.

Multicultural and Ethnic Affairs Commission of Western Australia (1988) *Ethnicity-*

related Data for Local Government Areas in Western Australia, Perth: MEAC.

Murray, M. (1975) *The Videotape Book: A Basic Guide to Portable Television Production for Families, Friends, Schools and Neighborhoods*, New York: Bantam Books.

Mužić, I. (1990) *Stjepan Radić u Kraljevini SHS* (Stjepan Radić in the Kingdom of Serbs, Croats and Slovenes), 4th edn, Zagreb: Nakladni Zavod Matice Hrvatske.

Nakhimovsky, A.D. and Nakhimovsky-Stone, A. (eds), (1985) *The Semiotics of Russian Cultural History: Essays by Jurij M. Lotman, Lidia T.A. Ginsbury and Boris A. Uspenskij*, introd. B. Gasparov, Ithaca: Cornell University Press.

Newcomb, P. (1990) 'Can video survive?', *Forbes* 145: 3: 39–40.

Newman, M. (1986) 'Revising modernism, representing postmodernism: critical discourses of the visual arts', *ICA Documents No. 4: Postmodernism*, London: Institute of Contemporary Arts, pp. 32–52.

Nichols, B. (1991) *Representing Reality: Issues and Concepts in Documentary*, Bloomington, Indiana: Indiana University Press.

Nightingale, V. (1989) 'What's "Ethnographic" about ethnographic audience research?', *Australian Journal of Communication* 16: 50–63.

Nikolić, V. (1988) *Bleiburg: Uzroci i posljedice* (Bleiburg: Causes and Consequences), Munich: Knjižnica Hrvatske Revije.

Njegoš, P.P. (1952) *Gorski vijenac* (The Mountain Wreath), Belgrade: Prosveta.

Nmungwun, A.F. (1989) *Video Recording Technology: Its Impact on Media and Home Entertainment*, Hillsdale, NJ: Lawrence Erlbaum Associates.

Noble, G. (1989) 'Exploring the concept of the polarised audience with the VCR in Australia', *Australian Journal of Communication* 15: 88–107.

Norris, C. (1992) *Uncritical Theory: Postmodernism, Intellectuals and the Gulf War*, London: Lawrence and Wishart.

O'Regan, T. (1986) 'Aspects of the Australian film and television interface', *Australian Journal of Screen Theory* 17–18: 5–33.

—— (1988) 'The background to television networking', in G. Lewis and E. Moore (eds), *Australian Communications Technology and Policy*, Sydney: Centre for Information Studies and AFTRS, pp. 126–43.

—— (1989) 'Towards a high communications policy: assessing recent changes within Australian broadcasting', *Continuum* 2, 1: 135–58.

—— (1990) 'TV as a cultural technology: the work of Eric Michaels', *Continuum* 3, 2: 53–98.

—— (1991) 'From piracy to sovereignty: international video cassette recorder trends', *Continuum* 4, 2: 112–35.

—— (1992) 'Too popular by far: accounting for Hollywood's popularity', *Continuum* 5, 2: 302–51.

—— (1993) *Australian Television Culture*, St. Leonards: Allen and Unwin.

O'Regan, T. and Batty, P. (1993) 'An Aboriginal television culture: issues, strategies, politics', in T. O'Regan, *Australian Television Culture*, St. Leonards: Allen and Unwin, pp. 169–92.

O'Regan, T. and Kolar-Panov, D. (1991) 'Marginal audiences', unpublished paper: Murdoch University.

O'Regan, T. and Kolar-Panov, D. (1993a) 'SBS-television: symbolic politics and multicultural policy in television provision', in T. O'Regan, *Australian Television Culture*, St. Leonards: Allen and Unwin, pp. 121–42.

—— (1993b) 'SBS-TV: A television service' in T. O'Regan, *Australian Television Culture*, St. Leonards: Allen and Unwin, pp. 143–68.

O'Regan, T. and Shoesmith, B. (eds) (1985) *The Moving Image: The History of Film and Television in Western Australia, 1896–1985*, Perth, Western Australia: History and Film Association.

O'Sullivan, T., Hartley, J., Saunders, D. and Fiske, J. (1983) *Key Concepts in Communication*, London: Methuen.

O'Toole, L.M. (1980) 'Dimensions of semiotic space in narrative', *Poetics Today* 1, 4: 135–49.

O'Toole, M. (1990) 'A systemic-functional semiotics of art', *Semiotica* 82, 3–4: 185–209.

—— (1991) 'The Bronze Horseman, looking East', *Australian Slavonic and East European Studies* 5, 2: 67–84.

—— (1992a) 'A functional semiotics for the visual arts', in J. Andrew (ed.), *Poetics of the Text*, Amsterdam: Rodopi, pp. 57–77.

—— (1992b) 'Institutional sculpture and the social semiotic', *Social Semiotics* 2, 1: 47–65.

—— (1994) *The Language of Displayed Art*, London: Leicester University Press, Pinter Publishers.

Obradović, D. (1992) *Suffering of Dubrovnik*, trans. M. Bašić, Dubrovnik: Naučna Biblioteka.

Omračanin, I. (1975) *The Pro-Allied Putsch in Croatia in 1944 and the Massacre of Croatians by Tito Communists in 1945*, Philadelphia: Dorrance and Company.

Ong, W.J. (1982) *Orality and Literacy: The Technologizing of the Word*, London: Methuen.

Ostojić, S. (ed.) (1977) *Rat, revolucija, ekran* (War, Revolution, Screen), Zagreb: Spektar.

Painton, F. (1993) 'Slaughtering the past and future', *Time*, 22 November, pp. 34–5.

Palmer, P. (1986) *The Lively Audience*, London: Allen and Unwin.

Pandevski, M. (1978) *Macedonia and the Macedonians in the Eastern Crisis*, Skopje: Macedonian Review Editions.

Panov, A. (1938/1983) *Pečalbari* (The Migrant Workers), Skopje: Kultura.

Panovski, N. (1991) *Teatarot kako oružje* (Theatre as a Weapon), Skopje: Kultura.

Paris, E. (1981) 'Genocide in satellite Croatia 1941–1945: a record of racial and religious persecutions and massacres', trans. L. Perkins, Melbourne, Aus., *Srpska misao* (The Serbian Thought): 65–6.

Pavković, A. (1993) 'Intellectuals into politicians: Serbia 1990–92', *Meanjin* 52, 1: 107–16.

Pearson, D.E. (1993) 'Post-mass culture', *Society* 30, 5: 17–22.

Peirce, C. S. (1932) *Collected Papers*, vol. 2, C. Hartshorne, P. Weiss and A.W. Burks (eds), Cambridge, Mass.: Harvard University Press.

Penušliski, K. (1992) *Narodna kultura na Egejska Makedonija* (Folk Culture of Aegean Macedonia), Skopje: Misla.

Petch, T. (1988) 'Belize', in M. Alvarado (ed.), *Video World-Wide: An International Study*, UNESCO, London: John Libbey, pp. 311–22.

'Picking over the pieces of war', (1992) *The Economist*, 17 October, p. 55.

Pink, B.N. (1992) *Demography West Australia 1990*, Canberra: AGPS.

Poliakov, L. (1974) *The Aryan Myth: A History of Racist and Nationalist Ideas in Europe*, trans. E. Howard, New York: Basic Books.

'Police called to brawl between Croat soccer fans' (1993) *Sunday Times*, 25 April, p. 11.

Pomorski, J.M. (1988) 'Poland', in M. Alvarado (ed.), *Video World-Wide: An International Study*, UNESCO London: John Libbey, pp. 181–96.

Poyatos, F. (ed.) (1988) *Literary Anthropology*, Amsterdam: John Benjamins Publishing Company.

Prcela, J. and Guldescu, S. (1970) *Operation Slaughterhouse: Eyewitness Accounts of Postwar Massacres in Yugoslavia*, Philadelphia: Dorrance and Company.

Price, C. (1989) 'Ethnic groups in Australia', in J. Jupp (ed.), *The Challenge of Diversity*, Canberra: AGPS, pp. 6–19.

Propp, V. (1968) *Morphology of the Folktale,* trans. L. Scott, Austin, Tex.: University of Texas Press.

—— (1971) 'Fairy tale transformations', in L. Matejka and K. Pomorska (eds), *Readings in Russian Poetics*, Cambridge, Mass.: Harvard University Press, pp. 94–116.

—— (1976) 'Study of the folktale: structure and history', *Dispositio Revista Hispanica de Semiotica Literaria: Soviet Semiotics of Culture*, Special Issue 3: 277–292.

—— (1984) *Theory and History of Folklore*, trans. A.Y. Martin and R.P. Martin, Manchester: Manchester University Press.

Provenzo, E. (1991) *Video Kids: Making Sense of 'Nintendo'*, Cambridge, Mass.: Harvard University Press.

Rabinow, P. (1977) *Reflections on Fieldwork in Morocco*, Berkeley and Los Angeles: University of California Press.

—— (1986) 'Representations are social facts: modernity and post-modernity in anthropology', in J. Clifford and G. Marcus (eds), *Writing Culture: The Poetics and Politics of Ethnography*, Berkeley and Los Angeles: University of California Press, pp. 234–61.

Radway, J. (1987) *Reading the Romance: Women, Patriarchy and Popular Literature*, London: Verso.

—— (1988) 'Reception study: ethnography and the problems of dispersed audiences and nomadic subjects', *Cultural Studies* 2, 3: 359–76.

Report of the Senate Select Committee (1987) *Television Equalisation*, Canberra: AGPS.

Republic of Croatia, (1991) *Constitution of the Republic of Croatia*, Zagreb.

Reuter, J. (1993) 'Policy and economy in Macedonia', *Balkan Forum* 1, 3: 135–76.

Ristić, S., Simić, Ž., Popović, V. (eds) (1973) *Enciklopediski englesko–srpskohrvatski rečnik* (Encyclopaedic English–Serbo-Croatian Dictionary), Beograd: Prosveta.

Rizvi, F. (1986) *Ethnicity, Class and Multicultural Education*, Deakin University, Victoria: Deakin University Press.

Robins, K. (1989) 'Reimagined communities? European image spaces beyond Fordism', *Cultural Studies* 3, 2: 145–65.

—— (1994) 'The haunted screen', in G. Bender and T. Druckrey (eds), *Culture on the Brink: Ideologies of Technology*, Seattle: Bay Press, pp. 305–15.

Robins, K. and Cornford, J. (1994) 'Local and regional broadcasting in the new media order', in A. Amin and N. Thrift (eds), *Globalization, Institutions, and Regional Development in Europe*, Oxford: Oxford University Press, pp. 218–28.

Robins, K. and Levidow L. (1995) 'Soldier, cyborg, citizen', in J. Brook and I.A. Boal (eds), *Resisting the Virtual Life: The Culture and Politics of Information*, San Francisco: City Lights, pp. 105–13.

Rogers, E.M. (1962) *Diffusion of Information*, New York: The Free Press, 1983.

Rosaldo, R. (1989) *Culture and Truth: The Remaking of Social Analysis*, Boston: Beacon Press.

Rota, J. (1990), 'Case studies of communication and identity', paper presented at International Communication Association Annual Conference (ICAAC), Dublin.

Rustin, M. (1987), 'Place and time in socialist theory', *Radical Philosophy*, 147.

Said, E. (1978) *Orientalism*, London: Routledge and Kegan Paul.

Santoro, L.F. (1988) 'Brazil', in M. Alvarado (ed.), *Video World-Wide: An International Study*, UNESCO, London: John Libbey, pp. 263–78.

257

Sazdov, T. (1986) *Folkroristički Studii* (Studies in Folklore), Naša Kniga: Skopje.
Sazdov, T. (1987) *Macedonian Folk Literature*, trans. S. Keesan, Skopje: Macedonian Review Editions.
Scannell, P. and Cardiff, D. (1991) *A Social History of British Broadcasting*, Vol. 1, *1922–1939: Serving the Nation*, Oxford: Blackwell.
Schapiro, M. (1973) *Approaches to Semiotics Words and Pictures*, The Hague: Mouton.
Scheglov, Y.K. and Zholkovskii, A.K. (1987) *Poetics of Expressiveness: A Theory and Applications*, Amsterdam: John Benjamins Publishing Company.
Scheper-Hughes, N. (1992) *Death Without Weeping: The Violence of Everyday Life in Brazil*, Berkeley and Los Angeles: University of California Press.
Schiller, D. (1986) 'Transformations of news in the United States information market' in P. Golding *et al.*, *Communicating Politics: Mass Communications and the Political Process*, Leicester: University of Leicester Press, pp. 19–36.
Schiller, H.I. (1973) *The Mind Managers*, Boston: Beacon Press.
Schiller, H. (1991) 'Not yet the post-imperialist era', *Critical Studies in Mass Communication*, 8: 13–28.
Schlesinger, P. (1987) 'On national identity: some conceptions and misconceptions criticized', *Social Science Information* 26, 2: 219–64.
—— (1991) *Media, State and Nation: Political Violence and Collective Identities*, London: Sage.
Schlesinger, P. *et al.* (1992) *Women Viewing Violence*, London: British Film Institute.
Schneider, C. and Wallis, B. (eds) (1988) *Global Television*, New York: Wedge Press, MIT Press.
Scholes, R. (1982) *Semiotics and Interpretation*, New Haven: Yale University Press.
Schou, S. (1992) 'Postwar Americanisation and the revitalisation of European culture', in M. Skovmand and K.C. Schrøder (eds), *Media Cultures: Reappraising Transnational Media*, London: Routledge, pp. 142–60.
Schrøder, K.C. (1992) 'Cultural quality: search for a phantom? A reception perspective on judgements of cultural value', in M. Skovmand and K.C. Schrøder (eds), *Media Cultures: Reappraising Transnational Media*, London: Routledge, pp. 199–219.
Schwarz, R. (1992) *Misplaced Ideas: Essays on Brazilian Culture*, London: Verso.
Secunda, E. (1990) 'VCRs and viewer control over programming: an historical perspective', in J.R. Dobrow (ed.), *Social and Cultural Aspects of VCR Use*, Hillsdale, NJ: Lawrence Erlbaum Associates, pp. 9–24.
Seiter, E., Borchers, H., Kreutzner, G. and Wanth, E.M. (eds) (1989) *Remote Control: Television, Audiences, and Cultural Power*, London: Routledge.
Seneviratne, K. (1992) 'Multicultural television: going beyond the rhetoric', *Media Information Australia* 66: 53–8.
Sepstrup, P. (1990) *Transnationalization of Television in Western Europe*, London: John Libbey.
Shafer, B.C. (1972) *Faces of Nationalism*, New York: Harcourt Brace Jovanovich, Inc.
Shils, E. (1981) *Tradition*, Chicago: University of Chicago Press.
Shishkoff, S. (1976) 'The structure of fairytales: Propp vs. Lévi-Strauss', *Dispositio Revista Hispanica de Semiotica Literaria: Soviet Semiotics of Culture*, Special Issue 3: 271–6.
Silverman, D. and Torode, B. (1980) *The Material World*, London: Routledge and Kegan Paul.
Silverman, K. (1983) *The Subject of Semiotics*, New York: Oxford University Press.
Silverstone, R. (1990) 'Television and everyday life: towards an anthropology of the

television audience', in M. Ferguson (ed.), *Public Communication: The New Imperatives*, London: Sage, pp. 173–89.

—— (1991) 'From audiences to consumers: the household and the consumption of information and communication technologies', *European Journal of Communication* 6, 2: 135–54.

Silverstone, R. and Morley, D. (1990) 'Families and their technologies: two ethnographic portraits', in T. Putnam and C. Newton (eds), *Household Choices*, London: Futures Publications, pp. 74–83.

Silverstone, R., Hirsch, E. and Morley, D. (1991) 'Listening to a long conversation: an ethnographic approach to the study of information and communication technologies in the home', *Cultural Studies* 5, 2: 204–27.

—— (1992) 'Information and communication technologies and the moral economy of the household', in R. Silverstone and E. Hirsch (eds), *Consuming Technologies: Media and Information in Domestic Spaces*, London: Routledge, pp. 15–31.

Simper, E. (1993) 'SBS to set up pay television service', *The Weekend Australian*, 26–7 June, p. 4.

Sims, J.B. (1989) 'VCR viewing patterns: an electronic and passive investigation', *Journal of Advertising Research* 29, 2: 11–18.

Singam, P.T. (1993) 'Macedonian rights fight a test of faith', *The West Australian*, 1 March, p. 11.

Singleton, F. (1976) *Twentieth-century Yugoslavia*, New York: Columbia University Press.

Šišić, F. (1975) *Pregled povijesti hrvatskog naroda* (History of Croatian People, An Overview), Zagreb: Nakladni Zavod Matice Hrvatske.

Skirrow, G. (1986) 'Hellivision: an analysis of video games', in C. MacCabe, (ed.), *High Theory/Low Culture: Analysing Popular Television and Film*, Manchester: Manchester University Press, pp. 115–42.

Skovmand, M. and Schrøder, K.C. (eds) (1992) *Media Cultures: Reappraising Transnational Media*, London: Routledge.

Slater, D. (1991) 'Consuming Kodak', in J. Spence and P. Holland (eds), *Family Snapshots*, London: Virago Press, pp. 49–59.

Sluga, G. (1993) 'Making multicultural mayhem', *The Independent*, 14 October, pp. 10–16.

Smith, A.D. (1979) *Nationalism in the Twentieth Century*, Canberra: Australian National University Press.

—— (1981) *The Ethnic Revival*, New York: Cambridge University Press.

—— (1988) *The Ethnic Origins of Nations*, New York: Basil Blackwell Inc.

—— (1990) 'Towards a global culture?', *Theory, Culture and Society*: 7: 171–91.

—— (1991) *National Identity*, London: Penguin.

Socialist Federal Republic of Yugoslavia (1974) *The Constitution of the Socialist Federal Republic of Yugoslavia*, trans. M.Vavičić, Belgrade: Government Publications.

Soja, E. (1989) *Postmodern Geographies: The Reassertion of Space in Critical Theory*, London: Verso.

Sorkin, M. (1986) 'Simulations: faking it', in T. Gitlin (ed.), *Watching Television*, New York: Pantheon Books, pp. 162–82.

Spence, J. and Holland, P. (eds), (1991) *Family Snapshots*, London: Virago Press.

Spindler-Brown, A. (1988) 'Red tape', *The Listener* 13: 23–4.

Splivalo, A. (1982) *The Home Fires*, Fremantle.: Fremantle Arts Centre Press.

Srebreny-Mohammadi, A. and Mohammadi, A. (1991) 'Hegemony and resistance: media politics in the Islamic Republic of Iran', *Quarterly Review of Film and Video* 12, 4: 35–59.

Stalin, J. (1953–5) 'Marxism and the national question', *Collected Works*, vol. 3, Moscow: Progress, pp. 300–84.

Starčević, M. and Petković, N. (1991) *Hrvatska '91: nasiljem i zločinom protiv prava* (With Violence and Crime Against Rights), Belgrade: Vojnoizdavački i Novinski Centar.

Stardelov, G., Grozdanov, C. and Ristovski, B. (eds) (1993) *Macedonia and its Relations with Greece*, Skopje: Macedonian Academy of Sciences and Arts.

Steiner, W. (ed.) (1981) *Image and Code*, Ann Arbor: University of Michigan.

Stratton, J. and Ang, I. (1994) 'Multicultural imagined communities: cultural difference and national identity in Australia and the USA', *Continuum* 8, 2: 124–58.

Sugar, P.F. and Lederer, I.J. (eds) (1969) *Nationalism in Eastern Europe*, Seattle and London: University of Washington Press.

Talbott, S. (1991) 'Fiddling while Dubrovnik burns', *Time*, 25 November, p. 37.

Tashkovski, D. (1976) *The Macedonian Nation*, Skopje: NIK Nasha Kniga.

Taylor, C. (1989) *Sources of the Self: The Making of the Modern Identity*, Cambridge, Mass.: Harvard University Press.

Taylor, P.M. (1992) *War and the Media: Propaganda and Persuasion in the Gulf War*, Manchester: Manchester University Press.

Theall, D.F. (1986) 'McLuhan telematics and the Toronto School of Communication', *Canadian Journal of Political and Social Theory* 10, 1–2: 79–89.

Thompson, J. (1990) *Ideology and Modern Culture: Critical Social Theory in the Era of Mass Communication*, Cambridge: Polity Press.

Thompson, M. (1992) *A Paper House: The Ending of Yugoslavia*, London: Vintage.

Threadgold, T. *et al.* (eds) (1986) *Language, Semiotics, Ideology*, Sydney: Sydney Association for Studies in Society and Culture.

Throsby, C.D. and Withers, G.A. (1978) *The Economics of the Performing Arts*, Melbourne: Edward Arnold.

Todorov, T. (1982) *Theories of the Symbol*, trans. C. Porter, Oxford: Basil Blackwell.

—— (1984) *Mikhail Bakhtin: The Dialogical Principle*, trans. W. Godzich, Manchester: Manchester University Press.

Tomlinson, J. (1991) *Cultural Imperialism: A Critical Introduction*, London: Pinter.

Toševski, I. (1993) 'United Nations Declaration on the Rights of Minorities', *Balkan Forum* 1, 2: 23–44.

Tracey, M. (1988) 'Foreword', in M. Alvarado (ed.), *Video World-Wide: An International Study*, UNESCO, London: John Libbey, pp. ix–xiii.

Tranhardt, D. (1989) 'Turkish headscarves and the "foreigner problem": constructing difference through emblems of identity', *New German Critique* 46: 27–46.

Tripalo, M. (1990) *Hrvatsko proljeće* (Croatian Spring), 2nd edn, Zagreb: Globus.

Tulloch, J. and Turner, G. (eds) (1989) *Australian Television: Programs, Pleasures and Politics*, Sydney: Allen and Unwin.

Turner, G. (1990) *British Cultural Studies: An Introduction*, London: Unwin Hyman.

Turner, V. (1974) *Dramas, Fields, and Metaphors: Symbolic Action in Human Society*, Ithaca, NY: Cornell University Press.

Tvrtković, P. (1993) *Bosnia Hercegovina: Back to the Future*, London: Polprint.

Tydeman, J. and Kelm, E. (1986) *New Media in Europe*, London: McGraw-Hill Book Company.

Tynyanov, Y.N. (1978) 'Plot and story-line in the cinema', trans. A. Shukman, *Russian Poetics in Translation* 5: 20–1.

Ulloa, Y. and Donoso, E.J. (1988) 'Chile', in M. Alvarado (ed.), *Video World-Wide: An International Study*, UNESCO, London: John Libbey, pp. 301–10.

United Nations High Commission for Refugees (UNHCR) (1992) Emergency, *Refugees* 91.

—— (1993) Human rights, *Refugees* 92.

University of Technology, Sydney (1990) *Racism, Cultural Pluralism and the Media*, Canberra: Office of Multicultural Affairs.

Uspenskij, B.A. (1973) *A Poetics of Composition: The Structure of the Artistic Text and Typology of a Compositional Form*, trans. V. Zavarin and S. Witting, Berkeley and Los Angeles: University of California Press.

Venner, M. (1988) 'Broadcasting for Remote Aboriginal Communities Scheme', *Media Information Australia* 47: 37–43.

Virilio, P. (1986) *Speed and Politics: An Essay on Dromology*, trans. M. Polizzotti, New York: Semiotext(e).

—— (1989) *War and Cinema*, trans. M. Polizzotti, London: Verso.

—— (1990) *Popular Defense and Ecological Struggles*, trans. M. Polizzotti, New York: Semiotext(e).

Virilio, P. and Lotringer, S. (1983) *Pure War*, trans. M. Polizzotti, New York: Semiotext(e).

Vološinov, V. (1930/1973) *Marxism and the Philosophy of Language*, trans. L. Matejka and I.R. Titunik, New York: Seminar Press.

Vujačić, V. and Zaslavsky, V. (1991) 'The causes of disintegration in the USSR and Yugoslavia', *Telos* 88: 120–40.

Walkerdine, V. (1986) 'Video replay: families, films and fantasy', in V. Burgin, J. Donald and C. Kaplan (eds), *Formations of Fantasy*, London: Methuen, pp. 167–99.

Wallden, S. (1993) 'Greece and its northern neighbours: impact of Balkan developments on the Greek economy', *Balkan Forum* 1, 3: 177–98.

Wallerstein, I. (1991) 'The construction of peoplehood: racism, nationalism, ethnicity', in E. Balibar and I. Wallerstein, trans. C. Turner, *Race, Nation, Class: Ambiguous Identities*, London: Verso, pp. 71–85.

Wark, M. (1990) 'Seeds of fire: media memory and the Beijing demonstrations', *Impulse* 15, 4: 30–40.

Webster, J.G. (1986) 'The television audience: audience behaviour in the new media environment', *Journal of Communication* 36, 3: 77–91.

Wedell, G., Luyken, G.M. *et al.* (1986) *Media in Competition: The Future of Print and Electronic Media in 22 Countries*, Manchester: The European Institute for the Media, and Hamburg: InterMedia Centrum.

West, R. (1943) *Black Lamb and Grey Falcon: The Record of a Journey Through Yugoslavia in 1937*, 2 vols, London: Macmillan.

White, N.R. and White, P.B. (1983) *Immigrants and the Media*, Melbourne: Longman Cheshire.

Wiesel, E. (1990) *From the Kingdom of Memory: Reminiscences*, New York: Summit Books.

Willener, A., Millano, G. and Ganty, A. (1976) *Videology and Utopia: Explorations in a New Medium*, trans D. Burifield, London: Routledge and Kegan Paul.

Williams, C.H. (1992) 'Identity, autonomy and the ambiguity of technological development', in Z. Mlinar (ed.), *Globalization and Territorial Identities*, Aldershot: Avebury, pp. 115–28.

Williams, R. (1974) *Television: Technology and Cultural Form*, London: Fontana/Collins.

—— (1976) *Culture*, Glasgow: Fontana.

—— (1989) *Resources of Hope: Culture, Democracy, Socialism*, London: Verso.

Winner, I. and Winner T. (1976) 'The semiotics of cultural texts', *Semiotica* 18, 2: 101–56.

Wolf, E. (1969) *Peasant Wars of the Twentieth Century*, New York: Harper and Row.

BIBLIOGRAPHY

—— (1982) *Europe and the People Without History*, Berkeley and Los Angeles: University of California Press.

'Woman regrets filming shooting by police' (1993) *The Straits Times*, 23 May, p. 8.

Young, C. (1986) 'Ethnic media and ethnic groups', *Media Information Australia* 40: 49–55.

INDEX

gypsies 148

hacking 170–1
Hall, S. 26–7, 176, 214, 215
Handler, R. 185
Harries, O. 97
Hartley, J. 22, 23–4, 160
hate campaigns 104, 149
Hayes, C. 37
Hechter, M. 36
Hegemonic State of Greater Serbia 132
helplessness 36
Helsinki Watch 188
high culture 25
Hill, P. 66, 67
Hill, S. 32
Hispanic communities, USA 17, 21, 45
historical dramas 124
history lessons 125–38
Hitler, A. 118, 214
Hobsbawm, E. 37, 92, 96, 111, 185
Hodge, R. 27
Holland, P. 148
Hollywood 15, 49
Holocaust 87
home-video terminals 14–15
homogenisation 122
Hong Kong 21, 45
Horowitz, D. 37
host cultures 46
Hristovski, J. 70
Hroch, M. 37
Hungary 129
hybridity 28, 176–7, 203, 209

iconic continuum 27–8
icons 109–11, 132, 175, 190–1, 206
identity 29, 48, 90, 112–13, 125, 178–80;
    destruction 201; diaspora 208–11;
    ethnic 21; hybrid 176; management
    25; negotiation 74; politics 32;
    renegotiation 76, 82; studies 37;
    symbols 181–3
ideology 26, 86–91, 98, 139; hybridity
    176; nationalism 37, 39, 122, 177, 214;
    semiotics 27
illegal screenings 19–20
immigration 38, 46, 49, 71
Imparja Television 20
imperialism 18, 211
imports 46, 50
incidental footage 33

independence 125–6, 158, 175
Independent Croatian State see
    Nezavisna država Hrvatska (NDH)
India 15, 21, 224
Indian communities: Australia 17–18,
    45; Britain 17; Malaysia 21
indigenous audiences 21, 40
Indonesia 15, 39
industry-oriented research 22
information 47, 155, 187, 217, 220;
    dissemination 167; monopolies 18,
    22; official channels 99; overload
    197–202
insanity 196–7
Inter University Centre for Graduate
    Studies (IUC) 193, 194
International Video Studios (IVS) 103,
    104, 146
Internet 20, 30
interpersonal dynamics 22
interpretation 26–7, 127, 138, 139
Inuit communities, Canada 20–1, 29
invisible audiences 17–22
Islam 21
Italian communities, Australia 17–18,
    20, 45
Italy 17, 142
Iyers, P. 19

Jameson, F. 196
Japan 16
Japan Victor Company (JVC) 22
Jasenovac concentration camp 149
Jelačić, B. see Ban Jelačić monument
Jews 148, 150
journalism 34, 93
Jugoslavenska Radio Televizija (JRT)
    99–100
Jugoslovenska Narodna Armija (JNA)
    93, 156, 157, 171, 179, 192, 199

King, R. 33
Kingdom of Serbs, Croats and Slovenes
    96
kinship 29, 82–3, 120–1, 144
Kohn, H. 36
Kolar-Panov, D. 167
Kosovo, Albanian communities 104
Kosovo, Battle of 96
Kouchner, B. 193
Kovač, M. 147
Krajina 104, 105, 149, 154, 155, 171

Printed in the United States
by Baker & Taylor Publisher Services